A LITHUANIAN HISTORICAL SYNTAX

William R. Schmalstieg

Slavica Publishers, Inc.

Slavica publishes a wide variety of textbooks and scholarly books on the languages, people, literatures, cultures, history, etc. of the USSR and Eastern Europe. For a complete catalog of books and journals from Slavica, with prices and ordering information, write to:

> Slavica Publishers, Inc.
> PO Box 14388
> Columbus, Ohio 43214

ISBN: 0-89357-185-7.

Copyright © 1987 by William R. Schmalstieg. All rights reserved.

This book was published in 1988.

Text set by Anna Mary Smalley and Mae Smith.

Printed in the United States of America.

TABLE OF CONTENTS

Foreword xi

1. Introduction to Participles 1
2. The Present Active Participle 4
   - 2.1 Attributive Use of the Participle . . . 5
   - 2.2 Attributive Use with Durative Intransitive Verbs 5
   - 2.3 Attributive Use to Denote Characteristics 6
   - 2.4 Lack of Diathesis in the Present Active Participle 7
   - 2.5 Postposed Participles and Nominalization 8
   - 2.6 Adverbial and Comparative Use of Participles 10
   - 2.7 The Origin of the Nominative Plural of the Participle; the Passive Meaning of Some Active Participles 11
3. The Past Active Participle 13
   - 3.1 Attributive Use of the Participle . . . 14
   - 3.2 Resultative Meaning of the Past Active Participle 14
   - 3.3 Adjectivization of Participles 15
   - 3.4 Participles to Translate Adjectives . . 15
   - 3.5 Preposed and Postposed Participles . . . 15
   - 3.6 Participles in Place of Subordinate Clauses 16
   - 3.7 Participles in Place of Substantives . . 16
   - 3.8 Adverbs and Comparative and Superlative Degrees from Participles 17
4. The Future Active Participle 18
   - 4.1 Participles in *-siant-* 18
   - 4.2 Participles for Indirect Speech; Rare Attributive Forms 18
   - 4.3 Attributive Use in 16th and 17th Centuries 19

	4.4 Limitations of Occurrence of Participles	20
5.	The Present Passive Participle	21
6.	The Past Passive Participle	30
7.	The Future Passive Participle	44
8.	The Semi-Predicative Use of the Participle	46
9.	The Origin of the Half-Participle	49
10.	The Half-Participle Used in Attributive Function	52
11.	The Appositional Use of the Past Active Participle	55
12.	The Appositional Use of the Passive Participles	60
13.	The Agent Nominative in a Participial Construction	62
14.	A Conjunction between the Participle and the Verb	66
15.	Constructions with Connective Words	73
16.	The Nominative with the Participle	76
17.	The Origin of the Nominative with the Participle	79
18.	The Development of the Nominative with the Participle	82
19.	The Accusative with the Participle	86
20.	The Origin of the Accusative with the Participle	89
21.	The Dative with the Participle	92
22.	The Predicative Use of the Present Active Participle	99
23.	The Predicative Use of the Past Active Participle	103
24.	The Predicative Use of the Passive Participles	108
25.	Origin of the Predicative Use of the Participles	111
26.	The Indirect Mood (reported speech, *modus relativus*) and Its Development	113
27.	The Origin of the Indirect Mood	117
28.	The Origin of Constructions with Indirect Cases	122
29.	The Nominative Case	128
	29.1 Nominative Case as Subject of a Verb	142

iv

29.2	The Nominative Case in Nominal Sentences	143
29.3	The Nominative Case in Predicate Position	143
29.31	The Semi-Predicative Use of the Nominative Case	144
29.32	The Nominative Case with Naming Verbs	144
29.4	The Nominative Case in Adverbial Expressions	145
29.5	The Nominative Plus Infinitive	145
29.51	The Origin of the Nominative Plus Infinitive Constructions	147
29.6	The Nominative Denoting Circumstances of Time and Place	152
29.7	The Nominative Case to Express Apposition	153
29.71	The Nominative Instead of the Vocative	154
29.72	The Nominative Case of the Noun Instead of a Pronoun	154
29.73	The Nominative Case for Titles	154
29.74	The Nominative Case for Greetings ...	155
29.8	Adverbialization of Nouns in the Nominative; The Origin of *gana*	155
29.81	The Fossilization and Adverbialization of the Noun	159
30.	The Adverbal Genitive Case	160
30.1	Verbs Requiring a Genitive Object ...	160
30.11	Verbs of Remembering	162
30.12	Verbs Denoting 'To Call, To Invite' ..	163
30.13	Verbs Denoting 'To Take Care of, To Watch out for'	164
30.14	Verbs with Various Meanings	164
30.15	The Partitive Genitive	166
30.16	Verbs with the Prefixes *pri-*, *at-*, *už-*, *pa-*	168
30.17	Temporally Limited Verbs	169
30.18	Verbs Denoting a Change of State ...	169
30.2	Verbs Denoting Existence with a Partitive Genitive Subject	170
30.21	Negated Verbs of Existence with a Genitive	172
30.3	The Genitive Direct Object of a Negated Verb	173

	30.31 The Genitive Direct Object of an Infinitive Governed by a Negated Verb . . .	173
	30.32 Expressions of Quantity in the Genitive with a Negated Verb	174
	30.4 The Genitive as the Direct Object of a Supine	174
	30.41 The Genitive of Goal in Competition with the Dative of Goal	176
	30.42 Discussion of the Genitive of Goal and Supine	176
	30.43 Infinitive Governing Genitive under the Influence of the Main Verb	178
	30.5 The Agentive Use of the Genitive . . .	180
	30.51 The Genitive with Verbs Denoting 'To Fill'	185
	30.6 Arguments for an Agentive Genitive . .	189
	30.61 Lithuanian *bijóti*	192
	30.62 The Indo-European Genitive of Goal . .	192
	30.63 Verbs Denoting 'To Need'	193
	30.64 Transitivization and Syntactic Reanalysis	193
	30.7 Replacement of a Nominative Subject by a Genitive Modifier	194
31.	The Adnominal Genitive	196
	31.1 The Genitive Denoting Relationship . .	196
	31.2 The Genitive in Adjectival Function . .	198
	31.21 The Genitive of Respect	199
	31.3 Adjectives with Genitive Complements	199
	31.4 The Genitive Denoting Quantity	200
	31.5 Numerals Governing the Genitive	200
	31.6 The Genitive Enhancing Quantitative or Qualitative Meaning	201
	31.7 The Genitive of Comparison	201
32.	The Adverbal Dative Case	203
	32.1 The Dative Object with Verbs Denoting Surprise	204
	32.11 The Dative Object with Verbs Denoting 'To Understand; To Obey; To Rule Over,' etc.	206
	32.12 The Dative with *gélbèti*	209
	32.13 The Passivization of Verbs Governing the Dative	210
	32.14 The Indirect Object	211
	32.2 The Dative Denoting Purpose of Existence of Something	213

	32.3 The Dative of Purpose with the Infinitive	214
	32.31 Classification of Dative of Purpose Constructions	215
	32.32 The Indo-European Origin of the Infinitive	219
	32.4 The Dative Subject of Impersonal Verbs	220
	32.41 The Dative Subject and Predicate of Copulative Verbs	222
	32.42 The Dative Subject of an Infinitive to Express Necessity	224
	32.43 The Dative Expressing the Whole and the Part	226
33.	The Adnominal Dative	227
	33.1 The Dative of Judgment	228
	33.2 The Dative of Comparison	228
	33.3 Dative to Express Time	229
	33.4 The Dative of Possession	229
34.	The Adverbal Accusative	231
	34.1 Klein's Definition of the Accusative	232
	34.11 The Cognate Accusative	232
	34.2 Verbal Prefixation Changing Government to the Accusative	233
	34.21 The Accusative Government of *tikė́ti*	233
	34.22 The Accusative Government of *liẽpti*	234
	34.3 Passive Participles Governing the Accusative	235
	34.4 The Accusative Government of *skelė́ti*	235
	34.5 The Accusative When the Governing Verb is Omitted	236
	34.6 The Double Accusative	236
	34.7 The Accusative Object of Negated Verbs	237
	34.8 The Accusative Object of Prefixed Verbs of Motion	239
	34.81 The Accusative of Direction	239
	34.82 The Accusative Object of *eĩti* in Certain Fixed Expressions	240
35.	The Independent Accusative	241
	35.1 The Accusative to Denote Extent of Space	242

36.	The Instrumental	243
	36.1 Verbs Governing the Instrumental	244
	36.2 The Instrumental of Manner	246
	36.3 Interpretation of the Instrumental of Manner as the Instrumental of Cause	247
	36.4 The Instrumental Denoting Spatial Relationship	248
	36.5 The Instrumental Denoting a Point in Time	249
	36.6 The Predicate Instrumental	249
	36.7 The Instrumental with the Nominalization of a Verb	255
	36.71 Instrumental of Association with Adjectives in -$inas$	255
	36.8 Instrumental with $mègti$ and Other Verbs	255
37.	Simple Locative	258
	37.1 Wider Use of Locative In Older Writings	261
	37.2 Influence of Other Languages on Use of Locative	262
	37.3 Locative Denoting Object of Motion	263
	37.31 Locative Denoting Direction	264
	37.32 Locative as Indirect Object	264
38.	Illative	265
	38.1 Illative Competing with Preposition i Construction	265
	38.2 Klein's Explanation of Illative	266
	38.3 Illative in Time Expressions	266
	38.4 Illative to Denote Manner	267
	38.5 Merger of Illative and Inessive	267
39.	Adessive	268
40.	Allative	271
41.	Prepositions	273
	41.01 ant	273
	41.02 Samogitian Usage of ant	277
	41.03 $apiẽ$	277
	41.04 Klein's Description of $apie$	277
	41.05 $bè$	277
	41.06 $dẽl(ei)$	278
	41.07 $dẽl$ to Denote Purpose	278
	41.08 iki	279
	41.09 ik with the Instrumental	280
	41.10 $ĩ$	280

	41.11 Dialect Use of various forms of *į*	281
	41.12 *iš*	282
	41.13 *iš* with the Dative	283
	41.14 *nuõg(i)*	284
	41.15 Samogitian *nu*	285
	41.16 *pagal̃*	286
	41.17 *pàs*	286
	41.18 *pas* with the Genitive in Samogitian	287
	41.19 *per̃*	287
	41.20 *po (pa)*	289
	41.21 *po (pa)* with the Genitive	289
	41.22 *po (pa)* to Denote 'under'	290
	41.23 *po* with the Accusative	290
	41.24 Klein's Explanation of *po*	290
	41.25 *po* with the Dative in Dialects	290
	41.26 *priẽ*	291
	41.27 Confusion of *priẽ* and *apiẽ*	291
	41.28 *priẽš*	292
	41.29 *príešais*	292
	41.30 *prõ*	293
	41.31 *prõ* with the Instrumental	293
	41.32 *sù*	294
	41.33 *sulìg*	294
	41.34 *tar̃p (ter̃p)*	294
	41.35 *tiẽs*	294
	41.36 *tiẽs* with the Dative	295
	41.37 *ùž*	295
	41.38 *ùž* with the Instrumental	297
42.	The Adjective	299
	42.1 Definite Adjectives Denoting Spatial, Temporal and Other Physical Characteristics	299
	42.2 Definite Adjectives Denoting Species	300
	42.3 Definite Adjectives Denoting Antecedent	300
	42.4 Definite Adjectives Emphasizing a Known Quality	301
	42.5 Klein's Explanation of Definite Adjectives	302
	42.6 Order of Personal Pronouns in Definite Adjectives	302
	42.7 Addition of Personal Pronouns to the Declined Adjective	303
	42.8 The Origin of the Definite Adjective	303

42.9	Valeckienė's theory of the Origin of the Definite Adjective	306
43.	Anatolian and Lithuanian Word Order	310
44.	Functional Sentence Perspective	312
45.	Position of the Adjective	317
46.	Position of the Adverb	321
47.	Conclusions about Word Order	325

Footnotes 328

References 333

Word Index 347

Abbreviations 412

FOREWORD

Herewith I should like to express my gratitude to the Fullbright Commission and the International Research and Exchange Board which made my four-month sojourn in Lithuania possible. I should also like to thank Professor Joseph Michels, Associate Dean for Research of the College of Liberal Arts of The Pennsylvania State University and Professor Michels' assistant, Ms. Irene Petrick, for their help in obtaining the Fulbright and the IREX awards.

I am also very grateful for my warm welcome by the members of the staff of the Institute of Lithuanian Language and Literature, its director, Professor J. Lankutis and its associate director, Professor V. Vanagas who were instrumental in supplying me with working space and the necessary assistance. But most of all I should like to thank my two patrons at the latter Institute, Professor Algirdas Sabaliauskas and Professor Vytautas Ambrazas, both of whom gave unselfishly and unstintingly of their time and helped with the preparation of this work. Professor Sabaliauskas was particularly helpful with questions of everyday living in Vilnius. Professor Ambrazas, undoubtedly the leading contemporary expert on Lithuanian historical syntax, was particularly kind in reading the entire text and making valuable comments and corrections. I am also grateful to Professor Ambrazas for many hours of stimulating discussions of problems of Lithuanian syntax. I am also thankful to Professor Antanas Klimas of the University of Rochester for comments and corrections.

I should also like to thank Professor Lea Sawicki of the Hebrew University of Jerusalem for comments and corrections. Many others, too numerous to mention, both at the Institute and the University of Vilnius gave valuable assistance also, but I must remain personally responsible for my own interpretations and any errors which may appear in the text.

I should like to express also my thanks to the Institute for the Arts and Humanistic Studies of The Pennsylvania State University for providing funds for the typing of part of the manuscript of this book.

Introduction to Participles

1. Ambrazas, 1979, 14, has pointed out that compared with other languages Lithuanian shows a considerably greater use of participles. In this respect Lithuanian is even superior to Classical Greek which has long been known as a language which likes participles (*philometokhḗ*). According to the calculations of Classen, 1879, 52, in the Iliad there are about 3500 participles, which would amount to about 200 in a text of 40,000 letters. On the other hand in a text of similar size from Donelaitis' *Seasons* there are about 395 and in a text like Bretkūnas' *Postilla* (I and II) there are about 345. One notes furthermore that in Lithuanian participles form a part of the living language and the usage was not influenced by literary styles as in such Indo-European languages as the Slavic, Germanic or classical Sanskrit and Latin.

Ambrazas, 1979, 16, notes that participles furnish the only means of expressing the contrast between active and passive diathesis in Lithuanian. The fundamental semantic and syntactic characteristic separating the active and passive voice is the relationship between the agent and the grammatical subject.

He writes also, 1979, 17, that a great number of the impersonal passive participles which have a genitive agent can have a genitive, accusative or nominative object:

(a) brólio   láukiama   svečių
    brother   awaits   guests
    (gen. sg.) (impersonal (gen. pl.)
                neuter pres.
                psv. prt.)

(b) rãšoma   láiškas   (or láišką)
    is written letter   letter
    (impersonal (nom. sg.)   (acc. sg.)
    neut. pres.
    psv. prt.)
'A letter is written.'

According to Ambrazas, 1979, 16, from the syntactic point of view the passive constructions are to be considered transforms of the corresponding active forms. In many cases one can derive from the same active construction two types of passives:

Active: (c)   tévas   skìna   óbuolius
                 father   picks   apples
                 (nom sg.)   (pres.)   (acc. pl.)

Passive I: (d)

obuoliaĩ   (yrà)   tévo   skìnami
apples   copulative   by father   picked
(nom. pl.)   (gen. sg.)   (nom. pl. masc.
                                       pres. psv. prt.)

Passive II: (e)

tévo   (yrà)   skìnama   obuoliaĩ
by father   copulative   picked   apples
(gen. sg.)   (neut. sg. pres.   (nom. pl.)
                          psv. prt.)

    In my view the oldest syntactic type is represented by passive II. There is no agreement between the grammatical subject (patient) and the originally intransitive verb *skìnama* because in the oldest type of sentence the adjective did not agree with the subject. The intrasitive verb came to be felt as passive once the active verb type was developed (see Chapter 6).
    From the point of view of modern Lithuanian, of course, the derivation appears to be from the active to the passive. The passive of modern Lithuanian merely represents the meaning induced at the time when certain of the old intransitive verbs became transitive. The original intransitive meaning is retained in many verbs, e.g., *miegóti* 'to sleep.' The similarity in derivation points up the fact that although the meanings of the

transitive and intransitive are different now, originally they were the same.

One notes, furthermore, that not only the direct, but the indirect object of a verb may function as the subject of the passive participle, e.g., both *obuolỹs* (nom. sg.) *dúotas* 'an apple (is, was) given' and *vaĩkas* (nom. sg.) *dúotas* (*óbuolį* {acc. sg.}) 'the child (is, was) given (an apple).' The fact that the dative may be passivized just like the accusative serves as additional evidence for the original identity of the two cases.[1]

According to Ambrazas, 1979, 18, contemporary Lithuanian has the following participial formations (all examples are given in the nominative singular):

A. Active

a) present tense with the suffix *-nt-* (*nešąs* or *nešantis*, fem. *nešanti* 'carrying')

b) simple preterit with the suffix *-us-* (*nẽšes*, fem. *nẽš-us-i* 'having carried')

c) frequentative past with the suffix *-(dav)us-* (*nẽš-dav-es*, fem. *nẽš-dav-us-i* 'having repeatedly carried')

d) future tense with the suffix *-(sia)nt-* (*nẽš-ias*, fem. *nẽš-iant-i* 'will be carrying')

B. Passive

a) present tense with the suffix *-ma-* (*nẽš-am-as*, fem. *neš-am-à* 'being carried')

b) preterit tense with the suffix *-ta-* (*nẽš-tas*, *neš-tà* 'having been carried')

c) future tense with the suffix *-(si)ma-* (*nẽš-im-as*, fem. *neš-im-à* 'which will be carried')

In addition to these we find the half-participle or special adverbial participle with the suffix *-dam-as*, *-dam-a* which is in the nominative case and co-ordinated with the subject of the sentence.

The Present Active Participle

2. The suffix *-nt-* is used to form a present active participle in the great majority of the Indo-European languages. This formant exists in the *-e-* grade, e.g., Doric Gk. nom. pl. masc. *ént-es*, Skt. acc. sg. masc. *sánt-am*, Lat. nom. sg. masc. *prae-sēns* (< *(-)sent-*) 'being,' the zero grade *-n̥t-*, Skt. nom. sg. fem. *sat-í* (< *sn̥t-*), and the etymological *-o-* grade, cf., Old Lith. *są̃s* (< *sont-s*), later *ẽsąs* 'being,' (Brugmann, 1906, 455-456). In Lithuanian the vowel of the participle depends on the stem vowel of the present tense, i.e., 1st conjugation verbs like *nẽš-ti* 'to carry' have the nom. sg. masc. participle *nẽš-ant-is* with the formant vowel *-a-* (< *-o-*) just like the 3rd person pres. *nẽš-a* 'carries, carry.' The form *nẽš-ant-is* is an analogical innovation, the older nom. sg. masc. being represented by *nẽš-ą-s* (< *neš-ant-s*); 2nd conjugation verbs like *tylė́ti* 'to be silent' have the nom. sg. masc. pres. act. participles *tyl-int-is* or *tyl-į̃-s* (< *tyl-int-s*), cf., the 3rd person pres. *tyl-i*. The 3rd conjugation participles have the same form as the 1st conjugation with the suffix *-ant-* as a result of the shortening of the last element of the mixed diphthong in proto-Baltic, i.e., *-ānt-* passed to *-ant-* whereas in open syllable the Baltic etymological *ā passed to Lithuanian *ō*, thus we encounter the 3rd pres. *laĩko* 'holds' but the nom. sg. masc. pres. act. part. forms *laĩk-ą̃-s* (< *laik-ant-s*) and *laĩk-ant-is*.

This participle has an active meaning and usually denotes a tense simultaneous with that of the main verb in the clause in most of the Indo-European languages. Amazingly enough this is not the case in Hittite where the participle in *-ant-* patterns semantically like the participle in *-t-* in the other Indo-European languages, e.g., Hittite *akkanza* denotes 'dead, having died,' i.e., it has a preterit or past meaning.

2.1 According to Ambrazas, 1979, 30, in the folk language the present active participle when used attributively is for the most part formed from unprefixed intransitive verbs with a durative meaning and stands before the modified noun, e.g., *bė́gantis vanduõ* 'running water,' *seȓgantis žmogùs* 'an ailing man,' *dė̃danti vištà* 'a laying (productive) hen.' More rarely the prefixed present active participle can denote the ability to perform an action, e.g., *pa-lôjantis šuõ* 'a dog capable of barking,' *nu-si-lėidžiąs žmogùs* 'a man capable of descending, i.e., making concessions.'

Sometimes the agent of the action of the participle is not the modified word, e.g., *lỹnanti naktìs* 'a rainy night' or *lỹnanti dienà* 'a rainy day, literally: a raining day' apparently derived from such an active sentence as *lỹja diẽną* 'it rains during the day' (Ambrazas, 1979, 30). Sometimes the relationship is even less clear, cf., *nemãtanti kepùrė̀* 'an unseeing hat, an invisible hat, i.e., a hat which makes its wearer invisible.'

2.2 According to Ambrazas, 1979, 31, in the writings of the 16th and 17th centuries almost one-half of the present active participles are attributively used (e.g., 48 percent in Bretkūnas' *Postilla* and 61 percent in Sirvydas' *Punktay sakimu*). The greater attributive use is to be explained by the fact that the adverbial active participle had taken over some of the functions of the present active participle in the nominative case.

In the old writings as in the contemporary language attributive present active participles are for the most part formed from durative intransitive verbs and can denote actions which are in progress at the time of speaking, e.g., (Bretkūnas' *Postilla* I 2612-14):

Budanti	szmogu	wagis	piggai	ne	apwogs/
being awake	man	thief	easily	not	will rob

o	mieganti/	snaudzanti	nesisaugaienti/
but	sleeping	drowsing	not taking care

iau	senei	prigawa.
already	long ago	deceived.

'A thief will not easily rob a man who is awake, but has long ago deceived the sleeping, drowsing (man) who does not take care.'

The affix *be-* can sometimes reinforce the concrete durative meaning, e.g., (Bretkūnas' *Postilla* II 4784):

szolie be-szelůienti / tuiaus gal pawisti.
grass now being green suddenly can fade.
'Grass which is green now can suddenly fade.'

2.3 More frequently, however, these participles denote characteristics which derive from continuous or constant actions, e.g., (DP 209$_{27}$; acc. pl.) *niežanczes ausis* 'itching ears,' (Bretkūnas' *Postilla* II 31$_{24}$; dat. pl.) *tikintiemus wirams* 'believing (= faithful) men,' (Morkūnas' *Postilla* 46; acc. pl. fem.) *galinczias* (= *galingas*) *rankas* 'powerful arms.' More rarely one runs across the participles formed from the prefixed verbs, e.g., (Bretkūnas' *Postilla* I 59; nom. sg.) *ischmanans* (= *išmintingas*) *Krikschczonis* 'wise Christian,' (DP 542$_3$) *priderąs žękłas*(= Polish *przystoyne známie*) 'suitable sign.' Some of the participles don't denote the duration of an action at all, but denote characteristics connected with the possibility or tendency to perform the action, e.g., (Bretkūnas' *Postilla* II 386$_6$; nom. sg.) *limpanti ir biauri ligga* 'a contagious (literally: sticking) and ugly sickness,' (DP 539$_{37}$; loc. sg.) *mirsztątime kűne* (= Polish *w śmiertelnym ciele*) 'in the mortal (literally: dying) body.' The tendency is particularly marked with the negative, e.g., (Sirvydas' *Punktay sakimu*; gen. sg.) *nederunčio daykto* (= Polish *nieprzystoyną rzecz*) 'unsuitable thing' (Ambrazas, 1979, 31).

Since present active participles which do not have any temporal significance are very close to adjectives the authors of old writings frequently used the Lithuanian participles to translate adjectives of other languages, cf., e.g., (DP 2433$_8$; inst. sg.) Polish *jasną świecą* = Lith. *žibancziąie žwake* 'bright candle,' (Morkūnas' *Postilla* II 52$_{30}$; gen. sg.) Polish *bez słusznej przyczyny* = Lith. *be prideránczios priežasties* 'without a valid reason.' Also with the negative particle (DP 5271$_6$; nom. sg.) Polish *ustawiczne gryzienie* = Lith. *nepaláubąsis krimtimas* 'incessant gnawing,' (Bretkūnas' *Bible, Numbers* 18, 19; nom. sg.) German *vnuerwesenlich Bund* = Lith. *nepagendansis Sudereghimas* 'indestructible union.' Likewise many of the participles derived from transitive verbs correspond to adjectives of the original texts, e.g., (DP 2245) Polish *zdradliwi odszczepieńcy* = Lith. *wilaiie / âtskalũnis* 'insidious apostates.' The adjectival usage of Lith. *sẽkantis* 'following' was stimulated by the cognate Latin *sequens*, German *folgender* and Polish *następujący* (Ambrazas, 1979, 32).

2.4 Ambrazas, 1979, 32, notes that the 16th and 17th century writings show no clearer regard for verbal diathesis than do the contemporary dialects. Thus there are many collocations which could not be put back into a nominative construction with a finite verb and then reflect the appropriate meaning, e.g., (Bretkūnas' *Postilla* I 125$_{14}$; inst. sg.) *tikincze wiera* '(literally) believing faith,' (DP 105$_{28}$; illative sg. fem.) Polish *grzechu śmiertelnego* = Lith. *nůdemen myrgtancżion'* 'mortal sin,' (*Margarita Theologica* 258a$_8^?$; acc. sg.) *abijoienti klausima* 'doubtful (literally: doubting) question,' (Giedraytis' *New Testament*, Matt. 17, 14; acc. sg.) *puolancię ligą* 'falling sickness,' (*Wolfenbütteler Postilla* 233$_4$; nom. sg.) *sussimilstas giwenimas* 'merciful life,' (*Kniga Nobaznistes*, 79$_{27}$; acc. pl.) *medžioiančius tinklus* 'hunting nets.'

Ambrazas, 1979, 32, writes that in some texts particularly popular is the present active participle (nom. sg.) *pakañkąs, -anti* 'being sufficient' used with the same meaning as the present passive participle (nom. sg.) *pakañkamas -à*, cf., e.g., (*Margarita Theologica* 42a$_{18}$; nom. sg.) *pakankąsis dczauxmas* 'sufficient joy.'

As Ambrazas mentions, 1979, 32, there are various relationships between the participle and the word modified, e.g., instrument, causality, time, etc. In such cases the use of the present active participle is indistinguishable from the present passive participle, cf., the following examples which replicate in meaning examples given above: *miřstamà nůodėmė* 'mortal (dying) sin,' *medžiójamieji tinklaĩ* 'hunting nets,' *abejójamas dalỹkas* 'doubtful (being doubted) affair,' *puolamóji ligà* 'epilepsy, falling sickness.' A few examples can be explained as the result of spread of meaning from forms where an agent is denoted, e.g., *susimilstąs gyvẽnimas* 'merciful life' on the analogy of *susimilstąs žmogùs* 'merciful person' or as a shift of meaning, but the correspondence with the examples from the contemporary popular speech and the semantic connection with the present passive participles lead one to conclude that some of the constructions are remnants left over from the time when the form represented now by the present active participle was neutral with regard to diathesis.

Preposed participles which denote constant qualities can be combined with governed or modifying words, e.g., (Bretkūnas' *Postilla* II 240-241):

nekenteia	....	piktai	giwenanczių	szmonių
hated		evilly	living	men

2.5 Ambrazas, 1979, 33, writes that postposed present active participles in original and compilational works are almost ten times as common as the preposed. Without dependent words they are rarer following the modified word and they may also denote permanent characteristics, e.g., (DP 314$_5$) *teisinikas didžiūias* 'the haughty righteous man,' (527$_{14}$) *liepsna žaizdącze* 'fiery flame.' Postposed present active participles are inclined to have governed or modifying words and have a clear connection with diathesis and tense. This usage in the old writings was apparently not under the influence of other languages. In Bretkūnas' *Bible* such forms frequently correspond to subordinate clauses in the original, e.g., (*Joshua* 6, 9):

ęija	pirm	Kunigų,	trubijenczių
went	before the	priests, who	blew

truba
with the trumpet (= German *die die Posaunen bliesen*); (*Exodus* 38, 3):

padare	wissokiu	Stotku	Altorui
he made	all the	vessels	to the altar

priderenczių
belonging. 'He made all the vessels for the altar' (= German *allerley gerete zu dem Altar* 'all kinds of vessels for the altar'). Postposed participial constructions and subordinate clauses can be used with the same meaning, e.g., (*Deuteronomy* 12, 12):

Leuitai	kurie	iusu	Wartůsų	ira
Levites	who (in)	your	gates	are (= German

die in ewren thoren sind); (*Deuteronomy* 12, 18):

Leuitas,   tawa   Wartosą   essansis
Levite (in) thy   gate   being.
'Levite who is in thy gate.' (*Numbers* 16, 14):

iwedei   Szemena   plustancze
thou hast brought   into a land   flowing

Pienu   ir   Maedumi
with milk   and   honey.
(*Deuteronomy* 11, 9):

Szeme,   kurioje   Pienas   ir   Maedus   plusta
land   in which   milk   and   honey   flow
(= German *da milch vnd honig innen fleusst*).
   A pronoun can also be modified by a postposed participle, e.g., (Bretkūnas' *Postilla* II 164$_{23}$):

Beda   iums   raschta   mokantiemus
Misfortune   to you   writing   knowing.
'Misfortune to you who know how to write' (Ambrazas, 1979, 33).
   Ambrazas, 1979, 33, explains the wide use of present active participles as substantives by the productivity of constructions with expanded postposed participles. In such cases a preposed noun or pronoun which denotes the generalized agent of the participial action is assumed (to have been deleted). The extended present active participles in the position of nouns in writings of the 16th and 17th centuries have the same clear verbal characteristics as the aforementioned postposed participles. In Bretkūnas' *Bible* translation the secondary members of the subjoined clauses are translated by these, e.g., (*Exodus* 32, 24): (The one)

Turinsis   Auksa   tenuplesch
having   gold   let him break (it) off (= German
Wer hat gold). One also finds sequences such as the
following: (*Numbers* 35, 19):

Pagieszansis   kraughi   tur   ghį
(The one) avenging   blood   must   him

smercziop   deti
to death   (to) put. 'The revenger of blood himself shall slay the murderer' (Ambrazas, 1979, 34).

The meaning of the participle used as an adjective is practically the same as when it is used as a noun, cf., e.g., from Sirvydas' *Punktay sakimu* (II 184$_{16}$) *žmogus pasituris* (= Polish *człowiek bogaty*) 'rich man' vs. (II 184$_{26}$) *Pasituris ir grinas* (= Polish *bogaty y vbogi*) *susitiko* 'The rich (man) and the pauper met' (Ambrazas, 1979, 34).

2.6 According to Ambrazas, 1979, 34, as a result of its nominal semantic characteristics forms of the present active participle can be supplied with the suffix -(*i*)*ai* and used as adverbs, cf., (Sirvydas' *Dictionary*, 345) *smirdunčiey* = Polish *smrodliwie* 'in a stinking way,' (DP 24$_{10}$) *ẽssanczei* = Polish *istotnie* 'indeed, really' (derived from pres. act. prt. of *būti* 'to be'). From various sources and particularly popular was the form *priderančiai* = Polish *słusznie* 'rightly, correctly.' Sometimes the active participles used adverbially do not have an active meaning, cf., (anonymous catechism 72$_{19}$):

neregiunčiey	ir	regiuncey	Diewu
invisibly	and	visibly	God

garbintumbime
we should honor. 'We should honor God both in visible and invisible things.' Note from the contemporary dialects:

nekuštėk	girdinčiaĩ	nemelúok
don't whisper	so it is heard,	don't lie

regin̄čiaĩ
when it can be seen.

Those participles which are used as adjectives occasionally have comparative and superlative degrees in some dialects. Cf., e.g., *lynantesnė vãsara* 'a rainier summer,' *džiūnantesnė širdis* 'a dryer heart,' *sijõnas degantesnis* 'a brighter dress,' (Morkūnas' *Postilla* I 77) *žmogus galincziausias* 'the most powerful man' (Ambrazas, 1979, 34).

Comparing the data from 16th, 17th century and later writings with the contemporary dialects one does not note that any particular present active participles or any group thereof has changed into adjectives. Those participles which denote constant characteristics in the contemporary language did so already in the earliest writings, e.g., *gãlintis* 'powerful, literally: being able,' *pakañkantis* 'sufficient, sufficing,' As in related languages, the evidence of old writings and contemporary dialects shows this to be an old feature.

2.7 The Lithuanian nom. pl. masc. forms (1st conj.) -*ą*, (2nd conj.) -*i̇̃*, (3rd conj.) -*ą* derive from the old 3rd pl. present tense form which I trace back to original *-*an* (< *-*on*), *-*in* (< *-*n̥* {?}), < *-*an* (< *-*ān* {?}) respectively. Cowgill, 1970, 30, has proposed that such a usage began in subordinate clauses such as *sakā (*kad*) *jai* (masc.) or *jās* (fem.) *vedan* 'he says (that) they lead.' When the 3rd singular form came to be used in the main clauses the etymological 3rd plural form remained for a longer time in subordinate clauses and was in competition with such sentences as *sakā (*kad*) *jai* (*esan*) *vedantes* 'they say that they lead' (or fem. *sakā (*kad*) *jās* (*esan*) *vedantjās*). From its predicative use in subordinate clauses *vedan* spread to attributive use. Cowgill, 1970, 29, would derive the -*an* from earlier *-*ont*, but I see no need for the final *-*t*. The Indo-European ending *-*on* consists of the thematic vowel *-*o*- plus the indefinite marker *-*n*.[1] The attested *-*t*, (*-*ti*, *-*to*) of 3rd plural forms, e.g., Latin (*ama-*)*nt* 'they love,' Gk. (*didó-*)*āsi* 'they give,' < *-*anti*, Skt. (*bhav-*)*anti* 'they are,' (3rd pl. middle imperfect) *á-bhava-nta*, derives from an analogical transfer from the 3rd singular, cf., Lat. (*ama-*)*t*, Gk. (*dídō*)*si* < *-*ti*, Skt. (*bhav-*)*ati*, (3rd sg. middle imperfect) *á-bhava-ta*, etc.

Ambrazas, 1979, 35, notes that the adjectival use of the *-*nt*- forms was explained as being the result of the adjectivization of the original participle. It had been thought that already in Indo-European times this participle had had active meanings. But as Ambrazas says, 1979, 36, Hittite evidence in the form of such passive forms as *kunanza* 'killed,' *adanza* 'eaten' (but also 'having eaten') vs. active intransitives, e.g., *panza* 'having gone,' *ašanza* 'being' caused this view to be reviewed. Many reliquary forms in other Indo-European languages must also be considered, e.g., Vedic *pŕ̥ṣant-* 'speckled,' *stavān* 'praised,' *járant-* 'having been made old,' Latin *ēuidēns* 'seen from a distance,' *uehēns* 'being carried,' etc. (see Watkins, 1969, 143-145). The Hittite distribution is more original and as stated above the passive meaning was adopted when the originally intransitive verbs came to be interpreted as transitives. In the non-Anatolian Indo-European languages the *-nt-* participle came to be specialized as transitive in contrast to the *-t-* participle which came to be specialized as passive. Note furthermore the noun of agent meaning of such forms as Latin *parentes*, Gothic *nasjands* 'savior,' *frijōnds* 'friend,' Old English *hǽland* 'doctor,' etc. (Ambrazas, 1979, 37).

As I have suggested before, Indo-European *-on* passed either to *-ō (if in word-final preconsonantal sandhi position) or remained as *-on (if in word-final prevocalic sandhi position). The Indo-European languages made use of this to differentiate between the nominative case of the *n*-stems in *-ō and the vocative case in *-on, cf., e.g., Sanskrit nom. sg. *śvā* 'dog' vs. voc. sg. *śvan*. In Greek the *-n was analogically added again to the nom. sg. giving *kúōn* (replacing an earlier *kúō = Skt. *śvā* and Lith. *šuõ*). This lengthened grade came to be considered an auxiliary marker of the nominative singular for certain stems, therefore the masc. nom. sg. *phér-ōn* 'carrying' replaced an earlier *phér-on (still retained in the neuter nom.-acc. singular).

3

The Past Active Participle

3. As Ambrazas, 1979, 37, points out, the Baltic past active participle is derived from the preterit stem with the suffix -us-, cf., e.g., acc. sg. masc. Lith. gím-us-į, Latv. dzim-uš-u 'born,' Old Prussian (ainan)gimm-us-in 'only born.' The only exception is the Lithuanian nom. sg. masc. (gím-)ęs and the nom. pl. masc. (gím-)ę. Cowgill, 1970, 32, has shown that the nom. pl. ending -ę derives from an old 3rd pl. pret. *veden which he derives from an earlier *vedent < *vedēnt. Although accepting in principle Cowgill's explanation, I see no need for supposing a final *-t. In fact the *-en replaces an earlier *-an, since the Lithuanian preterit in -ė results most probably from the remodeling of the Indo-European thematic aorist, see Schmalstieg, 1974a, 1976. The nom. sg. masc. vĕdęs is on analogy with the nom. sg. masc. pres. act. prt. vedą̃s as Cowgill, 1970, 32, suggests.[2]

Ambrazas, 1979, 37, writes that the suffix -us- is usually thought to be the zero-grade ablaut form of the suffix -wǫs-, cf., the nom. sg. masc. Homeric Greek (F)eid(F)ṓs 'knowing.' The nominative singular masculine shows a lengthening derived from other sources to set off this case from other cases, cf., the nom. sg. neut. eidós. Sanskrit also has the lengthened grade in the strong cases of the perfect participle, cf., e.g., nom. sg. masc. (cakṛ-)vā́n, acc. sg. masc. (cakṛ-)vā́ṃs-am vs. the nom.-acc. sg. neut. (cakṛ-)vát 'having made,' etc. The zero-grade is known, however, in the nom. sg. fem. (Homeric) Gk. iduĩa, Skt. vidúṣī OCS vĕdъši 'having known' (Specht, 1947, 345). The Old Prussian nom. sg. masc. ending -uns probably derives from *-ens with the adoption of the -u- vocalism from other declensional forms according to Cowgill, 1970, 34.

According to Ambrazas, 1979, 38, the evidence of such forms as Gothic *bērusjōs* 'parents' (cf. *bairan* 'to bear') and *weitwōps* 'witness' (cf. *witan* 'to know') and the lack of the participles as such in the Anatolian and Italic languages leads one to the conclusion that participles with the suffix -*us*- also developed from old verbal nouns which denoted for the most part the characteristics of the agent.

3.1 Ambrazas, 1979, 38, writes that the attributive past active participles both in contemporary Lithuanian and in the language of the 16th and 17th centuries is much less common than the attributive present active participles, e.g., in Bretkūnas' *Postilla* the proportion is 350 to 580 and in Sirvydas' *Punktay sakimu* the proportion is 114 to 271. On the other hand they are used more widely in other functions. In adnominal position they usually have a perfect meaning, i.e., they denote a state which is the result of a past action. Since in contemporary Lithuanian such a meaning is more characteristic of a prefixed verb, they are mostly formed from prefixed verbs in the contemporary language. Unprefixed verbs of completed aspect are, however, also used in the past active participle, e.g., *gimęs kūdikis* 'a baby having been born,' *lūžęs tekinis* 'a broken wheel,' *grįžęs kareivis* 'a returned soldier.' In dialects resultative-perfect meanings are found for non-prefixed verbs which in the personal conjugation denote an action lasting over a period of time, e.g., *džiūvusi mėsà* 'dried meat,' *áugęs* (= *su-áugęs*) *žmogùs* 'a grown man,' *bréndę* (= *su-bréndę*) *riešutėliai* 'ripe nuts,' *liñkęs arklỹs* 'horse with a sway back, literally: bent horse,' *siùtusi bóba* 'woman with a bad character, literally: mad woman.'

3.2 Such usage was also current in writings of the 16th and 17th centuries, cf., e.g., Daukša's *Postilla* 65_{26} inst. sg. masc. *bigusiu łápinimu* 'with hastened pace,' from Bretkūnas' *Postilla* II, 30: gen. sg. fem. *szuwies kepusias* 'gebraten Fisch, baked fish.' According to Ambrazas, 1979, 38-39, it is clear from such examples that the resultative meaning is derived from the participial form itself and is not dependent on the conjugated personal preterite. Furthermore, Ambrazas writes that for the earliest stages of the Baltic development one can assume that the contrast between the present and past participles was based on the resultative meaning of the latter.

3.3 With the denotation of a prior action and a non-resultative meaning the attributive participle is hardly used in the popular speech and indeed in old writings it is hardly found either. The meaning is sometimes found today by analogy with the meaning of the periphrastic tenses, e.g., *teñ gyvẽnęs kaimỹnas* 'a neighbor living there' from *kaimỹnas teñ (bùvo) gyvẽnęs* 'a neighbor was living there' (Ambrazas, 1979, 39).

The prefixed attributive past passive participles are formed for the most part from intransitive non-derived verbs and the resultative meaning is so dominant that its connection with a preceding action is almost lost. Thus in such sequences as *išdỹkęs vaĩkas* 'naughty child,' *ištvirkęs sẽnis* 'dissolute old man,' *išklẽrę láiptai* 'rickety stairs,' *ištìžus mergà* 'sluggish girl,' *apsiblaũsę ãkys* 'drowsy eyes' there is really no longer any direct connection with a prior action of the verbs *išdỹkti* 'to become naughty,' *ištvirkti* 'to become dissolute,' *išklẽrti* 'to become rickety,' *ištìžti* 'to become sluggish,' *apsiblaũsti* 'to become sleepy,' etc. (Ambrazas, 1979, 39).

3.4 Particularly many attributive past active participles are derived from verbs of which finite forms (except for the preterite) and other participles are not frequently formed. In old writings they frequently translated simple adjectives of other languages with the Lithuanian past active participles, cf., e.g., from Bretkūnas' *Bible* (*Deuteronomy* 33, 14) *nunokens Waisius* 'reiffe frūchte, ripe fruit,' (*Numbers* 25, 4) *inkirschusi Rustibe* 'der grimmige Zorn, the fierce anger.'

3.5 The preposed past active participle retains its verbal government and proximity to the modified word but in the popular speech and in the old writings it is usually by itself or else modified by a single adverb, cf., e.g., Bretkūnas' *Postilla* (I 1569) *nauiei uszgimens Karalius* 'newly born king.' In general, however, if there is a need to modify the participle by more words the participle follows the word modified. The postpositional participle is more common (about 70 percent of the cases). Without dependent words postpositional participles sometimes have the same meaning as participles preceding the word modified, e.g, Sirvydas' *Punktay sakimu* (I 144$_8$):

žmog'	nusideis	ira	kayp	medžias	žalas.
man	having sinned	is	like	tree	green.

'A man who has sinned is like a green tree.' There is a tendency to put a participle which is a second modifier in position after the word modified, e.g., Sirvydas' *Punktay sakimu* (I 51₉):

idant	piktus	darbus	praszakusius	gierays
so that	evil	works	having past	well

....	atpilditu.
	(he) would recompense.

'So that (he) would make amends for past evil works.' (*Piktus darbus praszakusius* = Polish *złe vczynki przeszłe*.) Most frequently postpositional past active participles have dependent words and form non-restrictive verbal constructions, e.g., (Bretkūnas' *Postilla* II 104₁₆):

szmogus	isch	moterischkes	gimens	trumpai
man	from	woman	born	short (time)

giwen.
lives.

'A man born from woman lives a short time' (Ambrazas, 1979, 40).

3.6 Just as do the corresponding present active participles, the past active participles are frequently used in place of subordinate clauses, e.g., (Bretkūnas' *Bible*, *Genesis* 17, 23):

eme	....	wisus	Tarnus,	namie
he (took)		all	servants,	at home

gimusius.
born.

'He took all the servants who had been born at home' (Ambrazas, 1979, 40).

3.7 According to Ambrazas, 1979, 40, some authors used past active participles more frequently in place of substantives than in place of adjectives, the proportion in Sirvydas' *Punktay sakimu*, e.g., being 64:50. But usually the same participles account for many of the examples, e.g., *pavar̃gęs* (indef.) 'the tired (one)' *pavar̃gęsis* (def.) *nusidė̃jęs* 'sinner, i.e., the one who has sinned,' *numir̃ęs* 'dead, the one having died,' the latter particularly common in the fossilized expression *iš numirusiu̧* 'from the dead,' which makes up about one-half the examples (120) in Bretkūnas' *Postilla*. Such participles can be formed from unprefixed durative verbs and be used in place of subordinate clauses, cf., e.g., Sirvydas' *Punktay sakimu* (II 78$_{18}$):

| pinkieto | duonos | miežienes, | kurie |
| five | loaves | of barley, | which |

| likos | walgiusiemus. |
| remained (to those having) | eaten. |

3.8 From adjectivalized past active participles one can also form adverbs with the aid of the suffix *-iai*, e.g., *apsnūdusiai* 'drowsily, in a somnolent fashion,' *igùdusiai* 'skillfully, in an experienced manner,' *išdỹkusiai* 'naughtily, in a naughty manner,' *pasiùtusiai* 'madly, ferociously,' etc. According to Ambrazas, 1979, 41, we find such adverbial constructions already in the oldest writings, for the most part, however, with prefixed participial stems, e.g., Dauksa's *Postilla* (441$_2$) *paklidusiâi giria* 'mistakenly, by error, praises.' One also encounters comparative and superlative forms, e.g., *pasiutesnis* 'madder,' *pašėlesnis* 'madder,' *suaugesnis* 'more grown up,' *pasiučiausias* 'maddest,' *padūkiausias* 'most furious.' Only rarely do we encounter participial adverbs from unprefixed stems which do not have a resultative meaning, e.g., (*Kniga Nobaznistes* 82$_8$) *siutusiay manę gundina* 'madly tempt me,' cf., the modern dialect form *siutusiai šoka* 'dance madly.'

4

The Future Active Participle

4. The future active participle seems to have two formants, either -*sint*- or -*siant*-. We encounter the forms in the Samogitian (Žemaitish) and neighboring High Lithuanian dialects, e.g., nom. sg. masc. *dirbsis* 'will be working' (Palangà), *važiuosis* 'will be traveling' (Akmẽnė) < *-*sint*-*s* (Ambrazas, 1979, 42). One also encounters the Latvian indeclineable dialect form *būsit* (Endzelīns, 1951, 938) and OCS *byšęšteje* = Gk. *to méllon* 'that which will be.' All of the above forms could be derived from *-*sint*- which in turn could come from *-*sn̥t*- presumably cognate with an athematic 3rd pl. future *-*sn̥t(i)*. It seems more likely, however, that the future participle is analogical to the 2nd conjugation present active participle in -*is*. Cf. 2nd conjugation present 1st pl. *gãl-ime* 'we can,' 2nd pl. *gãl-ite*, nom. sg. masc. pres. act. prt. *gal-ĩs*: fut. 1st pl. *dir̃bs-ime* 'we shall work,' 2nd pl. *dir̃bs-ite*, nom. sg. masc. fut. act. prt. *dir̃bs-ĩs*.
4.1 The participles in -*siant*- are characteristics of the literary language and many dialects, e.g., nom. sg. masc. *būsiąs*, fem. *būsianti* 'future, about to be' and cf., Latv. nom. sg. masc. *būšus* 'future' (also < *-*siant*-*s*). It was originally thought that a form like the Sanskrit nom. sg. masc. *dāsyán* was an exact cognate of Lith. *dúosiąs* 'will be giving, about to give' but this view has been profoundly questioned by Schmid, 1963, 47. I am not prepared to say whether his view is correct or not, but his notion that they are not connected would correspond with my general feeling that it is necessary to question the existence of a feature in the proto-language even if it exists in the daughter languages.
4.2 According to Ambrazas, 1979, 42, future active participles are used only here and there in Samogitia and

in a large part of eastern High Lithuanian where they
function in the nominative case to denote indirect
speech. The rare attributive forms are semantically
isolated, e.g., (Jõniškis) *bū́siantis* (= *bū́simas*) *výras*
'future husband,' (Varenãvas) *bū́siṇtis gyvẽnimas* 'future
life, life after death,' (Šãtės) *dė̃sianti bóba* 'pregnant
woman, literally: about to lay, put (*dė́ti*) woman,'
(Gargždaĩ) *vèsinti avìs* 'pregnant sheep, literally:
about to bear (*vèsti*) sheep,' *turė̃sianti kárvė* 'cow with
calf, literally: about to have (a calf) cow.' The Acad.
Dict., Vol. 7, 914, reports the sentence with the nom.
sg. masc. fut. act. prt.:

Matýsiantis	žmogus	bestypsinąs
Will be seeing	man	will be tiptoeing

par	Gegrė́nų	miẽstą.
through	of Gegrė́nai	town.

The sentence would seem to mean: 'A man whom I have
seen somewhere tiptoeing through the town of Gegrė́nai.'
The Acad. Dict. glosses the word *matýsiantis* with
matýtas so that the future active participle would seem
to have passive meaning.

4.3 According to Ambrazas, 1979, 42, a broader attributive use of these future participles is attested
in the 16th and 17th century monuments. They are
regularly correlated with the other tenses and they
usually precede the modified word, e.g., (Bretkūnas'
Postilla I 372₀):

Nes	wissi	prarakai	pranesche	ape
Because	all	prophets	prophesied	about

busenti	alba	ateisenti		Messioschu.
future	or	(will be)	coming	Messiah.

A	Ianas	kasani		saka /	ape
But	John	in a sermon		tells	about

ateijusi		/	ir	nu	po	akim
(having) arrived			and	now	under	eye

santi	Messioschu	Kristu.
being	Messiah	Christ.

'Because all the prophets prophesied about a future or coming Messiah, but John in a sermon tells about the Messiah Christ who has arrived and is now before the eye(s).' The attributive future active participle usually precedes the modified noun.

4.4 Ambrazas, 1979, 43, writes that most of the future active participles are formed from a few verbs, *ateĩti* 'to come,' *bū́ti* 'to be' and somewhat more rarely *mir̃ti* 'to die,' and only occasionally from other verbs. Cf., e.g., (Daukša's *Postilla* 62$_{17}$: dat. sg. masc. fut. act. prt.) *mìrsiancziam' žmóguy* 'to mortal man' (= Polish *śmiertelnemu człowiekowi*). It is interesting to note that elsewhere the same Polish adjective *śmiertelny* 'mortal' may be translated by a present active participle. In the later development of the literary language the attributive use of the future active participle was revived and stimulated by the earlier tradition and the need of the literary language to differentiate more accurately characteristics of phenomena connected with the verbal action. In contemporary Lithuanian future active participles are formed from various transitive and intransitive verbs, but they are used relatively rarely.

5

The Present Passive Participle

5. There is good evidence that the cuneiform and hieroglyphic Luwian participle in -*mi*/-*ma* had an original form -*ma* and that its force was medio-passive. This would parallel exactly the Balto-Slavic participle in *-*mo*- according to Hamp, 1973, 45. Cf. Luwian nom. sg. animate *ki-i-ša-am-m[i-iš]*, neut. *ki-ša-am-ma-an* 'combed,' see Laroche, 1959, 55, and hieroglyphic Hittite nom. sg. perfect prt. *á-š¹-za-mi-a-s* 'beloved' (person), see Meriggi, 1962, 36, and reading -*za*- instead of -*ī*- as suggested by Hawkins, Morpurgo-Davies and Neumann, 1973, 151. The Albanian participle *punuem* 'worked' and the Middle Albanian verbal adjectives derived from participles, e.g., *mish i pjekëm* 'roast meat,' *i dhanëm* 'devoted' belong here (Hamp, 1973, 46-47).

The participle in -*m*- is attested in Tokharian also, cf. Tokharian B *cämpamo* 'being able, capable' from AB *cämp*- 'to be able' which van Windekens, 1979, 48, compares with Lith. *tempiù* 'I stretch out.'

Also cited by van Windekens are B *pälkamo* 'shining,' *salamo* 'jumping,' *ynamo* 'going, running,' which van Windekens compares with Lith. *einù* 'I am going.' Van Windekens, however, derives these forms from *-*men*-, although it is not certain that this is necessary.

Ambrazas, 1979, 44, writes that the form *-*mo*- is to be noted in Skt. *bhī-máḥ* 'fearful,' (cf. Latv. *bîtiês*, Lith. *bijóti* 'to be afraid'), *pra-stī-maḥ* 'crowded together, swarming, clustering,' cf. Lith. *stŷroti* 'to be stiff; to stick out.'

Old Prussian is said to lack the participial form in -*mo*- but it seems likely that the single attestation *poklausīmanas* 'heard' shows the suffix -*m(e)n*- and is to be compared with the present passive participle forms Gk. *pheró-men-os*, Skt. *bhára-māṇ-aḥ* 'being carried.'

On the other hand if in the Old Prussian adjective *enimumne* 'acceptable' (= German *angeneme*) we assume a transposition of the last two letters and correct the form to *enimumen it can then be phonemicized as /enimaman/ and divided morphologically into the /en-im-a-ma-n/ in which the -ma- reflects the Indo-European *-mo-. Such a form could be compared directly with Lith. (prì-)ìmamas 'accepted, acceptable.'

Although the passive meaning of the *-m- participle is more abundantly attested in Slavic there are also traces of an original active meaning, cf. Polish *niewiadomi* = Latin *ignorantes* 'not knowing,' (Havránek, 1937, 31), Czech *lakomý* 'avaricious, greedy,' *nevidomý* = Polish *niewidomy* 'blind, i.e., not seeing. Note the Old Russian example (Havránek, 1937, 35): (a)

jepiskopi že,	egda xotętь		postavętь
bishops	when they want, they may		appoint
popa	ili	dьjakona ... da	prizovutь
priest	or	deacon let	them invite
znajemyja	susědi	jego že	znajutь	iz
knowing	neighbors,	him	know	since

dětьska
childhood, i.e., 'when the bishops wish, they will appoint a priest or a deacon ... let them invite knowing neighbors (i.e., neighbors familiar with the candidate), (those) who have known him since (his) childhood.'

Ambrazas, 1979, 52, compares the Russian *znaemyja susědi* with Lith. *žìnomas žmogùs* 'an intelligent, (knowing) man' where *žìnomas* is used in an active sense. (Of course, the passive sense of *žìnomas* is common, thus it more frequently means 'known; famous.')

According to Ambrazas, 1979, 44, the verbal characteristics of the attributive *-mo- participles appear more clearly in the Samogitian and western High Lithuanian dialects where the periphrastic passive and the half-predicative passive participles are widely used. Here the present passive participles are clearly correlated with other participles according to tense and diathesis and can denote characteristics arising from a clearly passive action, e.g., (b)

neraudók,	mergẽle ...	trejùs	meteliùs
don't cry,	oh girl ...	three	years

širdỹj	laikomóji
in the heart	held,

i.e., don't cry, girl, held three years in (my) heart (Klaipėda region folksong). The agent of the passive action, although rarely expressed, appears in the genitive, e.g., (c)

vėjo	girgždinamos	dùrys	neléido
by the wind	caused to squeak	doors	didn't allow

miegóti
to sleep, i.e., the doors squeaking in the wind didn't allow (one) to sleep. Especially in the older writings is it difficult to distinguish the agentive from the possessive use, e.g., (Bretkūnas' *Postilla* II 216$_2$): (d)

ius	mana	...	milimus	klausitoius ..
you	my (= by me)		beloved	listeners
(acc.)	(gen.)		(acc. pl.)	(acc. pl.)

meldziu ...
I implore.
It is unclear whether this means 'I implore you, my beloved listeners (or) listeners beloved by me.'

According to Ambrazas, 1979, 44, however, only a small portion of the attested present passive participles have a concrete passive meaning. Much more frequently they have a generalized meaning of lasting over a period of time and have no dependent words, e.g., *marìnamas ligónis* 'attended (dying) patient' (Mósėdis), *mýlimas svẽčias* 'beloved guest' (Veliuonà), *pažį́stamas žmogùs* 'an acquaintance, a man with whom one is acquainted.'
According to Ambrazas, 1979, 44-45, in texts representing the western High Lithuanian and Samogitian dialects which prefer the periphrastic passive, attributive participles are comparatively rare, but they have a clearer passive meaning and more frequently make up verbal type sequences with dependent words. On the other hand in the writings of authors from the eastern and southern High Lithuanian area where the periphrastic passive is not characteristic the adjectival use of the present passive participle predominates.

Ambrazas, 1979, 45, writes that the meaning of possibility is connected with that of a generalized passive action, e.g., *bredamà ùpè* 'fordable river, river which can be forded' (Endriejãvas), *válgomos úogos* 'edible berries' (Vilkavìškis), and from Sirvydas' *Punktay sakimu* II 197$_{16}$): *wisi dayktay regimi ir neregimi* (= Polish *widome y nie widome*) 'all things visible and invisible,' (Sirvydas' *Dictionarium* 350) *plaukiama upe* (= Polish *spustny*, Lat. *navigabile flumen*) 'navigable river.' Prefixed participles include the following examples: (Summa, 105) *su-prantamas žodis* 'comprehensible word;' (Sirvydas' *Dictionarium*, 268) *iž-manomas* (= Polish *pojętny rozumem*, Lat. *comprehensibilis, facilis ad intelligendum*) 'comprehensible, easy to understand.' The negative usage predominates with the attributive present passive participles. Examples: (Sirvydas' *Punktay sakimu* I 210$_2$) *ne-nu-sekami kieley* 'paths which cannot be followed, unfollowable paths' (= Polish *nie wybadâne*), (DP 325$_{35}$) *ne iž-bîloma žala* 'unspeakable damage.'

The meaning of possibility is closely bound to the meaning of aim or goal of the action, cf., e.g., (nom. pl.) *válgomieji burõkai* 'red beets, beets for eating,' (nom. pl.) *ariamì laukaĩ* 'fields for plowing,' (*Margareta Theologica* 181$_{a18}$) *awis piauiemosos* 'sheep for slaughtering,' (Bretkūnas' *Bible, Genesis* 6, 21; gen. sg.) *istrowos walgamosios* 'food for eating,' (id., *Exodus* 29, 40; nom. sg.) *gerama affiera* 'drink offering' (Ambrazas, 1979, 45).

In some dialects where the debitive participle in *-tinas* is unknown the **-mo-* participle has the function of the former, e.g., *ką ten girti negiriamą daiktą* 'why praise a thing which shouldn't be praised' (Pagiriaĩ), cf. also (Sirvydas' *Dictionarium* 180) *ambiguus = Abeioiamas, abejotinas* 'doubtful, to be doubted.'

When the present passive participle denotes possibility, necessity or goal, the genitive case is understood to denote the possessive meaning, e.g., (e)

mūsų	válgomi	burõkai	taĩ	jaũ	visái
our	eating	beets	they	already	completely

sušãlo.
have frozen.
'Our beets for eating have completely frozen' (Ambrazas, 1979, 45).

Ambrazas, 1979, 46, writes that the subject of the present passive participle under such circumstances is usually rendered by the dative case both in the modern language and in the old writings, (Bretkūnas' *Postilla* I 421$_{19}$): (f)

szmogui	neischkalbama	muka
for the man	unspeakable	torture

'Unspeakable torture for the man, the man is unable to speak of the torture'; (Sirvydas' *Punktay sakimu* I 128$_{27}$): (g)

ne	wienam	iż		żmoniu	nezinomas	ir
not	to one	from	among	men	not known	and

nepazistamas
not acquainted

'Not acquainted with or known to a single one of the men' (= Polish *żadnemu ... niewiadómy y nieznaiómy*); (Sirvydas' *Punktay sakimu* I 253$_{29}$): (h)

buday	pikti	regimi	wisiemus
manners	evil	visible	to all

'Evil manners visible to all.' It seems to me that each one of the datives in the examples can be understood as an experiencer, i.e., something is done to the person expressed by the dative case, in the first example 'torture to the man,' in the second 'unknown to anyone,' and in the third 'invisible to all.' Ambrazas gives the Latvian example *man aŗama cęlmu zeme* 'I am to plow the stumpy land.' For Ambrazas the notion of 'experiencer' can be included in the concept of subject.

According to Būga, 1958, 532, Jaunius said that such a sentence as: (i)

(Aš)	dúodu	vaĩkui		dúoną	válgyti
I	give	to the child		bread	to eat,

could be passivized in several ways:

(j) Vaĩkas   dúodamas
    The child is given

(k) Dúona   duodamà
    The bread is given

(I) Trobà   duodamà
    The hut is given
'The hut in which the event takes place.'

Verbs which require objects in cases other than the accusative may also be passivized. Thus the following verbs require genitive objects, *ieškóti* 'to search for,' *noréti* 'to want, to wish,' *bijóti* 'to fear,' *láukti* 'to wait for,' *pageidáuti* 'to desire,' *prašýti* 'to ask for,' *reikti* 'to be necessary.' Note then the following examples: (Juškevičius' *Wedding Songs* 256) *norimi ženteliai* 'wished for sons-in-law,' (Skiřsnemunė) *láukiamas dáiktas* 'a thing awaited,' (Veliuonà) *bijomas žmogùs* 'a feared man,' (Vydūnas) *geidáujama knygà* 'the desired book.' In the older writings sequences with the participle *reikiamas* are particularly widely used according to Ambrazas, 1979, 46. Cf. (Bretkūnas' *Postilla* II 360) *reikiamieghi daiktai* 'necessary things,' (Sirvydas' *Postilla* I 200$_{15}$, gen. pl.) *ne reykiamu žodžiu* 'not necessary words' (= Polish *niepotrzebnych*).

Note also the example from *Margarita Theologica* 50a$_{11}$: *žmones ... pagelbami* 'people (who are) helped.'

Likewise from DP 193$_{38}$ *dáiktas abéioiamas* 'doubtful affair' (= Polish *niepewna*), although *abejóti* requires an instrumental object (Ambrazas, 1979, 46).

There are various kinds of syntactic relationships expressed by the relationship of the *-mo-* participle to the word modified, according to Ambrazas, 1979, 46. Participles which denote the means of an action can be considered some kind of transformations of the instrumental case. Note the following examples: (Chyliński *Bible*, II *Samuel* 12, 31) *po kulameys gieležies važeys* 'under iron threshing machines,' (Bretkūnas' *Bible*, *Exodus* 29, 21) *imk ... Aleiu tepamaghi* 'take anointing oil,' (Sirvydas' *Dictionarium* 128) *Szaudomieij dayktay* 'charge for shooting, literally: shooting things' (= Polish *ładunek do strzelby*), (Mielcke's *Dictionary* II, 207) *mėžemoji szákė* 'dung fork, pitchfork used for spreading dung,' (id., II 561) *jáutis árams* 'plow ox, draught-ox,' etc.

Participles denoting place where an action takes place may be derived from transitive and intransitive verbs according to Ambrazas, 1979, 46. Note the examples: (Chyliński *Bible*, 97, 60) *raszomątobliczią* 'writing table,' (Bretkūnas' *Bible*, *Leviticus*

25, 29; acc. sg.) *giwenamą Trobą* 'dwelling house' (= German *Wonhaus*), Sirvydas' *Dictionarium* 136) *Kamara gulima* 'bedroom' (= Polish *sypialnia komora*), (Bretkūnas' *Bible* I *Samuel* 20, 19; acc. sg.) *dirbama diena* 'on the work-day' (= German *am Werckeltage*; note the King James English version 'when the business was *in hand*'). DP 111$_{39}$: (gen. sg.) *Vžgawimôsios Seredôs* 'fasting Wednesday, i.e., Ash Wednesday' (= Polish *wstępna Srzodę*), (Mielcke's *Dictionary* II 398) *sėjams cziėsas* 'sowing time' (= German *Saatzeit*).

According to Ambrazas, 1979, 47, participles denoting means derived from transitive verbs are frequently used with the genitive case which denotes the patient of the action, e.g., (Grūžiai) *avẽlių keȓpamos žirklės* 'sheep-shearing shears,' (Salantaĩ) *mẽdžių diegiamà dienà* 'tree-planting day,' (Joniškẽlis) *alaũs dãromas kùbilas* ' vat for making beer.' (Mielcke's *Dictionary* I, 81) *gėlmės jėszkomas Szwinnas* 'plummet, literally: depth seeking (sought for) lead' (German *Bleywurf*), (id., II 430) *skylẽlė prãkaitũ iszejemoji* 'pore, literally: small exit hole for sweat' (German *Schweissloch*), (id., II 445) *adata lãszinių įwãrstomà* 'larding-pin, literally: needle for lacing up bacon' (German *Spicknadel*). According to Ambrazas, 1979, 47, the Latvian correspondences confirm the antiquity of the construction (Barons' and Wissendorfs' *Latvian songs* 15956): (m)

Sirmi   zirgi ...   brūtes   vedamie
gray   horses ...   for the bride   brought

'Gray horses brought for the bride.' (The genitive case could be construed as the agent and one could imagine the construction as meaning 'by the bride' rather than the correct 'for the bride.') An example from the Mülenbach-Endzelīns' *Dictionary* II, 405, *linu plūcams laĩks* 'flax pulling time.' In the above example *linu* 'flax' is in the gen. pl. and the word *linu* can be understood as the object of *plūcams* 'pulling.' According to Ambrazas, 1979, 47, such a usage of the genitive case is most likely derived from the old adnominal genitive used with verbal adjectives (later participles) with the suffix *-mo-*. In a similar manner the adnominal genitive, understood as the subject of the verbal action came to function as the genetivus auctoris. Thus both the object and the subject constructions are to be connected with the nominal nature of the participle which is indifferent to verbal diathesis.

The relationships between the present passive participle and the modified word are sometimes very indirectly associated with the concept of the modified word, e.g., *mirštamà ligà* 'fatal illness' (from *mir̃ti* 'to die'), *puolimóji ligà* 'epilepsy' (from *pùlti* 'to fall'), *kimbamà môtriška* 'a woman attracting men, literally: a clung to woman' (from *kìbti* 'to cling to, to stick to'), *sėjamas vėjas* 'wind suitable for sowing, literally: sowing, sown wind,' *guliamà dúona* 'free bread, literally: lying down, recumbent bread,' from the notion that it is obtained by doing nothing, by lying down, derived from *gulėti* 'to lie down, to be lying down.' (Kuršaitis' *Dictionary* I, 526) *Giedamosios knygos* 'hymn books, literally: singing.'

According to Ambrazas, 1979, 47, sequences of words in which the participle denotes the action or the state of the subject form a special category. These are for the most part formed from intransitive verbs, cf., e.g., (Kudìrkos Naumiestis) *skaũdamas pir̃štas* 'aching finger,' (Svėdasaĩ) *limpamà ligà* 'contagious disease' (from *lìpti* 'to stick to'), (Kvėdarna) *žindamas ver̃šis* 'suckling calf' (from *žísti* 'to suck'). The relationship to the modified word corresponds very well with present active participles which denote constant characteristics, e.g., *skaũdantis pir̃štas* 'aching finger,' *lim̃panti ligà* 'contagious disease,' *žindantis ver̃šis* 'suckling calf.' Such a meaning is known in Lithuanian in the oldest writings, e.g., (*ChB, Phillipians* 4, 18 [310, 11-12]) *kwepiamas kwapas* 'sweet smell, literally: smelling, smelled (good) smell,' (Mielcke's *Dictionary* II, 402) *Kudikis žindams* 'suckling child' (German *Säugling*), (ib., I, 241) *skaudama koja* 'aching foot' (German *schlimmer Fuss*).

Ambrazas, 1979, 47, quotes also the following forms from the *ChB*: (*Mark* 12, 33 [86, 15]) *degamos - afieros* 'burnt offerings' (see also Latv. *dedzams upuris* 'Brandopfer'); (*Luke* I, 10; gen. pl.) *deganciu afieru* which appears to mean 'burning offerings' although the English King James version has 'incense,' Luther has *unter der Stunde des Räucherns* 'during the time of incense burning' from the Greek *têi hôrai toũ thumiámatos*. The example from Mark translates Greek (gen. pl.) *holokautōmátōn* '(than) burnt-offerings.' Although apparently two different concepts are being used the

Lithuanian examples do not necessarily justify the usage of the passive as opposed to the active on semantic grounds.

Transitive verbs also sometimes seem to use the *-mo- participle with active meaning, cf. gýdomas (gýdantis) vanduõ 'curative water,' kláusiamas (kláusiantis) žvilgsnis 'questioning glance,' pjáunamas (pjáunantis) peĩlis 'cutting knife.' Frequently according to Ambrazas, 1979, 47-48, these have an instrumental meaning, gýdo vándeniu 'cures with water,' kláusia žvilgsniù 'questions with a glance,' pjáuna peiliù 'cuts with a knife.'

Ambrazas, 1979, 48, writes that the actual agent or patient with the *-mo- participle is relatively more rare. Thus forms like the following are not so common: (Dùsetos) žìnomas žmogùs 'a knowing person, a person who knows,' (Panevėžỹs) suprañtamas žmogùs 'a man who understands,' (Tirkšliaĩ) griáunamas vėjas 'a destructive wind, a wind that throws (things) down,' laukiamà móteriška 'pregnant woman' (from láukti 'to wait').

The durative or iterative meaning of the Lith.-Latv. *-mo- participles from ancient times separated them from the participles in *-us- and *-to-. This distinction laid the foundation for the contrast of present versus past, a contrast which is much earlier than the active passive contrast, as is evidenced by the following forms which contrast for tense but not for diathesis: ẽsamas 'being, existing' vs. bū́tas 'having been;' gyvẽnamas 'living' vs. gyvéntas 'lived,' etc. As far as their durative meaning is concerned the *-mo- participles are close to those in *-nt- which in early Baltic were inclined to become active (Ambrazas, 1979, 50).

In my view all of the *-mo- participles were originally intransitive and only with the development of the active voice were some of them reinterpreted as passives of transitives.

6

The Past Passive Participle

6. D'jakonov, 1967, 105-107, suggests the following model for the possible development of the ergative construction. At first one might consider the possible simple apposition of the subject word with a predicate word, the latter not having any particular form of a finite verb, but rather being some type of diffuse word denoting a concept state. This would be more or less a pre-verbal condition of the language. Note the following constructions:

(a) Lith.
    rugiaĩ   pjáuta
    rye   cut
    (nom. pl.) (neut. sg.) 'The rye is (was) cut.'

(b) Russian
    batьka   ubito
    father   killed
    (nom. sg.) (neut. sg.)
'The father is (was) killed.'

Now according to Ambrazas, 1979, 204-205, such constructions as (a) and (b) are very ancient. They show no concord between the number and gender of the noun and the *-to participle.

It has long been known that the earliest form of the Indo-European adjective in predicate position did not agree in case, number and gender with the noun. Thus Hirt, 1937, 25-26, gives such examples: Gk. *ouk agathòn polukoiraníē* 'the rule of many is not good' (in which *agathòn* 'good' is in the neut. sg. and does not agree with the fem. sg. *polukoiraníē* 'rule of many'); *ápiston taĩs politeíais hē turannís* 'despotic rule is untrustworthy for the states' (in which *ápiston* 'untrustworthy' is in the neut. sg. and does not agree with the fem. sg. *turannís* 'despotic rule'); Lat. *varium et mutabile semper femina* 'woman is always diverse and changeable' (in which the neut. sg. adjectives *varium* 'diverse' and *mutabile* 'changeable' do not agree in gender with the fem. *femina* 'woman'); *turpe senex miles, turpe senilis amor* 'unseemly is an old soldier, unseemly is aged love' (in which the neut. sg. *turpe* 'unseemly' does not agree with the masc. sg. subjects *miles* 'soldier' or *amor* 'love'); Russian *grex sladko, a čelovek padko* 'sin is sweet and the human is susceptible' (in which the neut. sg. adjectives *sladko* 'sweet' and *padko* 'susceptible' do not agree with the masc. sg. subjects *grex* 'sin' and *čelovek* 'human').

At a later date agreement between noun and predicate was introduced giving such sentences as the following in Old Indic:

(c) rājā mr̥taḥ
    king dead, died
    (nom. sg.) (nom. sg.) 'The king died, is dead.'

(d) Yamaḥ prayātaḥ
    Yama set out
    (nom. sg.) (nom. sg.)
'Yama set out on the road' (Gonda, 1960, 90).

Sentences (a) and (b) are prototypical in that they show no grammatical concord between subject and predicate and sentences (c) and (d) are prototypical in that they are intransitive and cannot be considered passive. The passivization of sentences (a) and (b) is the result of a reinterpretation of an earlier simple intransitive and the shift of the notion of the subject of an intransitive to patient of a transitive.

The shift from intransitive to passive is not limited to the Indo-European family of languages. I would give here Hakulinen's, 1957, 175, comments on the Finnish passive: '... Auch aus anderen Gründen ist es wahrscheinlich, dass die Vorstufe des heutigen finnischen Passivs nicht unpersönlich war und dass somit das jetzt als Objekt aufgefasste Satzglied früher einmal als Subjekt auftrat (z. B. in einem solchen Fall wie (veralt.) *siemen quivettijn*, wo *siemen* 'Same' heute als Objekt aufgefasst wird, während es ursprünglich Subjekt war: der Same trocknete (der intrans. Charakter durch reflexiven wiedergegeben). [Also ursprüngliche Auffassung, der Same trocknete sich = wurde trocken, heutige Auffassung: "es wurde getrocknet = man trocknete den Samen"].'

There are actually two passive markers in Finnish, one having the strong grade in *-t-* (weak grade *-d-* or its representative) and the second having the strong grade in *-tt-* (and the weak grade in *-t-*). Examples of the first passive are: *saa-ti-in* preterit passive of *saada* 'to receive,' *juo-tu* preterit passive participle of *juoda* 'to drink,' *juo-da-an* present passive of *juoda*, etc. This passive participle, according to Hakulinen, 1957, 176-177, is the old original participle and the second one with the strong grade in *-tt-* and the weak grade in *-t-* is derived from the reflexive causatives within the history of Finnish. Thus such a causative as *pääs-tä-n* 'I free, cause to become free' (from the fundamental word *pääsen* 'I become free') developed a reflexive **päästäksen* 'he caused himself to become free, he freed himself' which came to mean 'he was freed.' Still Hakulinen writes in footnote 1, 176, that in Mordvin there is a passive which goes back to a **t* which cannot phonetically be connected with the causatives of the same language. On this basis some have wished to keep the Lappish and Hungarian *tt-* passive separate and derive the **tt-* passive as such from the Finno-Ugric proto-language.

The second **t-* participle whether derived from the causatives or not has left its trace in Hungarian, but one notices the similar distribution. Thus Károly, 1972, 111, writes: 'The main function of the participle with the formants *-t/-tt* is to express the antecedent passive action and the state which results from it.' It is passive if the verb is transitive, but active if the verb is mediopassive. Note the examples taken from Károly, 111:

(e) A   pénztáros   a   megszámolt   pénzt
    The   cashier   the   counted   money

   eltette.
   put away.
'The cashier put away the counted money.'

(f) A   kosár   megtelt   szeméttel
    The   basket   became filled   with litter.

Károly says that the participle is only rarely used with non-mediopassive verbs, but nevertheless he gives the examples:

(g) A   messziről   jött   ember.
    The   from afar   having come   man.
'The man who has come from afar.'

A parallel with the Indo-European situation is to be found in the fact that the participle in -t/-tt can be used in a subjective genitive construction (Károly, 1972, 119):

az   én   választottam
the (one)   my   chosen.   'The one chosen by me.'

Returning now to D'jakonov's, 1967, 107, concept, suppose that one introduces an agent to which the stative notion belongs. I propose then that in Indo-European the agent in the genitive case was introduced.

Next consider the following sentences in Old Indic (Delbrück, 1888, 153):

(h) pátyuḥ   krītā́   satī́
    by the spouse   bought   wife
    (gen. sg.)   (nom. sg. fem.)   (nom. sg. fem.)
'The wife bought by the spouse.'

(i) tā́   asya   prajā́ḥ   sr̥ṣṭā́ḥ
    the   by him   beings   created
    (nom. pl.)   (gen. sg. masc.)   (nom. pl.)   (nom. pl.)
'The beings created by him.

(j) tā́ny   asya   prītā́ni   devébhyo
    they   by him   gratified   to the gods
    (nom. pl.)   (gen. sg. masc.)   (nom. pl.)   (dat. pl.)

    havyā́ṃ   vahanti
    sacrifice   bring
    (acc. sg.)   (3rd pl. pres.)
'Having been gratified by him they bring the sacrifice to the gods.'

It is usually thought today that the forms *krītā́* 'bought,' *sr̥ṣṭā́h* 'created,' and *prītāni* 'gratified' are passive participles, but I would propose rather than they were originally intransitive in meaning and that a hypothetical original form of the sentences could have omitted the agent (in the genitive case) denoting 'belonging to.' The passive notion derives from the re-interpretation of the old intransitive. Such sentences as the above would then correspond to D'jakonov's second phase, i.e., the agent would be introduced. Note now the following almost parallel Lithuanian sentence:

(k) Senų miškaĩ mylėta
  ancients forests loved
  gen. pl. nom. pl. neut. sg.

'The ancients loved the forests' (Matthews, 1955, 354; See also 34a).

The Lithuanian sentence is parallel to the Old Indic sentences, the only major difference being that the *-to participle does not agree with the patient, although such would be possible and a later version of the same sentence could show the same type of grammatical concord:

(1) Senų miškaĩ mylėti
  ancients forests loved
  gen. pl. nom. pl. nom. pl.

Originally, of course, such an Old Indic sentence as the following showing the subject in the nominative case represents an earlier situation:

(m) rājā   gṛham gataḥ
  king   home   went
  nom. sg.   nom. sg.

'The king went home.'

In Lithuanian the use of the genitive as the agent with the *to- participle formations, led to its introduction as the subject of intransitive participles in *-to. Thus:

(n) karãliaus namõ eĩta
  king   home went
  gen. sg.   neut. sg.

'The king went home' (see 30.5 [r-w]).

Sentence (m) is innovative in that there is grammatical concord between the subject and the *-to participle, whereas sentence (n) is innovative in that the subject is in the genitive case. The Lithuanian situation has its parallel in West Georgian dialects which have introduced the ergative case, replacing the etymological nominative case with intransitive verbs in forms of the aorist, e.g., *kac-ma movida* 'the man (erg.) came,' *kac-ma mokvda* 'the man (erg.) died' (Boeder, 1979, 443).

Gołąb, 1975, 29, has introduced the term *activization* to denote the possibility of the complementation of a formerly passive verb by a direct object. If a Pole is faced with the task of translating an English agentless passive like *this house was built in 1915* he may either choose:

(o)	dom	ten	został	zbudowany
	house	this	was	built
	nom. sg.	nom. sg.	aux.	nom. sg. masc. past psv. prt.
	w	1915	
	in	1915	

or

(p)	dom	ten	zbudowano ...
	house	this	built ...
	acc. sg.	acc. sg.	neut. sg. past psv. prt.

According to Gołąb, he will most likely choose the latter sentence (p). In such a sentence the former subject in the nominative case has come to be understood as the object in the accusative case.

Note the similar reversal in Lithuanian where the difference between the nominative and accusative cases is clearly marked. Originally such apparent impersonal constructions were used with the Lithuanian nominative case, cf., e.g.,

(q)	Ant	šakelių	ant	žaliųjų	vainikai
	On	branches	on	green	wreathes
	prep.	gen.	prep.	gen.	nom. pl.
	(vainikus)	kabinta		
	(wreathes)	hung		
	(acc. pl.)	neut. prt.		

'Wreathes are hung on green branches' (Paulauskienė, 1979, 105). In the older form of the sentence the subject *vainikai* 'wreathes' was in the nominative plural which is interpreted as the subject of the neut. participle. Later as the feeling of *kabinta* 'hung' shifts from intransitive to transitive it becomes possible to use an accusative case *vainikus* 'wreathes' which is then felt as an object.

It is interesting to note that the famous Lithuanian language reformer, Jonas Jablonskis, 1957, 621-622, finds the following sentence culled from native Lithuanian sources as incorrect:

(r) Čià   jõ   surašýta   kèturis
    Here   by him   written   four
            gen. sg.   neuter sg.   acc. pl.

    sąsiuvinius
    fascicles
    acc. pl.

'Here four fascicles were written by him.' He would correct this to:

(s) Čià   jõ   surašýti   keturì
    Here   by him   were written   four
            gen. sg.   nom. pl.   nom. pl.

    sąsiuviniai
    fascicles
    nom. pl.

The incorrect portion is, namely, the substitution of the accusative plural (kèturis sąsiuvinius) for the nominative plural (keturì sąsiuviniai). And, in fact, Ambrazas, 1979, 17, writes that the etymological construction rãšoma laĩškas 'a letter is being written' with laĩškas 'letter' in the nominative singular is being replaced by rãšoma laĩšką, with laĩšką 'letter' in the accusative singular. The point is that we observe also in Lithuanian *activization*, i.e., the old passive is being reinterpreted as an active and is taking an accusative case. In other words, Jablonskis was fighting this trend of activization when he called sentence (r) in the preceding paragraph incorrect, see 29.51 (p).

In fact the connection between the 3rd sg. middle aorist in *-to* and the *-to* participles has long been recognized. Hirt, 1928, 102, wrote:

> Die 3. Sg. Med. des sogenannten Wurzelaoristes geht auf -*to* aus. Wir können die Formen des sog. starken Aorists im Griech., des Wurzelaorists im Indischen dem Kasus indefinitus des Verbaladjektivs auf -*to* gleichsetzen: ai. ákr̥ta: kr̥tás 'gemacht';

ai. avṛta: vṛtás 'gewählt'; ai. ārta: ṛtás
'geschickt'; ai. amṛta: mṛtás 'gestorben'; ai.
aspṛta: spṛtás 'gewinnen'; ai. ajukta: juktás
'anschirren'; ai. amata 'denken': matás; ai.
apṛkta 'mischen': pṛktás; ai. abhakta 'zuteilen':
bhaktás; ai. vikta 'zittern': viktás; ai. áspašṭa:
spašṭas; ai. asṛšṭa 'loslassen': sṛšṭás; gr.
étheto: ai. adhita: gr. thetós, ai. hitás; ai.
ásthita: sthitás von sthā 'stehen'; ai. astṛta:
astṛtás 'unüberwindlich'; ai. agū́rta: gūrtás
'begrüßt', l. grātus; ai. agata: gatás, gr.
batós 'gegangen'; ai. ávṛkta 'zusammendrehen':
vṛktás; ai. asakta 'hängen, haften': saktás; ai.
amatta 'fröhlich sein': mattas. Dazu kommen aus
dem Griech.: éphato: phatós; ksúneto: hetós;
gr. éssuto: ai. čjutás; (gr.) lékto: lektós;
ferner venetisch zoto: gr. dotós l. datus; got.
stōp, ahd. stuot: gr. statós, l. status, ai.
sthitás; gr. egéneto: l. genitus; abg. pitŭ: ai.
pītás usw.; gr. plẽto: l. com-plētus, ai. pūrtás;
gr. éphthito: ai. kšitás; gr. ékhuto: ai. hutás;
gr. blẽto: blētós u.a.

In the history of the Indo-European languages this
process of activization has taken place so that under
the influence of the active voice the middle voice which
represents the old ergative construction (cf. Lith. senŭ
miskaĩ mylẽta) has been 'activized' taking an accusative
patient and a nominative agent. The ending *-to could
either become part of the adjectival paradigm, in which
case it adopted the typical *-o (-ā) stem adjectival
endings or else it was incorporated into a new verbal
paradigm which came into existence under the influence
of the active paradigm.

An example from Marathi (as given by Elizarenkova,
1967, 123) shows the addition of an agent marker to the
ergative verbal form (which also shows concord with the
patient). Note the following sentence:

(t) Tũ   pustak   vācal-
    You   book   read
    Inst. sg.   nom.-acc. sg.

    ẽ-   s
    patient   agent
    marker   marker

Tũ pustak vācalẽs 'You read the book.'
In this sentence the *-ẽ-* encodes the neuter gender of
the noun *pustak* 'book' and the *-s* the 2nd sg. pronoun
tũ. It is in this manner that the middle-perfect endings
of the attested Indo-European languages were created.
Thus, for example, the Old Indic 2nd sg. middle aorist
was created by the addition of the active ending *-as* to
the 3rd sg. middle aorist ending (which originally showed
verbal concord with the neuter patient) *-ta*. Thus *-tās*
(< *ta* plus *-as*) and later with the adoption of the
aspiration typical of 2nd person forms it became *-thās*
(see Schmalstieg, 1980, 93-94).

Schmidt, 1972, 453, has given examples from Caucasian languages where there is a tendency to superimpose the agent concord on an older patient concord in the verb.

I have adapted slightly the Georgian examples from K. H. Schmidt, 1972, 452:

(u)   *vač̣ar-man*   *pov-n-a*   *margalit̩-ni*
       the merchant   found   the pearls
       erg. sg.   aor.   nom. pl.

(v)   *vač̣ar-ta*   *pov-n-es*   *margalit̩-ni*
       the merchants   found   the pearls
       erg. pl.   aor.   nom. pl.

In these examples the older concord is expressed by the *-n-* of the aorist tense which agrees with the *-ni* of the nominative plural. The historically younger concord is expressed by the singular personal ending *-a* which agrees with the ergative singular (*vač̣ar-*)*man* 'the merchant' and the plural ending *-es* which agrees with the ergative plural (*vač̣ar-*)*ta* 'the merchants.'

(Syntactically one could compare the following Lithuanian example:

(w)   *pir̃klio*   *surastì*   *smarãgdai*
       by the merchant   (were) found   emeralds
       gen. sg.   nom. pl. past   nom. pl.
                             psv. part.

From the point of view of contemporary Lithuanian this is interpreted as a passive participle, but this is only a result of the fact that we now have an active voice with which to contrast the passive. The agreement concord is between *surastì* 'found' [nom. pl.] and *smarãgdai* 'emeralds' [nom. pl.].)

As we have seen above the *-to-* participle is etymologically identical with the 3rd sg. middle aor. Old Indic *ádi-ta*, Gk. *édo-to* and in fact such a Lith. neut. sg. participle as *dúo-ta* corresponds exactly in form to the Old Indic and Greek middle forms given above. In Old Indic and Greek complete middle counterparts were developed, but the Lithuanian form *dúo-ta* never developed a full verbal paradigm as did Greek and Old Indic. Although the shift of the *-to* participle (or adjective forms) to a full verbal paradigm was accomplished in prehistoric times in Old Indic and Greek, the history of such a shift is actually attested in Farsi where we find the present paradigm:

    kard-am   kard-im
    kard-i   kard-id (kard-in)
    kard   kard-and (kard-an)

in which the root *kard* is derived from Old Persian *krtam* (see Watkins, 1962, 94 and Bogoliubov, 1982). The development of a full verbal conjugation from a participle is also attested in Polish, cf., e.g., *miał-em* 'I had,' 2nd sg. *miał-esz* etc.

Although originally there was no agreement between the *-to-* form and the patient of the action, when the forms came to be used as dependent parts of the sentence such adjectival agreement arose. The participial use had its origin in etymological sequences very much like what we would call subordinate clauses, and is surely a later development. The older forms are retained in clauses such as: *Senų miškaĩ myléta* 'the forests were loved by the ancients.' Once this was combined with a sentence such as *jis gyvẽno miškuosè* 'he lived in the forests' to give: *Jis gyvẽno senų mylétuose miškuosè* 'he lived in the forests loved by the ancients' the adjectival agreement became essential and the forms turned into full participles.

According to Ambrazas, 1979, 54, Lithuanian verbal derivatives with the suffix *-to-* derived from intransitive verbs are indifferent as to diathesis and tense. These are for the most part considered adjectives and not correlated with participles, e.g., *báltas* 'white' from *bálti* 'to become white, to be white,' *kìltas* 'stately, imposing, tall' from *kìlti* 'to rise,' *šáltas* 'cold' from *šálti* 'to become cold,' *rúgtas* 'sour' from *rúgti* 'to become sour,' *skýstas* 'liquid' from *skýsti* 'to liquefy.' We find in Latvian the corresponding words *balts* 'white,' *salts* 'cold,' *silts* 'warm,' and in Old Prussian *skijstan* 'pure,' *ructan-dadan* 'sour milk' (Elbing Vocabulary 690). Ambrazas, 55, writes that the coincidence of formation and meaning with corresponding words in other Baltic languages shows that these Baltic derivatives in *-to-* are not adjectivized participles or analogical formations formed according to the participles, but rather ancient verbal adjectives which never were true participles.

A somewhat different position is occupied by the following derivatives from intransitive verbs: *bùtas* 'past,' *gìmtas* 'native' (beside the more recent *gimtas*), *mirtas* 'dead.' According to Ambrazas, 55, etymological connections show that these words may be inherited from ancient times. Cf. Latv. *bûts*, OCS *bytъ*, Old Indic *bhūtáḥ* 'been, become, past,' Latv. *dzimts* 'native,' Old Prussian *nauna-gimton* 'newly born, neugeboren' (beside *naunagemmons* an apparent past active participle with the same meaning), Old Indic *gatáḥ* 'gone, departed,' Gk. *batós* 'passable, accessible,' Latin (*circum-*)*ventus* 'encircled, surrounded,' Old Indic *mṛtáḥ*, Avestan *mərəta*, Latin *mortuus* 'dead.' The Lithuanian words given above have no clear diathesis, but their semantic connection with the verbs *búti* 'to be,' *gìmti* 'to be born,' and *mirti* 'to die' is still felt by the speakers of the language.

For the participles the denotation of a prior or past action is secondary arising from the meaning of a realized or completed action, a notion close to that of the perfect tense, which in general according to Kuryłowicz, 1964, 90 ff. in the Indo-European languages forms the basis of a past action. Comparing the above forms with such derivatives as *báltas* 'white,' *šáltas* 'cold,' etc. we can see clearly how the verbal adjectives with the suffix *-to-* approach the system of verbal categories and become participles. Therefore with intransitive verbs the difference in meaning between the 'active' and 'passive' participles is frequently connotational rather than denotational.

There is a clear correlation between past and present participles for intransitive verbs:

gyvéntas   kambarỹs,   nãmas,   krãštas;
lived (in)   room,   house,   country, etc. vs.

gyvěnamas   kambarỹs,   nãmas,   krãštas;
being lived (in) room,   house,   country, or

eĩtas,   bégtas   tãkas,   kẽlias;
traveled,   run upon   path,   road, etc. vs.

eĩnamas,   bégamas   kẽlias
being traveled on,   being run on   road

 According to Ambrazas, 1979, 55, some of the transitive non-resultative verbal derivatives with the suffix *-to-, which have resultative characteristics also have adjectival meaning, e.g., drum̃stas 'troubled, turbid' (vanduõ 'water'), leñktas 'bent' (peĩlis 'knife,' piáutuvas 'sickle'), riẽstas 'bent, turned up or down' (kãklas 'neck'), pl. riesti ragaĩ 'turned up horns,' riestà nósis 'turned up nose,' sùktas 'sly, cunning; twisted' (tar̃nas 'servant,' siū́las 'thread'), mókytas 'educated' (žmogùs 'man'), mókytos 'scientific' (knýgos 'books'). Certain of the *-to- derivatives are no longer closely semantically connected with the verbs from which they were originally derived, e.g., griẽžtas 'strict, stern, demanding,' from griẽžti 'to cut, to draw,' and keĩstas 'odd, strange' from keĩsti 'to change, to make different.' There is no correlation between other active and passive participial forms.

 According to Ambrazas, 1979, 56, there is frequently a similarity of form between the past passive participles and adjectives derived from nouns with the suffixes -(i)uota-, -ota-, -yta- and -èta-. In some cases they can even be considered suffixed verbal participles, e.g., smalúotas 'tarred' (cf. smalà 'tar,' but there is also smalúoti 'to tar,'), auksúotas 'gilded' (cf. áuksas 'gold' but there is also auksúoti 'to gild'), vagótas furrowed' (cf. vagà 'furrow,' but also vagóti 'to furrow'), akýtas 'porous, spongy' (cf. akìs 'eye' and akýti 'to put holes into'), dėmė́tas 'stained, spotted' (cf. dėmė̃ 'spot' and dėmė́ti 'to make spots'). I see no reason, however, for not regarding these as etymological participles which have become adjectivalized.

 Other transitive verbal derivatives with the prefix *-to- also denote typical nominal characteristics but are correlated for tense and diathesis with the participles and are felt to be members of this system. They have a resultative meaning even when they are derived from non-resultative verbs, e.g., *keptà dúona* 'baked bread,' *virtà žuvìs* 'cooked fish,' *grį̃stas kẽlias* 'paved road,' *grū̃stà kõšė̃* 'ground porridge'. There are many from verbs with suffixes, e.g., *raug-in-ti agur̃kai* 'pickles, literally: pickled cucumbers,' *sūd-y-ta, rūk-ý-ta mėsà* 'salted, smoked meat,' *grūd-in-tas pliẽnas* 'hardened steel,' and with the negative *ne-tepti ràtai* 'ungreased wheels,' *ne-kultì šiaudaĩ* 'unthreshed straw.'

According to Ambrazas, 1979, 56, participles with resultative meaning were common even in the old writings, e.g., Bretkūnas' *Bible, Exodus* 12, 34: *nesche nekeptą Teschlą* 'carried unleavened dough' (German *rohen Teig*) beside (ib. 12, 39, gen. sg.) *ne-isch-kepto Teschlo* 'unleavened dough' and (ib. 12, 20, gen. sg.) *newalgikjte ... raugintos dūnos* 'do not eat ... leavened bread' (German *gesewrt Brot*); (ChB) *padare sau lieta telia* '(they) made themselves a molten calf' beside (Bretkūnas' *Bible, Exodus* 32, 4, acc. sg.) *nu-lietą werschi* 'molten calf.'

According to the statistics of Tamara Buch, 1962, 158, almost a half of the past active participles in Donelaitis' *Metai (Seasons)* are formed from unprefixed verbs, although most of them have resultative meaning, e.g., *rėdýti ponačiai* 'dressed up gentlemen,' *krõsytų marginių nekenčia* 'hates colored clothing,' *džiovytą pagalį skaldo* 'splits a dried stick,' *bùksvoms lopytoms ... užsidengia* 'with patched trousers, covers himself up.'

Ambrazas writes further, 1979, 56, that such unprefixed participles with a resultative meaning deriving from a prior action can occur with a genitive agent or have other governed or closely attached words, e.g.,:

(x) vilko   kąstà   avẽlė
     by the wolf   bitten   lamb
     gen.   prt.   nom.

     nebeĩs   rañkon
     will no longer go   into the hand
                               illative

Cf. Bretkūnas' *Bible, Numbers* 28, 12: *affiera su Oleumi sumaischita* 'offering mingled with oil.'

In the contemporary language, according to Ambrazas, 1979, 57, non-resultative past passive participles denoting a past action are relatively rare, but they are encountered, e.g.:

(y) turė́jo   senẽlis   žìlą   ožẽlį,
    had   old man   grey   kid

    kietõm   plùtom   penė́tą,
    (with) hard   crusts   fed

    išrūgė̃lėm   gìrdytą
    (with) whey   given to drink

'The old man had a grey kid which was fed with hard crusts and given whey to drink.'

Past passive participles, like the present passive participles, can be combined with the means of action or nouns denoting place or time, e.g., *piáutas peĩlis* 'knife with which bacon was cut,' (Pìlviškiai) *ártas arklỹs* 'horse which has plowed,' (Kùpiškis) *dirbtì arkliaĩ* 'horses which have worked,' *čiuõžtas lẽdas* 'slippery ice, ice which has been slipped on,' *gimtóji dienà* 'birthday' (cf., Latv. *dzimtā diena* 'id.'), *mirtóji dienà* 'day of death, day when a person died' (see Būga, 1959, 119).

The Future Passive Participle

7. The future passive participle is formed with the same marker *-mo- as the present passive participle, but it has rather a future stem and so two variants, viz. -sima- and -siama- have arisen. Differently from the future active participle which has the stem -sia- the literary language has generalized the stem -sim- most likely on the model of the present conjugation of the 2nd conjugation verbs, thus 2nd sg. *gali*, 1st pl. *gãlime*, 2nd pl. *gãlite* (from *galė́ti* 'to be able'), pres. psv. prt. *gãlimas* 'possible' is compared to 2nd sg. fut. *bùsi*, 1st pl. fut. *bū́sime*, 2nd pl. fut. *bū́site* (from *bū́ti* 'to be') and this explains the origin of the fut. psv. prt. *bū́simas* 'future.'

Forms in -siama- are encountered in dialects and older writings, cf. Samogitian *bū́siams* 'future,' and in Klein, 1653, 105, *vadisemas* 'will be called' (in contemporary orthography *vadinsiamas*), *sakýsemas* 'will be said' (c. orth. *sakýsiamas*).

Forms in -siama- derive from the addition of endings of the type of *-omo- to the future stem ending in -sj-.

The future passive participle is hardly used in the standard language except for the participle *bū́simas* which is used as an adjective with the meaning 'future.' Occasionally we encounter the formation from other verbs and A. Juška gives the examples.

(a) papenė́jęs   kárves   pardúosimas
     having fed   cows   which will be sold
     nom. sg. masc.   acc. pl.   acc. pl. fem.
     pst. act. prt.   fut. psv. prt.

     pardúok
     sell
     2nd sg. imperative
'Having fed the cows which will be sold, sell (them).'

(b) tekėsima   duktẽ
    who will be married   daughter

    nesibaĩdo   juomi
    is not frightened   by him.
'The daughter who will be married is not frightened by him' (Ambrazas, 1979, 59-62).

8

The Semi-Predicative Use of the Participle

8. According to Ambrazas, 1979, 67, the semi-predicative use of the participle is its fundamental area of usage and in this its specific characteristics become clearest. According to their syntactic position attributive participles correspond to adjectives and predicative participles correspond to conjugated verbal forms. Thus the semi-predicative relationships directly express its morphological nature, its intermediate position between the verb and the substantive. Being by origin a substantive the Indo-European participle is used first of all to define the conjugated verb of the sentence in which it is used.

This usage is primary in Lithuanian particularly in Western High Lithuanian and Samogitian dialects. In contemporary Lithuanian belles-lettristic style such participles make up from 35 to 55 percent of all participles. If one includes the half-participles (*pùsdalyvis*) the comparative weight would appear even greater.

According to Ambrazas, 1979, 67, the semi-predicative function is connected with the conjugated verb and the subject of its action, e.g., *tėvas grįžęs atsigulė* 'father, having returned, lay down) or the object of its action, e.g., *mataũ tėvą sugrįžusį* 'I saw father (who had) returned,' and thus forms a trinomial construction. Frequently the semi-predicative is characterized as a sub-group of the full predicate and the trinomial construction is considered binomial.

Ambrazas, 1979, 67-68, believes that it is best to consider the semi-predicative constructions as being derived from two sentences one of which is subordinate to the other, just as subordinate clauses are derived. Thus *tėvas grįžęs atsigulė* should be derived from *tėvas atsigulė* 'father lay down' (*tėvas grįžo* 'father returned'). In Ambrazas' view because of their

  and asiłayčio asliczios
  on ass's colt.
'Behold, thy king cometh sitting on an ass's colt.' Compare, however, Sirvydas' *Punktay sakimu* II 144: *atayti ... sededamas* 'comes ... sitting' with the half-participle.

 (c) Bretkūnas' *Postilla* I 401$_{26}$:

  ischeijo   ischgrabo
  (they) came out from the grave

  bijadamos ir didei
  fearing   and greatly
  half-participle

  dzaugenczies
  rejoicing
  pres. act. prt.

In this example one encounters both the half-participle and the present active participle with similar function.

  The appositional use of the present active participle was original in Latvian also, cf., Endzelīns, 1951, 1009:

  viņš jautā ļaunprātigi, labi
  he asks with evil intent well

  zinuots
  knowing
  pres. act. prt.

The phenomenon is well attested also in other Indo-European languages, e.g., Vedic:

  uṣā́ uchántī vayúnā kṛṇoti
  dawn dawning light creates.

'The dawn at day break creates light' (Ambrazas, 1979, 70-72).

complicated syntactic structure the semi-predicative constructions in the Indo-European languages are most likely to change. They are frequently subject to the syntactic regrouping of relationships, adverbalization, absolutization and similar phenomena. Thus in Lithuanian the most changes have taken place in this group even within the relatively short period of time encompassing the written history of Lithuanian.

Ambrazas, 1979, 68, writes that the nominative forms of the semi-predicative participles are used to differentiate the primary and the secondary actions connected with the same sentence subject. The primary action is denoted by the conjugated verbal form whereas the less emphasized action connecting with relationships of time, causality, etc. is expressed by the nominative of the participle. In most such constructions the participle plays a role similar to that of a second verb which has the same subject.

The new half-participle only gradually banished the old present active participle from its appositional function. Although this took place before the language began to be written down, in dialects, especially in Samogitia one encounters even now sayings in which the present active participle is used in the appositional function, e.g., (Veivirženai):

(a) kropštinėja   aplei   namus
    (he) walks   around   the house

    sergąs (sě.rgõ˙s)
    sick (pres. act. prt.).

(b) From a Lithuanian folk song:

    išeit   mergytė   graudžiai   verkianti
    comes out   girl   bitterly   crying
                                              pres. act. prt.

'Crying bitterly the girl comes out.' Such usage is also attested in 16th and 17th century writings (*ChB*, 171, 30-32):

Sztey	Karalus	tawo	ateyt	sedins
Behold	king	your	comes	sitting
				pres. act. prt.

9

The Origin of the Half-Participle

9. The half-participle is a specific Lithuanian and
Latvian innovation according to Ambrazas, 1979, 69.
Used only appositionally it has only nominative forms.
Examples are Lith. nom. sg. masc. $eĩ-da-mas$, fem.
$eĩ-da-mà$, nom. pl. masc. $eĩ-da-mì$, fem. $eĩ-da-mos$
'going.' It is commonly thought that the $-m-$ element
derives from the present passive participle and that
the $-da-$ element derives from the present stem suffix
$*-dho-$ found in such verbs as Lith. $vérd-amas$ 'cooking'
(as opposed to the infinitive $vìrti$ 'to cook'). From
such forms the suffix $-dama-$ was extracted which was
generalized to other verbs. Although the $-d-$ suffix
is not productive in contemporary Lithuanian, it is
possible that at an earlier time it was present in other
verbs, cf. Lith. $púti$ 'to rot, to decay' beside Gk.
$púthō$ 'to cause to rot.' Otrębski, 1956, 272, on the
basis of OCS $idǫ$ 'I go,' $jadǫ$ 'I travel' has proposed
that at one time there existed for Lithuanian $eĩti$ 'to
go,' $jóti$ 'to ride' a 1st sg. pres. $*eidō$ and $*jādō$
from which the half-participles $eĩdamas$ and $jódamas$ were
derived. Ambrazas, 1979, 69, objects, however, that the
appearance and the loss of such forms as $*eidō$ beside
the well retained old athematics like $eimì$ 'I go,' and
the later forms with the suffix $-n-$, cf. contemporary
$einù$ 'I go,' is hardly thinkable. In 1942, 205-206,
Stang considered the $-d-$ a hiatus filler, although he
himself realized some of the difficulties and thought
that in the distant past of the Baltic languages there
may have been a special verbal flexional element $-d-$.
The appearance of the $-d-$ was explained by Bech, 1971,
40-41, as having its origin in the reduplicating present
tense of verbs like $dė́ti$ 'to put,' $dúoti$ 'to give,' 1st
sg. pres. $dedù$, $dúodu$. Ambrazas, 1979, 69, writes that
notwithstanding the fact that the present passive participle

dúodamas 'being given' is homonymous with the half-participle there is no tendency to confuse the two forms cf. (pres. psv. prt.) *dúodamas im̃k* 'being given (something) take' and (half-prt.) *dúodamas vìsą turtą̃ išdalýsi* 'giving, you will divide up all the wealth.' Hofmann, 1970, 204, suggested that the *-d-* of the half-participle is somehow connected with the *-d-* of the suffix *-dav-*. He gives several examples from DP which, in his opinion, demonstrate that the usual view according to which the suffix *-dav-* could denote only a repeated action is wrong, e.g., *kim̃s-davo-s ir verž-davo-s spausdamies* 'they pushed and jammed crowding each other' (speaking of the crowd at lake Gennesaret [Luke 5.1]) which is a single action, durative, not a habitual action. One can think of cases where the imperfect denotes the secondary action just like the half-participle, according to Hofmann.

According to Ambrazas, 1979, 69, it is hardly to be doubted that the origin of the *-d-* in the half-participle is connected with the *-d-* in suffix **-dav-ā*, the causative-iteratives in Lith. *-dyti*, *-dinti*, *-dinoti*, Latv. *-dît*, *-dinât* and present forms with a secondary *-d-*, e.g., Lith. *mérdėti* 'to be dying,' *skélldėti* 'to be cracked,' Latv. *šķindêt* 'to ring.' Ambrazas, 1979, 70, suggests that maybe it is unnecessary to push the creation of the half-participles into the distant past of the Baltic languages and to connect it with the disappearance of verbs with the present stem in **-dho-*. Taking part in its creation may have been verbs with the secondary present stem in *-d-* (e.g., Lith. *skaũda* 'hurts, aches,' *mérda* 'dies, is dying,' *sver̃da* 'staggers, reels,' *skélda* 'splits, is split') which have a stative meaning tending towards an active use of the **-mo-* participles. Such passive participles are occasionally used with a meaning which is close to that of the half-participles, e.g., (Bretkūnas' *Hymnal* LXXIIII [124]):

Numirre	ir	tas	bagotas	/	Waitodams
died	even	that	rich		moaning

irgi	skaudamas
and	aching.

'Even that rich man died moaning and in pain.' *Waitodams* 'moaning' (for modern *vaitódamas*) is a half-participle of *vaitóti* 'to moan,' whereas *skáudamas* 'aching, in pain' is the nom. sg. masc. present passive participle of *skaudė́ti* 'to ache, to be in pain.' One notes the difference in formation of *waitodams* and *skaudamas*, but the similarity in usage.

Ambrazas notes, 1979, 70, that although the circumstances of the formation of the half-participle are still not completely clear the relationship to the present passive participle is important from the point of view of historical syntax, since it reinforces the notion that the participle was originally indifferent as to diathesis. Again I would assume an original intransitive active participle in *-m-* which began to be interpreted as passive when the new active voice was formed.

According to Ambrazas, 1979, 70, this new participle was used in order to differentiate between various functions of the participle. The newly formed suffix *-dama-* took on only an appositional function, whereas the attributive and predicative functions retained the old forms. Ambrazas objects to Hofmann's 1970, 204, statement that the Lithuanian and Latvian half-participle is an unusual and impractical innovation.

The Half-Participle Used in Attributive Function

10. A clear example of the half-participle in nearly attributive function comes from Donelaitis: *jūs niekus pliuškėdamos antys* 'you ducks splashing up nonsense.' One can see the lack of differentiation in such forms as Sirvydas' *Postilla* I 203$\frac{4}{6}$ where it is used with a form of the verb 'to be':

kur	Christus	ira	po	desiney	Diewo
where	Christ	is	at	right	of God

sededamas
sitting
(half-prt.)

'Where Christ is sitting at the right hand of God.'
This close relationship with the present active participle explains the appearance of the half-participle in other cases: *jám beeĩdamam* (dat. sg.) *pasitáikė* 'while he was still going it happened.'

Ambrazas, 1979, 72, finds evidence that prior to the formation of the half-participle present passive participles of some verbs (especially those denoting state) were used with a meaning similar to that of the half-participle. E.g.:

tánkiai		Pentepolėj	gyvẽno	o
often		in Pentepolė	lived	and

čià	nepàtelpams	kélės	į̃	kità
here	not fitting in (pres. psv. prt.)	moved	to	another

viẽtą
place

'He often lived in Pentepolė, but not fitting in there he moved to another place.'

In fact examples of the use of the half-participle with
the meaning of a present passive participle are also
encountered. Note the following example:

Áuga	ir	sūnytėlis	tėvužėlio	augìndamas
grows	even	son	by father	raised

'The son grows, raised by the father.' In this example
augindamas the half-participle functions in place of the
present passive participle **auginamas* 'raised, brought
up.' In Latvian folklore the present passive participle
also sometimes has the same emphatic meaning as the undeclined *-dams* (the half-participle), e.g., *ej, māsiņa,
ejamā* 'go, sister, go,' in which *ejamā* 'going' is the
present passive participle.

Ambrazas, 1979, 72, writes that already in prehistoric times, specialized as a means of expressing a
secondary action, the half-participle was regularly correlated with the nominative case of active participles,
cf., e.g., from Bretkūnas' *Postilla* II 224$_{16-18}$:

Awis	pabugusi	nůg	kitu	awiu /	ir
Sheep	frightened	by	other	sheep /	and

puschczoie	kleodama	iauczessi
in wilderness	wandering off	feels itself

negerai	esanti
not well	being

'The sheep, frightened by the other sheep and wandering
off in the wilderness, feels unwell.' Note the correlation of the past active participle *pabugusi* 'frightened'
with the half-participle *kleodama* 'wandering off.'

Although, according to Ambrazas, 1979, 72, the
majority of the half-participles have a durative meaning
and are formed from unprefixed verbs, in the old writings
half-participles formed from prefixed resultative verbs
were used. Some of them have no particular temporal
significance (Sirvydas' *Postilla* I 217$_{26}$):

Sużieduotine	nutekiedama	ażu wiro	/
(The) betrothed	marrying	(a) husband	/

apłaydżia	tewu	/	motinu	
leaves	(her) father	/	(and) mother	

The half-participle *nutekiedama* 'marrying' denotes no
special tense. Sometimes the half-participle even
denotes an action following that of the main verb
(Bretkūnas' *Bible*, *Genesis* 19, 4) ...

    ateija   Szmones...,   apstodami   namus
    arrived   men...,   surrounding house

'The men arrived and surrounded the house.' The half-
participle *apstodami* 'surrounding, surrounded' denotes
an action following that of the main verb *ateija*
'arrived.' Nevertheless according to Ambrazas, 1979,
73, some of the half-participles formed from resultative
prefixed verbs have the same durative meaning as the
corresponding unprefixed forms. In the writings of
Donelaitis the prefixed half-participles are even more
common than the unprefixed forms.

The Appositional Use of the Past Active Participle

11. According to Ambrazas, 1979, 75, the appositional use of the past active participle predominates in the writings of the 16th and 17th centuries just as it does today. Almost one half of all the past active participles in Sirvydas' *Punktay sakimu* are appositional, in the writings of J. Bretkūnas only the predicative participles, abundantly encountered in the compound tenses are slightly more common. Appositional past active participles are for the most part formed from verbs denoting a concrete action, especially from those denoting motion, although verbs of perception are common also.

Appositional past active participles characterize an earlier action as a finished process by which the state was achieved at the time denoted by the verb. Not only resultative verbs, but even unprefixed verbs may have this meaning, e.g., *dirbęs vėl nuėjo* 'having worked he left again.' Such participles, rather rare in the contemporary language, are abundantly attested in the old writings, e.g., (Bretkūnas' *Bible, Genesis* 38, 16):

(a) eiens   iospi   ant   kelio
    having approached   her   on the   way

    biloia
    (he) said ...

In this example *eiens* (= contemporary *ėjęs*) is the nom. sg. masc. past active participle and unprefixed it denotes an action prior to that of speaking. Note that *eiens* translates here a German finite *macht sich zu*. Cf. also from Bretkūnas' *Bible* I, *Genesis* 9, 21:

(b) gierens   Wyno,   gyrtas   tapa
    having drunk (of the) wine,   drunk   (he) became

'Having drunk of the wine, he became drunk.' In this

example *gierens* (= contemporary *gėręs*) 'having drunk' is an unprefixed past active participle.

Ambrazas, 1979, 75, writes that the appositional past participles are most frequently used to denote the sequence of actions and that in meaning are close to the use of a preceding verb either with or without a conjunction. In Bretkūnas' *Bible* translation almost two thirds of the appositionally used past active participles correspond to German constructions with two verbs conjoined with *und* 'and.' E.g.:

(c) (*Genesis* 27, 27)   Ghis   prieiens
                         He,   having approached,

    pabucziawa   ghi̇̀
    kissed   him.

This translates German *Er trat hinzu und küsset ihn.*

(d) (*Genesis* 37, 14)   Nueiens   weisdek
                         Having gone   see

'Go and see,' which translates German *Gehe hin vnd sihe.* Ambrazas, 1975, 76, writes that the translator correctly distinguished the primary action from the secondary, although in the original they are both described alike. I should like to point out, however, that for the two examples given above the Greek Septuagint has respectively (*Genesis* 27, 27) *kaì eggísas ephílēsen autón* and (*Genesis* 37, 14) *Poreutheìs íde* in which Greek participles correspond to their Lithuanian counterparts.

The past active participle has modal meaning (command, prohibition, negation, etc.) and expressive connotations in popular speech according to Ambrazas, 1979, 76, e.g.:

(e) gérk   gėręs,   brolyti,
    drink   having drunk,   brother,
    (imperative)   (prt.)

    dūmók   ir̃   namõ.
    think   even   homewards.
    (imperative)

'Even when drinking heavily, one must think about going home.'

(f) guliù   pasigùlęs   kàd ir̃
    I lie   having lain down,   although

neužmingù.
I don't fall asleep.
'I have been lying down, although I cannot fall asleep.'

(g) kad   šõks   nesõkęs   zuĩkis
    that   will jump   not having jumped   hare

    ir   kudì.
    and   runs off.
'Up jumped the hare and took to his heels.'

(h) eĩk   kàd   ẽjęs,   kàd   nẽr
    go   that   having gone,   that   there is not

    kuõ   apsiaũt.
    with which   to put on footwear.
'How can I go, since I have no footwear?'

(i) sakýk   jám   nesãkęs   - nuléidžia
    tell   him   not having said   - he lets go

    prõ   ausìs.
    by   the ears.
'No matter how many times you tell him, he does not pay any attention.'

(j) tylė́k   neburbė́jęs
    be silent   not having grumbled.
'Stop that grumbling.'

Ambrazas, 1979, 76, writes that in the writings of the 16th and 17th centuries just as now the neutral postional model has the order: noun, past active participle followed by conjugated verb, e.g., (*ChB*, 20, 7):

(k) O   ansjen   pats   kiełęs   nuejo
    And   he   himself   having arisen   went

    namosna.
    home.

A sentence with the order: noun, verb, in which the participle is moved to first place stresses the participle or the connection with the preceding context, e.g., (Sirvydas' *Postilla* II 21_{14}):

(1) Ir   ižgirdi   mokitiniey   puo*l*e
    And   having heard   the disciples   fell

    vnt   weydu   sawo.
    on   faces   their. 'And the disciples, having
heard, fell on their faces.' (*ižgirdi* = contemporary
išgir̃dę). In this position the participle occupies a
position customary for the attribute and as such in the
written language it is difficult to separate from the
attributive position. Such a stylistically marked position for the participle is encountered even in the contemporary language. In translated texts here and there
it owes its origin to Latin texts which in turn were influenced by New Testament Greek in which the participle
is much more frequently shifted to the beginning of a
construction.
    Much more rare, according to Ambrazas, 1979, 77, is
the word order: participle, verb, noun in which not only
the participle but the personal verb is placed before
the subject, e.g., (Bretkūnas' *Postilla* I 189₂₄):

    (m) Ir   schitokius   wargus   regeiens   ir
        And   such   troubles   having seen   and

        ischkenteiens   paskui   tur   kosznas
        having suffered   afterwards   must   everyone

        smerti   gauti.
        death   receive. 'And having seen such troubles
and having suffered afterwards everyone must die.'
Nevertheless frequently the object of the action of the
participle is shifted into position before the participle without any stylistic or contextual motives whatever, e.g., (Bretkūnas' *Postilla* I 166₁₉):

    (n) sluszba   atlikens,   kitas   dienas
        service   having performed,   other   days

        dirbti   neapleisk.
        to work   do not omit. 'Having performed the
service do not omit working on other days.'
    The fundamental order is noun, verb, participle,
e.g., (Bretkūnas' *Bible*, *Numbers* 13, [25] 26):

(o) Bei   anis   sugrįsza,   szemę   pertjrę.
    And   they   returned,   land   having searched.
'And they returned, having searched the land.' The
Septuagint has almost the same word order as the Lithuanian: *kaì apéstrepsan ekeĩthen kataskepsámenoi tḕn gḕn* 'and they returned thence having searched the land.'

The model with the word order: verb, noun, participle is noted in only a few cases (Bretkūnas' *Postilla* I 803):

(p) pirmiausei   apsake   Schwentas   Angelas
    first of all   said   holy   angel

    isch   dangaus   ateiens.
    from   heaven   having arrived. 'The Holy Angel, having arrived from heaven, said first of all.'

In general the postposed participles are less independent than the preposed. In the majority of cases they do not denote a second predicate and they go with the fundamental verb denoting either the characteristic of the action of the main verb or an immediately resulting state of the subject. More frequently than for the preposed they are formed from intransitive verbs of state and are used along with adjectives, although, to judge by the punctuation they sometimes retain their intonational independence.

12

The Appositional Use of the Passive Participles

12. According to Ambrazas, 1979, 78, appositional passive participles are much more rare (in the old writings approximately ten times less) than the active (including the half-participles). Ambrazas explains this with the notion that the passive meaning of the *-mo- and *-to- participles is relatively recent and not general. The relative rarity of the Slavic appositional passive participles is usually explained by their lesser predicativity.

In such constructions the predominating word order is: (noun), participle, verb, e.g., (Bretkūnas' *Postilla* II 87_6):

(a) Laurins.   Kepams   saka / Wersk   antra
    Lawrence   being baked   says / turn   on other

   schale.
   side. 'While he was being baked (tortured) Lawrence said, turn me on the other side.' Occasionally, however, one finds the order: participle, noun, verb, e.g., (Sirvydas' *Postilla* I 79_{26}):

(b) Ir   teyp   klausiamas   Anielas   ....   Atsakit
    And   thus   asked   the angel   answer

    turi.
    must. 'And thus asked, the angel must answer.'

The occasional postpositional use of the present passive participle retains its relative independence and the meaning of a secondary action, e.g., (Sirvydas' *Postilla* I 302_{22}):

(c) Grudas   garstičios   ira   karsztas   ir
    grain   of mustard   is   hot   and

    degina   gamuri   krimtamas
    burns   the palate   being chewed. 'A grain
of mustard is hot and burns the palate when chewed.'

The appositional past passive participle denotes a secondary passive action which took place before the fundamental action and is usually formed from prefixed resultative verbs, although sometimes they have their resultative meaning even when formed from durative verbs, e.g., (Sirvydas' *Postilla* II 1716):

(d) bus   kayp   miadžias / kuris   sodintas
    will be   like a   tree   which   planted

    stow ....
    stands ....

The usual word order is the same as that of the present passive participle, but special mention should be made of the postpositional participle, e.g., (Bretkūnas' *Postilla* II 361_7):

(e) muitenikas   pareia   namie
    (the) tax-collector   went   home

    apteisintas.
    justified.

According to Ambrazas, 1979, 79, the passive appositional participles are used much more frequently than the attributive participles with a genitive of agent, e.g., (Bretkūnas' *Postilla* II 243_{14}):

(f) Ir   ghi   augiwes   sawa   pamokita / biloia.
    And   she   by mother   her   taught   / says.
                 (gen.)
'And she, taught by her mother, says.'

13

The Agent Nominative in a Participial Construction

13. Ambrazas, 1979, 79, writes that the appositional participle when coming directly before the verb forms a close syntactic unit with the word denoting the subject. In the transcriptions of dialect texts and in general in the spoken language there is usually no pause between the nominative subject and the participle. The intonational division of the phrase is as follows:

(a) tévas   parẽjęs   namõ / atsigulė
    father   having arrived home / lay down

    pailsė́ti
    to rest.

Such a division is supported by the punctuational practices in the old texts which usually place the comma or slash (/) before the verbal syntagma.

    Constructions with the framed subject nominative usually follow the word order: participle, noun, verb. The participle is shifted to the beginning of the sentence and the elements governed by the participle follow the subject; Ambrazas, 1979, 79, quotes the following example from Basanavičius:

(b) Gãvęs   jìs   tókią   stáltiesę,
    Having gotten he   such a   table-cloth,

    aĩna   namõ.
    goes   home. 'Having gotten such a table cloth, he goes home.' Phrases subordinate to the participle also follow the subject and Ambrazas, 1979, 79, quotes the following example from Valančius:

(c) Pažinęs   vyskups   teisybę   juos
    Having recognized bishop   truth   them

kalbant, pastatydino koplyčią
saying, built chapel. 'Having recognized
that they were saying the truth, the bishop had a chapel
built.'

Ambrazas, 1979, 80, writes that 'framed' half-
participles are rarer than the past active participles,
but that they have also been used since the 16th century,
cf. Sirvydas' *Postilla* II 127-128):

(d) Regiedama   tádu   Bažničia   árti   iau
    Seeing   then   church   near   already
    (half-prt.)

    sunt   dienu .... skayto ....
    being   day   considers. 'The church seeing
that the day is already near, considers ....' One finds
similar examples in later writings and Ambrazas gives
the example from Basanavičius:

(e) nevalgydama   ana   vakarienės,   išbėgo   jo
    not eating   she   supper,   ran out   him
    (half-prt.)
    ieškoti.
    to search. 'Not eating supper she ran out to
search for him.' According to Ambrazas, 1979, 80, in
these constructions the participle is united into a
single group with the nominative of the subject as a
secondary semantically subordinated predicate and attributive constructions with a 'framed' subject case are
not used at all. The half-participles occurred in this
category apparently because of their correlation with
appositional participles, but not being as independent
as the latter, did not spread widely.

Only very occasionally does one encounter a subject
framed between a passive participle and syntactically
bound words, e.g., (from Grūžiai):

(f) mùšamas   bérnas   per   sprándą,
    being beaten   lad   on   the neck,

    tylėjo   kaip   negývas.
    was silent   as a   dead person. 'The lad, being
beaten on the neck, was silent as a dead person.'

Ambrazas, 1979, 80, writes that one encounters the
agent nominative in participial constructions with the
order: noun, participle, verb. In this latter case the

object or the adverbial member is placed before the noun, e.g., (Bretkūnas' *Postilla* II, 486$_{16}$):

(g) Schita   pamoksla   Schwentas   Petras
      This   sermon   Saint   Peter

      girdeiens   /   klause
      having heard / he asked. 'Having heard this sermon St. Peter asked ....' Such constructions are found in the later language and even in folklore, e.g.,

(h) Tą   sermėgą   laumė   rãdusi   suplėšė po
      That   coat   witch   having found   tore

      víeną   gìją
      one   thread. 'Having found that coat the witch tore one thread.' The adverbial or object is moved forward generally when one wants to connect it with a previous context, e.g., (Sirvydas' *Postilla* I, 90$_{19}$):

(i) Tas   ir   kitas   sawo   dusios   tobulibes
      Those   and   other   his   soul's   perfections

      żmogus   regiedamas / wisus   tos   żiemes
      man   seeing   all   this   world's

      dayktus... paniekins.
      things... will disdain. 'The man seeing those and other perfections of his soul will disdain all the things of this world.'

Ambrazas, 1979, 81, notes that the direct bond of the participle with the subject becomes clear even in those cases where the subject is repeated by a pronoun in the verbal group. Such sentences are particularly common in Bretkūnas' *Bible* where they translate sentences with a repeated subject, e.g., (*Joshua* 9, 3-4):

(j) O   Mieschczionis   Gibeona,   ischgirdę
      But   inhabitants   of Gibeon,   having heard

      ką   Josua ... darens   buwa,   pramane
      what   Joshua ... done   had,   thought up

      anis   wiliu
      they   trick, translating the German: *da sie hõreten* 'when they heard' ... *erdachten sie eine List*

'they thought up a trick.' Similar examples are to be encountered particularly in the folklore transcribed earlier, e.g.,

(k) Tas   ponas   luktelėjęs,
    That   gentleman   having waited a little

    eis   jis   pažiūrėt.
    went   he   to look.

'That gentleman, having waited a little bit, went to look.'

Ambrazas, 1979, 82, writes that an even more independent role is played by the participle in the nominative absolute construction, where the subject of the participle and the subject of the main verb are not identical. Ambrazas quotes the example from Schleicher II, 160:

(1) teip   abu   pasilabinusi,
    thus   both   having greeted (each other), the

    boba   meldė.
    woman   prayed.

Another possibility is that although the subject of the participle and the main verb are the same, the syntax of the sentence requires different cases.

14

A Conjunction between the Participle and the Verb

14. Ambrazas, 1979, 83, notes that the appositional character of the participle becomes particularly clear when a conjunction is placed between the participle and the main verb. Note the example from the dialect of Armõniškės:

(a) muzikañtas   atsisė́dęs   iř
    musician   having sat down   and

čyrúoja.
scrapes (on the violin).

In standard English we cannot translate this conjunction so we must say: 'the musician having sat down scrapes on the violin.' In such constructions the participle may be replaced by forms of the verb with the personal conjugation without changing the content of the sentence at all. The fact that such constructions are known in Baltic, Slavic, Celtic and Germanic has led Bednarczuk, 1966, 31-32, to consider them a northern Indo-European dialectal innovation.

According to Ambrazas, 1979, 83, the predominant word order in such constructions is: noun, participle, verb. The past active participle can be combined with various forms of the conjugated verb, e.g., present (usually with the meaning of a historical present). Ambrazas gives the following example from Basanavičius:

(b) jis prisiartinęs   prie lango   ir
    he   having approached   to   window   and

    veizd   par   langą   į   stubą.
    looks   through   window   at   room.

'Having approached the window he looks (looked) into the room.' Note the example with the preterit:

(c) vilkas iš   báimės   gãlą   pabėgė́jęs
    wolf   from   fear   a distance having run

   iř   nustìpo.
   and died.

'The wolf having run a distance died from fear.' The
construction is rare with other parts of speech, e.g.,
from a collection of proverbs:

(d) Gãvęs   į   sprándą, iř   eĩk   namõ.
    Having gotten   in   neck   and go   home.

'Having gotten it in the neck, go home.'
   The desemanticized past active participle (masc.
nom. sg.) ė̃męs, (fem. nom. sg.) ė̃musi (from the verb
im̃ti 'to take'), combined with the conjunction iř 'and'
and used with a verb, emphasizes and strengthens the
meaning of the verb. Note the example from Basanavičius:

(e) jì   ė̃mus   nuõ   jõ   iř   pabė́go.
    She having taken   from   him   and   ran off.

'She ran off from him unexpectedly (suddenly).'
   In the model with the word order: participle, noun,
verb, the conjunction iř 'and' goes between the subject
and the conjugated verb form, cf. the example from
Basanavičius:

(f) Išgiřdę   brolė̃liai iř   atjójа,
    Having heard   brothers   and   come,

   nèt   žẽmė   drẽba,   o   smãkas
   even   earth   shakes,   and   dragon

   išgiřdęs   kláusia...
   having heard   asks...

'The brothers having heard, come riding so that even the
earth shakes, and the dragon having heard (this) asks...'
   As in constructions without the conjunction the
subject nominative may be 'framed' between the participle
and its object or syntactically related element, cf. the
example from Basanavičius quoted by Ambrazas, 1979, 84:

(g) Išgélbėję   brolė̃liai sesẽlę   iř   jója
    Having freed   brothers   sister   and   ride

namõ,   o   jì   prãšo.
home,   and   she   asks.   'The brothers having freed (their) sister, ride home, and she asks.'

Ambrazas, 1979, 84, writes that the past active participles and the half-participles used with *ir̃* 'and' are similar in meaning to other appositional constructions, but that the constructions with *ir̃* are commonly used to describe something with more emotion or to emphasize the action denoted by the conjugated personal form of the verb, to show its exceptionality, its intensiveness, etc. In folk tales such constructions are frequently used to describe for the first time some more special or otherwise emphasized action. If the action is mentioned a second time the participle or half-participle construction is used without *ir̃*, cf., e.g.:

(h) Smãkas   devyngalvis   nusivijęs   ir̃
    Dragon   nine-headed   having chased after   and

    éda.
    eats.   'The nine-headed dragon having chased after (the pastry which has been thrown out) eats...' The second time in the same story when the pastry is thrown out we encounter *nusivijęs éda* 'having chased after, eats' without the inserted *ir̃* 'and.'

Lithuanian folklore has a fair number of such constructions and it is evident that the word *ir̃* not only joins the participle with the personal form of the verb, but also gives the statement some kind of special stylistic nuance such that *ir̃* has both the meaning of a conjunction and that of an expressive particle. This leads one to believe, according to Ambrazas, 1979, 84, that the older function of the conjunction *ir̃* may have been that of an emphatic particle and from this developed its meaning as a conjunction.

Lithuanian participial constructions with *ir̃* are attested, according to Ambrazas, 1979, 85, since the 16th century and in Bretkūnas' *Bible* they translate (along with asyndetic constructions) German personal verbs with *und* 'and.' (*Genesis* 33, 1):

(i) Jakubas   pakieles   akis   sawa
    Jacob   having raised   eyes   his

    ir   ischwida   Brolį   sawa.
    (emphatic)   saw   brother   his.   'Jacob

having raised his eyes, saw his brother.' This translates the German: *hub seine augen auff / vnd sahe*. One notes, however, that the Septuagint has a participle: *Anablépsas dè Iakōb toĩs ophthalmoĩs autoũ eĩde*.... 'Having looked up with his eyes he saw....' From the ChB we have the example (19, 15-16):

(j) Kiełęs   tada   ir   sudraude   wejus
    Having arisen then   (and) he rebuked   winds

    ir   marias.
    and   seas.

The Greek reads: *tóte egertheìs epetímēsen toĩs anémois kaì tẽ thalássę* with a participle also, but no conjunction (Matthew 8, 26).

Ambrazas, 1979, 85, writes that the constructions with *ir̃* 'and' between the participle and the verb clearly show that in a sentence the active participles were independent to such a degree that they could be coordinated with the personal forms of the verb. After the appositional participle came to be more subordinate to the verb the conjunction *ir̃* 'and' was kept in what then appeared to be stylistically marked sentences where it simultaneously had the role of an expressive particle. Following the model of the participial constructions it came to be used also in half-participle constructions, but did not become entrenched because of the lesser independence of the half-participle forms. Although the half-participles themselves are more frequent than the appositional past active participles, the constructions with the former and the conjunction *ir̃* 'and' are more rare. In the contemporary Lithuanian language appositional participles joined to a sentence with the conjunction *ir̃* are not characteristic. They are occasionally encountered in writings which reflect folk language or folkloristic style.

As Ambrazas, 1979, 86, points out that constructions with a conjunction joining a participial form with a full verb are richly represented in other Indo-European languages. For Slavic Ambrazas quotes Mark 6, 7 (Zograph):

i   prizъvavъ   oba na desęte   i
and   having summoned   the twelve   (and)

načętъ   ję   sъlati...
began   them   to send...

The Greek reads:

kaì	proskaleītai	toùs	dṓdeka,	kaì
and	he summoned	the	twelve	and

ḗrksato	autoùs	apostéllein
began	them	to send...

'And he summoned the twelve and he began to send them...' In Greek we have the finite verb *proskaleītai* corresponding to the Slavic *prizъvavъ* 'summoned.'

Although some scholars have tried to explain away the Slavic phenomenon by ascribing it to translation technique from Greek, it seems too persistent even in the oldest documents to account for it in this way. Cf., e.g., the example from Old Russian:

Sъdumavъ	knjazь	Smolenьskij	Mьstislavъ,
Having considered	prince	of Smolensk	Mstislav,

Dvdvъ	snъ,	i	prisla	v	Rigu...
David's	son,	(and)	sent	to	Riga

Eremeja.
Jeremiah. 'Mstislav, David's son, prince of Smolensk, having considered, sent Jeremiah to Riga.'

Likewise the construction is encountered in Gothic (*Matthew* 27, 53):

innatgaggandans	in	þo	weihon	baurg	jah
entering	into	the	holy	city	(and)

ataugidedun	sik	managaim
showed	themselves	to many

Note that although Gothic has the participle *innatgaggandans* 'entering (pl.)' in Greek we encounter two personal verbs in the sentence, viz. *eisēlthon* 'they entered' and *enephanísthēsan* 'they showed themselves.' The Gothic enclitic conjunction *-uh* is used in the same way, cf. Mark 8, 1:

athaitands	siponjans	qaþ-uh	du
calling together	disciples	said(-and)	to

im.
them. '(Jesus) calling together his disciples said

unto them.' In the Greek there is also a participle, but no connective. As in Lithuanian these conjunctions (especially -*uh*) have an expressive-emphatic meaning.

Ambrazas, 1979, 87, believes that it is most likely that such constructions arose independently in the various Indo-European languages as a result of an inherited tendency to use verbal nouns (later participles) as a second predicate in the sentence. The greater spread of participial constructions with conjunctions in the Baltic, Slavic and Germanic languages and their common characteristics are to be explained by the similarity of their grammatical structure which is reflected even in the syntax of these participles.

Ambrazas, 1979, 88, writes that in addition to the conjunction *ir̃* 'and' between the appositional past active participle or the half-participle and the fundamental verb one sometimes encounters the adversative conjunctions *õ* 'but,' *bèt* 'but,' *tačiaũ* 'however,' *vienók* 'nevertheless.' Note the example from Bretkūnas' *Postilla* II 744:

(j) szinnodams   ir   isch   tola   regedams
    knowing   and   from   afar   seeing

    wargus   ir   smerti   sawa   / o
    troubles   and   death   his   but

    tacziau   anu   newenge.
    nevertheless   them   not avoided.   'Knowing and seeing his troubles and death from afar, nevertheless he did not avoid them.'

Thus Ambrazas, 1979, 88, suggests that if one studies the usage of the Lithuanian appositional participles, especially the unmotivated usages of the syntactic system of the historical epoch, one can conclude that formerly these participles played a more independent role in the sentence and were directly connected with the nouns and pronouns denoting the subject as secondary subordinate predicates. The increasing bond between the appositional participles and their shift into circumstantial words prepared the ground for the formation and the enracination of the half-participle in place of the nominative present active participle. When the half-participle had gained a firm foothold the appositional participle of the present tense became morphologically separated from the corresponding predicative and attributive participles. Becoming more closely connected with the verb, the appositional participle loses its separate, although semantically subordinate, predicate role, even though up to now it retains its double syntactic relations, and in many cases its secondary meaning of action. The past active participles have retained the secondary meaning of action best, their formal connections with the predicative participles not having ceased.

Constructions with Connective Words

15. According to Ambrazas, 1979, 88, an intermediate position between the appositional and predicative usage is occupied by those constructions in which the participle, connected with the fundamental verb by a relational pronoun, relational adverb or a conjunction denotes a second action, but according to its syntactic position corresponds with a personal verb and can be replaced by it without changing the meaning, cf.:

(a) pàts nežinójo ką̃ dãrąs
    himself did not know what doing. 'He himself did not know what he was doing.' The form dãrąs 'doing' is a nom. sg. masc. pres. act. participle and could be replaced by the 3rd person present tense dãro 'does.' In the contemporary language the participial constructions are losing ground at the expense of the latter constructions. Such participial constructions were, however, more popular at an earlier period, cf. Bretkūnas' *Bible* (*Genesis* 24, 36):

(b) ghis padawe wis kan turrins.
    he gave all which having. 'He gave all that he had.' The pronoun *kan* 'which' is in the acc. sg. and *turrins* 'having' is the nom. sg. masc. pres. act. participle (Ambrazas, 1979, 89).

According to Ambrazas, 1979, 89, the most productive of such constructions now make use of the past active participles particularly with verbs denoting acts of communication or perception, cf., e.g.,:

(c) (bróliai)... neprasìtarė Ẽglei,
    brothers... did not reveal to Eglė,

ką̃ padãrę
what having done. 'The brothers did not reveal

to Eglė what they had done.' In the modern language such participial forms have been reanalyzed as forms of compound tenses with a zero auxiliary, i.e., *neprasĩtarė, kã bùvo padãrę*, in which *bùvo* is the auxiliary marking the pluperfect. With verbs of the same root we encounter certain fossilized phrases such as:

(d) mãtė kõ   nemãtęs.
    saw   what not seen.   'He saw what he had not (previously) seen';

(e) darỹk kã   nedãręs.
    do   what you (sg.) haven't done (previously).

With the disappearance of the present active participles which denoted a subordinated action, the half-participles began to take over the function of the former, e.g.,:

(f) daviaũ kã   turėdama.
    I gave what having.   'I gave what I had;'

(g) nežinaĩ   kã   galvódamas.
    you (sg.) don't know what (you are) thinking;

(h) galì prašýt   kõ   norėdams.
    you can ask for what wanting.   'You can ask for what you want.'

The relative pronoun *kàs* 'who, which' is sometimes used with the participle of *bū́ti* 'to be,' e.g.:

(i) žinójo   kàs ẽsąs.
    he knew who being.   'He knew who he was.'

Note further (Ambrazas, 1979, 90):

(j) nebùvo   kàs bedirbą̃s.
    there was not   who working still.   'There was no one to work.'

(k) kà(d) bū́t   kàs nueiną̃s.
    that   to be who going   'May someone go.'

Such sentences could be transformed into the type with a dative plus infinitive, e.g.:

74

(1) nerà   kám   dìrbti.
    there is not to whom   to work.   'There is no one to work.'

(m) kàd   bū́tų   kám   nueĩti
    that there may be   to whom   to come.   'May (let) someone come!'

The *nerà kàs darą̃* type construction can also be used with another type of meaning, i.e., 'there is nothing to do, there is nothing to be done.' Cf.:

(n) Nẽr   kàs   darą̃   sù   tókiu
    There is not which   doing   with   such

    karãlium - reĩkia   eĩt.
    king   it is necessary   to go.   'There is nothing one can do with such a king – one must go.'

The participle in constructions of both types is a former nominal sentence with *kàs* 'which, who' originally in an interrogative sense.

Constructions with relative adverbs and particles such as *kaĩp* 'as, like,' *kur̃* 'where,' *kíek* 'as far as, so far as,' *kadà* 'when,' *ikì* 'until,' *lìgi* 'until, as far as,' which have become conjunctions have the position of a secondary member of the subordinate clause which has circumstantial meaning, according to Ambrazas, 1979, 90.

The Nominative with the Participle

16. The participle may be in the nominative case, and modify the subject of the main verb and define more closely the meaning of the main verb. Examples:

(a) aš   nesijaučiù   niẽko   blõga
    I   don't feel myself nothing   bad

   padãręs.
   having done (prt.). 'I don't feel that I have done anything bad.'

(b) sãkės   daũg   dìrbdavęs
    he says himself (refl.)   much   having worked

   tenaĩ.
   there. 'He says that he used to work a lot there.'

(c) numanaũ   niẽko   gẽro   negáusiąs
    I think   nothing   good   will not be getting

   girdė́t.
   to hear. 'I don't think I will be getting anything good to hear' (Ambrazas, 1979, 96-97).

   Only certain semantic classes of verbs can function with the nominative participle: a. physical perception: *matýti*, *regė́ti* 'to see,' *matýtis*, *regė́tis* 'to be seen,' *jaũsti(s)* 'to feel (oneself),' *(pa-)ródyti* 'to show,' *ródytis* 'to appear,' *atródyti* 'to seem.' b. psychological perception or activity: *manýti*, *numanýti* 'to think,' *žinóti* 'to know,' *suprãsti* 'to understand,' *pa(si)tìrti* 'to experience,' *at(si)mìnti* 'to remember,' *už(si)mir̃šti* 'to forget.' One can include here verbs denoting a decision or a promise to act, e.g., *apsiim̃ti* 'to undertake,' *siū́lytis* 'to volunteer,' *nusprę́sti* 'to decide,' *žadėti(s)* 'to promise,' *ketìnti* 'to intend,' *grasìnti* 'to threaten,' *užtìkrinti* 'to check,' and verbs of belief or doubt, e.g., *tikė́ti* 'to believe,' *abejóti* 'to doubt.'   c. information, e.g., *sakýti(s)* 'to say (oneself),' *skélbti(s)* 'to announce (oneself),' *gìntis* 'to defend oneself,' *teisìntis* 'to justify onself,' *gìrtis* 'to boast,' *skų̃stis* 'to complain.'   d. emotional or simulated state, e.g., *džiaũgtis* 'to rejoice,' *bijóti(s)* 'to be afraid,' *rū́pintis* 'to take care of,' *gailė́tis* 'to be sorry for,' *verñkti* 'to cry,' *gė́dytis* 'to be ashamed of,' *stebė́tis* 'to be astonished at,' *apsimèsti* 'to pretend (to be),' *issidúoti* 'to betray oneself,' *dė́tis* 'to pretend (to be),' etc.

According to Ambrazas, 1979, 97, present active participles are used for the most part in the participle with nominative construction, but past active participles are encountered except with verbs denoting decision or promise to act.   Future active participles are not likely to be connected with verbs denoting an action limited to the present or the past or with verbs denoting remembering or forgetting.

Present and past passive participles depend on approximately the same semantic groups as the active participles, but the former are less common.   They are not usually combined with verbs of psychic perception (*at(si)miñti* 'to remember,' *užmir̃šti* 'to forget,') and they are not encountered at all with verbs denoting decision or promise to act.

Both the simple and the reflexive verb may be used as the main verb in conjunction with the participle. The reflexive forms are more customary in the Samogitian dialects.   The constructions with the simple non-reflexive verb are more characteristic for some northern Lithuanian dialects and are also productive in the standard language.   Some verbs are encountered only as reflexives, e.g., *prisimiñti* 'to remember,' *apsiim̃ti* 'to undertake,' etc. and some are encountered only as non-reflexives in this construction, e.g., *atródyti* 'to appear,' *abejóti* 'to doubt,' etc.

According to Ambrazas, 1979, 98, the Lithuanian construction of nominative with participle is equivalent to a subordinate clause.   Thus:

  (a) tė́vas   sãko-si   dìrbęs
     'father says himself having worked' is equivalent to: (b) *tė́vas sãko, kàd dìrbo* 'father says that he

worked.' Likewise the same construction with a present passive participle is equivalent to an infinitival construction, e.g., (c) *ligónis norėjo bū́ti lañkomas* 'the patient wanted to be visited' could be expressed by (d) *ligónis norėjo lañkomas*. Cf. also (e) *tė́vas žadė́jo grĩžti/ grĩšiąs* 'father promised to return' (also with nom. sg. masc. fut. act. participle).

The Origin of the Nominative with the Participle

17. There are several explanations for the origin of the nominative with participle. The first of these, according to Ambrazas, 1979, 107, goes back to Bielenstein (1863, 265) who compared the Latv.:

(a) šie   teicās   labi   strādājuoši.
    these   said themselves   well   working.
'They said that they work well,' with *viņš teicās bagāts* 'he said he was rich.' Both of these constructions according to Bielenstein, consist of a verb, its object, a reflexive participle -*s* and a nominal predicate. The nominal predicate got the nominative form instead of the accusative (as in Latin: (b) *dixit se divitem* 'he said himself to be rich' [where *divitem* 'rich' is in the accusative singular]) under the influence of the subject which is in the nominative case.

According to Ambrazas, 1979, 108, Potebnja, 1958, 156-157, has set forth the second view most clearly. The latter writes that already in the Baltic and Slavic languages there existed a second nominative with non-reflexive intransitive verbs. Potebnja writes that Old Russian (c) *tvoritьsja ida* 'he pretends (that) he is going' is the same kind of compound predicate as (d) *ostaneši tvorja* 'you stop doing,' cf. Lith. (e) *dědasi bemiẽgas* 'he pretends (that he) is still sleeping' and (f) *lĩko bemiẽgas* 'he remained sleeping still.' In such constructions the reflexive particle does not have the meaning of an object and is essentially a pure marker of the middle voice. Therefore the nominative form of the participle agrees regularly with the subject just as in Lat. (g) *nemo doctus nascitur* 'no-one is born learned.' Havránek, 1928, 160, 181, gives such examples as Old Russian:

(h) [Simonъ   volxvъ]   i   sam
    Simon   the sorcerer   himself

premĕnjašetsja,   ovo   starъ (nom.),   ovo
changed   first   old   then

molodъ (nom.).
young. 'Simon the sorcerer changed himself first
to young and then to old.'

Ambrazas, 1979, 109, writes, as far as its surface
structure is concerned the nominative with participle
construction resembles the predicate attribute construction used with verbs denoting state or change thereof,
cf., e.g., (i) žmogùs sédi pìktas (nom.) 'the man sits
(there) angry,' (j) gùli pãslìkas (nom.) '(he) is lying
(there) half-dead.' There are also many parallels from
other Indo-European languages, e.g., OCS (k) slĕpъ (nom.)
rodi sę 'he was born blind,' Goth. (l) galaiþ gaurs (nom.)
'he departed sad,' Lat. (m) felix (nom.) vivas 'may you
live happy,' Skt. (n) 'sthād ūrdváh, Gk. (o) stē̃ d'
orthós 'he stood straight.'

Ambrazas, 1979, 109-110, notes the correlation between the double nominative and the intransitive verb
on the one hand and the double accusative and the transitive verb on the other hand. Note the following
examples:

(p) tévas   bérė (tr.)   grúdą (acc.)   saũsą (acc.)
    father   sowed the   grain   dry vs.

(q) grūdas (nom.)   bìro (intr.)   saũsas (nom.)
    the grain   scattered   dry.

(r) tévas   pléšė (tr.)   áudinį (acc.)   skeř̃są (acc.)
    father   tore   the cloth   crosswise.

(s) audinỹs (nom.)   plýšo (intr.)   skeř̃sas (nom.)
    the cloth   tore   crosswise.

(t) tévas   (pà)vertė (tr.)   jį̃ (acc.)
    father   made   him

nelaimìngą (acc.)
unhappy.

(u) jìs (nom.)   (pa) vir̃to (intr.)   nelaimìngas (nom.)
    he   became   unhappy.

    Ambrazas proposes then that as the reflexive particle came to be a mark of intransitivity the nominative case came to be used in the predicate as with other intransitive verbs. Thus on the analogy of (v) dãro jį̃ (acc.) nelaimìngą (acc.) 'makes him unhappy' there arose the reflexive (intransitive) (w) jìs (nom.) dãrosi (intr.) nelaimìngas 'he is becoming unhappy' (see 34.6).

The Development of the Nominative with the Participle

18. Ambrazas, 1979, 112, writes that participial forms can be used with verbs denoting 'to stop, to cease,' e.g., *liáuti(s)* 'to cease,' *nustóti* 'to stop,' *baĩgti* 'to finish,' *mèsti* 'to give up.' Such constructions, characteristic of folklore and popular speech are being ousted from the literary language by constructions with the infinitive. Only rarely are they encountered (Krėvė, Rg, 152):

(a) bérnas   nesilióvė   beveřkiąs,   besiskùndžiąs.
    the boy   didn't stop   crying,   complaining.
Note *beveřkiąs* and *besiskùndžiąs* are nom. sg. masc. pres. act. participles. Note also the example with the nom. sg. masc. half-participle (Acad. Dict. Vol. 7, p. 395): (b) *Arklỹs neliáunas eĩdamas* 'the horse doesn't stop going (i.e., it is nervous, jumpy).' The present tense active participles and half-participles do not differ in meaning from the past active participles used in such constructions. In such nominative constructions one also finds such verbs as *nutìlti* 'to become silent,' *nurìmti* 'to calm down,' *nuščiūti* 'to become silent, calm,' *paĩlsti* 'to lose one's breath,' *sustóti* 'to stop moving,' *stàbtelèti* 'to stop briefly,' etc. Note the example: (c) *Nutìlo Jonìenė šaũkusi* 'Mrs. Jonas stopped shouting.' *šaũkusi* is the fem. nom. sg. past act. prt. of *šaũkti* 'to shout.'

Such constructions with verbs denoting 'to finish, to stop' are known in other Indo-European languages also, cf. Latv. (d) *nuostâja braucis* 'stopped riding,' Old Church Slavic (Luke 5, 4): (e) *prěsta gl(agol)ę* = Gk. (f) *epaúsato lalõn* 'left off speaking' (Ambrazas, 1979, 113).

At the very beginnings of the written tradition it seems that verbs of perception and information used with the nominative case of the participle are for the most part reflexive.

The existence of non-reflexive forms in Samogitian and West High Lithuanian dialects leads one to the conclusion that nominative participles could originally be used with non-reflexive verbs of perception and information also. Thus in some areas in addition to:

(g) brólis   sãko-s   atẽjęs
    brother   says himself   having come.   'Brother says that he came;' one may say also (h) *brólis sãko atẽjęs* with the same meaning (Ambrazas, 1979, 115).

The use of the nominative participle with forms of the Indo-European root *men- 'to think, to consider' is encountered in many languages according to Ambrazas, 1979, 116. Thus Lithuanian:

(i) jìs   mãnė   daugiaũ   žìnąs.
    he   thought   more   knowing.
'He thought he (himself) knew more.'   Old Church Slavic (Luke 24, 37):

(j) mьněaxǫ   d(u)xъ   vidęšte (nom. pl.).
    they thought   spirit   seeing.   'They thought that they were seeing a spirit.'   Old Indic (Rig Veda):

(k) sómam   manyate   papivā́n (nom. sg.).
    soma   thinks   having drunk.
'He thinks that he has drunk soma.'

In Lithuanian and Latvian the nominative with the participle, like the accusative with the participle is widely used even today, but the reciprocal relationships between these two structures have largely changed during the period of the written tradition (Ambrazas, 1979, 127). Since the gerund form has become widely spread in the accusative constructions, the participles are only retained in them when they are used as a modifier of a nominal or pronominal direct object. Therefore the use of the declined participial forms in the accusative constructions became much more limited. Similarly the contrast between the accusative vs. nominative constructions has simultaneously become weakened. Nowadays a nominative with participle construction such as (1) *sãkė-si grįžtą̃s* 'he said (himself) to be returning, i.e., he said he is returning' (or (m) *žinójo-si grįžtą̃s* 'he knew he is returning') can no longer be correlated with an accusative with participle construction (as in the

16th and 17th centuries) such as (n) *sãkė jį̃ grį̃žtantį* 'said him to be returning, i.e., said that he was returning' (or (o) *žinójo jį̃ grį̃žtantį* 'knew that he was returning'). The reason for this is that instead of the later constructions usually gerundive constructions such as (p) *sãkė (žinójo) jį̃ grį̃žtant* or subordinate clauses such as (q) *sãkė (žinójo), kàd jį̃s grį̃žta* 'he said (he knew), that he is returning' are used. The functional load of the reflexive pronoun *si* decreased under such circumstances. Thus in contemporary Lithuanian there came to be used more widely the nominative with participle with non-reflexive verbs of perception and information, e.g., (r) *jį̃s sãkė (žinójo) grį̃žtą̃s* 'he said (knew) he is returning.'

The nominative with participle and non-reflexive forms is particularly productive in north-east High Lithuanian dialects in which the accusative with participle is hardly used. In Sirvydas' *Punktay sakymų* (I 158₁₆) we find only one example of a non-reflexive verb out of 51 participle with nominative constructions:

(s) idant   žmogus... gailetus...   bewelidams
    so that man   should repent   wishing

    ing kuonorint   kito   pikto   impuolys
    in   whatsoever   other   evil   pits

    essus / negi   Diewu   pažieydis.
    being   than   God   to have injured. 'So that a man should repent wishing to be in the depths of some other evil than to have injured God.' Nowadays in the northeastern corner of Lithuania neither the nominative plus participle with reflexive verbs, nor the accusative with participle is encountered although with non-reflexive verbs one encounters such constructions with the nominative participle as:

(t) žmónės   kalbėjo   mãtę   Kraujelį.
    people   said   having seen   Kraujelis.
'People said they had seen Kraujelis.' The spread of the reflexive verbs and the nominative with participle, most characteristic of the Samogitian dialect for the most part only partially touched the nominative constructions of the eastern dialects. Some of these nominative constructions may have been old and the predominance of non-reflexive forms is evident.

Although in contemporary Lithuanian one notices a tendency to use the nominative with participle with certain non-reflexive verbs, the reflexive forms in this construction predominate up to now. The reflexive particle functions as a clear (although sometimes optional) grammatical marker denoting the identity of the subject of the personal form of the verb and the action of the participle (Ambrazas, 1979, 128).

The Accusative with the Participle

19. According to Ambrazas, 1979, 140, the accusative with the participle construction usually denotes constructions with main verbs of physical or psychological perception, information and an object in the accusative case along with a semi-predicative participle in the same case, e.g., (a) *mačiaũ brolýti grį̃žtantį* 'I saw (my) brother returning,' or (b) *girdžiù põną mirusį* 'I hear (that) the gentleman died.' Such constructions are very close to subordinate clauses in meaning.

In Old Lithuanian the accusative with participle construction was used extremely intensively and is most characteristic of Western High Lithuanian and Samogitian authors, Bretkūnas, Vilentas and Vaišnoras (Ambrazas, 1979, 141).

The accusative with participle is used much more in original and compilation works than in translations. In translations from the German it is used for the most part to translate secondary subordinate clauses. The Lithuanian construction of accusative with the participle often translates the Latin accusative with the infinitive. But the accusative with participle only translates Latin and Polish counterparts with verbs of physical perception, because this construction is not used in the latter languages with verbs of psychological perception or with information verbs. A detailed analysis of the relationship with the originals shows that neither the Polish nor the Latin accusative with participle had a noticeable influence on the Lithuanian accusative with participle construction, although the Latin accusative with infinitive construction sometimes activated a corresponding Lithuanian accusative with participle construction.

According to Ambrazas, 1979, 149, the syntactic synonymity of the subordinate clause and the accusative with participle constructions was very important in the development of the latter constructions. In addition to the accusative with participle constructions such as (c) *mataũ tėvą ateĩnantį* 'I see father coming' there also existed from early times paratactic constructions such as (d) *mataũ: tėvas ateĩna* 'I see: father is coming.' The latter constructions are still possible in Lithuanian, but with a stylistic connotation, as if to emphasize the unexpectedness of the action, to give the account a conversational nuance, etc. In the writings of the 16th and 17th centuries such constructions are encountered, but much more rarely.

From such paratactic constructions developed the subordinate clauses used in the same syntactic environments and they developed into syntactic synonyms of the accusative with participle constructions.

Although the subordinate clauses were wide spread they did not have the popularity of the accusative with participle construction. The former construction was supported by German, Polish and Latin originals, but the latter construction was more popular, particularly in original literature. Thus in the original Lithuanian Introduction of the *Margarita Theologica* beside ten accusative with participle and four nominative with participle constructions we encounter only six synonymous sentences with *jog* 'that' and one with *kad* 'that.'

A different situation is found in writings representing Eastern High Lithuanian and Kėdainiai dialects. Here subordinate clauses are much more common and exceed by far (some places by ten times as much) the accusative with participle constructions (Ambrazas, 1979, 150). Almost all the instances of the accusative with participle construction in the writings of the 16th and 17th centuries could be replaced by subordinate clauses with *jog* 'that' or *kad* 'that' without distorting the meaning of the text, although the reverse is not true since the sphere of use of *jog* and *kad* is considerably wider. Sometimes for stylistic considerations one clause would be translated by the accusative with the participle and another clause by a Lithuanian subordinate clause.

Since such subordinate clauses derive directly from a main clause by way of subject raising it is also possible in dialects to find examples with the so-called proleptic subject. Thus the sentence (e) *mataũ brólį grĩžusi* derives from (f) *mataũ brólį* 'I see (my) brother' and (g) *brólis grĩžęs* (prtc.) (*grĩžo* [3rd pret.]) 'brother returned.' One could then have a sentence with a proleptic subject, i.e., the subject of the subordinate clause might remain, e.g., (h) *mataũ brólį, kàd jìs grĩžęs* (*grĩžo*) 'I saw (my) brother, that he returned.' Such sentences are not characteristic of the contemporary language, but they are encountered in dialects and in old writings, e.g., (Bretkūnas' *Bible*, II *Samuel* 17, 8):

(i) Tu   gerai   paszinsti   sawa   Tiewa   ir
    You   well   know   your   father and

    io   Szmones,   annus   stiprus   sanczius (prtc.).
    his   men   them   strong   being.

(King James version) 'Thou knowest thy father and his men, that they be mighty men.' Note the proleptic *annus* 'them' in the Lithuanian accusative with participle construction.

According to Ambrazas, 1979, 152, when the subject of the main and the subordinate clause are identical one usually has the nominative with participle rather than the accusative with participle, i.e., not:

(j) jìs   sãko   savè (acc.)   žìnanti (acc.)
    he   says   himself   knowing, but rather

(k) jìs   sãko-si (refl. particle)   žìnąs (nom.).
    he   says himself   knowing.

'He says that he knows.'

The Origin of the Accusative with the Participle

20. The accusative with the participle is historically a subdivision of the double accusative case. Such double accusatives are most common with verbs of physical or psychological perception. Such constructions are common in the older Indo-European languages, e.g., Gothic:

(a) kunnands   ina (acc.)   wair (acc.)
    knowing   him   man

    garaihtana.
    righteous (Mark 6, 20).
'Knowing him to be a righteous man.' Latin: (b) *me ... tristem credas* 'you might believe me sad'; Greek:

(c) euergétēn   tòn Phílippon   hēgoũnto.
    benefactor   Philip   they thought.
'They thought Philip a benefactor.' (Goodwin and Gulick, 1958, 228.) Hittite:

(d) Arnuandan (acc.)   ŠEŠ-*ya*   irman (acc.)
    Arnuandas   brother my   sick

    ištamaššir.
    they heard (Friedrich, 1960, 164).
'They heard that my brother Arnuandas was sick.'

According to Ambrazas, 1979, 155, already in the 16th century the Lithuanian double accusative with a second noun was reliquary and a comparatively rare construction. Later it disappeared completely and is no longer used in the contemporary language. The double accusative with a second adjective is common only with factitive verbs and certain verbs of physical perception but with verbs of psychological perception and informational verbs already in the 16th century it was an archaism. Nevertheless, accusative with the participle is productive in the old writings and even ten times more common than all the other double accusative constructions. Because of the meaning of the verbal participle already in the 16th century the accusative with the participle tended to be differentiated from the double accusative with the adjectives and nouns, and was generalized as a specific construction, similar to the subordinate clause.

Ambrazas, 155, writes further that the development of the syntactic structure of the accusative with the participle is connected most of all with the strengthening of grammatical government and the grammaticalization of the meaning of the accusative case itself. This grammaticalization is noticeable even during the relatively short period of time which encompasses the history of the written tradition of Lithuanian. In the old writings and in folklore the grammatical meaning of direct object is still not clearly separate from the adverbial or concrete meanings of place, direction, time, means. As the verbal government became stronger the semantic and the grammatical meanings moved farther and farther apart. The expression of the direct and less direct objects became formally separate. The direct object came to be in the accusative case and the less direct objects came to be denoted with prepositional phrases. Such sentences as (e) *sãko jį, stebuklùs, príežastį* which already in the 16th century were syntactic archaisms were replaced by prepositional phrases with the preposition *apiẽ* 'about,' e.g., (f) *sãko apiẽ jį, stebuklùs, príežastį* 'say about him, miracles, the reason.' Thus in such constructions as:

(g) sake   ghiems   berneli   graszu,   gulinti
    said   to them   boy   handsome,   lying

    ant   ketu   edzu.
    on   hard   fence. (Mažvydas' Hymns 188_{10}), '...said to them that the handsome boy (was) lying on the hard fence' the noun could no longer be felt as the direct object of the verb. A decisive role for the further development of these constructions was played by the synonymy with the subordinate clauses which not only aided their survival, but also extended their use with verbs which did not require an accusative, but which could take a subsidiary secondary element modifying the sentence.

This synonymy lessened the motivation for case government to denote the relationship between the verb and the noun phrase, because the forms of the subject and predicate of the subsidiary element of the subordinate clause are not determined by the verb of the primary constituent element. In this manner the way was prepared for nominal case government to become a phrasal dependency on the verb of the entire noun phrase sequence. Already in the 16th and 17th centuries the primary syntactic division of the non-object accusative with participle in many cases had changed from (h) *žinaũ jį̃/ serganti̧* 'I know him/ ailing' to (i) *žinaũ / jį̃ serganti̧* 'I know / him ailing,' (i.e., that he is sick).

The tendency to generalize the accusative with participle constructions is noticeable also in other related languages where we find such constructions as Latvian:

(k) teicat   māsas   nieka   darba (gen. sg.)
    you say   the sisters no   work

nemâkuošas.
not knowing. 'You say that the sisters don't know how to do any work.' Old Russian:

(l) povědaša   jemu   otca   umerša (gen. acc. sg.)
    they told   him   father   having died.
'They told him that his father had died.'

The Dative with the Participle

21. Dative participles modifying nouns or other parts of speech dependent on the verb or another predicate are occasionally encountered in folklore or popular speech (Ambrazas, 1979, 129). Cf. the following example (Acad. Dict., Vol. 3, p. 267):

(a) jám pérsigėrusiam (dat. sg.) véidas (nom.)
    him having drunk too much   face

    tuĩžti   prãdeda.
    to become puffy   begins.

Originally the dat. sg. sequence *jám pérsigėrusiam* 'to him having drunk too much' was felt to be subordinate to the verbal predicate *tuĩžti prãdeda* 'begins to become puffy' and the sentence could be understood as meaning 'the face began to become puffy to him, who had drunk too much.' As the connection between the verbal predicate and the pronoun plus participle construction weakened, it came to be felt that the verb did not govern the latter sequence. Then the meaning of the dative absolute arises and the sentence is to be translated as 'since he had drunk too much, his face begins to become puffy.'

In the Lithuanian writings of the 16th and 17th centuries such constructions were used much more widely. As in the popular language the participle here is connected to nouns denoting persons or personal pronouns. Note the following example from Bretkūnas' *Bible* (*Mark* 14, 21):

(b) Geresnia   butų   tam   Szmogui, ne
    better   would be   to that   man   not

    gimmusiam (dat. sg.)
    having been born. (King James translation)
'Good were it for that man if he had never been born.'

Ambrazas, 1979, 130, writes that according to its syntactic composition the dative with the participle is a variant of the nominal double dative construction (dativus duplex) as in the following example from Bretkūnas' *Postilla* I 326$_{17}$):

(c) welinas   daug/   ir   mumus
    devil   much   and, even   to us

    nebagams (dat. pl.) per   daug   gal.
    unfortunate ones   too   much   can.   'The devil
can do much and even too much to us unfortunate ones.'
Nevertheless, since it expresses an action the subject of which is determined by a nominal or pronominal dative, the active participle contains the potential nucleus of a subordinate clause and sometimes in meaning comes close to the meaning of a subordinate clause of time or cause, as we can see from the following example from Bretkūnas' *Bible* (*Galatians* 2, 11):

(d) Bet   Petrui (dat. sg.) ataiusiam   ing
    But   against Peter   having arrived   in

    Antiochia,   passistengiau   esch   ing   akis,
    Antioch   I stood   I   in   eyes

    nes   buwa   ant   ia   skunsta.
    because   was   against   him   complained.
(King James version) 'But when Peter was come to Antioch, I withstood him to the face, because he was to be blamed.' Note the dat. sg. *Petrui ataiusiam* 'Peter having arrived,' functioning as a temporal clause, although formally subordinate to the verb *passistengiau* 'I stood (against), withstood.' Compare the following two sentences, both from Bretkūnas' *Bible* (I *Samuel* 17, 26):

(e) Tadda   kalbeia   Dowidas   Wirams,   pas
    then   spoke   David   to the men   near

    sawe   stowintiems (dat. pl.)
    him   standing.   'Then David spoke to the men standing near him.' (*Luke* 9, 57):

(f) O   staghisi   est,   eiantiemus   iemus (dat. pl.)
    and   it came to   pass   going   to them

93

kieliu,   bilaia   niekursai   iapi.
  on a path,   spoke   a certain (person)   to him.
'And it came to pass as they were going on a path a certain man said to him ...' In the first example, according to Ambrazas, 1962, 6, the dative *Wirams* 'to the men' is defined by a certain characteristic, i.e., he spoke to those men standing near him. In the second example, on the other hand, the participle of the absolute construction has lost its meaning of denoting a characteristic and the participial construction forms an independent sequence answering the question 'when did he speak to those going.' One can still see the original dative *eiantiemus iemus* 'to those going,' but it no longer functions as the indirect complement of *staghisi est* 'it came to pass' and it is not understood as meaning 'it came to pass to those going,' but rather 'it come to pass to them, as they were going.'

In fact the content of the predicate, the circumstantial function and the intonational unity weakens the dependence of such dative constructions on the predicate, so that sometimes in order to show the verbal government, the dative is expressed a second time in the sentence. Note the following example from Bretkūnas' *Bible* (Genesis 18,1):

(g) Ir   Ponas   passirode   iem (dat.)   Girioie
    And   Lord   appeared   to him   in forest

    Mamre,   sedinczam   iam   pas   ang̣a   sawa
    Mamre   sitting   him   at   door   of his

    Schẹtro.
    tent...   'And the Lord appeared unto him in the forest of Mamre, while he was sitting at the door of his tent.' Note that *iem* 'to him' functions as an indirect complement of *passirode* 'appeared,' but that the *iam* 'to him' (variant spelling) is repeated in the dative absolute expression *sedinczam iam* 'while he was sitting' (Ambrazas, 1962, 10).

Note the parallel from Old Church Slavic (*Codex Zographensis*, Matthew 27, 17):

(h) sъbъravъšemъ   že   sę   imъ
    having gathered   themselves   them

    reče imъ.
    said to them.
'When they were gathered together (Pilate) said to them.'
Note that *sъbъravъšemъ* ... *sę imъ* is an absolute construction with *imъ* in the dat. pl., but that the *imъ* 'to them' is repeated as the indirect object of *reče* 'said.'
  An example from Streitberg's edition of the Gothic *Bible* (*Matthew* 8, 5):

(i) innatgaggandin imma in Kafarnaum
   entering   him into Capernaum

   duatiddja imma hundafaþs.
   came   to him centurion.

'When he (Jesus) entered into Capernaum, a centurion came to him.' The sequence *innatgaggandin imma* is a dative absolute construction, but the *imma* 'to him' is repeated as the complement of *duatiddja* 'came.'
  Andersen, 1970, 9, writes that the supposed misinterpretation '... does not explain why absolute constructions, when they were lost, were not continually renewed in languages which preserved participial constructions.' But it seems to me that they are being continually renewed in languages with participial constructions. The so-called 'dangling participles' of the English freshman composition courses seem to be ample evidence of this general trend. An English sentence such as: (j) *Going down town it began to rain*, although formally incorrect, seems quite possible and even probable to me. Cf., e.g., Russian *Slušaja ego, u menja goreli glaza i ščeki* (lit.) 'Listening to him my eyes and cheeks burned,' and many examples from other languages listed by Jokojama, 1983, 373 and passim.
  Ambrazas, 1979, 137, notes the close relationship of the dative with the locative in the Indo-European languages and suggests a locative origin for some dative absolute constructions. Thus forms such as Lith. (k) *rýtui aũštant* 'while morning is dawning' can then easily be compared with Old Indic (1) *uchántyām uṣási* 'while dawn is dawning.'
  In contemporary Lithuanian dative absolute constructions with fully declined participles are hardly encountered. In some folk songs in places where it is necessary to keep the extra syllables for rhythmic structure some reliquary forms are retained:

(m) Beaustančiai   aušrelei,   betekančiai
    Dawning   dawn   rising

    saulelei,   siuntė   mane   motynėlė   į
    sun   sent   me   mother   to

    dunojų   vandenėlio.
    the river   for water. 'While dawn was breaking and
the sun was rising my mother sent me to the river for
water' (Ambrazas, 1979, 131). Already from the time of
the earliest literature the dative absolute with the
fully declined participle was beginning to disappear
(Ambrazas, 1979, 132). The gerund is distinguished from
the participle in dative absolute constructions in that
the latter is more clearly adverbial, but in the older
writings they were used side by side (Ambrazas, 1979,
132):

(n) Zmoguy   ánt   to   swieta   giwenáncziámuy
    to the man   in   this   world   living

    nera   daykta   reykalingiasnia   ánt
    is not   thing   more necessary   for

    iźgánima   káypo...   prisiartinti   Ponop...
    salvation   than...   to approach   to the Lord...

    o   prietam   grieku   átłaydimą
    and   in addition   of sins   forgiveness

    áptureius   sążinę...   nuráminti.
    having obtained   conscience...   to comfort. 'For
the man living in this world there is nothing more necessary for salvation than ... to approach the Lord and,
in addition, to comfort his conscience, having obtained
forgiveness of sins.' Note the syntactic parallelism
here between the dative participial *zmoguy ...
giwenáncziámui* 'for the man ... living' and the gerund
ápturejus 'having obtained, to have obtained.' In all
cases in which the half predicative dative forms of the
active participle can be used the gerund is also possible.
Such semantic proximity is to be found in those sentences
denoting the physical or psychological state of the subject with such impersonal verbs as *skaudėti* 'to hurt, to
give pain,' *pakàkti* 'to be sufficient,' *stigti*, *trúkti*

'to be lacking,' *derėti* 'to fit,' *regėtis, ródytis* 'to appear,' or the copula with adverbs such as *gẽra* 'well, good,' *sunkù* 'difficult,' *malonù* 'pleasant,' *gaĩla* 'sorry,' etc. Such gerunds from the old writings to the present times can be used as well as dative participle forms, e.g.,:

(o) Gẽra   yrà   keñčiančiam   (keñčiant)
    Good   is   for the suffering   (while suffering)
                   (dat. sg.)   (gerund)

    daũg   draugų̃   turė́ti.
    many   friends to have.
'It is good for a suffering person (while suffering) to have many friends.' Another example:

(p) niẽko   negė́rusiam
    nothing to the one (not) having drunk
             (dat. past act. prt.)

    (negė́rus)   tẽko
    (not having drunk)   it fell to the lot
    (gerund)

    mokė́t.
    to pay. 'It fell to the lot of the one who hasn't drunk anything to pay, or (with the gerund) not having drunk anything (one) had to pay' (Ambrazas, 1979, 132-133).

The very form of the gerund is genetically related to the dative singular active participle and in some old writings and dialects the original consonant-stem dative singular ending *-i* (later replaced by the **jo*-stem declension in modern Lithuanian) is encountered, e.g., in *DP* 302₃₃:

(q) iam'   giwám'   sánti
    him   alive   being.
'While he is alive' (Ambrazas, 1979, 133).

Helping to generalize the consonant stem dative of all genders and numbers were probably the forms in **-ei* with a locative-adverbial meaning, cf., e.g., Samogitian *lỹnantie* 'while raining,' *sniñgantie* 'while snowing,' *pašãlusie* 'having frozen.' Some of the gerunds of the impersonal verbs may have developed from old locative adverbs, especially those denoting natural phenomena, e.g., *aũštant* 'dawning,' *témstant* 'becoming dark,' *sutẽmus* 'having become dark,' *pašãlus* 'having frozen, become cold.' Still according to Ambrazas, 1979, 134, one could not derive all the dative absolute constructions from old locative adverbs.

The Predicative Use of the Present Active Participle

22. In standard Lithuanian the present active participle (always prefixed with *be-*) is combined with various non-present forms of the verb 'to be' in order to form the compound progressive tenses. The present tense forms of the verb 'to be' are not used with the present active participle in this function, because the present active participle is used to express indirect speech in standard Lithuanian.

Nevertheless in Samogitian and in Western High Lithuanian dialects bordering on the Samogitian area (from which the progressive tenses entered into the Lithuanian language) such forms are still productive. Here one encounters an almost complete paradigm, e.g., *esù* 'I am,' *esì* 'you (sg.) are,' *yrà* 'is' plus (masc. nom. sg.) *eiñąs*, (fem. nom. sg.) *eĩnanti* 'going.' Similarly with forms of the future tense *bū́siu* 'I will be,' etc.; *buvaũ* 'I was,' etc.; subjunctive *bū́čiau* 'I would be,' etc. Cf. e.g., (a) *ansy(rà) sergą̃s* 'he is (being) sick,' (b) *jìs bùvo bìskį sergą̃s* 'he was (being) a little sick,' (c) *tuojaũ bùs nesą̃ to lytaũs* 'right away won't be (being) that rain.' Such forms have a clear meaning of *infectum* (denoting an action lasting for a certain period of time).

In this sense they form a clear contrast to those compound tenses which have a perfect meaning. These in turn contrast with the non-compound tenses which are characterized in this regard (Ambrazas, 1979, 170-171).

Periphrastic infectum forms are attested from the 16th and 17th centuries especially in the writings of Bretkūnas and Vaišnoras who are representatives of Samogitian and Western High Lithuanian dialect areas. Cf. Bretkūnas' *Bible, Deuteronomy* 33, 3:

(d) Kaip   (Ponas)   ira   milins   Szmones.
    As   Lord   is   loving   people. 'As the
Lord loves (is loving) the people'; (*Margarita Theologica* 260a$_{21}$):

(e) ios...   pakaiuie   ir   linxmibaeie   jra
    they   in peace   and   happiness   are

    giwenanczes.
    living. 'They are living in peace and happiness';
Bretkūnas' *Bible, Genesis* 41, 1:

(f) Sapnawa   Pharaonas,   kaip   kada   stowins
    dreamed   Pharaoh   that   as   standing

    butu   pas   wandeni.
    was   by   water. 'And the Pharaoh dreamed that
he was standing by the water.' (Note that the Lith.
butu (*stowins*), a subjunctive seems to translate German
wie er stünde.)
    Forms of the pres. act. part. nom. sg. masc. *esą̃s*,
fem. *ẽsanti* 'being' are encountered in the old writings
where they may denote the independent existence of something, e.g., Bretkūnas' *Postilla* I 54$_{15}$:

(g) Szodis ...   iau   buwa   be
    word   already   was   (particle)

    esans / kada   Diewas   Dangu   bei   szeme
    being   when   God   heaven   and   earth

    sutwere.
    created. 'The word was already in existence (was
being) when God created heaven and earth.'
    Other complicated collocations are also encountered,
e.g., (Sirvydas' *Punktay sakimu* I 379$_9$):

(h) kayp   butu   anis   ne   galis
    as   if   he   not   being able
                                   (nom. sg. masc. pres.
                                   act. participle)

    essus   sunu...   apweyzdet.
    being   son...   to take care of.
'As if he were unable to take care of his son.'

Compound infectum tenses formed with the present active participles prefixed with *be-* are found in the old writings, e.g., Bretkūnas' *Bible, Exodus* 34, 26:

(i) Tu   awinaelio   newirk,   kolei   ira
    You (sg.)   lamb   not cook,   while   is

   beszindans.
   still sucking. 'Do not cook a lamb, while (it) is still sucking (from its mother).' (Modern Lithuanian *yrà be-žindą̃s* 'is still sucking.') (I *Samuel* 6, 13):

(j) O   BethSęmitai   buwa
    And   the men of Beth-shemesh   were

   bepiauia...
   harvesting... (Ambrazas, 1979, 171.)

The meaning of the prefix *be-* with its emphasis on the duration of an action prepared the meaning of the past progressive tense which becomes particularly clear when the latter action is interrupted by a second action, e.g., (Bretkūnas' *Bible*, I *Samuel* 17, 34):

(k) Tawa   tarnas   buwa   be-ganans   awis
    Your   servant   was   tending   sheep (of)

   sawa   Tiewo,   ir   ateija   Lęwas.
   his   father   and   came   lion. 'Your servant was tending his father's sheep and a lion came.'
The incomplete and semantically complex contemporary Lithuanian progressive tenses developed from the Samogitian and Western High Lithuanian periphrastic infectum which had a common durative meaning.

In dialects one encounters present tense forms in which the copula is absent:

(1) reik   numien   darbininko,   mama
    necessary   for us   laborer,   mama (is)

   serganti.
   ill. 'We need a laborer, mama is ill.' Likewise one encounters such tenses with the prefix *be-*, but differently from standard Lithuanian the participle does not have the modal nuance of disbelief, surprise, but

denotes a simple durative action. The antiquity of such a meaning is demonstrated by examples from Lithuanian folk songs: (m) *Aušrytėlė beauštanti* 'the dawn is dawning,' (n) *saulytėlė betekanti* 'the sun is rising,' (o) *galvelė beskaudanti* 'the head is aching.' The modal nuance of astonishment or amazement is only one of the meanings adhering to the use of the predicative participles in the history of Lithuanian (Ambrazas, 1979, 172).

This nuance is not necessarily connected with the presence of the prefix *be-*, e.g.:

(p) Jìs...   atsigręžęs   añ   kitą   pùsę,
    He   having turned   on   other   direction

    žiūri - stovįs   vélnias.
    looks - standing   devil. 'Having turned in the other direction, he looks - there the devil is standing.'

On the other hand, yet, participles with the prefix *be-* can also have the modal meaning of reported speech, e.g.:

(q) girdėjau   šienáuti   besiruošiąs.
    I heard   to mow hay   preparing.
'I heard he is preparing to mow hay.'

But the predicative present active participle can have even other modal meanings, even an imperative meaning, e.g., *einą* (= *eĩkim*) *namõ* 'let's go home' (in which *einą* is the nom. pl. masc. pres. act. participle).

The Predicative Use of the Past Active Participle

23. The periphrastic tenses formed with the past active participle have a perfect meaning, and are, in many cases close to that of the compound predicate. According to structure and form it seems clear that they developed from the past participles with nominal function used with the copula. The resultative meaning and the meaning of prior action derive from the grammatical meaning of the participle itself, a meaning encountered in the attributive and half-predicative constructions. They are very similar to other appositive constructions, e.g., (a) *bùvo paválgęs* 'had eaten,' (b) *sė̇dė̇jo paválgęs* 'sat, having eaten,' (c) *paválgęs atsisėdo* 'having eaten, he sat down,' They frequently have the resultative meaning when formed from unprefixed verbs; such a meaning is even more clear in texts of the 16th and 17th centuries where the participles of non-resultative verbs translate German perfect participles, e.g., from Bretkūnas' *Bible*, (*Exodus* 16, 18):

(d) tas...   daug   buwa   rinkens.
     that one... much   had   gathered. 'That one ... had gathered much.' The past act. part. *rinkens* (= contemporary *riñkęs*) 'having gathered' has no resultative prefix, and translates German *gesammelt hatte*. (*Genesis* 9, 24):

(e) ka   iam   io   maszas   Sunus   buwa
     what   to him   his   young   son   had

     darens.
     done. '... what his youngest son had done to him.' The past act. part. *darens* (= contemporary *dãręs*) 'having done' has no resultative prefix and corresponds to German *gethan hatte*.

Those past active participles which have retained the durative meaning of the verbal stem in the compound tenses denote a process which was finished before the moment of speaking. Such a meaning is possible with the past active participles of various verbs including *bū́ti* 'to be.' Note from Bretkūnas' *Bible* (*Judges* 21, 8):
(f) *Niekas ne biti buwens* 'No-one had been' (= German *da ward niemand gewesen*).

There exist even pluperfect forms consisting of the copula followed by a past active participle of the verb *bū́ti* plus another past active participle, e.g.:

(g) añs   visái   nẽr (< ne + yra)   vẽdęs   bùvęs.
    he   quite   is not   married was.
'He had never married';

(h) esù   bùvęs   nuvažiãvęs...
    I am   been   gone...   'I had gone...'

The predicative past participles are distinguished from the corresponding half-predicative and attributive past active participles in that the former denote a prior non-resultative durative action. This meaning is connected with the introduction of these forms into the verbal system. In order to correlate with the simple tenses originally the resultative past active participle began to be used to denote a durative prior action, although this latter meaning remains secondary until this day (Ambrazas, 1979, 173-174).

Past active participles without the copula have for the most part a resultative meaning, but they tend to be used mostly to denote a static situation, a state which is not connected with any particular moment of time, e.g.:

(i) víenas   brólis   žùvęs   ármijoj,
    one   brother   perished in the army,

    àš   vienà   atlìkus.
    I   alone   remained. 'One brother perished in the army and I have remained alone.' The English translation 'perished' is not quite accurate in that it puts too much emphasis on the action. The participle *žùvęs* stresses the timelessness and is more like 'is dead as a result of military action.' Similarly *atlìkus* denotes

'exist, am (alone).' This meaning of atemporal state is particularly characteristic of constructions with the archaic neuter participles, e.g.:

(j) Naktìs nepertamsì, alè màt iȓ
    Night not too dark, but (you see)

   apsidrum̃stę (neuter).
   overcast.
'The night is not too dark, but overcast.'

(k) apliñk vìsa apáugę (neuter)
    all around everything grown over,

   apstìrę (neuter).
   encrusted over.
'Everything all around (is, was) grown over, encrusted.'

With the spread of the periphrastic perfect newer forms with the present tense of *būti* 'to be' developed in sentences denoting a static situation. Such sentences are found in the Samogitian area (and vicinity) and in West High Lithuanian dialects, e.g.:

(l) vìskas apáugę su medùkais
    everything grown over with small trees

   yrà.
   is.   'Everything is grown over with small trees';
(m) *visì mìrę yrà* 'all are dead.' According to Ambrazas, 1979, 174, compound forms with the present tense of the copula are similarly generalized in old writings, particularly those with the aforementioned dialect characteristics, to which can be added the influence of the German perfect forms. In the writings of Bretkūnas and Vaišnoras, e.g., the predicative participles are differentiated from the appositional participles by their use with the copula. Bretkūnas' *Postilla* I 109[21]:

(n) O tassai Berneleis... ka buwa
    But that lad... something had

   pikta Herodui darens / alba darisens.
   bad to Herod done or will (have) done.
'But that lad ... had done or will have done something bad to Herod.'

Past active participles without the copula are used today in many unproductive phraseologically fossilized sequences which have a modal or an expressive nuance. The participles in these sequences correspond exactly in their syntactic position to forms of the personal conjugation of the verb. In order to emphasize the negation such participles (particularly with the neuter gender) are frequently used, e.g.:

(o) Nebebùvę,   kad   aš
No matter what would (will) happen   I

su   juõ   daugiaũ   besusieĩčiau.
with him   more   would meet. 'No matter
what will happen I will never be in social contact with him any more.' The neuter past act. participle *ne-bebùvę* emphasizes the negation. Note the idiom: (p) *balà jõ nemãtę* 'let's forget him, the heck with him,' an expression used when leaving something, giving something, dropping some subject. Literally it means 'the swamp not having seen it (him),' with *nemãtę* 'not having seen' a neuter past active participle. The idiom (q) *kõtas jõ nemãtę* means the same as the preceding idiom, *kõtas* meaning literally 'executioner.' A similar idiom is (r) *devýnios jõ nemãtę - jaũ iššibaigė*, literally 'the nine(fem.) not having seen him - everything is finished.' Other idioms include the following:

(s) Na,   kuř   nesìmeldęs,   anóks
    Well,   why   not praying   such

    maldiniñkas.
    prayerful person. 'Lo and behold, what a prayerful person, a real pilgrim (ironical).' *nesìmeldęs* 'not having prayed' is a nom. sg. masc. past act. participle.

(t) kuř   bùvę,   apsir̃go   põno
    where   having been,   fell ill   master's

    duktė̃.
    daughter. 'All of a sudden (unexpectedly, of all things) the master's daughter fell ill.'

(u) Ar   sãkęs,   ar šuniù
    Either   having said,   or like a dog

  lójęs   —   neklaũso,   ir   tíek.
  having barked   doesn't listen,   and   so much.
'No matter what you say to him, or how you put it (even barking like a dog), he won't listen, and that's all there is to it.' Both *sãkęs* 'having said' and *lójęs* 'having barked' are nom. sg. masc. past act. participles.

(v)   Kir̃tęs,   nekir̃tęs   -   kumẽlės
   Having hit,   not having hit   -   mares

   stóvi   saũ,   gálvas   nuléidusios.
   stand for   themselves   heads   having lowered.
'No matter whether you hit them or not (with the horsewhip), the mares just stand there with their heads hanging down.' *Kir̃tęs* 'having hit' is the nom. sg. masc. past act. participle.

(w)   Svíestas   mán   bùvęs   nebùvęs.
   Butter   to me   having been   not having been.
'I don't care whether there is any butter or not.' *bùvęs* 'having been' is the nom. sg. masc. past act. participle.

(x)   Žinaũ,   kur̃   nežinójęs.
   I know,   where   not having known. 'Of course I know, why wouldn't I know (I'm not stupid).' *nežinójęs* 'not having known' is the nom. sg. masc. past act. participle. In the preceding sentences note the modal feeling which the participles introduce.
  According to Ambrazas, 1979, 175, the phraseological fossilization, the peripheral and unmotivated use of the participles from the point of view of the contemporary literary language, and their stylistically marked character shows that the preceding sentences are syntactic archaisms, which have retained traits of the old predicative function of the participles.

24

The Predicative Use of the Passive Participles

24. According to Ambrazas, 1979, 175, present and past passive participles combined with a form of the verb *bûti* 'to be' form passive voice compound tense correlates of both simple and compound active voice forms. Such paradigms are based on Samogitian and partially on Western High Lithuanian dialects. In Eastern High Lithuanian dialects present passive participles are not used at all in such constructions. Past passive participles with forms of *bûti* (usually pret. fut. or subj.) are more like compound nominal predicates than compound tenses. This was probably the situation in the 16th and 17th centuries as the older writings show. In Sirvydas' *Punktay sakimu* forms of the present passive participle with the verb *bûti* are only found in a few cases where they could have been influenced by other writings of that time. The rare predicative present passive participles have a meaning similar to that encountered in attributive constructions. The predicative past passive participles are only a third more frequent than the attributive and correspond in meaning to those now used in Eastern High Lithuanian.

Ambrazas, 1979, 176, writes that in the periphrastic forms the present passive participle, as elsewhere, has for the most part a durative meaning and is formed from non-resultative verbs. In the old writings, just as today it commonly denotes a generalized, constantly repeated action, e.g., Bretkūnas' *Bible* (*Exodus* 5, 16):

(a) Ne   dů̃dami   ira   Schaudai   tawa
    not   given   is   straw (to)   your

    Tarnamus.
    servants. (King James version) 'There is no straw given unto thy servants.' When the participles are

formed from resultative verbs they also have an iterative meaning and are thus close to the non-resultative participles. An example from Bretkūnas' *Bible* (*Leviticus* 4, 12):

(b) Kur   Pellinai   ira   pakretami.
    where   ashes   are   poured out. Note that
with the prefix *pa-kretami* 'poured out' is a resultative verb.

According to Ambrazas, 1979, 176, the past passive participles in compound tenses are usually formed from resultative verbs and denote the state which results from a prior action. The resultative meaning is encountered even when the participles are derived from durative verbs, e.g., from Sirvydas' *Punktay sakimu* II 1887:

(c) (kojos)   tur   but   mazgotos.
    feet   must   be   washed.
From Bretkūnas' *Bible* (*Leviticus* 26, 17):

(d) busit   muschti   iusu   Neprieteliu.
    you will be   slain (before)   your   enemies.
In the old writings one also encounters the verb *tàpti* 'to become' as an auxiliary, e.g., from Bretkūnas' *Postilla* II 104_{20} (e) *pakasti tampa* 'are buried.'

In general the periphrastic passive with the past passive participle was formed earlier than periphrastic passive with the present passive participle and had already taken root in the 16th and 17th century Samogitian and Western High Lithuanian dialects. Old neuter participial forms had most likely been at the basis of such constructions, e.g., Bretkūnas' *Bible* (*Numbers* 18, 14):

(f) Wis   kas ...   uszkeikta   ira.
    everything   which   cursed   is. This
translates the German *Alles verbannete* 'everything banned' which is apparently a mistranslation of the original. Cf. also Bretkūnas' *Postilla* I 103:

(g) issipilde   kas   buwa   sakita.
    was fulfilled   what   was   said. In the two
previous examples *uszkeikta* 'cursed' and *sakita* 'said' are neuter sg. past passive participles.

Ambrazas, 1979, 177, notes that originally predicative participles were used with *bū́ti* 'to be' just like other adjectives, but already in preliterate times in some dialects there had been created compound tense forms which were correlated with simple tenses. Nevertheless this correlation was not overall and the compound tense forms retained a close bond with the substantival predicative constructions.

Along with the compound tense forms there have remained until today predicative participles without a copula having a stative atemporal meaning or specific modal connotations in reliquary fossilized phrases. The predicative function came closer to the verbal function, but not all such participles turned into compound tense forms, particularly those which had some kind of qualitative meaning, cf., such examples as *jìs* (*yrà, bùvo* ...) *tìkintis, ištvìrkęs, nepakeĩčiamas, paténkintas* 'he (is, was) faithful, debauched, irreplaceable, content.' As far as their meaning is concerned they correspond to attributive forms.

25

Origin of the Predicative Use of the Participles

25. According to Ambrazas, 1979, 183-184, comparison with other Indo-European languages shows that the Lithuanian use of predicative participles both with and without the copula is an ancient Indo-European feature. In contemporary Lithuanian some of the predicative constructions without a copula are felt to be variants of constructions with the copula. Just as (a) *tėvas sveĩkas* 'father is healthy' without the copula can be considered a variant of (b) *tėvas yrà sveĩkas* with the copula, so can (c) *tėvas pavar̃gęs* 'father is tired' without the copula can be considered a variant of (d) *tėvas yrà pavar̃gęs* with the copula.

Ambrazas notes that etymologically the Indo-European root **bheu-* meant 'to grow, to thrive' and assumes that the root **es-* originally had the concrete meaning of 'to live.'

The construction of noun plus participle without the copula reflects an earlier nominal sentence. Thus such Lithuanian sentence types with neuter forms of the participle are quite archaic, e.g., (e) *jaũ pasnigę* (past act. prt.) '(it) has already snowed' or (f) *rugiaĩ sėjama* (pres. psv. prt.) 'rye is being sowed.'

On the other hand constructions with the copula originally had a different meaning. Thus a sentence such as (g) *tėvas bùvo liñksmas* 'father was happy' originally meant something like 'father lived happy (as a happy person).' Thus today even a sentence such as (h) *mẽs dabar̃ bū̃nam anam̃ galè kaĩmo* can be understood to mean 'we live at the other end of the village now' with *bū̃nam* which ordinarily means something like 'we frequent, we frequently are' translated as 'we live.' As the verbs **es-* and **bheu-* lost their semantic function and gradually took over the syntactic function of connective, sentences with the copula approached the meaning of sentences without the copula. In the course of time many of the old nominal sentences were drawn into the system of verbal sentences as constructions with zero copula. Still some of the predicative participles without the copula remained outside of the tense system and have an atemporal stative meaning or have specific modal nuances (Ambrazas, 1979, 185). Thus, e.g., the nom. pl. present act. prt. (i) *einą̃* (= *eĩkim*) *namõ* 'let's go home' and cf. also the examples in para. 24.

According to Ambrazas, 1979, 185-186, the use of participles in the nominal sentence is based on their nominal characteristics. Nevertheless, the participle differs from other adjectives by its verbal meaning, which enables it to express action or process in nominal constructions. Neither the data of Lithuanian or other related languages gives us any reason to think that the verbal meaning of the participle should have developed later in the history of the separate languages. The deeper one penetrates into the Proto-Indo-European past, the clearer the nominal morphology and the verbal semantics of the participle become. This is most clearly visible in the predicative and half-predicative constructions. This is somewhat hard to understand from the point of view of the structure of the attested Indo-European languages, but may derive from an epoch when the distinction between the verb and the noun was not as clearly marked as in historical times and forms denoting a process and having morphological markers common to substantives (or perhaps the pure stem) were used in meanings close to that of the verbs.

In order to explain the verbal function of these forms it is not necessary, in Ambrazas' opinion, 1979, 186, to assume the complete identity of noun and verb in Proto-Indo-European times. The Baltic predicative substantives and participles (and those of other Indo-European languages) have specific functions separating them from verbs. In addition to the atemporal, stative function, there is a clear tendency to use them in semantically dependent phrases, subordinate clauses and with various modal meanings. It is thus possible that even in the late common Indo-European period substantive predicates stood in relationship to the verbs as marked forms which had a clearly defined sphere of use.

26

The Indirect Mood (reported speech, *modus relativus*) and Its Development

26. Nominative case forms of the active participles are used to denote the indirect mood (reported speech), e.g., (a) *jìs gyvẽnąs* (nom. sg. masc. pres. act. prt.) *káime* 'he (they say) lives in a village' vs. the direct or ordinary indicative (b) *jìs gyvẽna káime* 'he lives in a village.' There is a complete paradigm of forms of indirect mood paralleling the forms of the ordinary direct indicative mood. The forms of the indirect mood, however, being nominative active participles, agree with the subject in number and gender, but not in person.

The forms of the indirect mood differ from the predicative participles used in the periphrastic tense in that the former never have a conjugated auxiliary verb. Cf., the indirect (c) *jìs rãšęs láišką* 'he (they say) wrote a letter' as opposed to the direct indicative forms (d) *jìs yrà (bùvo, bùs) rãšęs láišką* 'he has (had, will have) written a letter.'

The clearest formal contrasts are offered by the forms of the frequentative past and the future which are never used without an auxiliary verb, thereby opposing the indirect mood which never uses an auxiliary. Likewise present tense participles with the auxiliary verb *bū́ti* 'to be' are almost unused, and if they are used with the simple preterit, frequentative preterit and future tenses they have the prefix *be-* and denote the progressive tenses. Thus when the present active participles occur in the position of a finite verb without the copula (or auxiliary) they are always understood as denoting the indirect mood. On the other hand, since the past active participles, particularly prefixed perfective forms are used to denote compound perfect tenses, when these occur there is homonymy with forms of the indirect mood, e.g., (e) *jìs pavar̃gęs* 'he is tired' or 'he (they say) is tired.' The homonymy is observed also if the verb in question is a compound form with the past act. prt. *bùvęs* plus a pres. psv. part. such as *mẽtamas* 'being thrown' or a past psv. part. such as *mèstas* '(having been) thrown.' Only in these three aforementioned cases is there homonymy in which the opposition between the direct indicative and the indirect mood is neutralized. In such cases, however, the homonymy can be disambiguated by inserting the appropriate participle of the verb *bū́ti* 'to be.' Thus, instead of *jìs pavar̃gęs* one could say (f) *jìs esą̃s* (*bùvęs*) *pavar̃gęs* 'he (they say) is (was) tired.'

Likewise the neuter participial form *esą̃* can be inserted to show the indirect mood. Sometimes one encounters even the neuter future participle of *bū́ti*, cf., e.g., Acad. Dict. I, 1209:

(g) Dár, màt, bū́sią nežìnanti Lazdiẽnės
    Even, you see, as if not knowing Lazdiẽnė's

liežùvio.
tongue.
'Just as if she didn't know Lazdiẽnė's tongue.'

Ambrazas, 1979, 190, gives the following meanings for indirect speech. (1) It may denote an action which is being retold, an action which is not directly experienced by the speaker, or somebody else's speech or thought, e.g.,:

(h) Àš girdė́jau, kàd añs geraĩ ìšgeręs.
    I heard that he well drinks.
'I heard that he drinks well, gets pretty drunk.'

(i) Kitì sãko, kàd jám kliùvę.
    Others say that to him befell. 'Others say that he really got it (e.g., some kind of punishment).' (2) It may denote a doubtful, uncertain action, or one which is thought unreal.

(j) benè nuõ žmonõs jìs atsiskýręs
    perhaps from wife he divorced

esą̃s.
is.
'Perhaps he is divorced from his wife.'

(k) ródos,   iš   kapų   svíetas   suvėjęs.
    it seems, from   graves   people   gathered 'It
seems as though a crowd gathered out of the graves.'
(3) It may denote a sudden, unexpected action which
causes surprise, e.g.:

(1) išeinù   į   laũką,   ogi
    I go out   outside   and (surprisingly
                                          enough)

    belỹnąs   šìltas   lytẽlis.
    raining   warm   rain.
'I go outside and to my surprise a warm rain is falling.'

(m) einù   žiurét,   kàs   tám   šùnie,
    I go   to look   what   to that   dog,

    žiūriù   ẽži   rãdęs.
    I look   -- hedgehog   has found.
'I go to look what has happened to the dog, I look - he
has found a hedgehog.' (4) It may denote an action
which is assumed from the results, e.g.:

(n) tiẽ   katinaĩ   nè   sàvo   bliũdo
    those   cats   not   their   dish

    neišsilaĩžę   besą̃.
    licked out   apparently.   'Those cats have not
yet licked out their dish apparently.'

(o) jaũ   matýtis,   tiẽ   vaikaĩ
    already   evident,   those   children

    rupliùkai   pùpose   bùvę.
    little devils   in beans   have been.
'It looks like those devilish little children have been
in the beans.'

Thus the indirect mood does not have a single
unitary meaning, but has a number of different meanings
unified into a single paradigm. The most common meaning
is that of reported speech, with which is closely connected the dubitive connotation (since what one hears
from others may seem open to doubt to the speaker).
Participles of all the tenses have these moods. The
meaning of the suddenly experienced action is more common

for the present active participle (especially with the prefix *be-*) and also for the simple preterit (more rarely). The action assumed from the results, the most rare of all the meanings, is also found with the present and simple preterit active participles. The last two meanings are rather close also.

The Origin of the Indirect Mood

27. Delbrück, 1897, 491, considered the origin of the indirect mood the accusative plus participle construction. Such sentences as (a) *sãkè tévą ateĩsianti̯* (*ateĩsiant*) '(he) said father will come' in which *tévą* 'father' and the fut. act. prt. *ateĩsianti̯* 'will be coming' are in the accusative case, were used alongside of synonymous sentences such as (b) *sãkè, (kad) tévas ateĩs* 'he said (that) father will come.' From some kind of a mixture of the two preceding sentences a sentence such as (c) *sãkè tévas ateĩsią̃s* became possible and then (d) *sãkè, (kad) tévas ateĩsią̃s* '(he) said (that) father will come.'

Potebnja, 1958, 230f, connected the indirect mood with the nominative plus participle constructions, proposing that the meaning of indirect mood and the nuance of doubt could have arisen as the result of the lexical meaning of the verb used in such constructions, e.g., 'to think, to pretend,' which was later strengthened by such particles as *bũk* 'as if, apparently' (etymologically the 2nd sg. imperative of *bũti* 'to be'), *nêi* 'as, as if' etc. Examples:

(e) bijojos,   dūmodami,   bũk   dwase
    they were afraid, thinking,   as if   spirit

    kokę   regį.
    some   seeing. 'They were afraid, thinking they might have seen some kind of spirit.'

(f) dėtis   turėjo,   ney   esą   teisũs.
    to pretend they had to   as if being   right.
'They had to pretend they were right.' Supposedly such constructions would have originally been neutral as to mood. They would correspond exactly with Slavic.

(g) mьněaxǫ (aky) ᲃuxъ viděšte
    they thought (as if) spirit seeing. 'They
thought they saw a spirit.' The problem with this theory
is that Baltic differs from Slavic in that in Baltic the
participles are widely used when the participial subject
does not correspond with the subject of the main verb,
e.g., (h) *aš nežinaũ, ar jis ateĩsiąs* 'I don't know if
he will come.'

E. Tangl, 1928, 50-51, derives the indirect mood
from the nominative with participle used with non-
reflexive verbs, which, in his view, were created later
and in the 16th and 17th centuries could not yet have
succeeded in becoming widespread. J. Marvan, 1962, 36-
37 and 1969, 18, suggests a similar origin adding that
the nominative with participle constructions were a
variant of subordinate clauses, and under the influence
of the latter could have gotten conjunctions and a different subject of the action. Since both of the aforementioned authors derive the nominative with participle
from accusative constructions, one can postulate the
following series of developments for the origin of the
indirect mood:

(i) sãko savè atẽjusį (acc. sg. masc.).
    says himself having come.
'He says that he has come.'

(j) sãkosi atẽjęs (nom. sg. masc.).
    says himself having come.
'He says that he has come.'

(k) sãko (kad) atẽjęs
    says (that) having come.
'He says that he has come.'

(l) sãko (kad) tévas atẽjęs.
    says (that) father having come.
'He says (that) father has come.'

(m) tévas atẽjęs.
    father having come.
'(They say), father has come.'

Kazlauskas, 1961, 86-87, 1968, 402-403, suggests
that the indirect mood may be the relic of a periphrastic
optative such as (n) **bi negelbąs* 'would not have helped,'

(o) *bi nekẽlęs 'would not have arisen.' These reconstructions are predicated on Stang's suggestion, 1970, 155, that the -b in the conjunction jéib 'if' derives from a 3rd person optative *bi from the verb būti 'to be.' Stang quotes the following examples from Mazvydas:

(p) Jeib   Christus   ne   keles...
    If   Christ   not   arisen.
'If Christ had not arisen...'

(q) Jeib   Pons   Diews   mums   nepagelbas...
    If   Lord   God   us   not having helped.
'If the Lord God had not helped us...'

In other Indo-European languages indirect speech is frequently put in the optative mood, so it is possible to imagine that it could have been so in Lithuanian as well. Once the optative meaning had been transferred from the particle bi to the participle, the particle itself could have disappeared.

Although some of the early literature does not have clear examples of the indirect mood, some does and in this respect the writings of Vaišnoras are particularly important.

According to Ambrazas, 1979, 193, except for one example with optative meaning all of the forms of the indirect mood in Vaišnoras' translations are accompanied by the particle būk (2nd sg. imperative of būti 'to be') emphasizing nuance of uncertainty and doubt. The indirect mood is even now widely used with this particle in Samogitia, in northern Lithuania and sometimes even in southern dialects in which the indirect mood is in general very rare. Vaišnoras usually uses these participles in subordinate clauses with the conjunctions jóg 'that,' kaĩp 'as' and with the relative pronouns kuris, kursaĩ 'which.' When the indirect mood occurs in a compound sentence in which there is no conjunction, the same particle būk fulfills the function of the conjunction. Indirect (reported) speech is used with such verbs as sakýti 'to say,' pérkalbėti 'to dissuade,' tarýti 'to pronounce, to say,' pastiprinti 'to emphasize, to affirm,' rašýti 'to write,' e.g.:

(r) Teipaieig   saka   ghie   ...   iog   spawiedniie
    Thus   say   they   that   in confession

buk priwalingas essąs ischskaitimas
allegedly necessary being enumeration

wissu grieku.
of all sins. 'They say that an enumeration of all sins is necessary in confession' (Ambrazas, 1979, 193).

Those ideas and notions which the author feels to be unreal and incorrect are rendered by the indirect mood with such verbs as *dūmóti* 'to think,' *klajójime laikýtis* 'to believe erroneously,' e.g.:

(s) Popieżischkei ...... klaiojme laikosi /
    papal supporters erroneously believe /

    iog buk dūna ... butischkai
    that allegedly bread ... in essence

    persimainanti.
    changes. 'The papal supporters believe erroneously that the bread in essence changes.'

Ambrazas, 1979, 194, writes that in the writings of Vaišnoras the indirect mood is most frequently formed with the present active participle (25 examples), and more rarely with the past active participle (5 examples). Participial forms of the verb *búti* 'to be' acting as a copula are combined with nouns, adjectives (including neuter forms) and prepositional phrases. There are four examples of its use with the meaning of the indirect mood in constructions with present passive participles. Vaišnoras' translations contain phrases with the gerund *esant* 'being, allegedly' and the neuter form of the adjective *priwalu* 'necessary, required' along with the predicate adverb *gana* 'enough' and the impersonal gerunds *reikent, tereikiant* 'necessary' corresponding to the neuter participial forms (*reikią, tereikią*), e.g.:

(t) noraetu tu (for tů = tuo) perkalbeti/ghiems
    (they) would wish in such a way to convince them

    nebereikent walgjti / bet buk
    no more necessary to eat but allegedly

    essant ganna.
    being enough.

'(They) would wish in such a way to convince them that they should not eat more, but that there is enough.'

In this sentence the forms *nebereikent* and *essant* are gerunds.

Such sentences used with verbs having an explanatory meaning are close to the use of the accusative with gerund. The gerund began to penetrate into impersonal constructions of the accusative with participle, ousting the neuter form of the participle.

Ambrazas, 1979, 194, writes that in the writings of the 16th and 17th centuries the constructions with the indirect mood both in structure and meaning correspond to those of contemporary Lithuanian. Their appearance in the writings of Vaišnoras is to be explained by the author's Samogitian origin and the nature of the books themselves. Since the Latvian indirect mood is also used beginning with writings of the 17th century there is no doubt that its formation goes back to prehistoric times in East Baltic dialects.

According to Ambrazas, 1979, 195, evidence from the Lithuanian dialect atlas allows us to locate the chief center for the origin of the indirect mood as the Samogitian dialect, although a second center is the northeastern corner of the Lithuanian dialect area. A narrow band running along the northern border with Latvia unites the two centers. The areas where the indirect mood and the nominative plus participle are used are largely the same areas, but Ambrazas, 1979, 196, disputes the notion that the indirect mood is derived from the nominative plus participle. Such an assumption would require that from old constructions with a single subject such as (u) *sãkė(si) grĩžęs* 'he said (himself) having come, i.e., he said that he had come' one would have to derive sentences with two clauses such as *sãkė(si), grĩžęs* 'he said, he had come' and *sãkė, tėvas grĩžęs* 'he said, father had come.' But in fact, it seems quite uncommon for a single clause to split up into two clauses. The history of the Indo-European languages shows just the opposite, viz., that several clauses are rather united into a single clause. It seems more likely to Ambrazas, 1979, 198, that the indirect mood developed from an older nominal participial sentence without a copula. When the copula began to be used with the participles the reliquary form without the copula took on a modal meaning.

The Origin of Constructions with Indirect Cases

28. Ambrazas, 1979, 167-169, writes that all of the absolute constructions with indirect cases are originally variants of nominal appositional constructions. In such constructions the participle has the same syntactic position as the second noun or the adjective. The first noun (N) is directly subordinated to the verb (V), but the second verbal noun (N_1) or the participle (P) is connected with the first noun by a half predicative relationship. Thus:

(1) V ———> N <———> N_1/P

This model supposes that a sentence in which along with the indirect case forms subordinate to the verb there could also be secondary nominal predicates. In such a sentence the meaning is not so centralized or compact and flows from one part of the sentence to the next. Such sentences are to be found in older Indo-European languages, e.g., Old Indic:

(a) tasmāt   putrasya   jātasya
    therefore   of the son   having been born

    nāma   kuryāt.
    name   may he create.
Etymologically this seems to mean 'let him create a name for the son who has been born,' but actually the meaning for us would be 'when a son will be born.' Cf., Gk.:

(b) eirōtā̰s   m'   elthónta.
    you ask   me   coming.
Literally this means 'you ask me why I have come.'
    Because of the verbal characteristics of the participles and their meaning conditioned by a secondary

action the constructions with the indirect cases separated from the nominal constructions and followed their own path of development. The sequence of participle with the indirect case of a noun, understood as the equivalent of a subordinate sentence synonymous with the subsidiary element of a subordinate clause came to be used in those cases where the noun could no longer be felt to be governed by the verb. The constantly increasing feeling for verbal government and the differentiation between the syntactic and the semantic cases created the conditions for this shift in interpretation. Thus in a sentence such as: (c) *juõkiasi brõliui sergančiam* 'he laughs at (his) ailing brother' the dative *brõliui* 'at (his) brother' comes to be felt as less natural than the prepositional expression *iš brõlio* with the verb *juõkiasi* 'laughs (at).' Therefore the expression begins to mean 'he laughs when (or since) his brother is sick.' Another example is: (d) *sãko brõli grįžusi* 'he says (his) brother (has) returned.' In the two aforementioned constructions the former semantic bond of the noun with the verb was replaced by a new bond in which the entire noun phrase as a unit is linked with the verb. In constructions with the accusative and genitive there arose a relationship of phrasal government between the verb and the noun phrase, cf. the preceding example *sãko brõli grįžusi* with *brõli grįžusi* '(his) brother (having) returned' in the accusative case. In constructions with the dative, which from early times had a semantic function an adverbial relationship arose, but in both types of examples given above the same forces were at work. The difference between the dative absolute and the non-object accusative with the participle and genitive with the participle is to be explained by the semantic characteristics of the government and the fact that in Lithuanian the subsidiary members of subordinate explanatory clauses cannot occupy the dative position.

In other Indo-European languages participial constructions with cases having a semantic function (ablative, adverbal genitive, dative, instrumental and locative) tend to turn into absolute constructions, but constructions with the accusative of the direct object are most frequently restructured on the basis of phrasal government. Absolute constructions in which the noun is no longer so closely bonded with the verb are represented in the altered model of syntactic relationships. Thus:

(2) V ────> (N <────> P)

According to this model the dative absolute was created. Note the example from the *Contiones Litvanicae*:

(e) Jam   bezaydziantiam   gryżo   atgalos   isz
    Him   still playing   returned   back   from

    dangaus   anoy   strela.
    sky   that   arrow.   'While he was still playing that arrow returned from the sky.' Likewise the non-object accusative and genitive with participle. Note the example of the accusative with participle construction from Bretkūnas' *Bible* (*Joshua* 8, 6):

(f) Nesa   anis   tars,   mus   nog   iu
    Because   they   will say,   us   from   them

    beganczius.
    fleeing.   'Because they will say that we are fleeing from them.' Note the example of the genitive with participle from Bretkūnas' *Bible* (*Exodus* 9, 14):

(g) idant   ischtirtumbei,   man
    so that   you (sg.) may learn,   to me

    ligaus   nesanczio.
    equal   not being.   (King James version) 'that thou mayest know that there is none like me.'

In such constructions the verb governs the noun and participle together as a group.

As a result of the centralization of the sentence the half predicative constructions, which formerly had played a rather independent role, became even more dependent on the verb. Under these circumstances those constructions, in which there had been an object relationship between the verb and noun, could not remain unaltered either. The contradiction between the reciprocal relationship between the noun and the participle on the one hand versus the unidirectional relation of the verb with the noun had to surface in these constructions. This contradiction was removed by bonding the verb and the participial construction, thereby giving the typical trinominal construction:

(3)

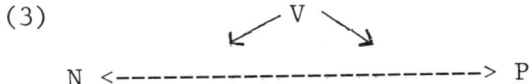

N <----------------------> P

This model furnishes the analysis of such constructions as the following:

(h) Ir   vil̃kui (dat.) pasẽnusiam   dañtys
    Even   the wolf   having become old teeth

išlãksto.
fall out. 'Even when the wolf becomes old his teeth fall out.' Presumably, according to Ambrazas, 1979, 168-169, there is a relationship of subordination between the verb išlãksto 'fall out' and the noun vil̃kui 'wolf' on the one hand and the dative participle pasẽnusiam 'having become old' on the other hand. In other words both elements are directly subordinate to the verb. An example with the accusative plus participle:

(i) išgir̃do   bitùtę (acc.)   atgaũdžiančią.
    (he) heard   the little bee   buzzing closer.

An example with the genitive plus participle:

(j) Ar   nejuntì   merguẑele,   manẽs (gen.)
    Don't   you (sg.) feel,   girl,   me

parjójančio?
riding home? 'Don't you, girl, have a presentiment that I am riding home?'

Because of similar syntactic restructurings in constructions with all three indirect cases the same undeclined forms of the gerunds which arose in the dative absolute became established and spread rather later to the accusative and genitive with the participle. In constructions with model number (2) above the gerunds took root first and at the present time have ousted the declined participial forms. In model number (3) above the gerunds are still optional and sometimes not used at all.

The establishment of gerunds in the place of declined participles in turn had an effect on the reciprocal relationships of the members of the absolute constructions. In constructions with gerunds the former dependence of the participle on the noun, which had been shown by grammatical agreement, was completely lost. The gerund, which derived from an old participle, began to be felt as the fundamental member of the old participle plus noun sequence. In this way the gerund came to stand in the fundamental syntactic relationship with the verb. The indeclineable form of the gerund could be used even without the noun or pronoun in a certain case, e.g.:

(k) láukiant   visuomèt   prailgsta.
    while waiting   always   becomes tiresome.

'(While) waiting (it) always becomes tiresome.' (1) *pajutaũ lãšant* 'I felt drops' (literally '[it] dripping.'

Under these circumstances the noun which had become syntactically unnecessary came to be felt as dependent on the gerund. A negated gerund governs the case of the dependent noun, e.g.:

(m) Áukso   kilpẽlės   šalià   siūbúoja,
    Golden   stirrups   at the side   sway,

    raiteliùko   nebẽsant.
    rider   no longer being.
    (gen.)   (gerund)

'The golden stirrups sway at the side, there no longer being any rider.' In this example the negated gerund *nebẽsant* 'no longer being' takes a genitive complement, *raiteliùko* 'rider.' Another example:

(n) sãko   blùsų   peř   kiáurą   mẽtą
    say   fleas   through   entire   year
            (gen.)

    neẽsant.
    not being.

'They say that there are no fleas during the entire year.' The negated gerund *neẽsant* 'not being' takes a genitive complement, *blùsų* 'fleas.'

The following syntactic model illustrates the newly formed syntactic relationships of the absolute constructions:

(4) V --------> P --------> N.

That is, the verb governs the gerund (which derived from a participle) and the gerund in turn governs the noun.

The Nominative Case

29. For most types of nouns the Indo-European nominative case derives from an earlier absolute case, a case without any marking whatsoever. The possible exception is the class of *o-stem nouns which are characterized by an ending *-os, the origin of which will be discussed below. The consonant-stem nouns show most clearly the earlier nominative case which was completely unmarked. The attested vocative case corresponds well with the stem form of the consonant-stem noun. Thus Gk. páter, Skt. pítar 'oh father' reflect the stem form of this Indo-European noun. The absolute case of those consonant stem nouns with the final resonants in the liquid *-l or *-r, or the nasals *-n or *-m developed a sandhi alternant in which the final resonant was lost and the preceding vowel lengthened. Thus for nouns with the suffix *-ter there developed an alternative stem *-tē (see Schmalstieg, 1980, 40-41). The ending *-tē is represented, for example, in the Old Indic nom. sg. mātā́ and in the Gk. mḗtēr (with the addition of the -r to *mḗtē from other forms of the same stem). Thus nominative singular forms such as Old Indic mātā́ Slavic mati 'mother,' Lith. mótè 'wife' (< *mātē < **māter) are etymologically older than the Greek form mḗtēr

In order to clarify my notions of agent and patient in Indo-European I shall discuss briefly and in a somewhat schematic fashion the syntactic relationships of the noun with the verb.

I propose that structurally the earliest stages of Indo-European syntax were very much like Georgian in that the functions of agent and patient were different depending upon the verbal tense/aspect. In other words the Indo-European antipassive or active voice is etymologically connected with the present tense of the verb and the ergative or medio-passive is connected with the preterite tenses of the verb. I omit here the Indo-European perfect system, although I suspect that the Indo-European perfect may have had even different methods of expressing the agent and patient relationships. (I would recall here Georgian again which has even a third way to express the agent and patient relationships in the perfect tense.)

The following diagram illustrates this:

		Thus:	Antipassive (> Active)
Present:	1st sg.		$*pek^w$-om
	2nd sg.		$*pek^w$-es, -et
	3rd sg.		$*pek^w$-et, -es

			Ergative (> Medio-Passive)
Present:	1st sg.	---	(did not exist
	2nd sg.	---	at this period)
	3rd sg.	---	

			Antipassive (> Active)
Preterite:	1st sg.	---	(did not exist
	2nd sg.	---	at this period)
	3rd sg.	---	

			Ergative (> Medio-Passive)
Preterite:	1st sg.		$*pek^w$-(t)é/ó(i)(r)
	2nd sg.		$*pek^w$-(t)é/ó(i)(r)
	3rd sg.		$*pek^w$-(t)é/ó(i)(r)

The three hyphens denote verbal categories which did not exist at this early stage. The identity of the 2nd and 3rd sg. present denotes that at first *-es denoted animate and *-et inanimate subjects. The complete identity of the ergative preterite forms merely means that there was no agreement for person with the subject. Originally there was no agreement for gender or number, but later agreement was for the most part adopted in those forms which became adjectives or *-tó participles.

A present tense antipassive sentence would be such as the following:

| A(1) | *māter
mother
(absolute
case) | pek^w-et
cooks away
(intransitive
verb) | ovi-m
at the sheep
(dat.-loc. or
benefactive case) |

Preterite ergative sentences might be of the following type:

| A(2) | *ovi
sheep
(absolute
case) | pek^w-tó
cooked
(intransitive
verb) | mātros
by mother
(erg. case) |

| A(3) | *medhu
honey
(absolute
case) | pek^w-tó
cooked
(intransitive
verb) | vīros
by the man
(erg. case) |

(As Shaumyan points out, 1985, 312, "so-called mixed ergative languages must have both ergative and accusative syntactic structures as counterparts of their ergative and accusative morphologies.") In this schematic representation I ignore problems of word order.

In sentences A(1), (2), and (3) the verb is intransitive. The subject of these sentences is the noun in the absolute case and the predicate is the intransitive verb. In other words in each of these sentences it is the first two words which are fundamental. The third word in sentence A(1) was originally an adverbial complement. The third word in sentences A(2) and A(3) is the agent. I interpret sentence A(1) as intransitive because it does not take an accusative direct object case, it takes an indirect object. Note that to this day one may say in Lithuanian either (a) *mótè kèpa ãvį* 'the wife bakes the sheep' or merely (b) *mótè kèpa* 'the wife bakes' without a direct object. The verb *pek^w-et* in A(1) may be interpreted as being of imperfective aspect also, and an imperfective by nature might not take an accusative object. I interpret sentences A(2) and A(3) as intransitive because the subject of the verb and the verb itself may stand as sentences by themselves without an agent. The agent in sentences A(2) and A(3) is secondary and not an essential part of the sentence. Note that in the preterite verb we may have to do with a perfective aspect and in the perfective aspect the accomplishment of the action, the goal and the patient are more important. In the imperfective aspect, on the other hand, the action itself, the agent and the performer of the action are more important.

One feature of stage A which must be emphasized is that in the present tense there was agreement for verbal person with the subject, viz., there existed a 1st sg. *pek^w-om* 'I cook.' Although originally the form *pek^w-es* was used with an animate subject and the form *pek^w-et* was used with an inanimate subject, eventually this was straightened out so that *pek^w-es* for the most part became the second person singular and *pek^w-et* became the third person singular. In a few residual cases the reverse distribution is observed, e.g., Tocharian A 2nd sg. *pälkät*, 3rd sg. *pälkäṣ* 'shines.'

In the preterite the agreement with the subject was either absent or else the agreement was according to gender and number. (Note the similar type of agreement in modern Russian, although, of course, the agreement in modern Russian has a completely different origin.) At this stage there was no agreement for person as there was in the present tense.

Now let us proceed to the next step in the development:

B.   Active (< Antipassive)

Present: 1st sg.   *pek^w-ō
           or   *pek^w-om-i
           2nd sg.   *pek^w-es-i, -et-i
           3rd sg.   *pek^w-et-i, -es-i

           Medio-Passive (< Ergative)

Present: 1st sg.   *pek^w-(t)é/ó(r)(i)
           2nd sg.   *pek^w-(t)é/ó(r)(i)
           3rd sg.   *pek^w-(t)é/ó(r)(i)

           Active (< Antipassive)

Preterite: 1st sg.   *pek^w-om
           2nd sg.   *pek^w-es, -et
           3rd sg.   *pek^w-et, -es

Medio-Passive (< Ergative)

Preterite: 1st sg.   *pek^W-(t)é/ó(r)(i)
            2nd sg.   *pek^W-(t)é/ó(r)(i)
            3rd sg.   *pek^W-(t)é/ó(r)(i)

The medio-passive preterite is represented by the *-to 3rd sg. middle aorist of Greek and Old Indic. Hirt, 1928, 102, noted the similarity in formation with the participle in *-to (see Chapter 6).
The original lack of number and gender concord is discussed in Chapter 6. I see no evidence that Baltic ever had a complete medio-passive paradigm.
Let us return now to a further explanation of the developments of B. above.
The first step in the creation of an active preterite came when the new imperfective aspect *pek^w-et-i began to take over the function of the present tense, pushing the old imperfective aspect *pek^w-et into the function of a preterite. The Old Indic injunctive uses of this form (future, imperative, wish) are a relic from the time prior to its taking over the preterite function (Burrow, 1965, 298). The augment (3rd sg. imperfect) in Old Indic (and in Greek, partially in Armenian) solidified *e-pek^w-et > a-pac-at in the preterite function.
As a counter-balance to the existence of a present and a preterite in the active voice, the old medio-passive split into a present and a preterite also. But in addition to splitting into two separate tenses, the medio-passive fell under the influence of the active voice and began to agree with the subject in person, whereas formerly if it agreed with the subject at all, it was only according to gender and number. Thus personal forms for the present medio-passive are created. Cf. Gk. 1st. (phér-)om-ai, 2nd sg. (phér-)eai < *-es-ai, 3rd sg. (phér-)et-ai (in which the final -ai replaces earlier *-oi, see Ruipérez, 1968). In Old Indic the 1st sg. retains the older *oi uncontaminated, cf. (bhár-)e, but the 2nd sg. (bhár-)as-e and the 3rd sg. (bhár-)at-e correspond exactly to the Greek. The corresponding forms in Latin are passives or deponents. The 1st sg. (reg-)or 'I am ruled' reflects the etymological *-or plus the length from the active 1st sg. (reg-ō); the 2nd sg. (reg-)er-is represents *-er (with a e-grade ablaut) plus *-es, cf. active 2nd sg. (reg-)is; the 3rd

sg. (*reg-*)*it-ur* represents the active *regit* plus **-or*. The Tocharian A present middle endings are: 1st sg. (*tränk-*)*mār* 'I say,' 2nd sg. *-tār*, 3rd sg. *-tär* or *-trä*; Tocharian B 1st sg. (*kolok-*)*mar* 'I follow,' 2nd sg. *-tar*, 3rd sg. *-tär* or *-trä* (Krause and Thomas, 1960, 262). All of these seem to result from a contamination of the 1st sg. *-m*, non-first sg. *-t* plus some sequence of **-(ō)r* (**-ōr* is derived from a contamination of **-ō* < **-or* in preconsonantal word-final sandhi position plus **-or* in prevocalic word-final sandhi position {Schmalstieg, 1973, 104; 1980, 32}). The Hittite 1st sg. middle ending *-ḫa*(*-ri*) is of obscure origin. The 2nd sg. ending *-ta*(*-ri*, *-ti*) and the 3rd sg. endings *-a*(*-ri*), *-ta*(*-ri*) derive from the suffixes **-o* or **-to* which could be augmented by either *-ri* or *-ti* (Sturtevant, 1951, 165). The Old Irish 1st sg. absolute deponent ending is represented by *midi-*(*ur*) 'I judge,' where *-ur* has the same explanation as Latin *-ōr*, the 2nd sg. (*suidig-*)*ther* 'you place' derives from **-te* plus **-r* (it is usually connected with Old Indic **-thās* < **-thēs*), the 3rd sg. (*suidigi-*)*dir* also represents the original dental element plus **-r* (Thurneysen, 1946, 365-368). I will not discuss the difference between the absolute and conjunct endings, because I think that Cowgill, 1975, 67, has shown that this does not reflect the difference between the primary and secondary endings of Indo-European.

In addition to a deponent Old Irish offers a present passive which is conjugated as follows:

	Singular	Plural
1st	no-m·charthar 'I am loved'	no-n·carthar
2nd	no-t·charthar	no-b·carthar
3rd	carth(a)ir, ·carthar	cart(a)ir, ·cartar

(Thurneysen, 1946, 349).

I assume this also to derive from the medio-passive of stage B above. I have proposed that there is no original agreement for person, so the only question arising here is why the 1st and 2nd plural have been replaced by the singular. The Gothic 1st and 3rd sg. present passive (*nasj-*)*ada* has its starting point in the 3rd person singular of the Indo-European middle perfect (Collitz, 1888, 42ff and 1891, 227ff). The 2nd sg. (*nasj-*)*aza* is undoubtedly somehow contaminated with the

-*s*. The Old Armenian present passive is formed on a completely different principle, viz., the use of the stem vowel -*i*- thus *var-i-m* 'I am led' vs. *var-e-m* 'I lead' (Godel, 1975, 47).

Just as the medio-passive present fell under the analogical influence of the active present, so did the medio-passive preterite fall under the influence of the active preterite. Thus 1st and 2nd person singular medio-passive preterite endings were developed to correspond to the 1st and 2nd person singular active preterite endings.

The Old Indic 1st sg. medio-passive aorist ending (*ad-*)*i* (Whitney, 1885, 71) may derive from an original *-*i*, one of the medio-passive endings found in all persons. The Old Indic 2nd sg. medio-passive aorist ending (*adi-*)*thās* is discussed in Chapter 6 (see 6(t)).

I note here that even the traditional comparative grammars would not connect the Gk. 2nd sg. middle aorist ending (*édou* < *édo-*)*so* with the Old Indic form. The Greek ending is clearly analogical to the 3rd sg. ending (*édo-*)*to*. Kerns and Schwartz, 1972, 27, maintain that the Gk. 2nd sg. passive (*e-dó-*)*thē-s* is formally cognate with Old Indic (*á-di-*)*thā-s*. I suspect rather that the passive value is connected with the stative value of Indo-European *-*ē*- and the use of the intransitive in passive meaning (Schwyzer, 1966, 224). The creation of a passive different from the old medio-passive in certain of the older Indo-European languages is new also. Thus Schwyzer, 1966, 224, writes: '... im ältesten Griechischen und im frühen Arischen war der Passivgebrauch medialer Formen ausgedehnter als später.' The Greek 1st sg. middle aorist ending (*ed-*)*óm-ēn* is completely new and has nothing to do with the Old Indic (*ád-*)*i*.

The Latin passive imperfect (1st sg.) *regēbar* 'I was ruled,' (2nd sg.) *regēbāris*, (3rd sg.) *regēbātur* seems to be clearly based on the present.

Friedrich, 1960, 109-110, gives the following Hittite 2nd and 3rd sg. medio-passive preterite forms: (*ar-*)*tat* 'stood,' (*kiš-*)*at* 'became'; the 2nd sg. (*iₓa-*)*ttati* 'you went' and 3rd sg. (*kiš-*)*ati* 'became' are also listed. These also derive from *-(*t*)*o* plus a preterite ending -*t* or -*ti*. The 1st sg. medio-passive preterite is represented by (*ar-*)*ḫaḫat* 'I stood,' (*iₓa-*)*ḫḫaḫat*, *ḫḫat*, from *-*ḫa* plus the preterite *-*t*.

The Tocharian 3rd sg. medio-passive preterite {B} (*kautā-*)*te*, {A} (*kota-*)*t* 'split' as expected, derives from *-*to* (Krause and Thomas, 1960, 260). The 2nd sg. {B} (*kautā-*)*tai*, {A} (*kot-*)*te* would appear to derive from a contamination of the *-*t(o)* with the 1st sg. (*kautā-*)*mai*, {A} (*kot-*)*e*. One notes immediately the 1st sg. endings appear not to presuppose a common source. Krause and Thomas, 1960, 260, compare the Tocharian B ending -*mai* with the Gk. 1st sg. medio-passive ending -*mai*, but the Greek -*mai* may come from *-*moi* and the Greek ending is for the present and the Tocharian ending for the preterite. Similarly they compare Tocharian A -*e* with the Old Indic (thematic) (*bhar-*)*e*, both of which could reflect *-*oi*.

The origin of the Armenian preterite endings is complex and unclear so I will not go into that matter here. In the Old Irish passive preterite the 3rd sg. relative absolute form of the (strong) verb *breth(a)e* 'born' seems to reflect IE *-*tos* and the 3rd pl. conjunctive ·*bretha* may reflect the fem. pl. *-*tās* (Thurneysen, 1946, 440; Kerns and Schwartz, 1972, 55). Note the agreement by number and gender rather than person.

Obviously the question of the origin of the medio-passive and passive endings is very complex and I have given here only a superficial survey of some of the possibilities of development. The problems of the creation of the medio-passive and passive endings could be the subject of a monographic investigation in each of the languages mentioned.

In general, however, I analyze the verbal forms of Indo-European as deriving from the concatenation of minimorphemes rather than from the phonological decay of morphemic monsters. I think that in principle both the concatenation of minimorphemes and the phonological decay of endings are possible. To perform deletions on morphemic monsters seems more scientific, because one can apply rules more easily. There is no reason to believe, however, that ease in the application of rules reflects historical processes any better. Indeed, unless the Indo-European languages came straight from God with their highly developed inflections, they must have gotten them through the addition of morphological elements at some point in their history.

Let me propose next that a sentence such as A(1) comes to be interpreted as B(1) below:

$$\left[\begin{array}{l}\text{*māter}\\\text{mother}\\\text{(nom. sg.)}\end{array}\right]\left[\begin{array}{l}\text{pek}^w\text{-et}\\\text{cooks}\\\text{(transitive}\\\text{verb)}\end{array}\right]\left[\begin{array}{l}\text{ovi-m}\\\text{the sheep}\\\text{(acc. sg.)}\end{array}\right]$$

In other words the shift of antipassive to active voice has created the possibility of a transitive verb. Thus (1) the absolute case has passed to the nominative case, (2) the intransitive verb has become transitive and (3) the dat.-loc. case has become the accusative case.

When the antipassive sentence becomes active the old ergative sentence becomes passive. Thus:

B(2) $\left[\begin{array}{l}\text{*ovi}\\\text{sheep}\\\text{(nom. sg.)}\end{array}\right.$ $\left.\begin{array}{l}\text{pek}^w\text{-to}\\\text{cooked}\\\text{(passive)}\end{array}\right]$ $\left[\begin{array}{l}\text{mātros}\\\text{by mother}\\\text{(gen. of agent)}\end{array}\right]$

B(3) $\left[\begin{array}{l}\text{*medhu}\\\text{honey}\\\text{(nom. acc.}\\\text{sg.)}\end{array}\right.$ $\left.\begin{array}{l}\text{pek}^w\text{-to}\\\text{cooked}\\\text{(passive)}\end{array}\right]$ $\left[\begin{array}{l}\text{vīros}\\\text{by the man}\\\text{(nom. of agent)}\end{array}\right]$

As Shaumyan, 1985, 319, has remarked: "the *basic voice* in ergative languages corresponds to the *derived voice* in accusative languages, and the *derived voice* in ergative languages corresponds to the *basic voice* in accusative languages." Thus in Indo-European the derived antipassive has become the basic active voice and the basic ergative has become the derived passive.

There was a split in the development of the *-to forms. The *-to forms either began to function as part of the new verbal paradigm which furnished the basis of the Indo-European medio-passive (and passive in some languages) or they became adjectivalized. In the case of the adjective the original syntactic relationships are attested in extant Indo-European languages. With the shift of the antipassive to the active, in some cases, the old intransitive was reinterpreted as passive. Passives seem to have two possible origins, either they arise from the reinterpretation of an intransitive or else they come from a transitive plus reflexive. It has long been known that the Indo-European passive derives from the middle or medio-passive voice (e.g., Paul, 1920, 281). Many of the modern Indo-European languages retain traces of the passive from the old participles, cf., e.g., French (c) *les livres ont été vendus* or Russian (d) *knigi byli pródany*. On the other hand the new forms with the reflexive are also encountered, (e) *les livres se vendent*, (f) *knigi prodajutsja*.

The use of the genitive as agent with the participles in *-to* is discussed in 30.5.

Originally that form of the nominative case (which developed from the older absolute case) could be the subject only of an intransitive verb. A relic of this older syntactic norm is retained in Hittite in which an inanimate noun can be the subject of an intransitive verb, but not the subject of a transitive verb (Tchekhoff, 1978; Laroche, 1962; Benveniste, 1962; Ivanov, 1963, 132).

There are two problems with the theory presented so far: (1) If the nominative case derives from an Indo-European absolute case, why are some of the nouns marked with the morpheme *-s* (*$*\bar{v}iros$*); (2) If the accusative case in *-m* derives from some kind of locative or benefactive why doesn't it occur in all neuters (e.g., *medhu*). I will discuss question (2) first.

Once the passive voice has been created it is susceptible to what Gołąb, 1975, 15, calls 'activization,' viz., its reinterpretation as an active and the simultaneous reinterpretation of the subject of the passive as the object of an active verb. Bogoljubov, 1982, 20-21, has noted this phenomenon in many languages of the world and gives such examples as North Russian:

(g) u   volkóv (gen. pl.)   tut
    by   wolves   here

    koróvu (acc.)   jídeno (past psv. prt.).
    cow   eaten.

'A cow has been eaten by wolves here' = 'Wolves have eaten a cow here.' Or standard Russian (h) *ètu bašnju* (acc.) *vidno izdaleka* 'this tower is visible from far away.' Or Polish (i) *pracę* (acc.) *rozpoczyna się o ósmiej* 'work begins at 8.'

Thus a phrase such as B(3) *medhu pek^w-tó* 'the honey is (has been) cooked' could be interpreted as '(someone) cooked the honey.' I.e., the interpretation of *medhu* as a nominative singular could shift to accusative singular. Traces of possible ambiguity exist in ancient Greek. Compare the following sentence (Iliad, XIII, 597):

(j) tò   d'ephélketo   meílinon
    the   dragged after   ashen

   égkhos (neut. sg.).
   spear.

The Murray translation, 1976, 47, reads 'and the ashen spear trailed after him.' Schwyzer, 1966, 237, writes that the sentence could be translated in several ways: (k) *der eschene Speer schleifte nach* (cf. the Murray English translation), or (l) *wurde nachgeschleift* 'was dragged after' or even (m) *er schleifte den e. Sp. hinter sich nach* 'he dragged the ashen spear after himself.' If one accepts translation (k) or (l), then the neuter *meílinon égkhos* 'ashen spear' is in the nominative singular. But if one accepts the 'activized' translation (m), then the neuter is in the accusative singular.

There came to be then two possibilities for the interpretation of neuters. Since in general neuters or inanimates were low on the agentivity index, for the most part, they did not need the extra mark *-m* to mark them as direct objects. Following the pattern established in preterite forms the direct objects of the activized passives were substituted as direct objects of the original preterite active and thence to the present tense of both the active and the mediopassive. Thus sentences of the type C(l) became possible:

*māter pek^w-et-(i)   medhu
mother   cook-ed, (-s)   honey
(nom. sg.)   (transitive   (neut. acc. sg.)
                verb)

Comrie, 1981, 212, has written that accusative marking is more likely in noun phrases that are high in animacy. It also characterizes the acquisition or loss of accusative case marking. I assume that even the inanimates (neuters) may have originally had an *-m* marker in the accusative (when used as the object of the active verb), but that they lost it whereas the animate nouns (masculine and feminine) retained it.

The situation could have been somewhat similar to that of the Spanish personal *a* marker of the direct object. Only in recent times has this personal *a* begun to penetrate to the inanimates and now it is frequently a matter of choice to the speaker of Spanish whether he will use the *a* or not, according to Villar, 1983, 188. Villar gives the following example of the use of the personal *a* to mark an inanimate direct object (fn. 3): (n) *ningún rasgo morfológico diferencia a los géneros* 'no morphological feature differentiates the genders.' In the *$*o$*-stem neuters then there seems to have been vacillation, since some of the Indo-European languages show the accusative (and nominative) ending $*-m$, whereas Balto-Slavic apparently does not, cf., the Slavic nom.-acc. neuter (*měst-*)*o* 'place,' Lith. neuter sg. adj. (*gěr-*)*a* 'good.' The evidence of Hittite *tannattan* and *tannatta* 'empty' is ambiguous (Neu, 1979, 180). I assume a vacillation or a partial spread of the accusative marker $*-m$ to the $*o$-stem neuter category. In principle it would be less necessary to mark the neuter direct object since it would be less likely to conceive of the neuter as the agent. In some languages with the loss of the feeling for the need for the distinction between subject and object marking in the inanimate (neuter) $*o$-stem nouns the marker $*-m$ was substituted back into the nominative singular (cf., nom.-acc. sg. Gk. *dzugó-n*, Lat. *iugu-m*, Old Indic *yuga-m*, but Slavic *ig-o* 'yoke').

It is not at all certain, however, that the neuter singular form $*-om$ is to be identified with the $*o$-stem accusative singular $*-om$. Burrow, 1965, 173, notes that ancient thematic neuters are very rare in Indo-European. Furthermore, he writes (loc. cit.):

> The *m* in the neuter *yugám* was originally the *m*-suffix, but owing to similarity with the accusative singular of thematic stems (originally all adjectival and of common gender), it came, by an easy process of adaptation, to be treated as a termination, with the consequence that formations of this kind were turned into neuter thematic stems and declined accordingly. The neuter

thematic type then became productive, particularly
in forming extensions of neuter consonantal stems
(*-ana*, *-atra*, etc., ...).

See also the discussion in Villar, 1983, 133-139. Thus
it may not even be necessary to explain from a syntactic
point of view the appearance of *-m* in the *o*-stem neuter
nominative singular.

The existence of a marked allomorph for animate
accusatives as opposed to a zero allomorph for inanimate
accusatives has a parallel in the Čan (Laz) dialect of
the Zan language (South Caucasian). According to Klimov,
1962, 78, in common Khartvelian on the eve of its split
into separate languages the morpheme *-s* functioned as
a grammatical marker of the oblique case in all groups
of tenses and as a marker of the direct object in the
first group of tenses (i.e., present tense group - WRS).
As a result of various changes on the way towards nomina-
tivization in the Čan dialect there are two allomorphs
of the accusative, one deriving from the old nominative
and a second from the etymological *-s*. This second
allomorph is limited to a small group of verbs, the object of which is generally an animate noun. Thus,
e.g., (o) *biči-k* {erg. > nom.} *qozops kulani-s* {acc.}
'the fellow loves the girl.'

I shall return now to the first question. Since I
have proposed that in principle the nominative case derives from the absolute case I must try to explain away
the sigmatic forms of the nominative. One notes first
of all the identity of the *o*-stem nom. and gen. singular in Hittite, e.g., *an-tu-uḫ-ša-aš* 'man,' and the
identity of the *jo*-stem nom. and gen. singular in
Gothic *harjis* 'army,' *haírdeis* 'shepherd,' Vedic *ve-s*
'bird' (beside the usual nom. *vis*; Specht, 1947, 362).
One possible explanation is that with the reorganization
of the syntax as Indo-European passed from partially
ergative to nominative, the *o*-stem ergative agent passed
into nominative function (Ivanov, 1963, 132). This
explanation identifies the sigmatic nominative singular
with the sigmatic genitive singular. In Baltic the
o-stem ergative *-os* has been restricted to the nominative case (Lith. *výr-)a-s* 'man, husband,' and the old
ablative has taken over the additional function of genitive (Lith. *výr-)o* (< *-ā*). Mažiulis, 1970, 80, pro-
fesses to see the etymological *o*-stem gen. sg. in Old
Prussian (*deiw-)as*, which is, of course, possible,

although I am in general inclined to discount Old Prussian evidence. The multiple origin reveals the two fundamentally different functions of the Indo-European nominative case, viz. (1) the subject of an intransitive verb (originally expressed morphologically by the absolute case) and (2) the agent of an ergative verb form (originally expressed by the ergative case, the sigmatic nominative singular and the genitive singular in *-s).

The ending *-os or better, thematic vowel plus marker *-s took over the function of the simple thematic vowel by itself, still represented in the *-e of the *o-stem vocatives, e.g., Skt. (vr̥k-)a, Lith. (vilk-)e, OCS (vlьč-)e, Gk. (lúk-)e, etc.

Another explanation which also identifies the sigmatic nominative and genitive singular suggests the genitive singular came to be used as an adjective. Thus a nom. sg. *i̯ātḗr 'physician' would have a gen. sg. *i̯ātrós 'relating to a physician, physician's' which in turn could be substantivized as a noun and understood as a nominative singular (Villar, 1974, 250-263). A possible parallel to this could be seen in the use of the Hittite gen. sg. waštul-aš (nom. sg. waštul 'sin') in the meaning of 'sinner,' or the gen. sg. tayazil-aš (nom. sg. tayazil 'theft') in the meaning 'thief' (Friedrich, 1960, 123). See 30.7.

The *o-stem nouns then supplied the final *-s which became one of the markers of the Indo-European nominative singular. The spread was gradual and was never, indeed, completed. Hittite personal names occur sometimes with a final -š, sometimes without it. This phenomenon is usually ascribed to Akkadian influence, but this is an unnecessary assumption (Kronasser, 1956, 99). Čikobava, 1948, 223, noted that in Old Georgian the indefinite case was originally used for the agent with proper names and one encounters Abraam šva Jsaak 'Abraham bore Isaac' in the indefinite case rather than the expected Abraam-man (ergative). Since proper nouns are more likely to function as agents than patients, the marking with the *-s in Indo-European was later.

In sum then Indo-European is perhaps typologically unusual in that sometimes there exists marking for the agent (nominative case in *-s in some instances) and marking for the patient (accusative case in *-m in most instances). But neither the marking in *-s nor the marking in *-m was thorough-going. I explain the zero-marking of the nominative and the *-m marking of the accusative from the nominative-accusative (< absolute-indirect) syntax of the original present tense. The *-s marking of the nominative and the zero-marking of the accusative may derive from the ergative syntax characteristic of the preterite tense. Indo-European was originally a mixed ergative language which became almost completely nominativized in the course of its extant history, possible traces of the original ergativity being retained in some of the modern Indo-Iranian languages.

In the present tense (or imperfective aspect) the performer of the action and the action itself were the most important elements of the sentence. In the preterite tense (or perfective aspect) the action and the goal of the action were the most important elements. Therefore in the present (imperfective) the performer of the action was morphologically unmarked and in the preterite (perfective) the goal of the action was morphologically unmarked.

Following tradition we will use the term *subject* to denote both the agent of the transitive verb and the subject of the intransitive verb.

29.1 Note the following examples of the use of the nominative case for the subject of a verb (Acad. Gram., Vol. 1, 182) from modern Lithuanian:

(a) Ir   klùpo   žìrgas,   ir
And   stumbled   steed   and
                          (nom. sg.)

nupúolė   Ilgis   nuõ   žìrgo,
fell   Ilgis   from   steed
           (nom. sg.)

kaĩ   vãkaras   tẽmė   girià.
as   evening   darkened forest.
       (nom. sg.)

'And the steed stumbled and Ilgis fell from the steed as evening darkened the forest.'

According to Palionis, 1967, 151, the use of the nominative case in old Lithuanian differed little from the contemporary use. An example of the nominative case used as the subject of a transitive verb is from Mažyvdas Catechism (10, 11).

(b) Tassai   maxlas (nom. sg.)   roda
    This   doctrine   shows the

    tikra   kiely...
    true   way...

An example of the nominative case used as the subject of an intransitive verb is also from Mažyvdas' Catechism (49, 1):

(c) tawesp   eit   szmagus (nom.)   gressnasis
    to you   comes   man   sinful.
'A sinful man comes to you.'

29.2 The nominative case of the noun is used also in nominal sentences, i.e., those sentences without a verb (Acad. Gram., Vol. 1, 182): (a) *Juodà naktìs*. 'A dark night.' (b) *Jaũ vėlỹvas ruduõ* 'it is already late autumn.' Sometimes a single word is used: (c) *Krañtas. Ẽglė žìno čià visùs keliùs.* 'The bank. Eglė knows all the paths here.' Such a use of the nominative case shows only the existence of the object or phenomenon in question.

29.3 The use of the nominative case in predicate position with the verbs *bū́ti* 'to be,' *algõtis* 'to be called,' *pramiñti*, *vadìnti* 'to name, to call,' *vadìntis* 'to be called,' *tàpti* 'to become,' *stóti(s)*, *pastóti* 'to become' is common (Palionis, 1967, 151): (Mažvydas' Catechism 31, 12-13):

(a) Jr   ghadnas   esti   darbinikas   algas
    And   worthy   is   laborer   of hire

    saua
    his.

'And the laborer is worthy of his hire.' Note the predicate *ghadnas* 'worthy' as predicate nominative with *darbinikas* 'laborer.' Cf. from Sirvydas' *Punktay sakimu* I 177[10]: (b) *Diewas algoiasi stebuklingas* (nom.) 'God is called miraculous' (Palionis, 1967, 151; Zinkevičius, 1981, 210). From Bretkūnas' *Bible*:

(c) (*Genesis* 38, 11): ikki   didis   taps
                                 until   big   will become

     mana   sunus
     my   son.
'Until my son becomes grown up.' *didis* 'big, grown up' is a predicate nominative.

29.31 An older semipredicative use of the nominative is represented by such a Lithuanian sentence as (a) *stăčias stoviù* 'I stand straight' which is similar to Gk. (b) *stē̃ d'orthós* 'stood up straight' and Old Indic (c) *Savitā sthād ūrdhvas* 'Savitā stood up straight.' Lith. *stăčias*, Gk. *orthós* and Old Indic *ūrdhvas* 'straight' are all nom. sg. forms (Zinkevičius, 1981, 210). The function of such adjectives is both to modify and to predicate, i.e., they have a double function. Fraenkel, 1928, 20-21, terms such constructions as 'appositive-predicative constructions in competition with adverbs,' cf., e.g., (d) *ištisas gulėti* 'to lie stretched out,' (e) *púolęs į̃ klãną saũsas nekélsi* 'having fallen into the swamp you won't get out dry.' In the above expressions *ištisas* 'stretched out,' *saũsas* 'dry' are in the nom. sg. and are closely bound up with the verb and yet they function as a predicate also.

29.32 The nominative case is attested with the meaning 'to give a name' in Pietkiewicz' Catechism (159, 2): (a) *Jėzus wardą iam dawė* 'they gave the name Jesus to him.' This may be on the model of Polish *Jezus mu imię dali* in which the noun *Jezus* is also in the nominative singular (see Fraenkel, 1947, 60). From Brētkunas' *Postilla* I, 134, 19:

(b) to   warda   tu   praminsi   Jesus
     his   name   you   will call   Jesus.
'You will call his name Jesus.' The noun *Jesus* is in the nom. sg. From *Punktay sakimu* I, 254, 21-23:

(c) todryn   raupuoti   patogiey   wadinasi
     therefore   lepers   justly   are called

     heretikay
     heretics.

'Therefore the lepers are justly called heretics.' The noun *heretikay* is in the nom. pl. Cf. Pol. *przeto trędowaći słusznie śię zowią heretycy* (Palionis, 1967, 152).

29.4 The nominative case is also encountered in adverbial expressions which originally consisted of a pronoun or adjective plus a predicate noun in the nominative case. Thus an adverbial expression such as *kàs rýtas* 'every morning' derives its meaning from an older nominal sentence with zero copula, i.e., originally with the meaning 'which(ever) is the morning.'

29.5 Kiparsky, 1969, 148, was on the right track with his suggestion that the nominative plus infinitive in Baltic is a relic of the Indo-European situation.
    Palmaitis, 1977, 117, puts it in the following way: In utterances of the type (a) *langaĩ uždarýta* 'the windows are closed,' (b) *vãgos išárta* 'the furrows are plowed' if one replaces the participle with participle plus infinitive one obtains the following sentences:

(c)   langaĩ   reĩkta (turéta)
       windows   are necessary

       uždarýti
       to close.
'The windows must be closed.'

(d)   vãgos   reĩkta (turéta)
       furrows   are necessary

       išárti
       to plow.
'The furrows must be plowed.'

Since neuter participles with the suffix *-ta* are characterized by neutrality in respect to diathesis, in these examples *reĩkta (turéta)* 'necessary' must be regarded as a simple expression of necessity similar to the impersonal *reĩkia* '(it is) necessary' {(e) *vãgos reĩkia išárti* 'the furrows must be plowed'} without any nuance of active or passive voice.

According to Palionis, 1967, 153, the nominative plus infinitive construction was used relatively rarely in East Prussian Lithuanian in comparison with the use in contemporary Lithuanian. Palionis records only two examples, both from Bretkūnas' *Postilla* I. The first is (180, 2):

(f) kosznam   wirui   pareitissi   schie
    for every   man   are appropriate   these

    keturi   daiktai   dariti
    four   things   to do.

'These four things are appropriate for every man to do.' Note that *schie keturi daiktai* 'these four things' is nom. pl. The second example (138, 6):

(g) teipo   pareitis   mums,   wissa
    so   is appropriate   for us   all

    teisibe   ischpilditi
    right action   to fulfill.

'So all right action is appropriate for us to accomplish, it is appropriate for us to do the right thing.' In this sentence, however, according to Palionis, it is unclear whether *wissa teisibe* is in the nominative or accusative singular. One can find a few examples of the nominative with infinitive, according to Palionis, 1967, 153, in 16th and 17th century writings of the Lithuanian Grand Duchy, but even here the construction is not common. Thus in Daukša's Catechism (42, 7) (h) *kas pridera darit* 'what is fitting to do.' In Pietkiewicz' Catechism (3, 13-14) (i) *kas vžgul mokieti?* 'what is fitting to know?' According to Palionis, 1967, 153-154, the rarety of such constructions in writings of the early periods is probably to be explained by the fact that the nominative with infinitive construction at that time, even as now, was more characteristic of the Eastern High Lithuanian and certain Samogitian dialects.[3]

Sirtautas, 1971, 78, writes that in contemporary Lithuanian the nominative with infinitive is widely used, but there is a tendency to replace the simple infinitive with the reflexive infinitive, thus *girdėtis*, *matytis*, *regėtis* tend to replace *girdėti* 'to hear,' *matyti*, *regėti* 'to see.' Thus both *kas girdėti?* 'what is to be heard' and *kas girdėtis* (same meaning) are encountered. The subject of the infinitive can be a special gerund, e.g.:

(j) Ūž   miško   buvo   matyti   dẽgant.
    Beyond   forest   was   to see   burning.
'(Something) burning could be seen beyond the forest' (Sirtautas, 1971, 76).[4]

29.51 Continuing with the notion that the earliest form of the Indo-European verb is intransitive one arrives at a natural interpretation of the origin of the nominative plus infinitive constructions. Thus Disterheft, 1980, 187, notes that voice is not morphologically marked for the infinitive in most of the Indo-European languages (notable exceptions being Latin and Greek). According to Disterheft voice is only indicated syntactically by marking the relationship of the noun phrase to the infinitive. The patient is the object when the infinitive is active, but the subject when the infinitive is passive. I suggest that the verbs in such constructions are old non-diathetic intransitives which have come to be interpreted as passives as a result of the emergence of the new active voice. Note the examples from various Indo-European languages:
    Tocharian A:

(a) wsā-yok-   yats...   sūk
    gold-colored   skin (is)...   pleasant
                       (nom.)

    lkātsi
    to see.
'The gold-colored skin is pleasant to see' (Krause and Thomas, 1960, 79).
    Vedic:

(b) havyaír   agnír   mánuṣa
    by the sacrifices   Agni   of the man
    (inst.)   (nom.)   (gen.)

147

īrayádhyāi
is to be brought to life
(inf.)

'Agni is to be brought to life through the sacrifice of a man.' Avestan: (c) *gāuš jaⁱdyāi* 'The cow is to be killed' (Brugmann-Delbrück, 1916, 923-924). Hittite:

(d) ...nepisas   daganzipas-a   uddār
        heaven   earth and   word
        (gen.)   (gen.)   (nom.)

     kattan   arha   petummanzi
                      bring-forth
                      (inf.)

'May the word of heaven and earth be brought forth.'

(e) ...1   GA.KIN.AG   parsiwanzi
       one   cheese (?)   break
                                (inf.)

'One cheese(?) should be broken' (Disterheft, 1980, 165).
    Kiparsky, 1969, has given an excellent brief review of the vast literature on the subject as it concerns the Baltic and Slavic languages and one must agree with him that the construction is retained from early Indo-European, although Tocharian and Hittite evidence seems to have escaped him. From dialect Russian Kiparsky, 1969, 142, gives the example: (f) *ryba nado lovit'* 'a fish is to be caught' < Old Russian (g) *ryba na době estь loviti* 'a fish is at this time to be caught.' From Vsevelod Miller, Kiparsky quotes the example:

(h) znat'   sova   po perju
     to be recognized   an owl   by the feathers,
     (inf.)   (nom.)   (prep. dat.)

     sokol   po   polëtu
     falcon   by   flight.
     (nom.)   (prep.)   (dat.)

'An owl is (to be) recognized by its feathers, a falcon by its flight.'
    From Endzelīns, 1922, 409 (= 1951, 553), para. 392, Kiparsky quotes the Latvian example:

(i)   nuosûnuojis   akmins   grūti
      covered with moss   stone   difficult
                           (nom.)

      kustinât
      to move
      (inf.)

'A stone covered with moss is difficult to move.'

A typical Lithuanian example is furnished by the Academy Grammar, Vol. 1, p. 183:

(j)   Kitíem   láiškai   rašýti   buvo
      For others   letters   to write   was
      (dat. pl.)   (nom. pl.)   (inf.)   (past
                                                tense)

      daũg   lengviaũ
      much   easier
      (adv.)   comparative

'For others letters were much easier to write.'

Thus the use of the nominative case (mostly derived from the old indefinite case) as the patient of the apparently passive (although originally non-diathetic) infinitive is well represented in many Indo-European languages. Disterheft, 1980, 115, has argued that in the Rig-Veda the use of the passive voice with the negated infinitive is a reflection of a more archaic passive use of the infinitive. One would expect the earlier form of the intransitive verb to be understood as a passive, once the new transitive verb is developed.

The common feature of the Armenian transitive and intransitive perfect forms is that they are expressed by a periphrastic construction, but that in the intransitive perfect the subject is in the nominative case and in the transitive perfect the agent is in the genitive case. Note the following forms:

(k)   es   cneal   em
      I   born   was.

'I was born.'

(l)   žamanak   haseal   ē
      the time   come   has.

'The time has come.'

(m) Yisus   ekeal   ēr
    Jesus   come   had.
'Jesus had come.' Armenian examples with a transitive perfect:

(n) z-ayn   nšan   arareal
    this   miracle   accomplished
    (acc.)   (acc.)   (*eal*-participle)

    ēr   nora
    had   he
           (gen. sg.)
'He had accomplished this miracle.'

(o) ēr   nora   hraman   aŕeal
    had   he   a promise   received
           (gen.)   (acc.) (?)   (*eal*-prt.)
'He had received a promise' (Benveniste, 1971, 156-157; Godel, 1975, 54).

Although in the examples given above the object of the transitive verbs is in the accusative case (*z-ayn nšan* 'this miracle,' and *hraman* 'promise') it seems probable that originally such forms were in the nominative. Thus, according to Benveniste, 1971, 159:

(p) z-gorc   gorceal   ē   nora
    operam   factum   est   eius
    (acc.)   (acc.)   (gen.)
'He accomplished this work' shows the replacement of an old nominative case by an accusative and was originally rather like the Latin *eius* (gen.) *facta* (nom.) *est opera* (nom.). The transitive government was adopted under the influence of the earlier *fecit* 'he accomplished.' The phenomenon is exactly comparable to the Lithuanian situation where *rãšoma láiška* replaces *rãšoma láiškas* (see 6) under the influence of the prevailing transitive pattern.

According to Benveniste, 1971, 175, 'the form of the transitive perfect active in Armenian is distinguished from that of the perfect passive only if the object is specified as such by the particle *z-*; otherwise, the two forms coincide.' Note the example from Mark 15:46:

(q) ed   i   gerezmani   z-or
    he laid (him)   in   sepulchre   which one

ēr	p'oreal	i	vimē
had	hewn	out of	rock.

'He laid him in a sepulchre which one had hewn out of a rock.' But if the particle z- is omitted, the expression or ēr p'oreal must be translated by the passive which corresponds exactly with the Greek: (r) hò ên lelatomēmenon ek pétras 'which was hewn out of a rock.' An example from Luke 2:5:

(s) Maremaw   handerj   z-or   xawseal
     Mary   with   whom   espoused

ēr   nma
had   to him.

'With Mary whom one had espoused to him.' If again one deletes the z- from the relative pronoun the sentence would read: 'With Mary espoused to him' and corresponds exactly with the Greek (t) sùn Mariàm tễi emmēsteumēnēi autõi.

Benveniste, 1971, 175, writes further: 'Examples can be found in which nothing except the context allows us to decide whether the perfect is active or passive.' Some examples: Luke 19:15:

(u) .....   z-caraysn   oroc'   tueal
     .....   the servants   to whom   given

ēr   z-arcat'n
had   money.

'...servants to whom he had given money.' Since the relative pronoun oroc' is genitive-dative-ablative plural it could logically be understood as the subject, i.e., 'who have given the money.' It is only the context which allows us to decide on the true agent of the action of giving.

Typologically the Armenian syntactic shifts are extremely instructive. In the first place it is evident that the use of copulative verb with the -eal participle was originally only intransitive, as is evidenced by the older constructions such as es cneal em 'I was born.' Later by contrast with the new active constructions, e.g., aṙnem 'I make, do' such an original intransitive form as arareal 'accomplished' came to be understood as a passive and the old possessive genitive is understood as the agent. While it was still a passive one assumes with Benveniste, 1971, 159, that the patient was in the nominative case. When the interpretation shifted from passive to active, following the pattern of the active verbs the patient shifted to the accusative case. This is, as we have seen above, exactly what happened with the Indo-European medio-passive in such languages as Greek and Sanskrit (see Chapter 6).

Thus both the Vedic infinitive and the Armenian participles in *-eal* show complementary distribution, i.e., they originally denoted either (a) intransitive or (b) the passive of a transitive. This renders it likely that the latter (b) developed from the former (a) through syntactic/semantic reanalysis at the moment when the new active voice was being created.

29.6 The nominative case can also be used to denote circumstances of time and place (Acad. Gram., Vol. 1, 184):

(a) Mán   su   žéntu   gál
    To me   with   son-in-law   perhaps

    dár   mẽtai   kitì   teks,
    still   year   another   will fall to the lot,

    o   jái   su   výru   -   ìlgas
    but   to her with   husband -   long

    ámžius   ateitỹ.
    age   in the future.

'I will have to live with (my) son-in-law perhaps another year, but she will have to live (her) whole life with her husband.' Note that the adverbial expressions *mẽtai kitì* 'some years' and *ìlgas ámžius* 'long age' are in the nominative case.

(b) Atvažiãvo   į   stõtį   peñkios
    Arrived   at   station   five

    minùtės   priẽš   išeĩnant   tráukiniui
    minutes   before   departing   train.

'(He) arrived at the station five minutes before the train left.' The expression *peñkios minùtės* 'five minutes' is in the nom. pl. Such adverbial constructions are usually in the accusative rather than the nominative case in the literary language.

The nominative of place usually shows the distance from the action or the place where the action is occurring (Acad. Gram., Vol. 1, 184):

(c) Dabar̃   kàs   žiñgsnis   –   atsìveria
    Now   each   step (nom.)   opens

    nematýti   vaizdaĩ
    unseen   views.

'Now at each step (previously) unseen views are opening up.' The adverbial expression kàs žiñgsnis 'at each step,' is in the nom. sg. The nominative case is used only with words which express a certain quantity and the words with which they agree syntactically, e.g., penkì žiñgsniai (nom. pl.) 'five paces,' kelì mètrai (nom. pl.) 'a few meters,' devynì kilomètrai 'nine kilometers.'

29.7 According to the Acad. Gram., Vol. 1, 183, apposition is also expressed by the nominative case of the noun. Examples:

(a) Kur̃   jìs   vargšèlis   ràs
    Where   he   poor fellow   will find

    sáu   prieglaudė̃lę   be   tė́vų̃
    himself   shelter   except   parents'

    nãmo?
    house?

'Where will he, the poor fellow, find for himself any shelter except his parents' house?' The noun vargšė̃lis 'poor fellow' in the nom. sg. is in apposition with jìs 'he.' With naming constructions the noun may be either in the nominative case or in the case of the noun to which it refers, e.g.:

(b) Jiẽ   turė́jo   dùkteri̇̀,
    They   had   daughter (acc.)

    vardù   Onýtė   (or)
    by the name of (inst.)   Anna (nom.)

    Onýtę
    (acc.).

'They had a daughter by the name of Anna.' Here the name 'Anna' could be expressed either by the nom. *Onýtė* or the acc. *Onýtę* to agree with *dùkteri̇̀* 'daughter' in the acc. sg. (c) In Pietkiewicz' Catechism (Fraenkel, 1947, 72) we encounter appositional expression *krikščionis žmogus* 'Christian man' (but see also 31.2).

29.71 The nominative case also functions in place of the vocative (Acad. Gram., Vol. 1, 185):

(a) Àš   apiẽ   reĩkalą   ir   kalbù,
    I   about   affair   even   am talking,

    draũgas.
    comrade.

'I am indeed talking about the affair, comrade.' Here the noun denoting the person addressed, *draũgas* 'comrade' is in the nom. sg., not the vocative as might be expected.

(b) Kàs   tiesà,   põnas,   taĩ   tiesà.
    What   true,   sir,   that   true.

'What is true, sir, is true.' Here *põnas* 'sir' is in the nom. sg., not the vocative.

29.72 Sometimes the nominative case of the noun is used with the meaning of a 2nd person pronoun:

(a) Bėdà,   jùk   põnas   pìnigus
    Too bad,   indeed   you (sir)   money

    surinkaĩ.
    have gathered.

'Too bad, you have gathered the money.' In this example *põnas* 'you, sir' functions as the subject of the verb *surinkaĩ* (2nd sg. pret.) 'you (sg.) have gathered.'

29.73 The nominative case is typically the case for titles (Fraenkel, 1928, 8), cf. Mažvydas 1, 1:

(a) catechismusa   prasty   szadei,
    of the catechism   simple   words
                                       (nom. pl.)

makslas	rašta	yr	giesmes.
art	of reading	and	song.
(nom. sg.)			

The expressions *prasty szadei* 'simple words' and *makslas* 'art' are in the nominative case.

29.74 Greetings may be in the nominative case (a) *lãbas vãkaras* 'good evening,' (b) *labà dienà* 'good day,' (c) *labãnaktis* 'good night' (cf., Pol. *dobranoc*), (d) *lãbas rýtas* 'good morning.' According to Fraenkel, 1928, 8, the rationale behind the use of the nominative is the notion 'may the (evening, day, etc.) be good.'

   According to Fraenkel, 1928, 27, as in other Indo-European languages the so called 'nominativus pendens' is not rare. Note the example from Pietkiewicz' Catechism (Fraenkel, 1947, 62):

(e)	tas,	kurs	wakar	numirė,
	he	who	yesterday	died
	(nom. sg.)			

negali	iam	padėt	tay	šią	dieną,
cannot	him	help	that	this	day

o	tas,	kurs	šią	dieną
but	he	who	this	day
	(nom. sg.)			

numirė,	teypag	iam	nepadest	tas
died	also	him	doesn't help	this

žodis	šią	dieną.
word	this	day.
(nom. sg.)		

'He who died yesterday, this cannot help him today, and he who died today, this word doesn't help him today.' Cf., the equivalent Polish: (f) *ten, co wczora umarł, nie służy mu to dzisia, a ten, co dzisia umarł, także mu to iuż nie służy słowo dzisia*. In such a case the nominative case establishes the theme which is then later picked up by some other case in the sentence.

29.8 According to Ulvydas, 1969, 7, nouns in the nominative case are not likely to be adverbialized; those that are, usually function not to denote additional circumstances in the sentence, but rather as predicates of impersonal sentences.

Ulvydas, 8, divides up those adverbs which derive etymologically from the substantival nom. sg. into three groups: (1) the adverbs *ganà* 'enough' and *gaĩla* 'sorry' which have left no trace of any other case in contemporary Lithuanian and have lost all connection with the nouns, (2) the adverbs *valià* 'it is allowd, one may' (and the negated *nevalià*) and *žinià* 'it is known, certainly, surely' (and the negated *nežinià*) which when used as predicates cannot be modified by any adjective and (3) the hybrid noun-adverb group including, e.g., *garbẽ* 'honor' (*negarbẽ*), *gė́da* 'shame' (*ne gė́da*), *laĩkas* 'time' (*ne laĩkas*), etc. Note the following examples: (a) *Niẽkam* (dat. sg.) *nevalià kéikti* 'no-one is allowed to curse.'

(b) Nedìdelė garbẽ svetimomìs kalbomìs
    not great honor foreign languages

    kalbė́ti, didì gė́da savõsios
    to speak, great shame one's own

    geraĩ nemokė́ti.
    well not to know.

'It is not a great honor to speak foreign languages, it is a great shame not to know one's own well.' The adverb *gaĩla* may be derived from the old nom.-acc. neuter form of the adjective:

(c) Mán mótinos gaĩla.
    To me of mother sorrow.
    (dat. sg.) (gen. sg.)

'I am sorry for mother.'

The adverb *ganà* 'enough, rather' is cognate with the verb *ganė́ti* (3rd sg. pres. either *ganė́ja* or *gãna*) and probably Slavic *gonė́ti* 'to suffice' (Ulvydas, 1969, 7). Note the examples: (d) *jìs ganà dìdelis* 'he is rather large,' (e) *ganà dúonos* (gen. sg.) 'enough bread.' Differently from other adverbs formed from the nominative *ganà* is distinguished by the fact that it cannot only be used in predicate function, but also as an adverb of manner or quantity. In addition *ganà* is the only one to have a truncated form *gañ* which for the most part has already become a particle.

Although Ulvydas has suggested that the adverb *ganà* is the old noun nominative singular it seems to me that it may be derived rather from the verb *ganė́ti* 'to be sufficient.' According to the Acad. Dict. (Vol. 3, 100) the preferred 3rd person present of *ganė́ti* is *ganė́ja*, but the form *gãna* is also apparently possible.

The Acad. Gram. (Vol. 2, 239) gives a list of thematic verbs with the suffix -ė- in the infinitive and preterit, e.g., 3rd pres. *tẽka* 'runs, flows,' inf. *tekė́ti*, 3rd pret. *tekė́jo*. Such verbs, called the mixed type, seem less numerous than the completely productive verbs with the -ė- suffix in the infinitive and all tenses, e.g., *akmenė́ti* 'to turn to stone' (3rd pres. *akmenė́ja*, 3rd pret. *akmenė́jo*; Acad. Gram., Vol. 2, 258). Historical linguistics shows that the less regular verbs are more likely to be archaic than the more regular verbs, so a 3rd present *gãna* is probably more archaic than a 3rd present *ganė́ja*.

Būga, 1961, 57, proposes that at one time Lithuanian did indeed have an oxytone verbal paradigm. Doubting the primacy of etymological end-stress Stang, 1957, 156-157, assumes an original etymological mobility for certain Lithuanian verbal paradigms. Nevertheless he thinks there are some cases where the Old Prussian thematic vowel was stressed, e.g., 2nd sg. *giwassi* 'you live,' 3rd person *giwa*, 1st pl. *giwammai*, pres. part. *giwantei*. He suggests further that an Old Prussian paradigm *$gív\bar{o}$, *$gívasei$, *$gíva$, *$gívamái$, *$gívat\acute{e}$ has been leveled according to the plural forms as in Slavonic. This gave rise to a 3rd person *gīvà*, which in turn produced *$gīvàsei$, *$gīvàmai$. I would certainly dispute in principle heavy reliance on Old Prussian evidence, but in other cases there does seem to be a macron written where one would expect a short vowel. I interpret the macron to denote an etymological stressed short vowel. Thus *perweddā* 'lead' and *popaikā* 'deceive' are not conjunctives (Trautmann, 1910, 397, 405), but are simple 3rd person present forms which are to be phonemicized as {per-vedá} and {pa-paiká} respectively (Schmalstieg, 1974a, 173, 170).

Old Prussian *per-weddā* would be compared with Lith. *prì-veda* 'leads' (a mobile paradigm which could reflect an earlier end-stress, if Būga is right; *pér-veda* 'leads across' cannot be used as evidence, since *pér-* is always stressed). The Lithuanian cognate of Old Prussian *po-paikā*, viz. *paĩkti* 'grow foolish' cannot be used as evidence since the present has an *-st-* suffix, viz. 3rd person *paĩksta*, although the circumflex root is compatible with accentual mobility (or end stress) if we are dealing with a root-type thematic verb.

Skardžius, 1935, 195, notes the following vacillations in Dauksa's accentuation: *nèbjauris, nopkeñčia, praleñkia* beside *nebjaũris, n,opkenčia* (i.e., *neãpkenčia*) and *prãlenkia*. He writes further that such forms as *neãpkenčia* and *prãlenkia* might not be mistakes, but reflect the linguistic facts, as is shown by the contemporary hesitation between *àtgręžia* beside *atgręžia*. Again following Skardžius the accentuation *(ne) turimė* is attested (10X) and *tùrime* (4X). In fact a marginal end-stress is well attested in the 1st and 2nd pl. present forms in Dauksa's Postilla. Skardžius, 1935, 199, writes, however, that the forms *daliiê, gadinâ, giwenâ, iszriszâ, kelauiâ*, etc. are clear errors and compares the attested *gãdina, wãdina*, etc. It would appear to me, however, that if *turimê, žinomê*, etc. can reflect an earlier end stress, then the 3rd person forms *daliiê, gadinâ*, etc. could also reflect an earlier end stress.

ganà is then a reliquary form from the 3rd person present originally meaning 'it is sufficient.' The government of the genitive case is to be expected, because the verbal successor *ganėti* governs the genitive case, cf. the example from the Acad. Dict. (Vol. 3, 100):

(f) Sveikám   žmõgui   ir   prastèsnio
     For a healthy   man   and   worse

     val̃gio   ganėja.
     food   suffices.
     (gen. sg.)

Used in short predicative sentences *ganà* lost its connection with the verbal paradigm and was reinterpreted as an adverb of quantity. No longer a member of the verbal paradigm it was able to retain its final stress when oxytone paradigms became mobile. This explains also why there is no oblique case for *ganà*. Being an etymological 3rd person present verb rather than a nom. sg. *$\bar{a}$-stem noun it could, of course, have no oblique case.

The adverbial forms *daũgi*, *daũgia* 'much, many' could also have been 3rd person forms of the verb *daugė́ti* 'to increase, to be abundant.' Although the Acad. Dict. (Vol. 2, 314) does not list these as possible 3rd person pres. forms for *daugė́ti*, the pattern of *i*-stem or **je/o*-stem presents for verbs with the suffix *-ėti* is attested elsewhere. For example, the 3rd present of the verb *skaudė́ti* 'to hurt' according to the Acad. Dict. (Vol. 12, 769) in addition to standard *skaũda* may be also *skaũsta*, *skaũsti*, *skaũdžia* or *skaũdi*.

Since verbs in *-ėti* are frequently denominatives in many cases it may be impossible to know whether the adverb is derived from a verb or a noun.

29.81 The fossilization and adverbialization of the noun is illustrated by the fact that it can sometimes even have a comparative degree, e.g., from *sarmatà* 'shame' one encounters a comparative *sarmačiaũ* 'more shameful.' Cf. also:

(a) Anksčiaũ   jíem   vìskas   bùvo
    Earlier   to them   everything   was

   valiaũ (= labiaũ valià).
   more allowed.
'Earlier more was allowed to them' (Ulvydas, 1969, 10).

From Lithuanian dialects Zinkevičius, 1966, 391, reports that the meaning 'a lot, very many' is found for certain adverbialized nominatives such as (in Luokė)
(b) báimės (nom. pl.) žmonių̃ (gen. pl.) 'lots of people,'
(in Kalnãlis) (c) galýbės (nom. pl.) vaikų̃ (gen. pl.)
'many children.' (Ordinarly *báimė* and *galýbė* mean 'fear' and 'possibility' respectively.) From Ukmergė̃:

(d) gývas   vélnias   kiaušìnių
    living   devil   eggs
               (nom. sg.)   (gen. pl.)

   turgùj
   at the market.
'There are a lot of eggs at the market.'

30

The Adverbal Genitive Case

30. The Indo-European genitive case was originally probably some kind of locative case from which the notion of belonging developed. It is from this 'notion of belonging' that the agentive notion developed (the action belongs to X).

30.1 According to the Lithuanian Acad. Gram., Vol. 1, 186, there are certain verbs which consistently require a genitive object: (a) *bijóti sunkùmų* 'to fear difficulties,' (b) *láukti draũgo* 'to wait for a friend,' (c) *norė́ti miẽgo* 'to wish for sleep,' (d) *prašýti (ką̃ nors) knỹgos* 'to ask (somebody) for a book' (note that the person asked *ką̃ nors* 'somebody' is in the acc. sg. whereas the thing requested *knỹgos* 'book' is in the gen. sg.). Some examples from Vilentas' Catechism (Ford, 1969, 118) are the following:

```
(e)  (48, 22):  iey      tô              nůg      musu
                if       this            of       us
                         (gen. sg.)
```

    nores.
    will wish.
'If they will wish this of us.'

```
(f)  (24, 1):   tũ       daiktu...,      kuriu
                those    things          which
                                         (gen. pl.)
```

    męs   praschom.
    we   ask for.

(g) (16, 7): Todelei   turim   biotiesi
              Therefore   we should   fear

   rustibes   jo.
   wrath   his.
   (gen. sg.)
'Therefore we should fear his wrath.'
   According to Klein, 1653, 152, when the verb (1st sg.) *klausau* denotes 'obey' it is used with the gen. or the dat., but when it denotes 'hear' it is used with the gen. or the acc. Thus (h) *klausyk man* (dat.) 'obey me'; (i) *Klausyti žodi* (acc.) *Diewo* or (j) *Klausyti žodžio* (gen.) *Diewo* 'hear, listen to the word of God.'
   According to Zinkevičius, 1981, 210-211, most probably in earlier times the meaning was important for the choice of the case, not the syntactic government. Thus verbs did not require a certain case as they do now, but they were used with this or that case depending upon the meaning of the sentence. Thus in the phrase (k) *išklausiaũ vìsą kaĩbą* 'I listened to the whole speech' the acc. (sg.) complement is used to denote the direct object of the listening. On the other hand in the phrase (l) *klausiaũ sàvo tėvo balso* 'I listened to my father's voice' the noun *balso* 'voice' is in the gen. sg. to denote the source of the voice.
   One notes that with the Greek and Old Indic verb 'to hear' the accusative case is used as the object of the verb when it denotes the thing heard, but the genitive case when it denotes the producer of the sound. Thus, Gk. (Iliad 4, 455): (m) *doũpon* (acc. sg.) *éklue poimēn* 'the shepherd heard the din' vs. (n) (Iliad 1, 357): *toũ* (gen. sg.) *d'éklue pótnia mētēr* 'his queenly mother heard him.' Similarly Old Indic (o) *vácam* (acc. sg.) *śṛṇóti* 'he hears a voice' vs. (p) *devásya* (gen. sg.) *śṛṇóti* 'he hears a god' (Humbert, 1954, 272).

   Compare the following sentences:

(q) Vilko   bebėginėdamas   užbėgsi
    Wolf   fleeing   you will run across
    (gen.)

    lóki.
    bear.

'Fleeing (from) the wolf, you will run across the bear' (Jablonskis, 1957, 589). The tendency is, however, to reinforce the simple case form with prepositions so we also find:

(r) Nuõ   vilko   bėgsi,   ant
    From   wolf   you will run   on

    meškõs   užbėgsi.
    bear   you will run.

'You will run from the wolf, (but) you will run on to the bear' (Acad. Dict., Vol. 1, 731). It is impossible then to list all the verbs used with a genitive complement, and a few selected examples are given from the older and modern language. See 30.6 and 30.62.

30.11 According to Palionis, 1967, 154, in writings of the 16th and 17th centuries the verbs of remembering are encountered with a genitive as well as an accusative complement: (a) (Bretkūnas' Bible, Joshua 1, 13) *atminkite szodzio* 'remember the word' (cf. Luther's Bible) *gedenket an das Wort*. The word *szodzio* (= modern *žõdžio*) is gen. sg.; (b) (Bretkūnas' Bible, Genesis 40, 14) *atmink manęs* (gen. sg.) 'remember me,' cf. Luther's Bible, *gedencke meiner* in which *meiner* is gen. sg.; (c) (Bretkūnas' Bible, Deuteronomy 24, 19) *pædo uszmirschai ant lauko* 'thou hast forgotten a sheaf in the field,' note that *pædo* 'sheaf' is gen. sg. (cf. Luther's Bible, *eine Garbe vergessen hast auf dem Acker*); (d) (Rėza's Psalter 45, 11) *vszmirschk tawo szmoniû ir nammû tewo tawo* 'forget thine own people and thy father's house' note that *szmoniû* 'people' and *nammû* are gen. pl. (cf. Luther's Bible, *vergiss deines Volcks, und deines Vaters Hauss*); (e) (Punktay sakimu II, 3, 22-23) *ažumirszk žmoniu tawo, ir namu tewo tawo* = Pol. *zapomni narodu twego, y domu oyca twego*, the same as example (d) as far as the use of gen. is concerned.

Klein, 1653, 152, writes that with verbs denoting 'to remember' and 'to forget' one may use either the gen. or acc. object, thus: (f) *atmenu žodžiū* (gen. pl.) and *žodžius* (acc. pl.) 'I remember the words'; (g) *užmiršk namū* (gen. pl.) and *namus* (acc. pl.)... 'forget the house...' The genitive case here seems to denote the sphere of the remembered object, whereas the accusative would denote the objects in their entirety (Fraenkel, 1928, 78). One notes, however, genitive usages in German and Polish also cf. (h) *vergiss deines Volcks* (gen.) and (i) *zapomni narodu twego* (gen.), so there may be influence of other languages. Modern Lithuanian usage would be, e.g., (j) *atmiñk màno žodžiùs* (acc. pl.) 'remember my words,' and (k) *visaĩ užmiršaũ jõ pãvardę* (acc. sg.) 'I forgot his name completely.' Both *žodžiùs* and *pãvardę* are acc. rather than gen.

In general the replacement of the genitive by the accusative case can be understood as an increase in transitivity of the verb which formerly could only encompass part of its object, but can now be understood to encompass the entire object (Hopper and Thompson, 1980, 252). But see also 30.6 [g, j], 30.62 and 30.64.

30.12 Palionis, 1967, 154, writes that the genitive complement is also encountered with verbs meaning 'to invite, to call,' etc. We encounter in Pietkiewicz' Catechism (161, 19):

(a) Eliosiaus   tas   szaukia.
    Elias   he   calls.
    (gen.)

'He is calling Elias' (= Pol. *Heliasza ten woła* [Fraenkel, 1947, 65]); (b) (Daukša's Postilla, 279, 10-11):

o   atêięs   namů̃sn,   suwadina
but   having arrived   home (he)   invites

gencziu   ir   susiédu
friends   and   neighbors.
(gen. pl.)   (gen. pl.)

This is apparently not a result of Polish influence because in Polish the corresponding words are acc. pl., cf. *a przyszedszy do domu, wzywa przyaćioły, y sąśiady*. (c) (Sirvydas' *Punktay sakimu* I, 261, 10):

pawadino...   bado   unt   žiemės
called forth   famine   on   earth
                 (gen. sg.)

'(he) called forth a famine on the earth' (= Pol. *zawołał głodu na ziemię* = Lat. *invocavit famam super terram*; Fraenkel, 1947, 65). Modern Lithuanian would use the accusative case under such circumstances, e.g., (d) *Šaũk vaikùs namõ* 'Call the children home.' On the other hand with the reflexive even in modern Lithuanian one encounters the genitive, e.g., (e) *Ligónis šaũkėsi dãktaro* 'The patient called for a doctor (for himself).'

30.13 According to Palionis, 1967, 155, in addition to an accusative complement in the texts of the 16th and 17th centuries verbs denoting 'to care for, to watch out for' also could take a genitive complement:

(a) (Pietkiewiecz' Catechism, 91, 10-11): Ponas... Lord

serkti	tawęs	pats.
watches over	you	himself.
	(gen. sg.)	

'The Lord himself watches over you' (Fraenkel, 1947, 65).

(b) (Vilentas' Catechism, 3, 2): tò this (gen. sg.)

saugotusi,	ir	lenktu.
may guard against,	and	avoid.

'that he may guard against and avoid this' (Ford, 1969, 118).

30.14 Palionis, 1967, 155, writes that in the texts of the 16th and 17th centuries a genitive (as well as an accusative) complement may be used with verbs denoting 'to fall in love with, to confess, to laugh at, to teach, to touch, to enrich, to use, to know' and others.

(a) (Bretkūnas' Bible, Deuteronomy 10, 19): todelei therefore

ir	ius	turit	Ateiwiu	mileti
also	you	should	strangers	love
			(gen. pl.)	

'Love ye therefore the strangers.' (= [Luther's Bible] *darum sollt ihr auch die Fremdlinge lieben*).

(b) (Daukša's Postilla 508, 41-42): Christus,
                                                               Christ

teip	didžei	įsimiłejo	to	pasáulo
so	greatly	loved	the	world.
				(gen. sg.)

'Christ loved the world so greatly.'

(c) (Bretkūnas' Bible, Genesis, 21, 6): nesa
                                                       because

kursai	tatai	girdes,	manens
whoever	that	will hear,	at me
			(gen.)

iuksis.
will laugh.

'Because whoever will hear that will laugh at me.' (= German [Luther's Bible] *denn wer es hören wird, der wird mein lachen*).

(d) (Vilentas' Catechism, 29, 3): Kuriū   ghrieku
                                        Which   sins
                                                        (gen. pl.)

reik	tada	ischpaszinti.
it is necessary	then	to confess.

'Which sins then is it necessary to confess?' (Ford, 1969, 118).

(e) (Mažvydas' Catechism, 67, 1): mokik   manes
                                            teach   me
                                                      (gen.)

kieliu	tawa.
path	your.

'Teach me your path.'

(f) (Daukša's Postilla, 368, 9): palitêio
                                        touched

žambo	rubo	io
edge	of garment	his.
(gen. sg.)		

'He touched the edge of his garment.' (= Pol. [Wuyek's Postilla, I, 422, 12-13] *dotknęła się kraiu szaty iego*).

(g) (Daukša's Postilla 420, 53): o   kiti
                                  but   others

   norėdami   pražobint   waikų   sawų
   wishing   to enrich   children   their
                              (gen. pl.)   (gen. pl.)

'But others, wishing to enrich their children.' (= Pol.
{Wuyek's Postilla II, 45, 7-8} *a drudzy chcąc zbogacić
dzieci swoie*).

(h) (Daukša's Postilla 294, 51): iog
                                  that

   piktái   wartôie   wárdo
   with evil intent   use   name
                                   (gen. sg.)

   diéwo.
   of God.
'that he uses the name of God with evil intent.' (= Pol.
{Wuyek's Postilla I 311, 6-7} *że źlie vżywa imienia
bożego*).

(i) (Punktay sakimu I 146, 24-26): reykia .....
                                    it is necessary

   żinot   skayčiaus   ir   sunkibes
   to know   number   and   gravity
              (gen. sg.)   (gen. sg.)

   nusideimu
   of sins.
'it is necessary...to know the number and gravity of
the sins.' See 30.64.

30.15 The use of the genitive as the direct object of
a verb may also derive from the partitive meaning of
the genitive. The use of the genitive in such circumstances is much more common in Lithuanian than in
Russian. Thus we encounter:

(a) mokinỹs   padãrė   klaidų̃
     pupil   (some) mistakes.
                             (gen. pl.)
'The pupil made (some) mistakes.' Russian, on the other

hand, would use the acc. pl. direct object in a similar situation: *učenik dopustil ošibki* (acc. pl., Musteikis, 1972, 51).

Nouns denoting a material may have a genitive object (Bulygina, 1959a, 96):

(b) Vienì,   sukū̃rę   žẽmėje
    Some,   having lighted   on the ground

    ùgnį,   vérda   val̃gio,   kẽpa
    fire,   cook   food   roast
                    (gen. sg.)

    šašlỹkų
    shashliki.
    (gen. pl.)
'Some, having lighted a fire on the ground, cook (some) food, roast (some) shashliki.'

Note the following examples with an abstract meaning.

(c) mergáičių   gražùmas   padãrė   atvažiãvusiems
    girls'   beauty   made   (on the) arriv-
                                    als

    į́spūdžio
    impression
    (gen. sg.)
'The girls' beauty made an impression on the new arrivals.'

(d) Vis dėltõ   miẽstas   turė́jo   sàvo
    Nevertheless   city   had   its

    reikšmė̃s...
    significance...
    (gen. sg.)
'Nevertheless the city had its (certain) significance...'

On the other hand the noun *į́spūdis* 'impression' may occur in the accusative case also.

(e) aukštà   tẽkintojų   kvalifikãcija
    high   lathe operators'   qualifications

jám	padãrė	gìlų	íspūdį
on him	made	deep	impression
			(acc. sg.)

'...the high qualifications of the lathe operators made a deep impression on him' (Bulygina, 1959a, 101-102).

If the noun *reikšmẽ* can be translated by English 'denotation' then the accusative case may be used.

(f) Taĩp,   kai   kuriẽ   žõdžiai   tùri
    Thus   some   words   have

    siaũrą,   speciãlią   réikšmę
    narrow,   special   meaning.
                            (acc. sg.)

'Thus some words have a narrow, special meaning' (Bulygina, 1959a, 101).

The same verb may have two direct objects, one of which is in the genitive and the other of which is in the accusative.

(g) pàdavė   vandeñs   ir   kẽdę
    gave   (some) water   and   a chair.
              (gen. sg.)   (acc. sg.)

'(He) gave (him) some water and a chair' (Grenda, 1979, 34).

30.16 Transitive verbs with the prefixes *pri-*, *at-*, *už-*, *pa-* (those which either increase or decrease the sphere of action of the verb) usually take direct objects in the genitive case (Grenda, 1979, 34).

(a) Prisìkepė   senẽliai
    baked   (for themselves)   old people

    pyrãgų
    (some) cakes.
    (gen. pl.)

'The old people baked (some) cakes for themselves.'

(b) atsikándo   dúonos
    bit off (for himself)   some bread.
                                 (gen. sg.)

'He bit off some bread for himself.'

Grenda, 1979, 34, writes that although such verbs are indeed for the most part used with a genitive, they can also take an accusative of a word denoting a certain quantity.

(c) pririñko   úogų
    (He) gathered (some)   berries.
                           (gen. pl.)

(d) pririñko   krẽpšį   úogų
    (He) gathered (a)   bag (full)   of berries
                        (acc. sg.)   (gen. pl.)

30.17 According to the Acad. Gram., Vol. 3, 24-25, in eastern Lithuanian dialects certain transitive verbs can take a concrete noun as a genitive direct object, the sequence denoting that the action of the verb is temporally limited.

(a) Dúok   mán   peĩlio
    Give   to me   knife.
                    (gen. sg.)
'Give me a knife' (i.e., for a short time, I will return it immediately).

(b) Paskõlink   pieštùko
    Lend   pencil.
                (gen. sg.)
'Lend (me) a pencil' (for a short time...).

(c) Paskõlink   žirklių̃
    Lend   scissors.
                (gen. pl.)
'Lend (me) (a pair of) scissors' (for a short time...).

30.18 Verbs denoting a change of state may have a genitive subject (Acad. Gram., Vol. 3, 25):

(a) Vándenio   padaugė̃s,   lietùs
    Water   will increase,   rain
    (gen. sg.)

    lỹja.
    rains.
'The water will increase, it is raining.'

(b) Šulnỹ   vándenio   pasidáugino.
    In the well   water   has increased.
                    (gen. sg.)
'The water in the well has increased.'

(c) Dabař   ir   válgytojų   paudaugėjo.
    Now   even   boarders   has increased.
                     (gen. pl.)
'Now even the (number of) boarders (eaters) has increased.'

(d) Miškų   ir   žuvų   mažėja.
    Forests   and   fish   are decreasing.
    (gen. pl.)   (gen. pl.)
'The (number of) forests and fish are (is) decreasing.'

30.2 Verbs denoting existence and certain verbs of motion can have a subject in the partitive genitive (Labutis, 1981, 198).

(a) klãsėje   yrà   gerų   mokinių
    in the class   are (some)   good   pupils.
                                              (gen. pl.)
'There are (some) good pupils in the class.' Such a sentence shows that there are some good pupils in the class and would be translated into Russian by the sentence: (b) *V klasse est' xorošie učeniki* (nom. pl.). To show that all of the pupils in the class are good one would use the nom. pl. in Lithuanian:

(c) klãsėje   (yrà)   gerì   mokiniaĩ
    in the class   (are)   good   pupils.
                                              (nom. pl.)
'(All) the pupils in the class are good.' In Russian the existential *est'* would be omitted to give the same meaning: (d) *V klasse xorošie učeniki* (Musteikis, 1972, 51).

(e) atvažiãvo   svẽčių
    arrived   guests.
                    (gen. pl.)
'(Some) guests arrived.' In Russian the nom. pl. would be used in a corresponding construction: (f) *priexali gosti* (Musteikis, 1972, 51).

(g) miškè   yrà   vilkų̃,   lãpių,
    in the forest are   wolves, foxes,

   kiškių,   ir   kitų̃   žvėrių̃.
   hares,   other   animals.

'There are wolves, foxes, hares, and other animals in the forest.' (h) *rañdasi úogų* (gen. pl.) '(some) berries are found.'

(i) Darbè   pasitáiko   klaidų̃
    In the work are encountered   (some) errors.
                                    (gen. pl.)

'In the work (some) errors are encountered.'

(j) Dárbo   visadà   ràsis.
    (Some) work always   will be found.
    (gen. sg.)

'Some work will always be found.'

Frequently it is possible to use a nominative or a genitive as the subject when an indefinite quantity is to be denoted. (k) *susiriñko žmonių̃* (gen. pl.) or *žmónės* (nom. pl.) 'people gathered,' (l) *apsigyvẽno amatiniñkų* (gen. pl.) or *amatiniñkai* (nom. pl.) 'Artisans took up residence,' (m) *užplū́do pirkė́jų* (gen. pl.) or *pirkė́jai* (nom. pl.) 'shoppers came in droves' (Acad. Gram., Vol. 3, 25-26).

Sometimes a co-ordinated nominative and a genitive can function as the subject of the same verb.

(n) belìko   avižų̃,   linaĩ
    there remained oats,   flax
                    (gen. pl.) (nom. pl.)

   ir   bùlvės
   and   potatoes.
         (nom. pl.)

'There remained some oats, flax and potatoes' (Grenda, 1979, 34).

The partitive genitive with a verb of existence can take a genitive predicate also:

(o) Vietų̃   bùs   laisvų̃
    (Some) places will be   free.
    (gen. pl.)   (gen. pl.)

(Acad. Gram., Vol. 3, 371.)

According to Labutis, 1981, 198, the genitive case in place of a nominative or an accusative is a marked member of the opposition and frequently only by means of a search of the deeper context can one decide whether to use either the genitive case on the one hand or the nominative or accusative case on the other hand.

30.21 Negative verbs of existence are used with the genitive case: (a) *nelìko žẽmės* (gen. sg.) 'no land remained,' (b) *nèrà reĩkalo* (gen. sg.) 'there is no need' (Acad. Gram., Vol. 3, 23). Such usage is attested in Vilentas' Catechism (Ford, 1969, 132):

(c) (43, 19): ir   nera   weisdeghima
               and   there is not   respect
                                                (gen. sg.)

        ant   personu   yemimp.
        for   persons   with him.

'and there does not exist respect of persons with him.' In Bretkūnas' Bible (John 11, 10) one encounters a nominative case with a negated verb of existence (Fraenkel, 1928, 54):

(d)   nesa   nera   schwiesibe   iamije
      because   there is not   light   in him.
                                      (nom.)

'because there is no light in him.' Negated forms of the so-called 'nominative plus infinitive construction' (see 29.5) replace the nominative with the genitive case:

(e) Negirdė́t   neĩ muštỹniu,   neĩ
    Not to be heard   neither fights,   neither
                        (gen. pl.)

        vagỹstės   nematýt   girtuokliãvimo
        thievery,   not to be seen   drunkenness.
        (gen. sg.)   (gen. sg.)

'Neither fighting nor thievery is to be heard and drunkenness is not to be seen' (Sirtautas, 1971, 77-78). Strictly speaking *girdė́ti* 'to hear' and *matýti* 'to see' could from the point of view of the contemporary language be classified as 'active,' but such usage seems to derive from a pre-diathetic state.

30.3 The genitive also functions as the direct object of a negated verb. Such usage is attested from the earliest texts, e.g., Vilentas' Catechism:

(a) (11, 6): Ne   turek   kitu   Diewu
              Not   have   other   gods
                                    (gen. pl.)

   prieg   manes.
   before   me.
'Do not have other gods before me.'

(b) Niẽkas   neįvértino   Mykoliuko
    Nobody   appreciated   Mykoliukas'

    mùzikos
    music.
    (gen. sg.)
(Acad. Gram., Vol. 1, 187.)

(c) Àš   neskaičiaũ   šìtos   knỹgos
    I   didn't read   this   book.
                                   (gen. sg.)
Such a sentence can be compared in form exactly with Russian *ja ne čital ètoj knigi* (Musteikis, 1972, 50; see 34.7).

30.31 The direct object of an infinitive which in turn is the object of a negated main verb may also be in the genitive case:

(a) Negaliù   užmir̃šti   víeno   atsitikìmo
    I cannot   forget   one   incident.
                                      (gen. sg.)
(Acad. Gram., Vol. 1, 187.)

(b) Žmónės   neįveĩkia   bùlbių
    People   don't succeed   potatoes
                               (gen. pl.)

    kàsti.
    to dig up.
'The people don't succeed in digging up the potatoes' (see 34.7). [5]

30.32 In clauses with negated verbs certain expressions of quantity occur in the genitive case:

(a) nevažiúoja   valandõs
     (He) does not travel an hour.
                          (gen. sg.)
'He travels less than an hour.'

(b) nenuẽjo   kilomètro
     (He) didn't go   a kilometer.
                         (gen. sg.)
'He went less than a kilometer' (Acad. Gram., Vol. 3, 26).

30.4 The genitive case is also used as the direct object of a supine:

(a) ateis   suditu (supine)   giwu
     (He) will come   to judge   (the) living
                                         (gen. pl.)

     ir   numirusiu
     and (the)   dead
                    (gen. pl.)
(Vilentas' Catechism, 18, 8; Ford, 1969, 118.) Modern Lithuanian:

(b) eĩti   láimės   ieškótų (supine)
     to go   happiness   to seek.
             (gen. sg.)
'To go to seek happiness.'

(c) parvažiãvo   suknẽlės   pasiim̃tų (supine)
     (She) came   dress   to get.
                  (gen. sg.)
'She came to get her dress.'
    Musteikienė, 1967a, 24, writes that constructions with the supine in the contemporary Lithuanian literary language are no longer productive and are met only in writers of the older generation and in certain eastern High Lithuanian (*rytų aukštaičių*) dialects. Everywhere the supine is being replaced by the infinitive and the differences which formerly existed between the supine and the infinitive have been lost. The supine which had previously been used only with verbs of motion began to

be used with other verbs, just like the infinitive, e.g.,
siũsti 'to send,' *varýti* 'to chase,' *kviẽsti* 'to invite,'
etc. On the other hand, the goal is expressed not only
by the supine, but also the infinitive. The commonality
of syntactic function between the supine and the infinitive led to the loss of the supine as an unnecessary
category. The most common pivotal words in such constructions are verbs of motion such as *važiúoti* 'to
travel,' *eĩti* 'to go,' *bėgti* 'to run,' *grĩžti* 'to return ' verbs of motion with special stylistic nuances
such as *tráukti, kiūtinti* 'to drag oneself along,'
léistis 'to drop,' hortatory verbs such as *siũsti* 'to
send.' Thus one encounters phrases such as:

(d) eĩti   vasarójaus   séti
    to go   spring crops   to sow.
              (gen. sg.)   (infinitive)

'To go to sow (for the purpose of sowing) the spring
crops.'

(e) nubė́go   ūkvedžio
    (She) ran off   the farm manager
                        (gen. sg.)

    ieškóti
    to search for.
    (infinitive)

'She ran off to search for the farm manager' (Musteikienė,
1967a, 28).

According to Musteikienė, 1967a, 31, one may suppose
that the sequence of verb with an object in the genitive
case to denote purpose arose from the sequence of verb
plus genitive case plus infinitive with loss of the infinitive. Thus (f) *eĩti pietũ* (gen. pl.) 'to go to
(for) dinner' means the same as (g) *eĩti pietũ válgyti*
(infinitive) 'to go to eat dinner.' In sentence (f) the
infinitive *válgyti* 'to eat' may be assumed. Nevertheless the loss of the infinitive in such constructions
can lead to a difference in meaning. Thus a sequence
such as (h) *atėjaũ dvìračio* (gen. sg.) 'I came for the
bicycle' merely means that the bicycle is necessary.
On the other hand a sentence such as (i) *atėjaũ
atsiim̃ti dvìračio* means 'I came to take back my bicycle'
and (j) *atėjaũ pasiskólinti dvìračio* means 'I came to
borrow a bicycle.' In sentences (i) and (j) the attention

is centered on the meaning of the infinitive verb. Musteikienė, 1967a, 32, writes that in those sequences which retain the infinitive the goal of the action is expressed twice, once with the genitive of object and the second time with the infinitive. A sentence such as (f) above can only be understood as a reduction of (g). Other infinitives could be added to (f), thus one could have (k) *eĩti pietų̃ gamìnti* 'to go to make dinner,' or (1) *eĩti pietų̃ vìrti* 'to go to cook dinner,' but (f) would not be understood as a reduction of (k) or (1) (Musteikienė, 1967a, 37).

30.41 Sometimes the genitive of goal can be used in the same circumstances as the dative of goal (Musteikienė, 1967a, 34):

(a) Į   Mãskvą   oficialaũs vizìto
    In   Moscow   for an official visit
                       (gen. sg.)

    atvỹko...
    arrived...

(b) Vãkar   į   Var̃suvą   atvỹkęs
    Yesterday in   Warsaw   having arrived

    oficialiám vizìtui
    for an official visit...
    (dat. sg.)

30.42 In 1893 in an article *Medega sintaksiui* 'Material for syntax' published in the newspaper *Varpas* Jablonskis suggested that when the main verb of the sentence is a verb of motion such as *eĩti* 'to go,' *važiúoti* 'to ride,' *siųsti* 'to send,' *varýti* 'to drive' it is not always appropriate to use the genitive as the direct object of a dependent supine (or infinitive). The genitive is only appropriate if the sentence is correct even without the supine or infinitive. Thus (a) *einù vandeñs* (gen.) *sémti* 'I am going to draw water' is correct because (b) *einù vandeñs* 'I am going for water' is correct.[6] When the genitive is impossible without the supine (or infinitive), then the accusative object is to be used. Consider the following sentences:

(c) púolė   visì   bučiúotų   rankàs
    fell   all   to kiss   hands
                        (sup.)   (acc.)

   senėliui
   of the old man.
   (dat.)
'All fell to kiss the old man's hands.'

(d) Stankūnas   nubėgo   sudėtų   pinigus
    S.   ran off   to get   money
                           (sup.)   (acc.)

   advokãtui
   for the lawyer.
   (dat.)

In sentence (c) *púolė rañkų 'fell the hands' would be impossible because the 'hands' are not the goal of the action of falling. In sentence (d) Stankūnas did not *'run the money' but was carrying it back to the lawyer (Pirockinas, 1972, 131).[7]

Pirockinas, 132, writes that for the genitive to be used the apparent object of the infinitive must be the goal of the main verb of the sentence in certain areas of Lithuania (Veliuonà, Jùrbarkas). According to the rule the genitive object of the infinitive (replacing the supine) is retained in (e) važiúoja árklio (gen.) pir̃kti 'comes to buy the horse' and (f) eĩna algõs (gen.) pasiim̃ti 'goes to get (his) salary' but the accusative object is encountered in (g) važiúoja árklį (acc.) pardúoti 'comes to sell the horse' and (h) eĩna mókesti (acc.) mokėti 'goes to pay (his) tax.' In (e) and (f) the genitive is considered the object of the main verb (as well as the infinitive), whereas in (g) and (h) the accusative is only the object of the infinitive. Zubatý, 1889, 64, wrote that originally both the genitive object and the supine were directly dependent on the main verb of the sentence.

There is a common belief that the genitive in such expressions derives from the ellipsis of an accusative of goal (e.g., Kuryłowicz, 1964, 185). Thus sentence (a) above was supposedly preceded by (i) *einù vandeñs sémtų in which the supine sémtų represents an old accusative of goal of the intransitive verb.

In order to maintain this belief one must presuppose a period during which the genitive adopted a meaning of the goal of the action, presumably by semantic transfer before the ellipsis of the supine. Perhaps during the time when the infinitive replaced the supine the genitive came to be understood as the goal of the action of the main verb.

Ambrazas, 1979, 57, reports the phrase from Panevėžỹs and Kùpiškis:

(j) mė́šlo   vežti   rãtai
     of dung   transported   wagon.
     (gen.)   (nom. pl. past   (nom. pl.)
                psv. prt.)

'Wagon used for the transportation of dung.' I interpret this also as an original genitive of purpose on analogy with the sentence:

(k) àš   išvažiavaũ   (vèžtų {sup.})
     I   went out   (to transport)

     ({su} rãtais {inst.}) mė́šlo
     ({with} wagon)   dung.
                             (gen.)

'I went out to get dung with the wagon.'

Since originally the meaning of the *t- participle was intransitive and active it was quite natural that it would adopt the syntactic pattern of the intransitive verbs of motion with a genitive of goal.

30.43 The infinitive object of a main verb sometimes governs an object in the genitive case, even when finite forms of the verb would govern an accusative object.

(a) Saulỹs   jį̃   mókė   ir   kalavìjo
     Saulys   him   taught   both   sword
                                       (gen.)

     vartóti, ir   kìlpinio   tampýti.
     to use   and   bow   to pull.
                    (gen.)

'Saulys taught him both how to use a sword and to pull a bow.' Under ordinary circumstances both *vartóti* 'to use' and *tampýti* 'to pull, to stretch' govern an accusative direct object, but in this sentence the influence of *mokýti* 'to teach' which governs the accusative object of person, but the genitive object of the thing taught is felt. Such a sentence runs counter to the norm of the literary language (Grenda, 1965, 43). Note the examples:

(b) pašaukė   ją   tvarkýti
    (Someone) called her   to tidy up

    kambariũ
    the rooms.
    (gen. pl.)

(c) paprãšė   jį   akėčių   apveřsti
    asked   him   harrow   to turn over.
                      (gen. pl.)

'(Someone) asked him to turn the harrow over.' Ordinarily *tvarkýti* 'to tidy up' and *apveřsti* 'to turn over' govern an accusative direct object. Grenda, 1965, 45, suggests that such sentences may have developed as the result of an omitted verb of motion which has left a nuance of goal oriented activity. This in turn has determined the replacement of the accusative by the genitive direct object. Thus originally (b) was *pàšaukė ją eĩti* (to go) *tvarkýti kambariũ* and (c) was *paprãšė jį eĩti* (to go) *akėčių apveřsti*. Still the verb *prašýti* 'to ask' ordinarily requires the genitive of person and accusative of thing (see 30.1), so one could assume the influence of this verb in sentence (c) above.

(d) Jį̃   palìksim   namũ
    him   we shall leave   house
                                (gen. pl.)

    prižiūrėt
    to look after.

'We shall leave him to look after the house.' Grenda, 1965, 49, writes that *palìkti* in the meaning 'to continue someone's stay in a single place, not to release' may be used with an infinitive object which in turn governs a genitive object. The construction is similar to the genitive object of the supine, but here the verb *palìkti* is used as an antonym of a verb of motion.

30.5 The agentive use of the genitive case is inherited from Proto-Indo-European, cf., 6(h) and ff. (Palmaitis, 1977, 115, 119).

(a) (Latin) attonitus serpentis
            astonished by the serpent.
                       (gen. sg.)

(Kühner-Stegmann, 1962, 443.) In Slavic the original genitive case was supplemented with the preposition otъ, cf. OCS (Savvina kniga; Luke 2, 18):

(b) diviše sę   o   glagolanyxъ   otъ
    marveled   about said   by

    pastuxъ   kъ   nimъ
    shepherds to   them.
    (gen. pl.)

'They marveled at those things which were told to them by the shepherds' (Paternost and Schmalstieg, 1977). The genitive case of agent was also used in Tocharian according to Krause-Thomas, 1961, 82-83. In the ancient Greek name *Diósdotos* 'given by Zeus' the initial element *Diós-* 'by Zeus' is in the gen. sg. and the second element *-dotos* 'given' is a past participle in *-t-* and would have as its exact correspondent Lith. *Diẽvo* (gen. sg.) 'by God' *dúotas* 'given.' An example from Bretkūnas' Postilla II, 19:

(c) Diewo   paszadetu   Messioschu
    by God   promised   Messiah.
    (gen. sg.)

'The messiah promised by God' (Ambrazas, 1979, 57; Fraenkel, 1928, 95). Fraenkel, 1947, 66, writes that only in those instances in which the possessive meaning is still clear do we encounter the genitive by itself in Pietkiewicz' Catechism, e.g., (d) *tawo* (gen. sg.) *išrinkti* 'chosen by you' (or 'your chosen...') which translates Pol. *twoi wybrani*. Otherwise, according to Fraenkel the preposition *nuog* plus the genitive is used, e.g.:

(e) pastatitas   nuog   Pona   Christusa
    established   by   Lord   Christ.
                                (gen. sg.)

'established by Christ the Lord' = Pol. *postanowiony od Pana Chrystusa*. One suspects Polish influence with the addition of the preposition *nuog* 'by, from.'

Zinkevičius, 1977, 368, writes that Mažvydas acted like a person stemming from a Polish rather than a German cultural milieu. Thus, the following four examples from his Catechism might be considered to be under Polish influence also.

(f) (25, 23) testamentas nogi kieturiu
                testament   by   four (gen.)

    Enangelijstu (for Euangelijstu)   paraschitas
    apostles   written.
    (gen.)
'Testament written by the four apostles.'

(g) (31, 20) kurias   patam   ijra
                which   moreover   are

    maczes,   nogi   Dewa   ijngistatitas
    powers   by   God (gen.)   ordained

    ijra
    are.
'Moreover the powers which exist are ordained by God.'

(h) (50, 9) Kurs   est   nog   tawęs
              which   is   by   you
                          (gen.)

    pamektas
    liked.
'Which is liked by you.'

Nevertheless a clear case of Polish influence is encountered in the use of *per* plus the accusative as the agent of a participle construction.

(i) (20, 18) PER   APASCHTALUS   SCHWENTOSIUS
                by   apostles   holy
                     (acc. pl.)

    SUGULDITU
    put together.
'Put together by the holy apostles.'

Although the usual agent of the passive in Lithuanian is the genitive case alone, in dialects one finds examples where it is supported by a preposition, e.g.:

(j) Čià   tù   gyvénsi   nuõ   výro
    Here   you   will live   by   husband
                                             (gen. sg.)

   myléta
   loved.

'You will live here loved by your husband.' In this example the preposition *nuõ* 'from' is added, although from the point of view of the standard language the *nuõ* is not necessary (Acad. Gram., Vol. 2, 601).

Although one usually assumes Polish influence one can note that in Slavic an original genitive case was replaced first by *отъ* plus the genitive apparently without foreign influence. Thus one might view the Slavic influence as the catalytic agent which led to the adoption of the use of the preposition *nuõ* 'from' plus the genitive case.

Interesting examples illustrating just how the instrumental case could replace the genitive case come from Lithuanian as reported by Paulauskienė, 1979, 99:

(k) ...kur̃   devýnis   ménesius per̃ metùs
    ...where   nine   months in a year

    žẽmė   ẽsti   (sniẽgo)   sniegù
    earth   is   (by snow)   with snow
    (nom. sg.)   (gen. sg.)   (inst. sg.)

    muklóta...
    covered...
    (nom. sg. fem.
      past psv. prt.)

'...where nine months in a year the earth is covered by (with) snow...'

(1) Daiktìnis   ar̃   veiksmìnis   sim̃bolis
    Material   or   active   symbol

    bùvo   užstelbtas   ir̃   užtémdytas
    was   choked off   and   eclipsed

    žõdiniu   ãpvalkalu   (žõdinio ãpvalkalo)
    verbal   cover   (gen. sg. gen. sg.)
    (inst. sg.)   (inst. sg.)

'The material or active symbol was choked off and eclipsed by the verbal covering.'

(m) Bendrúomenės istòrijos
    of the community of the history
    (gen. sg.) (gen. sg.)

    kūrimas   neįžvelgiama   paslaptim̃
    establishment by an impenetrable secret
    (nom. sg.) (inst. sg.)   (inst. sg.)

    (neįžvelgiamos paslaptiẽs)   pridengtas...
    (gen. sg.   gen. sg.)   (is) hidden...
                                 (nom. sg. past
                                 passive prt.)

'The establishment of the history of the community is hidden by an impenetrable secret...'

In sentences (k), (l), and (m) the use of the genitive may be somewhat surprising because one expects an animate being as the agent. In fact, however, the tendency for an instrumental to be used in the function of agent is found in many Indo-European languages. In Russian it seems clear that the old *ot* plus genitive construction to express agent has been ousted by the instrumental. Curiously enough, however, in some impersonal constructions only an inanimate object can be admitted as agent, cf., e.g., (n) *šljapu unosilo vetrom* (inst.) 'the hat was carried away by the wind,' but not (o) **šljapu unosilo oficiantom* (inst.) 'the cap was carried away by the waiter.')

Schwyzer, 1942, 14, points out the use of the *genitivus auctoris* with verbal adjectives and passives participles in Greek, Lithuanian, Armenian and Tocharian, and identifies this genitive with the *genitivus possessivus*. In spite of Schwyzer, 1942, 29-42, I see no reason for not assuming that the use of *hupò* plus the genitive does not reflect an earlier agentive use of the genitive, cf., e.g., Xenophon, Hellenica 2, 3, 15: (p) *ei tis etimãto hupò toũ dẽmou* (gen. sg.) 'if anyone was honored by the people.' Similarly perhaps with *apó*, cf., e.g., Thucydides, 1, 17: (q) *eprákhthē ap' autõn* (gen. pl.) *oudén* 'nothing was done by them' (Goodwin and Gulick, 1958, 261, 255). Even if the use of the genitive of agent (strengthened with a preposition) with the Greek finite verbal forms does not reflect the Indo-European syntactic relationships, certainly the adjectival forms do.

The use of the genitive case as an agent of passive verbs was extended to the subject usage of intransitive verbs, see 6[n] and ff. Thus one encounters, e.g.:

(r) čià   jõ   búta
     here   he   was.
               (gen. sg.)

'He was here.'

Note the following sentence in which both the subject and predicate are in the nominative case:

(s) Jìs   bùvo   negudrùs
     He   was   stupid.
     (nom. sg.)   (nom. sg.)

On analogy with such sentences the genitive case could then appear in predicate position as well:

(t) Jõ   búta   negudraũs,   didelio
     He   was   stupid,   a great
     (gen. sg.)   (gen. sg.)

     tìnginio
     lazy-bones.
     (gen. sg.)

Compare then the following sentences:

(u) Brólis   išlìko   gývas
     Brother   remained   alive.
     (nom. sg.)   (nom. sg.)

(v) Tàs   brólio   gývo   išlikìmas...
     That   brother's   alive   remaining...
              (gen. sg.)   (gen. sg.)

     tavè   nudžiùgino
     you   gladdened.
     (sg.)

'The fact that brother remained alive gladdened you.' (Lit.: 'that remaining alive of brother gladdened you.') The predicate *gývo* 'alive' of the action of the verbal noun *išlikìmas* 'remaining' is in the gen. sg. because the subject *brólio* 'brother' is.

(w)
Jõ	pasiródyta	dìdvyrio
He	appeared	a hero
(gen. sg.)	(neut. sg. past psv. prt. refl.)	(gen. sg.)

ir,	jõ	dìdvyrio	ẽsama,
and,	he	hero	is,
	(gen. sg.)	(gen. sg.)	(neut. sg. pres. psv. prt.)

apsimesta	negývo,	ir	jõ
played	dead,	and	he
	(gen. sg.)		(gen. sg.)

ilgaĩ	ìšdriko	guléta [8]
a long time	stretched out	lay.
	(gen. sg.)	

'He appeared a hero, and he is a hero, he played dead and lay stretched out a long time' (see Jablonskis, 1957, 587-589). The predicates *dìdvyrio* 'hero,' *negývo* 'dead, not alive,' and *ìšdriko* 'stretched out' are all in the gen. sg. because the subject *jõ* 'he (of him)' is in the gen. sg.

30.51 It is commonly stated that in the Indo-European languages words denoting 'full' may take a partitive genitive complement, thus Vedic (a) *sómasya jathāram pṛṇati* 'he fills his stomach with soma,' Lat. (b) *aquae plēnus* 'full of water' (Meillet, 1964, 345-346).

According to Schwyzer, 1966, 110-111, the partitive in Greek is parallel with the instrumental in the meaning of an indefinite but concrete quantity especially with verbs denoting 'to be full, to abound in (of vegetation), to fill, to make full, etc.' Examples: (c) *oínou* (gen.) *enípleion* 'full of wine,' (d) *plēsámenos d' oínoio* (gen.) *dépas* 'filling a cup with wine.' Note the vacillation between the instrumental use of the dative and the genitive: (e) *dakrúoisi* (dat. pl.) *gàr Hellád' hápasan éplēse* 'filled all Greece with tears' vs. (f) *dakrúōn* (gen. pl.) *d' éplēsen emé* 'filled me with tears' (Schwyzer, 1966, 166).

In Latin the ablative and the genitive compete, e.g., (g) *deus bonis omnibus* (abl. pl.) *explevit mundum* 'god has filled the world with all good things' vs. (h) *convivium vicinorum* (gen. pl.) *cotidie compleo* 'I fill up my company with neighbors every day' (Woodcock, 1959, 55).

Consider the following sentence from Acad. Dict. (Vol. 9, 977):

(i) Baltramiejaus   lytùs   pìldo   bũrams
    Baltrameus'   rain   fills   for the peasants
                                                      (dat. pl.)

    arúodus
    bins.
    (acc. pl.)

'Baltrameus' rain fills the peasants' bins.' A passive of this would be:

(j) Bũrams   arúodai   pìldomi
    (nom. pl.)   (nom. pl. pres. psv. prt.)

    Baltramiejaus lytaũs (gen. sg.)

'The peasants bins are being filled by Baltrameus' rain.'

The common conception is that the use of the genitive with verbs and adjectives denoting 'full' falls under the heading 'partitive genitive.' I propose, however, that such usage is not partitive but rather reflects the old ergative, which in addition to denoting an animate agent could also be used with an instrumental meaning. Commonly in the Indo-European languages inanimate things can function as the agent or at least as the performer of an action. Thus such English sentences as *The wind (key) opened the door* with instrumental subjects are possible (Fillmore, 1968, 24-27).

The categories of agent and instrument are not exclusive dichotomous categories. At one end of the scale an animate being is considered clearly agent, but at the other end of the scale an inanimate object seems to be clearly an instrument. But in such a sentence as *The robot fed the cats* the assignment of agent or instrument category depends upon the amount of free will one is willing to ascribe to the robot, and the matter becomes a complex philosophical issue (Moulton and Robinson, 1981, 86).

I propose that the Indo-European ergative (expressed by the genitive case) denoted agent if used with clearly animate beings, but could denote instrument if used with inanimate objects.

Consider then the following Lithuanian sentences.

(k) žėmė   primirko   lietaũs
The earth   became soaked   with rain.
    (gen. sg.)

This intransitive sentence can be understood as a paraphrase of the transitive sentence:

(1) lietùs   primerkė   žėmę
The rain   soaked   the earth.
    (acc. sg.)

Thus the genitive *lietaũs* of sentence (k) is not partitive, but instrumental in force. (Stepanov, 1978, 343 and passim shows that the zero grade verb is ordinarily intransitive whereas the -*e*- grade is ordinarily transitive.)

I analyze then the genitive in the following Lithuanian examples as instrumental rather than partitive:

(m) kiẽmas   pribìro   pelų̃ (gen. pl.)
The yard   became strewn   with chaff.
This sentence can be understood as meaning 'Chaff covered the yard.'

(n) pridrìbo   rugiaĩ   sniẽgo
was covered   rye   with snow.
    (gen. sg.)
'The rye was covered with snow,' but which can also be understood as 'Snow covered the rye' (Acad. Dict., Vol. 2, 702).

My colleague Vytautas Ambrazas objects (letter dated 1983,I,30) that it would be impossible to paraphrase sentences (m) and (n) in the same way that I have paraphrased (k) with sentence (1). In other words sentences such as (o) *pelaĩ pribėrė kiẽmą and (p) *sniẽgas pridrėbė rugiùs are impossible. I suggest that the reason for this is a fundamental difference in meaning (in addition to that of verbal diathesis) between the intransitive verbs *pribìrti* 'to be strewn with, full of,' *pridrìbti* 'to become full of (as the result of falling)' on the one hand and the transitive verbs *pribeŕti* 'to strew,' *pridrė̃bti* 'to add, to shake into' on the other hand. The English translation of sentence (o) would be 'chaff threw about the yard' and the English translation of sentence (p) would be 'snow threw about the rye.' Sentences (o) and (p) (like their English translations) are impossible because the meanings which they express are impossible under ordinary circumstances. The same analysis holds even for the formal passive voice of *pribeŕti*.

Consider the following sentence (Acad. Dict., Vol. 1, 774):

(q) Pribertas   pìlnas   pẽčius   kiaũliaberio
    strewn   full   stove   with pig fodder.
                                  (gen. sg.)

'The stove was strewn full with pig fodder.' The apparent active paraphrase (r) **kiaũliaberis pribère pìlną pẽčių* 'pig fodder strewed the stove full' would be impossible.

In sentences (q) and (r) even the formal active and passive forms cannot be considered paraphrases of each other. As far as meaning is concerned the active paraphrase of sentence (m) is (s) *pelaĩ nuklójo kiẽmą* 'The chaff covered the yard' and the active paraphrase of (n) is (t) *sniẽgas nuklójo rugiùs* 'The snow covered the rye.'

Note the following sentences:

(u) Užsimérk,   kad   ăkys   smilčių̃
    Close   so that   eyes   with sand
                                     (gen. sg.)

    nepridulkétų
    do not become full of.

'Close your eyes so that they do not become full of sand' (Acad. Dict., Vol. 2, 825). I would understand *smilčių̃* 'sand' as the instrument for filling your eyes, not as a part of the total amount of sand.

(v) Trobà   priẽjo   žmonių̃. . .
    The cottage   filled with   people. . .
    (nom. sg.)   (gen. pl.)

(w) Laĩvas   priẽjo   vandeñs
    The ship   filled   with water.
    (nom. sg.)   (gen. sg.)

(x) Duobė̃   pribégo   vandeñs
    The hole filled   with water.
                         (gen. sg.)

(Jablonskis, 1957, 576-577.)

Ordinarily the verb *priẽjo* denotes 'approached, reached,' and *pribė́go* denotes 'arrived (running)' but in the preceding examples the prefix *pri-* alters the meaning to denote the action of filling, so that the meaning is only indirectly connected with the notion of 'approaching, reaching, arriving at.'[9]

30.6 The agentive genitive is attested in various Indo-European languages, but probably most important are those cases where a genitive is used where it would have been possible to use some other case such as an instrumental or ablative. In Old Indic according to Renou, 1952, 353, the genitive of agent is encountered in such a construction as (a) *máméd* (< gen. *mama* plus *id*) *vardhasva suṣṭutaḥ* 'grow (as a result of the fact that) you are praised by me' (see also 6 [h-j]). There existed also an Old Indic instrumental *mayā* 'by me' and an ablative *mat* 'from me' which were available if the genitive had not been perfectly satisfactory. The genitive of agent is also encountered in such Old Armenian perfect constructions as (b) *ēr nora* (gen. sg.) *hraman aŕeal* 'he had received a promise' (see 29.51 [o]). Old Armenian has an instrumental *novaw* and an ablative *i nmanē* (Godel, 1975, 26) which were also available to serve as agent, but which were not used as agent in this kind of construction. In Latin one encounters (c) *attonitus serpentis* (gen.) 'astonished by the serpent' where it would have been perfectly possible to say *ā serpente* (see 30.5 [a]). (See 30.51 (a-h) also where I assume the etymological older syntactic structures to contain the genitive case.) It seems then that it is not necessary to trace the Old Bulgarian *otъ* plus the genitive of agent back to an Indo-European ablative. The genitive may indeed be the original case of the agent, represented only in a fragmentary fashion. But one should keep in mind Meillet's dictum that it is in just such fragments that older structures are retained.[10]

The attested Indo-European languages are, of course, for the most part nominative-accusative languages, i.e., the nominative case functions as the agent and the accusative case functions as the patient. This is, of course, what I have assumed for the Indo-European present tense syntax. On the other hand, for the preterite tenses I have assumed an ergative syntax, i.e., one in which the patient is in the nominative case and the agent (originally) in the genitive case (see 29). There were, however, also some present tense verbs (mainly statives), which also seem to have had ergative syntax, i.e., the patient was in the nominative case and the agent in the genitive (= ergative) case. In grammars of the various Indo-European languages these are usually referred to as verbs requiring the genitive case for the direct object and in fact from the point of view of the speakers of the languages in question this is probably a correct analysis. This correct analysis is the reason for either (1) the reinterpretation of these originally agentive genitives as verbal objects with a special meaning or (2) the replacement of the genitive case of the object by the accusative case. Many states reflecting human perception, attitudes, desires, needs, fears, etc. can be understood either as the action of the human being on the outside world or as the outside world impinges upon the human being. This is obvious even in English where one can say *I hear the rock music* or *The rock music deafens me*; *I need the book* or *The book is necessary for me*; *I want the book* or *The book is very desirable for me*. I should like to give a few examples from Georgian where for many such concepts the ordinary syntactic structure reflects the effect of the outside world on the human being. The constructions in question are not (with the exception of sentence [k]) ergative constructions, they are constructions with the 'indirect verbs' in which the person affected is in the dative case and the source of the emotion or sensation is in the nominative case (Aronson, 1982, 332).

(d) mṭer-s   ešinoda   kartvel-
    enemy   frightened   Georgian
    (dat.-acc.)

    eb-   is   šeertebul-   i
    (pl.)   (gen.)   united   (nom.)

    jalisa.
    forces.
    (nom.)

'The enemy was afraid of the united force of the Georgians' (Aronson, 1982, 351).

(e) mas   unda   čemgan
     to him   is desirable   me from
     (dat.-acc.)

     erti   çign-i.
     one   book.
               (nom.)
'He wants a book from me' (Tschenkéli, 1958, Vol. 2, 269).

(f) [Old Georgian] esmis   deda-
                     is audible to   mother

     sa   qma-   y   qom
     (dat.-acc.)   voice   (nom.) of child

     isa-   y
     (gen.)   (nom.)
'The mother hears the child's voice' (Schanidze, 1982, 67).

(g) qvelaper-   i   maxsovs
     everything   to me is recalled
     (nom.)
'I remember everything' (Aronson, 1982, 349).

(h) tkven-i   saxel-i   ar   da-
     your   name   not   prefix
     (nom.)   (nom.)

     m-   vicqebia.
     to me   was forgotten.
'I haven't forgotten your name' (Aronson, 1982, 349).

(i) deda-   s   uqvars
     to mother   (dat.-acc.)   inspires love

     švil-   i
     child   (nom.)
'The mother loves the child' (Tschenkéli, 1958, Vol. 1, 454).

(j) mela-   s   jilšidac
     to fox   (dat.-acc.)   even in sleep

     katam-   i   axsovso.
     hen   (nom.)   is recalled.
'The fox thinks of the hen even in his sleep'
(Tschenkéli, 1958, Vol. 2, 269).

    One notes that in the Georgian sentence (d) above the agent in the nominative case is causing fear in the patient in the dat.-acc. case. One may reinterpret the syntax of the Lith. sentence (k) *tévas* (nom.) *bìjo vilko* (gen.) 'father fears the wolf' in such a way as to suggest that originally the genitive agent *vilko* 'wolf' caused fear in the nominative patient *tévas* 'father.'

30.61 The assumption that the Lithuanian verb *bijóti* 'to fear' originally required an ablative case is based on Old Indic where we have, e.g., (a) *bhayate vṛkāt* (abl.) 'he fears the wolf.' One could easily imagine, however, that the Old Indic ablative replaced the genitive in the sentence (b) **pitā* (nom.) *bhayate vṛkasya* (gen.) 'father fears the wolf.' The construction was originally ergative with the nominative expressing the patient and the genitive expressing the agent. When the nominative case came to express the agent, the genitive of the agent was replaced by the ablative to denote the source of the fright.

30.62 The Indo-European genitive of goal is represented by Latin (a) *quae* (nom. pl.) *cupiunt tui* (gen. sg.) 'who want you'; (b) Gothic [Matthew 5, 28] *du luston izos* (gen. sg.) 'to lust after her'; Old Church Slavic (c) *zapovědei* (gen. pl.) *tvoixъ* (gen. pl.) *želěxъ* 'I desired thy commandments' (Vaillant, 1964, 182). The Lithuanian phrase (d) *jìs* (nom. sg.) *nóri miẽgo* (gen. sg.) 'he wishes for sleep' belongs here. One notes that in the Georgian sentence (e) in 30.6 the book brings about the desire in the patient *mas* 'him.' I propose then that in Lithuanian sentence (d) the word *miẽgo* 'sleep' was originally agentive acting on the patient *jìs* 'he.' Mutatis mutandis the same holds for the verbs of goal in other Indo-European languages. In 30.11 one notes examples of verbs denoting 'to remember' and 'to forget' requiring the genitive case. Similarly

I propose that there was originally an agentive genitive causing the subject (= patient) to remember or to forget. Compare Georgian examples (g) and (j) in 30.6 above. The contemporary replacement of the genitive by the accusative is the expected tendency for a language changing from ergative to nominative-accusative, since the genitive is no longer felt as the agent. In 30.14 one notes that in texts of the 16th and 17th centuries the verb *mylẽti* 'to love' may take the genitive case (see 30.14 a, b). Cf. Georgian sentence (i) above. I propose again that the feeling of love was inspired by the genitive agent acting on the nominative subject (= patient).

30.63 Hermann, 1926, 284-286, compares the Greek collocation (a) *khrẽ mé* (acc.) *tinos* (gen.) 'I need something' with the Lithuanian -*è*- stem verbs, which he would derive from nouns. One should note, however, that in the Greek collocation a dative as well as an accusative is possible, and that Schwyzer, 1966, 72, gives the example (b) *khrẽ sé* (acc.) or *soí* (dat.) *tinos* 'you need something.' Syntactically this can be compared exactly with the Lithuanian collocation (c) *táu* (dat.) *reĩkia kõ* (gen.) 'you need something.' In the Greek example one can suppose the replacement of the nominative case by the accusative or dative and in the Lithuanian example one can assume the replacement of the nominative case by the dative.

I speculate that all the denominative verbs in *-*ē*- and *-*ā*- in the Indo-European languages originally had ergative syntax and denoted an atemporal stative condition. In the course of time such verbs were incorporated into the regular verbal paradigms and adopted the same tense system as the other verbs. Note that in Georgian the verb 'to be necessary' patterns like the indirect verbs, e.g., (d) *araperi* (nom.) *ar gvč̣irdeba* 'we don't need anything, nothing is necessary for us' (Aronson, 1982, 348).

30.64 One can see the transitivization and syntactic reanalysis in the following examples. Indo-Iranian verbs of the fourth class (-*ya*) were originally statives, but some developed into passives probably already in the Indo-Iranian period according to Erhart, 1980, 148. Note the following Old Persian sentence showing ergative syntax reanalyzed as a passive:

(a) avaiya   ūvjiyā   arikā   āha
    the   Elamites   faithless   were

   utā͡sām   auramazdā   naiy   ayadiya
   and by them   Ahuramazda   not   revered
   (gen. pl.)

   auramazdām   ayadaiy.
   Ahuramazda   I revered.
   (acc.)

'The Elamites were faithless and Ahuramazda was not revered by them. I revered Ahuramazda' (Cardona, 1970, 2; Kent, 1953, 133). Compare now the Old Indic sentence with a stative verb of the same class: (b) *ánnasya* (gen. sg.) *tṛpyati* 'he refreshes himself with (some) food' (Macdonell, 1916, 319). If one understands 'food' as being the genitive of agent, then sentence (b) is to be interpreted as 'he is refreshed by the food' or 'the food (agent) refreshes him (patient).' In other words for the Indo-Iranian verbs in *-ya* represented in sentences (a) and (b), the same original syntactic interpretation is possible. Sentence (b) merely shows the transitivization and reversal of the role of agent and patient. The reversal of roles of agent and patient undoubtedly led to the creation of the Slavic genitive-accusative, which spread from those verbs which originally seemed to require the genitive case. Thus verbs such as *želěti, iskati, xotěti* 'to wish' originally had agents in the genitive and patients in the nominative. (Cf. the Georgian sentence [not, however, ergative] 30.6[e].) Klenin, 1983, 16, writes that speakers of Slavic never had to accept a radical change in form such as the substitution of genitives for accusatives, since the '... genitive-accusative replaced not accusative objects, but genitive ones.'

30.7 Sometimes the nominative subject of a sentence appears to be replaced by the genitive modifier, which stands in place of the subject.

(a) Čínoko   dar   neišvirė,   ----   o
    Čínokas'   still   didn't cook   but
    (gen. sg.)

Baltarãgio	jaũ	susė́do	válgyti.
Baltaragis'	already	sat down	to eat.

'The Cinokas (family, farm workers?) still haven't finished cooking, but the Baltaragis (family, farm workers?) have already sat down to eat' or 'At the Cinokas' (place) they haven't finished cooking, but at the Baltaragis' (place) they have already sat down to eat.'

(b)
Kaimýnų	jaũ	ir	linùs
The neighbor's (gen. pl.)	already	even	flax

nurõvė,	ir	roputės	nùkasė,	o
harvested	and	potatoes	dug up	but

mū́sų	dár,	antaĩ	vasarójus
our (gen. pl.)	still,	behold	summer crops

añt	laũko.
on	field.

'At the neighbor's (farm) they have already harvested the flax and dug up the potatoes, but on ours, lo and behold, the summer crops are still on the fields.' According to the Acad. Gram. (Vol. 3, 291) in these examples the genitive could be replaced by the nominative without any change in the meaning. Thus instead of sentence (b) one could have (c): *Kaimýnai* (nom. pl.) *jaũ ir linùs nurõvė*... The use of the genitive attribute in place of another noun is common in other languages, cf., e.g., the Hittite gen. sg. *waštul-aš* 'of the sin' to denote 'sinner' (Friedrich, 1960, 123).

The Adnominal Genitive

31. A noun in the (adnominal) genitive case defines or limits a second noun.

31.1 According to the Acad. Gram., Vol. 1, 188, it may denote an object, person, organization, institution, etc. to which something belongs or with which another object is somehow connected, e.g., (a) *Anglijos* (gen. sg.) *karãlius* 'the king of England,' (Vilentas' Catechism, 32, 13), (b) *Sacramentas Altoriaus* (gen. sg.) 'sacrament of the altar.' Note the following examples from Mažvydas' Catechism:

(c) (35, 8) Vredas   tiewu   prijsch
             The duty   of fathers   toward
                         (gen. pl.)

Sunus.
sons.

(d) (36, 1) Vredas   wijsakiu   weschpatu,
             The duty   of all   masters

alba panu   priesch   tarnus.
or   lords   toward   servants.
      (gen. pl.)

(e) (37, 11) Vredas   sennu   wiru   ijr
             The duty   of old   men   and

iaunikaicziu.
youths.
(gen. pl.)

(f) (38, 6) Naschliu   vredas.
             of widows   the duty.
             (gen. pl.)
'The duty of widows.'

(g) (38, 19) Vissu   szmaniu   vredas.
             of all   men   duty.
                       (gen. pl.)
'The duty of all men.'

(h) (1, 1)   Catechismusa   prasty
             of the catechism   simple
             (gen. sg.)

   Szadei.
   words.
'The simple words of the Catechism.' (i) (10, 4)
Dągaus (gen. sg.) karaliste 'the kingdom of heaven.'

(j) (8, 13) żadis   dągaus   karalistas.
             word   of heaven   of kingdom.
                       (gen. sg.)   (gen. sg.)
'The word of the kingdom of heaven.' In examples (f),
(g), (h), and (i) above we encounter the expected preposed genitive of possession. Examples (b), (c), and
(d) show a postposed genitive of possession which may
be attributed either to Polish or German influence.
In example (j) the attributive genitive dągaus 'of
heaven' is preposed to the head noun karalistas 'of the
kingdom' which, however, is postposed with respect to
its own head noun żadis 'word.' In Sirvydas' Postilla
49, 7 (Fraenkel, 1928, 94) one encounters the preposed
genitive in (k) dangaūs (gen. sg.) karalÿstė 'the
kingdom of heaven' whereas Vilentas' Catechism (62, 10)
had the postposed genitive in the similar expression
(1) karalista dąngaus. See Zinkevičius, 1981, 216. In
the title of Mažvydas' Catechism we encounter the phrase
(m) Knigieles Paczias byla Letuuinikump jr Szemaicziump
which Ford, 1971, 15, translates as 'The Little Book
Itself Speaks to the High Lithuanians and Low Lithuanians.' Such a translation assumes that Knigieles
Paczias 'the little book' is a nom. plurale tantum and
is subject of the verb byla 'speaks.' Bammesberger,
1971, 185, proposes that Knigieles Paczias is gen. sg.
and defines the noun byla 'speech.' If this is accepted

then one must translate the phrase as 'The Speech of the Little Book Itself to the High Lithuanians and Low Lithuanians.' The adnominal genitive may denote the material from which something is made, e.g., (n) *akmeñs* (gen. sg.) *kójos* 'legs of stone, stone legs,' (o) *stiklo* (gen. sg.) *ãkys* 'eyes of glass, glass eyes.'

The genitive may denote the purpose or the content of the object under discussion, e.g., (p) *geležiẽs* (gen. sg.) *fabrikaĩ* 'steel factories,' (q) *tekstilès* (gen. sg.) *fabrikaĩ* 'textile factories.'

Examples of the objective genitive are encountered in Mazvydas' Catechism: (r) (55, 14) *krauia* (gen. sg.) *ischlegimu* (inst. sg.) 'with the shedding of blood.'

(s) (40, 9) Greku   musu   pazinimas.
             of sins   our   confession.
             (gen. pl.)

'The confession of our sins.' (t) (22, 10) *greku* (gen. pl.) *atleidima* 'the forgiveness of sins.' From modern Lithuanian (Acad. Gram., Vol. 1, 190) (u) *uždavinio* (gen. sg.) *issprendimas* 'the solution of the problem.'

The genitive case can also be used to denote an indirect object: (v) *Birùtės* (gen. sg.) *dainà* 'Birutė's song,' i.e., song about Birutė,' (w) *tévo* (gen. sg.) *padėjėjas* 'father's helper' (*padėti* 'to help' is construed with an indirect object in the dat.), (x) *rañku* (gen. pl.) *dárbas* 'hand work,' i.e., work done with the hands, cf. *dìrba rañkomis* (inst. pl.) 'works with the hands' (Acad. Gram. Vol. 3, 204).

An example of a subjective genitive from Mazvydas' Catechism (40, 7): (y) *Diewa* (gen. sg.) *prisakimas* 'commandment of God.' From modern Lithuanian (z) *paũkščio* (gen. sg.) *čiulbėjimas* 'chirping of birds.' According to the Acad. Gram., Vol. 3, 204, the subjective genitive is usually derived from intransitive verbs.

Appositional names of places may be in the genitive case, e.g., (z1) *Vilniaũs* (gen. sg.) *miẽstas* 'the city of Vilnius.' Occasionally in dialects and in belles lettres such usage is encountered with personal names as well, e.g., (z2) *Klìmo* (gen. sg.) *Antãnas* 'Antanas Klimas,' (z3) *Kazakáusku Anùpras* 'Anupras Kazakauskas.' Usually the genitive plural is used in such constructions (Acad. Gram., Vol. 1, 190).

31.2 Sometimes the genitive can be synonymous with an adjective, e.g., (a) *prõto* (gen. sg.) *žmogùs* 'a man of intelligence' is almost the same as (b) *protìngas žmogùs* 'an intelligent man.' See 29.7. Mažvydas has (c) *kriksczianių* (gen. pl.) *žmagus* 'Christian man' whereas Pietkiewicz' Catechism has also the adjectival expression (d) *krikščioniškas žmogus* (Fraenkel, 1947, 72). Frequently the possessed object is of an abstract nature as in the preceding examples, although it can be concrete as in (e) *mẽno* (gen. sg.) *kūrinỹs* 'an art work, composition' (Acad. Gram., Vol. 3., 191). As in English a characteristic of the modifying noun can be expressed by the genitive, e.g., (f) *lìno* (gen. sg.) *plaukaĩ* 'flaxen haired,' (lit. 'hair of flax'; Acad. Gram., Vol. 3, 192). Klein, 1653, 154, gives the example: (g) *esmi gẽrôs szirdiês* (gen. sg.) 'I am of a good heart' (Lat: *sum bonae mentis*).

31.21 The genitive of respect is commonly used with such nouns as *didùmo* 'size,' *aukštùmo* 'height,' *ilgùmo* 'length.'

(a) Nýkščio   nagà,   didùmo
    of the thumb nail,   in respect to size
                          (gen. sg.)

    sulìg   gerù   kauseliù...
    according to a good   scoop...
                             (inst. sg.)

'A thumb nail about the size of a good scoop.'

(b) puikì   pilìs,   ilgùmo
    marvelous   castle,   in respect to length
                           (gen. sg.)

    peř   kelìas   mylìas
    through   several   miles.

'...a marvelous castle, several miles long' (Acad. Gram., Vol. 3, 419).

31.3 Adjectives such as *pìlnas*, *kùpinas* 'full,' *veřtas* 'worth,' *reikalìngas* 'necessary,' *turtìngas* 'rich,' *godùs* 'greedy' take complements in the genitive case. Note the following examples from Vilentas' Catechism:

(a) Pone   Diewe   Tiewe   wissokios   malones
    Lord   God   Father   of all   grace
                                         (gen. sg.)

          pilnasis (10, 6).
          full.
'Oh Lord God, the Father, full of all grace.'

(b)   wertas   ira   darbinikas   algos
       worthy   is   worker   of pay
                                                    (gen. sg.)

          sawa (39, 16).
          his.
'A worker is worthy of his pay.' From modern Lithuanian (Acad. Gram., Vol. 1, 191): (c) *Jis enèrgijos* (gen. sg.) *kùpinas* 'he is full of energy.' (d) *Ar nesì turtìngas šiẽno?* (gen. sg.) 'aren't you (sg.) rich in hay?'

31.4 As one can see from the preceding examples ordinarily the adnominal genitive precedes the noun it modifies, but in the case of the genitive denoting quantity it follows the noun it modifies resembling the English order, e.g., (a) *kilogrãmas úogų* (gen. pl.) 'a kilogram of berries.' According to the Acad. Gram., Vol. 3, 202, sequences with the postposed genitive accent the quantity itself, whereas the preposed genitive accents the object quantified, thus ordinarily (b) *kilogrãmas svíesto* 'a kilogram of butter,' whereas (c) *svíesto kilogrãmas* 'a kilogram of butter' with emphasis on the butter, to show that it isn't, e.g., a kilogram of meat or a kilogram of potatoes. Ordinarily one uses the expression (d) *puodẽlis kavõs* 'a cup of coffee.' The expression (e) *kavõs puodẽlis* could mean either (1) that it is a cup for coffee drinking or (2) that it is a cup that has just the amount of coffee that will fit into a cup (Acad. Gram., Vol, 3, 203).[11]

31.5 According to the Acad. Gram. (Vol. 3, 268) the following numbers require the genitive case: the decades from *dẽšimt* (*dešimtìs*) 'ten' - *devýniasdešimt* 'ninety'; *vienúolika* 'eleven' - *devyniólika* 'ninety'; *šim̃tas* 'hundred,' *tū́kstantis* 'thousand,' *milijõnas* 'million,' *milijárdas* 'billion'; the collectives *dvẽjetas* 'two, a group of two,' - *devýnetas* 'nine, a group of nine.' In a compound expression each numeral in turn can govern a genitive case, e.g., *šim̃tas* (nom. sg.) *tū́kstančių* (gen. pl.) *žmoníų* (gen. pl.) 'a hundred (of) thousand (of) people.' The situation was apparently not different in Old Lithuanian, cf. from Mažvydas' Catechism:

(10, 16) deiwiu   schimta...
          goddesses   hundred...
          (gen. pl.)

turinczias.
having.
'Having a hundred...goddesses.';

(10, 18) schimty   szmaniu   wena
          in one hundred   people   one
          (loc. sg.)   (gen. pl.)

negaleczia   atrasti.
I would not be able   to find.
'...I would not be able to find one in a hundred people...';

(17, 11) Deschimtis   Diewa   prisakimu.
          Ten   of God   commandments.
                                   (gen. pl.)

'Ten commandments of God.'; (17, 13) *Dwilika straipscziu* (gen. pl.) 'Twelve articles.'

31.6 The same noun may be repeated with the first member of the sequence in the genitive plural case. This enhances the quantitative or the qualitative meaning of the second noun (Acad. Gram., Vol. 3, 203), e.g., (a) *minių* (gen. pl.) *minios* (nom. pl.) 'large crowds' (lit: 'crowds of crowds), (b) *draugų* (gen. pl.) *draũgas* 'a real friend' (lit: 'a friend of friends'). From Mažvydas' Catechism (48, 16) (c) *Ant amsziu* (gen. pl.) *amszia* 'forever' (lit: 'for ages of ages').

31.7 An example of a genitive of comparison from Daukša's Postilla 168, 29-30 is given by Fraenkel, 1928, 88:

(a) Barabôsziu   augszczéus   Christaus
     Barabas   higher (than)   Christ
                                         (gen.)

201

kelame.
we raise.

'We raise Barabas higher than Christ.' Jablonskis, 1957, 593, gives the following examples which he feels to be incorrect:

(b) Laimėjo   daugiaũ   dešimtiẽs
    (He) won   more (than)   ten
                                        (gen. sg.)

lìtų.
litas.
(gen. pl.)

'He won more than ten litas (unit of money).'

(c) Bùvo   ne   mažiaũ   penkiũ
    There were   no   fewer (than)   five

arkliũ
horses.
(gen. pl.)

Jablonskis would correct sentences (b) and (c) respectively to:

(d) Laimėjo   daugiaũ   *ne* (or *nekaip, negu, kaip*)
    (He) won   more   than

dẽšimtį   lìtų
ten   litas,
(acc. sg.)   (gen. pl.)

and

(e) Bùvo   ne   mažiaũ   *kaip*   penkì
    There were   no   fewer   than   five

arkliaĩ
horses.
(nom. pl.)

The use of the genitive of comparison is felt to be due to Slavic influence and Jablonskis would replace such usage with a native word for 'than.'

32

The Adverbal Dative Case

32. The dative case is primarily the case of the 'indirect' object, but there are some verbs which require the only object in the dative case. Quoting Comrie, 1979, 15-17, and Givón, 1976, Hopper and Thompson, 1980, 260, write: 'a dative morpheme is often re-analysed as a marker of definite and/or animate o[bject]s.' Thus the Spanish personal *a* is etymologically a dative marker. Likewise both in Ge'ez and Neo-Aramaic, the Semitic dative marker *l-* has spread to become a marker of the definite accusative (Givón, 1976, 160). Similarly the **o*-stem Indo-European dative **-om* underwent a phonological split such that the sandhi form **-ō* came to function for the most part in the dative case and the form **-om* took on the accusative function (Schmalstieg, 1974b, 196-197; 1980, 44). Etymologically the dative case predates the accusative case which is a semantic specialization of the former. It is therefore not surprising that most of the verbs which require the dative case will be used with an animate and/or definite indirect object. Examples of various verbs requiring the dative case object come from Mažvydas' Catechism:

(a) (10, 1) Tassai   kasznam   szmagui
            He   every   man
                                 (dat. sg.)

     wenas   gal   padety.
     alone   can   help.
'He alone can help every man.'   (b) (35, 2) *nosytikiedamas Diewui* (dat. sg.) 'trusting in God.'   (c) (36, 22) *sluszidamy Panui* (dat. sg.) *ir ne szmanemus* (dat. pl.) 'serving the Lord and not men.'

(d) (50, 6) Idant   mes   tau
             So that   we   thee
                              (dat. sg.)

         tarnautumbim.
         may serve.
'So that we may serve thee.'

(e) (50, 18) Kure   tik   sawa
             Who   believe   their

         ischmintiei,   Sawa   silams   ir
         wisdom,   Their   strength   and
         (dat. sg.)   (dat. pl.)

         schwentibei.
         sanctity.
         (dat. sg.)
'Who believe in their wisdom, Their strength and sanctity' (see 34.21f and h).

(f) (52, 3) Artimims   sawa   atleidem
             Neighbors   our   we forgive.
             (dat. pl.)
'We forgive our neighbors.'

(g) (54, 12) Pagal   darbu   mums
             According to   works   us
                                           (dat. pl.)

         neatwersk.
         do not reward.
'Do not reward us according to our works.' (h) (54, 13) *mums* (dat. pl.) *susimilk* 'have mercy on us.'

(i) (57, 13) Liepk   panams   teisei
             Order   lords   righteously
                        (dat. pl.)

         rediti.
         to rule.
'Order the lords to rule righteously.'

32.1 According to Palionis, 1967, 156, in the writings of the 16th and 17th centuries reflexive verbs denoting surprise or to look at something are common with a dative complement. Cf., e.g., (Punktay sakimu I, 16, 28-29):

(a) dabokites   liliamus   lauko.
    look at   the lilies   of the field.
                  (dat. pl.)

From Morkūnas' Postilla, 259, 26-27:

(b) negaliu   prisiweyzdet   tiemus
    I cannot   look at   these

    stebuklamus.
    miracles.
    (dat. pl.)

Palionis writes that the use of the dative in such circumstances may be under Polish influence, cf. a corresponding sentence from a Polish Postilla: *nie mogę przypatrzyć tym dziwom* (dat. pl.). Sometimes in the 16th century the verb *dabotis* in the meaning 'to look at, to give attention to' is used with the genitive case, thus from Daukša's Postilla 16, 34: (c) *dabókites to* (gen. sg.) 'look at that.' Further examples of dative: (Chyliński's Bible, Matthew 22, 33): (d) *diwijos jo mokslui* (dat. sg.) 'they were astonished at his doctrine,' (id., Matthew 7, 28):

(e) stebeiosi   pulkey   moksłuy
    were astonished   people   at doctrine
                                     (dat. sg.)

    jo.
    his.

'The people were astonished at his doctrine.' Palionis, 1967, 156, writes that in writings of this time the dative was used with the verb *stebėtis* 'to be surprised at, to wonder at.' Contemporary usage would require an instrumental case with this verb, cf. (Acad. Gram., Vol. 1, 200; Vol. 3, 51):

(f) nusistebėjau   tókiu   jõ
    I was surprised   at such   his

reikalãvimu.
demand.
(inst. sg.)
'I was surprised at such a demand of his.' Nevertheless according to Palionis at the earlier time the dative case was the universal norm, although in many cases it may have arisen under Polish influence. In general it is difficult to determine to what extent Polish influenced the language of the people and to what extent an individual feature is due to the influence of the text in question. Verbs denoting 'to laugh at, to rejoice' were also construed with a dative object in 16th and 17th century writings, e.g., from Pietkiewicz' Catechism (Fraenkel, 1947, 67; Palionis, 1967, 157):
(g) *tamuy* (dat. sg.) *džiaugies* 'they rejoiced in (at) that.'

Note, however, that Klein, 1653, 151, has both (h) *džaugiůs to* (gen.) and (i) *džaugiůs isz to* (prep. plus gen.) 'I rejoice at (from) that.' Usually the contemporary verb *džiaũgtis* 'to rejoice' is construed with the instrumental or the preposition *iš* (plus gen.), cf., e.g., (Acad. Dict., Vol. 2, 1014): (j) *Nesidžiaũk pažadais* (inst. pl.) 'don't rejoice at promises,' (k) *Nesidžiaũk iš kito nelãimės* (gen. sg.) 'don't rejoice at another's misfortune.' Also from Pietkiewicz' Catechism (Fraenkel, 1947 67):

(1) sawa   iszganima   akmeniuy
     our   salvation's   rock
                                (dat. sg.)

     linksminkim (for *linksminkimės).
     let us rejoice.
'Let us rejoice in the rock of our salvation.'

32.11 According to Palionis, 1967, 157, in certain of the 16th and 17th century writings the dative is sometimes still used as the object of the verbs *išmanýti* 'to understand,' *klausýti* 'to obey,' *(pa-)šlõvinti* 'to glorify,' *viešpatáuti* 'to rule over.' Thus from Morkūnas' Postilla: *iszmanidamas tamuy* (dat. sg.) 'understanding that'; cf. Pol. *rozumieiącz temu* (dat. sg.); Bretkūnas' Bible (Genesis 21, 12): (a) *tam klausik* 'obey that.' From a Polish-Lithuanian gospel (Palionis, 1967, 157-8):

(b) kurie   io   klause   iszmanimuy
    who   his   listened to   thought
                                  (dat. sg.)

    ir   atsakimams   io.
    and   answers   his.
           (dat. pl.)

Cf. Pol. (c) *ktorzy go słuchali rozumowi y odpowiedźiom iego* 'who listened to his thought and his answers.' Note the following from Bretkūnas' Postilla (II, 50):

(d) kas   iusu   klausa,   tassai
    whoever   you   listens to   that one
               (gen. pl.)

    mane   klausa
    me   listens to.
    (acc. sg.)

'Whoever listens to you, that one listens to me.' In Pietkiewicz' Catechism one finds either dative or accusative government according to the Polish model for the verb *slóvinti* 'to glorify.' (Fraenkel, 1947, 67):

(e)   paszławina   dieną   nedėlios
    (Pol.)   błogosławił   dzień   odpoczynienia
               glorified   day   of rest

               Ponas.
               Pan.
               Lord.

'The Lord glorified the day of rest.' (f) *szławina iems* (dat. pl.) = Pol. *błogosławił im* (dat. pl.) 'glorified them.' On the other hand Pietkiewicz uses the accusative sometimes where Polish has the dative, e.g., (g) *paszławink mus* (acc.) = Pol. *błogosław nam* (dat.) 'glorify us' and only once do we encounter the reverse, viz., (h) *giemus* (dat. pl., *žmonėms tikroms*) *szławint* = Pol. *iy* (acc. sg., *lud wierny*) *błogosławić* 'to glorify them (faithful people).' According to Fraenkel, 1947, 67, the dative government with verbs denoting 'to glorify' etc. is due to Polish influence. (i) *wisam swietuy* (dat. sg.) *wieszpatauia* 'governs the entire world.' Palionis, 1967, 158, suggests that the dative usage with *viešpatáuti* may be original and not under Polish influence.

Note the examples of dative of interest and indirect object from Mažvydas' Catechism:

(j) (53, 9)   Piktas   dienas   mums
              Evil   days   for us
                                 (dat.)

ateia.
have come.
'Evil days have come for us.';

(k) (57, 21) Paschak   sylpnams
              Help   the weak
                        (dat. pl.)

bei   sergancziams.
and   ill.
       (dat. pl.)

The following examples with verbs of various meanings are taken from Vilentas' Catechism:

(l) (40, 18) kurs   wirausibei
              whoever   authority
                        (dat. sg.)

prieschtarau,   tas   prieschtarau
contradicts,   he   contradicts

jstatimui.
law.
(dat. sg.)
'Whoever contradicts authority, contradicts the law.';

(m) (45, 11) tada   neužgul
              then   it does not behoove

mums   Duchawniems
us   pastors;
        (dat. pl.)

(n) (12, 2): *yamui* (dat. sg.) *dekawotumbim* 'so that we may thank him.';

(o) (35, 20) idant   taw   wissi
              so that   you   all
                         (dat. sg.)

       mana   darbai,   ir   žiwatas   passidabotu.
       my   works   and   life   may please.
'So that all my life and works please you.' An example
from Mažvydas' Catechism:

(p) (37, 6)   gimus   pamegdamij,   ne
              them   pleasing   not
              (dat. pl.)

       prischtariaudamij.
       not contradicting.
'Pleasing them, not contradicting them.'

32.12 The history of the verbal government of *gélbèti*
'to help' is rather unclear. Hermann, 1926, 70, considers it possible that *gélbèti* is derived from *galéti* 'to
be able' in which case *gélbèti* would have originally
been intransitive and with the dative may have had the
meaning 'einem etwas können, to make something possible
for someone.' Then the accusative government may have
been adopted on analogy with *šelpti* 'to help.'
     Klein, 1653, 157, writes that *gélbmi* which he translates as Lat. *juvo* 'to help' governs the accusative case,
whereas the prefixed compound *pagélbmi* which he translates as Lat. *adjuvo* 'to help' governs the dative:

(a) jis   kitiemus   pagélbejo,   a   sawę
     he   others   helped   but   himself
            (dat. pl.)   (acc. sg.)

       negal   gélbeti.
       cannot   help.
'He helped others, but he cannot help himself.' (Lat.:
aliis opem tulit, seipsum autem juvare neqvit.) He
claims that the quotation is from Matthew 27, but all of
the versions of Matthew 27, 42, at my disposal give:
Alios salvos fecit, seipsum non potest salvum facere 'He
saved others; himself he cannot save.' It seems possible
that *gélbeti* here means 'to save' just as in modern Lithuanian, but the origin of Klein's version of Matthew 27,
42 and his interpretation of the Lithuanian sentences remain unclear. Klein writes further that sometimes the

simple verb governs the dative, especially when the meaning of the verb is somewhat different. (b) *negelbt man* (dat.) *nieka* (gen.) 'nothing is of benefit to me' (Lat.: *nihil prodest mihi*);

(c) kam   gelbt   puikyste   szo   swieto.
    for what   is useful   splendor   of this   world.
    (dat.)

'What is the use of the splendor of this world' (Lat.: *ad qvid facit fastus hujus mundi?*). Vilentas' Catechism (13, 6) shows the dative case *iem* (dat.) *pagelbetumbim* 'we might help him.'

Contemporary Lithuanian has accusative government for *gélbėti* with the meaning 'to get (somebody) out of trouble, to save from evil; to cure.' E.g.

(d) Gélbėk   manè (acc.)   iš   bėdõs
    Save   me   from   evil.

For the most part one encounters dative government with the meaning 'to help,' e.g., (e) *Gélbėk nenùjėgančiamui* (dat. sg.) 'Help the one without strength.' Nevertheless accusative government is also encountered, e.g.,

(f) Ar negalì   gélbėti   manè (acc.)   su pinigaĩs...?
        you can't help   me   with money ...?

'Can't you help me with some money? (Acad. Dict., Vol. 3, 211)

32.13   In contemporary Lithuanian verbs governing the dative case can be regularly passivized with the nominative replacing the dative:

(a) Jõnas   atstováuja   institùtui.
    John   represents   the institute.
    (nom.)   (dat.)

(b) Institùtas   atstováujamas   Jõno.
    The institute   is represented   by John.
    (nom.)   (gen.)

(c) Fãktai   prieštaráuja   téiginiui.
    The facts   contradict   the statement.
    (nom.)   (dat.)

(d) Teiginỹs   prieštaráujamas   fãktų.
    The statement   is contradicted   by the facts.
    (nom.)   (gen.)

(Grabauskas, 1971, 57.) This is evidence that the dative and accusative were originally the same case.

32.14 Many verbs require a direct object in the accusative case but have an indirect object in the dative case. Note the following examples from Mažvydas' Catechism:

(a) (23, 11) Dona   musu   wyssu-
             bread   our   of all
             (acc. sg.)

    dienu   dodi   mumus.
    days   give   us.
                   (dat.)
'Give us our daily bread.';

(b) (62, 1) Apreisskie   mums   kielius
            reveals   to us   ways
                         (dat.)   (acc. pl.)

    sawa.
    his.
'He reveals to us his ways.';

(c) (67, 15) Paradik   mums   malane
             Show   us   grace
                       (dat.)   (acc. sg.)

    sawa.
    your.
'Show us your grace.';

(d) (65, 11) Szadeiei   malane   wisims.
             You promised   grace   to all.
                             (acc. sg.)   (dat. pl.)

It is almost impossible to separate such usage very clearly from the usage of the dative of person (or thing) affected:

(e) (63, 11) platink   Cziesti   ir   garbe
             Extend   honor   and   praise
                         (acc.)   (acc.)

211

                Dewui
                to God.;
                (dat.)

(f)   (52, 16) kure   mums   szabągha
                who   for us   trap
                          (dat.)   (acc. sg.)

        spend.
        set.
'Who set a trap for us.';

(g)   (51, 14) Gieisk   mums   wisu
                Wish   for us   all
                          (dat.)
        priwalimu.
        all necessities.;
        ([partitive] gen. pl.)

(h)   (31, 11) Jauczui   kulantem   ne
                to an ox   thrashing   not
                (dat.)

        vszrischi   nasru.
        you will bind   mouth.
                          (gen. pl. [of negation])
'You will not bind up the mouth of a thrashing ox.'
     According to the Acad. Gram. (Vol. 3, 41) either
the nom. or the acc. case can be used in such sentences
as the following:

(i)   skaũda   mán   gálvą
      aches   to me   head
                          (acc. sg.)

(j) skaũda mán (dat.) galvà (nom. sg.). Both sentences
are to be translated as 'my head aches.' In sentence
(i) it can perhaps be understood that etymologically
the meaning was that some outside agency was bringing
pain to the head, whereas in sentence (j) the head
indeed is causing pain to the sufferer. Note similarly:

(k)   maũdžia   marčiai   dañtį   [or]
      aches   daughter-in-law   tooth
                                  (acc.)

         dantìs.
         tooth.
         (nom.)
'The daughter-in-law's tooth aches.'

(1)   nupiŕko   dùkteriai   siúlų
      bought   for daughter   some thread
                   (dat.)   (gen. pl.)

      megztìniui.
      for a sweater.
      (dat.)
'(He) bought (his) daughter some thread for a sweater'
(Acad. Gram., Vol. 3, 31).
    Sentences (h)-(1) may be considered to show a
dative of possession which is in competition with the
genitive of possession.

32.2 The dative for whom or for which something exists
or should exist is also encountered in Mažvydas'
Catechism.

(a)   (67, 17)   Garbe   testa   Diewui
                 Glory   may be   to God
                                       (dat.)

      tewui.
      the father.
      (dat.)
'May glory be to God the Father.'

(b)   (74, 19)   buki   cziestis   ir   garbe
                 may be   honor   and   glory

      Dewui   amszinamui.
      to God   eternal.
'Honor and glory be to eternal God.'

(c)   (65, 13)   Tu   essi   tiews   mums
                 You   are   father   to us
                                                 (dat.)

      malanus.
      merciful.
'You are a merciful father to us.'

213

32.3 The dative of purpose with the infinitive is attested in the following examples:

(a) pirkaũ   daĩgį   šiẽnui   pjáuti.
    I bought   scythe   hay   to mow.
                   (acc.)   (dat. sg.)

'I bought a scythe (in order) to mow the hay.' Such constructions are relatively independent of the main clause. Thus the definition of the noun *daĩgis* 'scythe' is (Acad. Dict., Vol. 2, 240):

(b) įrankis   žőlei   ar   javáms
    instrument   grass   or   grain
                   (dat. sg.)

    pjáuti.
    to mow.

'An instrument to mow (for mowing) grass or grain.' The object of the main verb of the clause is not necessarily in the accusative case, e.g.:

(c) íeško   árklio   žẽmei
    (He) is looking for   horse   earth
                                  (gen. sg.)   (dat. sg.)

    árti.
    to plow.

'He is looking for a horse to plow the earth' (Acad. Gram., Vol. 3, 171-173). The construction is well known in other Indo-European languages, cf. Czech:

(d) kúpichu   pole   pútníkóm   hřésti.
    they bought   field   pilgrims   to bury.
                                  (dat. pl.)

'They bought the field to bury the pilgrims in' (Fraenkel, 1925, 60). Cf. Vedic:

(e) brahmā́ṇa   índram   maháyanto   arkáir
    Brahmans   Indra   magnifying   songs
    (nom.)   (acc.)   (nom. pl.)   (instr.)

    avardhayann   áhaye
    they-have-strengthened   snake
                                  (dat.)

214

       hantavā   u   (V.31.4cd)
       kill
       (inf.)
'The magnifying Brahmans have strengthened Indra with songs so that (he) would slay the snake' (Disterheft, 1980, 61). Cf. Avestan:

(f)   maθrəm   spənəm   maraēta . . .
      word   holy   they-speak
      (acc.)   (acc. sg.)

   . . .   uxšne   xraθwe   (Vd 4.45bd)
            increase   wisdom
            (inf.)   (dat.)

'They speak the word in order to increase wisdom' (Disterheft, 1980, 96). Cf. Hittite:

(g)   nu   SAL.MEŠ   ukturiya   hastiyas
      Pt   women   bones
             (nom.)   (dat.)   (dat.)

      lessuwanzi   pānzi   (KUB XXX 15 I 1-2)
      collect   they-go
      (inf.)

'The women go to the *ukturiya* to collect bones.'

(h)   ^DUTU-ŠI-ma   EGIR-an   EGIR-pa   *ANA*
      Majesty-my   again   back   to

      DINGIR.MEŠ.ŠU   iyauwanzi   uizzi
      gods   his   honor   he-comes
                                 (inf.)

      (KUB XXVI 17 I 10)

'My majesty comes back again in order to honor his gods' (Disterheft, 1980, 167).

    According to Disterheft, 1980, 108, in Indo-Iranian 'only dative infinitives used in purpose clauses without conjunction regularly have dative object.' Thus there is a syntactic rather than a morphological reason for choosing the dative object in purpose clauses.

32.31 According to Ambrazas, 1981, 15, one can divide the dative plus infinitive constructions into three types as follows: (1) the construction refers to the

(a) object or (b) the subject of the sentence, thus:

(a) Kamārą   daiktáms   pasidéti
    Room   for things   to put away for oneself
              (dat. pl.)

    vìsiškai   àtėmė.
    completely   took away.
'(He) took away completely the store-room to put things away.'

(b) Tàs   kiřvis   málkoms   kapóti
    That   axe   fire-wood   to chop
                       (dat. pl.)

    visái   atšìpo.
    completely   became dull.
'That axe for chopping firewood became completely dull.'
(2) The construction refers to the noun or pronoun and simultaneously to the main verb (or the predicate of the sentence):

(c) Atvežiaũ   kárčių   tvõrai
    I brought   some poles   fence
                                 (dat. sg.)

    tvérti.
    to make.
'I brought some poles to make the fence.' (3) The construction refers only to the main verb:

(d) Šóvė   į̃   órą   pagą̃sdinti
    Shot   into   the air   to frighten

    žmonė́ms.
    people.
    (dat. pl.)
'(They) shot into the air in order to frighten the people.' Ambrazas writes further that it is quite possible to derive type (1) constructions from type (2) and that one can compare type (1) constructions with such common sentences as (e) *pastačiaũ kamārą daiktáms pasidė́ti* 'I built a store-room to put things in' and (f) *atsinešiaũ kiřvį málkoms kapóti* 'I brought an axe to chop wood.' Sentences of type (1) are rare

in the folk language and refer only to the noun or pronoun if it stands in some kind of adverbial relationship to the main verb or to the nominal predicate of the sentence. In the latter case a predicative *tiñkamas* 'suitable (for)' or *skìrtas* 'destined (for), devoted (to)' is implied. Thus the saying:

(g) Ne visų̃ bùrnos pùtrai
    Not of all mouths meal soup
                                   (dat.)

srẽbti.
to eat,

can be translated literally 'Not everyone's mouths are for eating meal soup.' Still the notions *bùrnos tiñka* 'the mouths are suitable (for),' *gẽros* '(are) good (for),' *skìrtos* '(are) destined, prepared (for)' are implied in (g). Sentences such as:

(h) Šìtas tiñklas yrà žuvìms
    This net is for fish
                               (dat. pl.)

gáudyti.
to catch.

'This net is for catching fish' do not answer the question *Kàs taĩ?* 'What is that?' but rather *Kám (yrà skìrtas) tàs tiñklas?* 'What is the purpose of that net?' Ambrazas continues, 16, saying that sentences both of type (2) and (3) are variants of a construction type in which the dative with infinitive stands in some relationship with the main verb (with or without the expression of the subject or the object). In contemporary Lithuanian the dative with infinitive functions as the equivalent of a subordinate clause of purpose. For the most part one encounters this construction in sentences which also permit the occurrence of the dative of purpose (even without the infinitive). This limitation of the use of the dative with infinitive derives from the character of the original relationship of both members of the construction (that of the dative and that of the infinitive) to the main verb, which can be seen even today. Either the dative or the infinitive taken separately can be used in meaning similar to that of the entire construction. Example:

(i) Tévas   parsìvežė   málkų
    Father   brought   some fire-wood

    trôbai   kūrénti.
    cottage   to heat.
    (dat. sg.)

'Father brought some fire-wood to heat the cottage.'
The word *trôbai* 'cottage' could be omitted giving the
meaning 'Father brought some fire-wood for heating' or
the word *kūrénti* 'to heat' could be omitted giving the
meaning 'Father brought some fire-wood for the cottage.'
This shows that the dative with infinitive offers two
additions to the sentence, viz. the dative and the
infinitive and the infinitive corresponds directly to
the verbal noun and in many cases can be replaced by the
verbal noun in the dative case, e.g.:

(j) àtvežė   bùlvių   paválgyti
    (He brought)   some potatoes   to eat

    (or)   paválgymui
    (or)   for eating.
           (dat.)

This shows that the infinitive can have its origin
directly in the verbal noun. Cf. then:

(k) pirkaũ   árklį   laukáms   árti.
    I bought   a horse   fields   to plow.
'I bought a horse to plow the fields' which can be
paraphrased in Lithuanian as:

(l) pirkaũ   árklį   laukáms   /
    I bought   a horse   for the fields   /
                              (dat. pl.)

    arìmui
    for (their) plowing.
    (sg.)

Many opinions have been expressed concerning the relationship between the infinitive and the dative itself,
but Ambrazas, 17, ascribes a central role to the dative
and a more marginal role to the infinitive. This is
supported by the usual position of putting the dative

before the infinitive. According to Ambrazas, 17, the fact that the dative usually denotes the object of the infinitive action has led some researchers to the mistaken conclusion that the dative replaces an accusative case in such constructions. Nevertheless, the multiplicity of semantic relationships between the dative and the infinitive speaks against such a notion. The dative can denote the subject of the infinitive or some kind of circumstantial relationship to the infinitive:

(m) Įpýliau   píeno   kačiùkams
    I poured   some milk   for the kittens (subject)
                                (dat. pl.)

    užlàkti.
    to lap up.

(n) Pasiẽmė   verpalų   nãkčiai
    (She) took   some yarn   for the night
                                (dat.)

    verpti.
    to spin.

'She took some yarn to spin during the night.' Furthermore, Ambrazas, 19, points out that that one finds the dative of subject in Old Indic also:

(o) átho   indrāya   pátave   sunú
    therefore   for Indra   to drink   press
                 (dat.)

    sómam.
    soma.

'Therefore press soma for Indra to drink.' Ambrazas, 20, concludes that the dative with infinitive construction is a special case of double dative with appositional relaionships between its members. The replacement of the object dative with the accusative is a later development of Latvian, the Slavic languages (Ambrazas, 1980, 21) and Avestan (Disterheft, 1980, 109-110).

32.32 In the Indo-Iranian languages the infinitive is derived from the verbal nouns in the dative, accusative, and locative cases and in Iranian the instrumental case as well (Disterheft, 1980, 12-15). In Balto-Slavic the

infinitive derives from the dat. sg. ending *-t-ei.
The use of the dative as the direct object of the verb
(where ordinarily one might expect an accusative) attests
to the age of the construction. Both the supine (acc.
sg.) in *-t-um and the infinitive (dat. sg.) in *-t-ei
originally functioned in much the same way and the functions became separate in the history of Balto-Slavic.
(In fact, of course, the comparatively free use of cases
in the infinitive as apparent direct objects of verbs
reflects an earlier situation.)

32.4 The apparent subject of many impersonal verbs is
expressed by the dative case. Such subjects in the
dative case are relatively weak in agency and can in
fact be interpreted as patients acted upon by some
exterior agent or force. With verbs denoting 'to be
necessary, to lack, to be sufficient' the thing which
is necessary, lacking or of which there is a sufficient
quantity is in the genitive case.

(a) Mán   reĩkia   kaṁbario.
    I   need   a room.
    (dat.)   (gen.)

Fraenkel, 1925, 37, suggests a nominal origin for the
verb reikėti 'to be necessary' and quotes the example
from Mažvydas' Catechism:

(b) (77, 3) liekariaus   sweikims
             physician   for the healthy
             (gen.)   (dat. pl.)

    ne   esti   reika.
    not   is   necessity.

'There is no need of a physician for healthy people,
i.e., healthy people don't need a physician.' As a
parallel Fraenkel quotes the verbal forms možnẽs (3rd
fut.) 'will be possible' and možnė́tų (3rd subj.) 'would
be possible' derived from Polish można '(it is) possible'
(Acad. Dict., Vol. 8, 377). The predicate of the copula
governed by reikėti is also in the dative case:

(c) Víeną   kartą   pamókytam   reikė́jo
    one   time   taught   it was necessary
                      (dat. sg.)

```
       būti        gudrèsniam
       to be       more clever.
                   (dat. sg.)
```
'Once taught he had to be more clever.' (Lit: 'it was necessary for him [having been taught] to be more clever.') Even if the dative subject is not explicitly expressed the predicate is in the dative:

```
(d)  reĩkia              bū́ti       visaĩ
     it is necessary     to be      completely

     bukám               ar         fanãtikui,      kad
     obtuse              or         fanatic         in order that
     (dat. sg.)                     (dat. sg.)

     tikė́tum                   tà         pačià       maldà.
     you would believe         that       same        prayer.
```
'You (one) would have to be obtuse or a fanatic in order to believe that same prayer.' Examples of other verbs with a dative subject and a genitive object include the following.

```
(e)  Sáulės         mùms         užteñka.
     sun            for us       is enough.
     (gen.)         (dat.)
```
'We have enough sun.'

```
(f)  Jám           stiñga         pìnigų.
     He            lacks          money.
     (dat.)                       (gen. pl.)
```
(Literally: 'to him there is a shortage of money.') The reflexive verb *norė́tis* 'to wish, to want' has a similar syntax.

```
(g)  Mán           baĩsiai        norė́josi
     I             desperately    wanted
     (dat.)

     fìgų.
     figs.
     (gen. pl.)
```

(Acad. Gram., Vol. 3, 613.)

32.41 The dative can be used as both the subject and predicate with the copula to express the notion of necessity, e.g., from Daukša's Postilla:

(a) neger   yra   žmõgui   wienam
    not good is   for man   alone
                      (dat. sg.) (dat. sg.)

    buti.
    to be.

'It is not good for a man to be alone' (Fraenkel, 1928, 120; Ford, 1969, 121). This is equivalent to the Polish expression: *nie iest dobrze człowiekowi być samemu.*

According to Elzbutas, 1967, 146, the second dative constructions consist of four elements: (1) the initial dative, (2) the linking element, i.e., the part which remains when the infinitive and second dative are removed, (3) the infinitive and (4) the second dative. In sentence (a) the first dative is *žmõgui*, the linking element is *neger yra*, the infinitive is *buti* and the second dative is *wienam*. The initial dative element can be omitted either if it is implied by the context or if its omission is a sign that we are dealing with a general statement (Elzbutas, 147):

(b) per̃   mišką   žmõgui   basám
    through forest   for a man barefoot
                        (1st dat.) (2nd dat.)

    eĩti   nepatõgu.
    to walk uncomfortable.

'It is uncomfortable for a man to walk barefoot through the forest.' The element *žmõgui* could be omitted in the Lithuanian original and its counterpart 'for a man' could be omitted in the English translation. The linking element is absent in the sentence:

(c) Kodẽl   jám   vikriám
    Why   for him quick
               (dat. sg.) (dat. sg. masc.)

    nebúti?
    not to be.

'Why shouldn't he be quick?' Such sentences are ordinarily interrogative or negative. With the exception of *bū́ti* 'to be' the infinitive may never be omitted. The exception:

(d) Mán   perdaũg   sunkù   vienám.
    To me   too   difficult alone.
    (dat.)   (dat. sg.)

'It is too difficult for me to be alone.' One could always restore the element *bū́ti* in such a sentence. There is, however, an example where the omission of the infinitive seems possible:

(e) Iř   mū́sų   giriečiui   įkyrė́jo
    Even our   forest dweller   became tired of
                  (dat. sg.)

    nuolačiai̇̃   vienám   bebū̃nant.
    constantly   alone   being.
                  (dat. sg.)

'Even our forest-dweller became tired of constantly being alone.' One gets the impression that here we have to do with the replacement of *bū́ti* by *bebū̃nant*. Actually the expression is derived from a former dative construction *vienám bebū̃nančiam* and originally there were three datives, viz. *giriečiui*, *vienám* and *bebū̃nančiam*. The fourth element, the second dative, may never be omitted from such sentences.

According to Elzbutas, 145, in the contemporary language there is a tendency to replace the participial forms by the gerundial forms:

(f) Vaikáms   į   mišką
    For the children   to the   forest
    (dat. pl.)

    reĩkia   eĩti   apsiãvusiems
    it is necessary   to go   having put on shoes.
                                      (dat. pl. past act.
                                      prt.)

'The children must have shoes on when they go into the forest.' The participle *apsiãvusiems* could be replaced by the gerund *apsiãvus* with the same meaning. In principle a noun may be used as the second dative:

(g) Nereik   bū́t   tokiám
    It is not necessary   to be   such

besõčiui.
a greedy person.
(dat. sg.)

Other nouns which might function in this position include *vėpla* 'gaping fool,' *begėdis* 'shameless person,' which (as well as *besõtis*) could easily be replaced by adjectives (Elzbutas, 146; Jablonskis, 1957, 604). In fact, however, instead of the second dative case one ordinarily encounters the instrumental if a noun is used:

(h) Táu   tèks   bùti
    For you   it will happen   to be
    (dat. sg.)

    pìrmininku.
    president.
    (inst. sg.)

'You will have the duty (honor, etc.) of being president.' With nominalizations of the verb the second dative is possible with adjectives, but rare, e.g.:

(i) ...   nóras   lìkti
    (her)...   wish   to remain

    nepastebimaĩ.
    inconspicuous.
    (dat. sg. fem.)

With the noun also the dative is rare, so that instead of:

(j) ... nóras   išlìkti   šeimininkams
    (their)...wish   to remain   masters...
                                   (dat. pl.)

one would find *šeimininkais* (inst. pl.) (Elzbutas, 152).

32.42 The dative case is used as the subject with an infinitive to express the notion of necessity or requirement:

(a) Rùgio   dáigui   áugti   ir
    of rye   sprout   to grow   and
               (dat.)

   žaliúoti.
   to turn green.
'A sprout of rye should (is to) grow and turn green.'

(b) ... žinódami,   kad   jíems   čià
        knowing   that   for them   here
                           (dat.)

   ne   ámžius   gyvénti.
   not   ages   to live.
'... knowing that it is not for them (that they will
not) live here forever' (Acad. Gram., Vol. 3, 36-37).
Quoting Balkevičius, 1963, 143-145, Elzbutas, 1967, 147,
writes that the dative of necessity has arisen under
Russian influence.
   Grenda, 1967, 81-82, proposes that such infinitive
sentences are reduced variants of impersonal sentences
which contain an impersonal verb. E.g., such a sentence
as (c) *Ką mán* (dat.) *darýti* 'What am I to do, what is
there for me to do?' does not differ essentially from:

(d) Ką   mán   reĩkia   darýti?
    What   for me   is necessary   to do?
             (dat.)
'What is it necessary for me to do?' Supporting this
thesis Grenda, 83, writes that in any infinitive sentence an impersonal verb may be restored. Thus *reĩkia*
'it is necessary' could be inserted in the sentence:

(e) Taĩ   kám   mùms   (reĩkia)
    So   why   for us   (is it necessary)
                       (dat.)

    tólintis   nuo   kits   kìto.
    to separate   from   each   other.
'Why (is it necessary to) separate from each other.'
Similarly in such infinitive sentences usually the
present tense is understood, e.g.:

(f) Kám   gáinioti   be   reĩkalo
    Why   drive   without   need

    árklius?
    the horses?

Other tenses could use some form of the verb *reikė́ti* 'to be necessary,' thus the preterit: (g) *Kám reikė́jo* ([frequentative past] *reikė́davo*; [future] *reikẽs*; [subjunctive] *bū́tų reikė́ję*) *gáinioti*... 'Why was it necessary (did it used to be necessary, will it be necessary, would it have been necessary) to drive...'

32.43 The expression of the whole and the part is also known, e.g., from the Lithuanian author Žemaitė:

jam	lengviau	esą
to him	lighter	being, is
(dat. sg.)		

širdžiai.
to the heart.
(dat. sg.)
'He feels lighter in his heart; (lit.): to him, to (his) heart, (it) is lighter' (Fraenkel, 1928, 120).

33

The Adnominal Dative

33. The dative case accompanies many adjectives and nouns with various meanings. Note the following examples from Mažvydas' Catechism:

(a) (65, 13) Tu   essi   tiews   mums
              You   are   father   to us
                                    (dat.)

   malanus.
   merciful.
'You are a merciful father to us.';

(b) (31, 18-19) Kaszna   duscha   maczems
                 Every   soul   to powers
                                   (dat. pl.)

   wiresniams   testawi   padota.
   higher   may stand   subject.
'Let every soul be subject to the higher powers.';

(c) (71, 4) Macze,   garbe,   ligus
             In power,   in glory   equal

   est   Diewui.
   is   to God.
         (dat.)
'He is equal to God in power and glory.' From Vilentas' Catechism:

(d) (50, 15) padarisiu   yem
              I shall make   for him a
                              (dat.)

           pagalba   werta   yamui.
           helpmate   worthy   of him.
                                     (dat.)

(e) (40, 9) Paklusni   bukit   yussu
            Obedient   be   your

      mokitojems.
      teachers.
      (dat.)
'Be obedient to your teachers.'; Mažvydas' Catechism:

(f) (32, 5) Diewa   abawem   tarnas
            of God   for   servant

      esti   tau...
      is   to thee...
                (dat.)
'For he is the servant of God to thee...'

33.1 The dative is also used with a special meaning called 'dative of judgment,' i.e., the attitude of the person is indicated by the dative case.

(a) Diẽvui   visì   žmónės   lýgūs.
     For God   all   men (are)   equal.

From the point of view of the grammar this could be interpreted as meaning 'All men are equal to God.' It is only the meaning which assures us of the correct translation (Fraenkel, 1928, 129).

33.2 An example of the dative of comparison comes from Vilentas' Catechism:

(a) (40, 5) kurie   wiresnieghi   yums
            who   higher   than you
                                        (dat. pl.)

      jra   wieschpatije.
      are   in the Lord.
'Who are higher than you in the Lord' (Ford, 1962, 122; Fraenkel, 1928, 126).

33.3 The dative is used to express the length of time for which an event is supposed to last:

(a) Aš išėjau minùtei.
    I went out for a minute.
    (dat. sg.)

(b) Atvažiãvome dvýlikai dienų̃.
    We arrived for twelve days.
    (dat. sg.) (gen. pl.)

(Acad. Gram., Vol. 3, 35-36.) (See paragraph 35.)
There are also contexts which render it ambiguous as to whether one has to do with the dative of time or the dative of purpose.

(c) Jõnas sugrį̃š vãsarai.
    Jonas will return for the summer.
    (dat. sg.)

This could be interpreted to mean either 'Jonas will return for the entire summer' or 'Jonas will return to spend the summer' (Grabauskas, 1971, 52).

33.4 An example of the dative of possession:

(a) Nẽr mán tėvẽlio nẽr
    There is not to me father there is not
    (dat.) (gen.)

    mán močiùtės.
    to me mother.
    (dat.) (gen.)

'I have no father nor mother.' Jablonskis, 1957, 600-601, wrote that the more common contemporary usage would be (b) *Aš neturiu tėvẽlio*...with the verb *turėti* 'to have.' The dative of possession is the normal mode of expression in Latvian, however, e.g.:

(b) Man ir nams
    To me is house.
    (dat.) (nom.)

'I have a house' (Fennell and Gelsen, 1980, 18).

Grabauskas, 1971, 55, points out that the dative of possession occupies an intermediate position between the semantic and syntactic cases. On the one hand it has an attributive nuance (it defines a characteristic) and on the other hand it denotes an indirect object. Thus if we emphasize the meaning of the indirect object and leave out the possessive meaning we can receive distorted information. Cf.:

(c) padėjo   viĺkui   kójas
    He helped   (to the) wolf   legs
                 (dat. sg.)

    ráišioti.
    to tie up.

In this sentence it is clear that the meaning is 'he helped tie up the legs of the wolf.' Note, however:

(d) padėjo   Jõnui   kójas
    He helped   Jonas   legs
                 (dat. sg.)

    ráišioti.
    to tie up.

For sentence (d) there are two possible translations, either (d.1) 'he helped Jonas tie up (somebody's) legs' or (d.2) 'he helped (somebody) tie up Jonas' legs.' Essentially one cannot tell whether the dat. sg. *Jõnui* is the object of the verb *padėjo* 'helped' or whether it denotes the possessor of *kójas* 'legs.' According to Grabauskas there is a tendency in contemporary Lithuanian for the dative of possession to oust the genitive of possession. Grabauskas seems to consider this to be an adverse tendency since it apparently adds to the possibility of confusion.

34

The Adverbal Accusative

34. Typically the accusative case is the case of the direct object of the verb. As I have pointed out in para. 29 and 32, the accusative case marker *-N has its origin in an old dative-locative or benefactive case. I refer here to Villar's, 1983, 191-196, view that the accusative marker *-m spread gradually to proper names, then to humans, then to animates and finally to a portion of the inanimates. Particularly interesting and valuable in this regard is Villar's comparison with the spread of the Spanish 'personal a,' 187-188. Before the beginning of the literary tradition the use of a as a mark of the patient had been firmly established with proper nouns denoting a person. The a was sometimes omitted if the patient followed the verb, i.e., in the unmarked SVO order. In the *Mio Cid* the personal a was not used to express the patient relationship with common personal nouns if the order was SVO. On the other hand with other word order possibilities which do not clarify the role of agent and patient the personal a was obligatory. Personal a was not used with generic significance. Although personal a was not originally used with other animate nouns, Cervantes used it in *Don Quixote* with a certain frequency. With words denoting inanimate objects the preposition was not used.

In more modern times the personal a spread to domestic animals, higher animals and to those which are highly individualized. The personal a was still not used with inanimate nouns.

In the most recent times, however, the use of personal *a* has become common with animals and it is widely used with words of inanimate reference in many cases depending on the simple preference of the speaker. In fn. 3, 188, Villar writes that any native speaker of Spanish can check the frequency of the use of *a* with nouns of inanimate reference. In Villar's own book one encounters such sentences as 88; '...soluciones que satisfagan por igual *a* los datos comparativos y *a* las exigencias de la tipología'; and, 110, 'ningún rasgo morfológico diferencia *a* los géneros.' (See 29.51 and 32.)

34.1 Klein, 1653, 156-157, writes that verbs denoting an action, as in Latin, require the accusative case, e.g., verbs of helping, exhortation, requesting, asking, having, following, finding, etc. Examples (Mažvydas' Catechism):

(a) (36, 5) iuss turit   Pana   Dangui.
              you have a   Lord   in heaven.
                           (acc.)

(b) (11, 8) Balsus   tus   iusu   ssmaniu
              Voices   those (of)   your   people

       ischgirskiet.
       hear.
'Hear those voices of your people.'

34.11 The so-called 'cognate accusative' with intransitive verbs is encountered (Klein, 1653, 157):

(a)   miegmi   géra   miega.
      I sleep a   good   sleep.
                             (acc. sg.)

(b)   eimi   géra   kela.
      I am going (on the)   good   path.
                                    (acc. sg.)

Klein remarks that the instrumental case could also be used here and gives the example:

(c)   geru   / teisu   kelu   eiti.
      on the good   just   path   to walk.
                                (inst. sg.)

'To walk on the good/just path.' The 'cognate accusative' usage is known in modern Lithuanian also, e.g., (d) *šókti šóki* 'to dance a dance,' (e) *keliáuti kẽlią* 'to travel a road,' etc. (Acad. Gram., Vol. 3, 41). Fraenkel, 1928, 147, points out that if we understand *kẽlią* simply as a component of the activity of going, we have an accusative of content, whereas if we understand *kẽlią* as a specific road, then it is an accusative of spatial relationship. Fraenkel, 1928, 148, writes that the noun *kar̃tas* 'time, event' originally denoted 'chop (of an axe)' so that (f) *kir̃to tris kartùs* (acc. pl.) originally meant 'chopped three chops' cf. the zero-grade ablaut in the verb *kir̃t-o* [< *kr̥t-] and the *-o-grade in the noun *kart-ùs* [< *kort-]. Thus the originally cognate accusative came to be interpreted as an accusative of time.

34.2 A simple verb which does not ordinarily govern the accusative may, when prefixed, take an accusative object. Thus *ieškóti* ordinarily governs the genitive case, e.g., (a) *ieškójau kepùrės* (gen.) 'I hunted for my cap' as opposed to (b) *apieškóti namùs* (acc.) 'to search the house.' Under ordinary circumstances the verbs *áugti* 'to grow,' *brìsti* 'to wade' and *gulė́ti* 'to lie' are intransitive but note the following expressions: (c) *pér-augti tė́vą* (acc.) 'to outgrow father,' (d) *iš-brìsti batùs* (acc.) 'to get (one's) shoes soaked by wading,' (e) *nugulė́ti rañką* (acc.) 'to put one's arm to sleep (i.e., cut off the circulation in the arm)' (Acad. Gram., Vol. 3, 41.) The increase in transitivity occasioned by the addition of the prefix makes the accusative case possible in these circumstances.

34.21 The verb *tikė́ti* 'to believe (in)' can govern the accusative case (Mažvydas' Catechism):

(a) (22, 10) Tikiu   greku
              I believe   of sins

atleidima.
forgiveness.
(acc.)

'I believe in the forgiveness of sins.' According to Fraenkel, 1947, 76, the Polonism *tikė́ti į̃ ką̃* 'to believe in something' is common in Pietkiewicz' Catechism. In modern Lithuanian (b) *tikė́ti Diẽvą* and (c) *tikė́ti į̃ Diẽvą* 'to believe in God' are both possible. It is attested in Mažvydas' Catechism:

(d) (22, 5)   Tikiu   ingi   dwase
              I believe   in   spirit
                                   (acc.)

            schwentąge.
            holy.
'I believe in the holy spirit.' The verb is also construed with the instrumental:

(e) (22, 7) Tikiu   surynkimu
             I believe   in the assembly
                           (inst.)

            schwentu   kriksczianiu.
            holy   of Christians.
'I believe in the holy assembly of Christians.' The dative is also encountered:

(f) (27, 11) Kas   tems   żadems
             Whoever   these   words
                                     (dat. pl.)

            taip   tik.
            so   believes.
'Whoever so believes these words' (see 32b and e). Modern Lithuanian shows a similar distribution:

(g) Nètikiu   sàvo   ausimìs.
     I don't believe   my   ears.
                                   (inst. pl.)

(h) Netikėk   nè   vienám
     Don't believe   not even one
                                   (dat. sg.)

     jõ   zõdžiui.
     his   word.
             (dat. sg.)
'Don't believe a single word of his' (Kruopas, 1972, 849). Šukys, 1978, 39, advises the construction with the accusative or instrumental rather than the construction with *į* plus the accusative. See also 41.10h.

34.22 The verb *liẽpti* 'to order, to command' may govern the accusative case of the person, cf. Bretkūnas' Postilla I, 83:

(a) liepe   jos   buti   linksmos
    commanded   them   to be   of happy
                  (acc. pl.)   (gen. sg.)

    schirdies.
    heart.
    (gen. sg.)

(Fraenkel, 1928, 108; Acad. Dict., Vol. 7, 430.) The dative of the person commanded is also encountered:

(b) ... ką   jám   prõtas
        what   him   mind
        (acc. sg.) (dat. sg.)

    ir   širdìs   liẽpia.
    and   heart   command.
'...what mind and heart command him...' (Acad. Dict., Vol. 7, 430).

34.3 According to the Acad. Gram. (Vol. 3, 37) only in rare cases do passive participles which denote a secondary action govern the accusative case.

(a) Niaũzgia   kaĩp   kãtinas   úodegą
    caterwauls   like   cat   tail
                            (nom.)   (acc.)

    láužomas.
    being twisted.
    (nom. sg. pres. psv. prt.)
'(He) is caterwauling like a cat whose tail is being twisted.'

(b) Šìrdį   sópamas   palikaũ   sàvo
    heart   aching   I left   my
    (acc.)   (nom. sg. pres.
                   psv. prt.)

    tėvỹnę.
    fatherland.
'(With) aching heart I left my fatherland.'[12]

34.4 The verb *skelėti* 'to owe' requires the accusative case of the thing owed, cf. Mažvydas Catechism 32, 17-18:

(a) Attadokiet   tadrin   wissems   ką
     Give   therefore   to all   what
                                              (acc.)

   skielat.
   you owe.

On analogy with such verbal constructions an accusative is used with *skolìngas* 'indebted, owing,' *kaĺtas* 'guilty, responsible; indebted' (Fraenkel, 1928, 149-150). Cf. Chyliński's Bible:

(b) (40, 23) užmokiek   mi   ką   essi
              pay   me   what   you are
                                     (acc.)

   kaltas.
   indebted.

34.5 The accusative case may be used in certain constructions in which the governing verb is omitted. Thus the expressions *labą dienq* 'good day,' *labą rýtą* 'good morning,' *labą nãkti̧* 'good night' are all in the accusative case.

34.6 The double accusative is encountered with causative verbs, e.g., (Vilentas' Catechism):

(a) (11, 2) kaipo   anus   Hukinikas
             how   them   father of a
                        (acc. pl.)   household

   Scheimina   ir   waikus
   to his household   and   children
   (acc. sg.)   (acc. pl.)

   sawa...   tur   mokinti.
   his...   should   teach.

'How a father of a household should teach them to his household and his children' (Ford, 1969, 122). According to Palionis, 1967, 161, the double accusative is particularly common in 16th and 17th century documents with verbs of making, especially (*pa-*)*darýti* 'to make' (Mažvydas' Catechism):

(b) (78, 10) Ir   kuns   ... Kaltus
              And   body   ... guilty
                                       (acc.)

       mus   nepadaritu.
       us   may not make.
       (acc. pl.)

'And may (our) body not make us guilty.' The double accusative is also commonly encountered with verbs denoting 'to name, to give a name to' (Bretkūnas' Postilla II):

(c) (234, 3-4) ape   schi   Jana,   kuri
                about   this   John,   whom
                                          (acc. sg.)

       wadinam   krikschtitoghi.
       we call   the Baptist.
                  (acc. sg.)

See also 17p-t.

34.7 Palionis, 1967, 161-162, writes that in 16th and 17th century documents the direct object of negated verbs was frequently accusative rather than genitive (especially in the works of East Prussian authors), cf. Bretkūnas' Bible:

(a) (Genesis 37, 22)   nedeket   ranką
                       Lay not   a hand
                                     (acc. sg.)

       ant   io.
       upon   him.

(b) (Genesis 14, 23)   nei   siulą
                       neither   thread
                                     (acc. sg.)

       nei   kurpių   dirsą   neimsiu.
       nor   shoe   lace   I will not take.
                        (acc. sg.)

'I will take neither thread nor shoelace.' Musteikis, 1972, 50, writes that in Russian the accusative object

237

of a negated verb is common, but in Lithuanian such usage is rather rarely encountered.

(c) Tõdėl   nerãgina   šẽšuras
    Therefore does not press father-in-law

    martẽlę   grį̃žti   į̃ vidų̃.
    daughter-in-law   to return   to the house.
    (acc. sg.)

'Therefore the father-in-law does not press the daughter-in-law to return to the house.' The Russian counterpart, however, would not have the genitive object either: *Poètomu ne toropit svekor nevestku vernut'sja domoj.*

According to the Academy Grammar (Vol. 1, 187) in contemporary standard Lithuanian the direct object of a negated verb is always in the genitive case, but in Samogitian and in southwestern High Lithuanian dialects the accusative is sometimes encountered. Cf. the following examples from Donelaitis' Seasons:

(d) Nemùšk   be   reikalo   kuiną
    Don't beat   without   purpose   the old nag.
                                     (acc. sg.)

'Don't beat the horse uselessly.'

(e) Àš,   dar   tokias   biaurybes
    I,   still   such   disgusting things
                           (acc. pl.)

    kol   gyvs   neregėjęs...
    while   living   not having seen...

'I, still not having seen such disgusting things during my lifetime...' Still the accusative direct object of a negated verb is encountered in Mažvydas' Catechism:

(f) (8, 18) Jei   bralei   seseris   tus
            If   brothers   sisters   these

    ssadzius   nepapeiksit.
    words   you will not scorn.
    (acc. pl.)

'If you brothers and sisters will not scorn these words.' According to the Acad. Gram. (Vol. 1, 187) the genitive case is usually used as the object of an infinitive which is in turn the object of a negated verb (see 30.31). On the other hand the accusative is also encountered under such circumstances, cf. the example from Donelaitis' Seasons:

(g) Viežlybus   lietuvininkus   išpeikt
    respectable   Lithuanians   to defame
                   (acc. pl.)

    nesigėdi...
    is not ashamed...
'...is not ashamed to defame respectable Lithuanians.'
Cf. also from Mažvydas' Catechism:

(h) (30, 8) idanti   negaletu   ne   wenas
             so that   can (not)   not   one

    ius   kaltinti.
    them   to blame.
    (acc. pl.)
'...so that no one can blame them.'

34.8 According to the Acad. Gram. (Vol. 3, 42), certain prefixed verbs of motion may be used either with an accusative direct object or with a preposition requiring the accusative with no difference in meaning. (a) *apeĩti* (*apiẽ*) *nãmą* (acc. sg.) 'to go around the house,' (b) *pėreiti* (*peř*) *kẽlią* (acc. sg.) 'to go across the road, to cross the road.'

34.81 According to Fraenkel, 1928, 164, relatively few examples of the accusative of direction are attested in Lithuanian. He gives the following example from a folk song:

(a) upitela   ežerelį   tek.
    river   into the lake   flows.
                 (acc.)
'The river flows into the lake.' He writes also that certainly the accusative of direction is at the basis of the expression (b) *bitès* (acc. pl.) *kôpti* 'to take honey from the bee-hives.' Since this expression means literally 'to climb bees' one could understand it as having the meaning, 'to climb to the bees.'
    Eckert, 1981, 32, 51-52, has noted the cognate Latvian expression (c) *bites* (acc. pl.) *kâpt* and, 7, similar

expressions in the Slavic languages: 16th century
Pol. (d) *pszczoły* (acc. pl.) *łażbić*, Russ. (Dal') (e)
lazit' pčel (gen. pl. [animate, replacing acc.]). The
Lithuanian expression can be passivized, e.g., (f) *Jų̃
bìtès dár nekõptos* '(literally) their bees have not been
climbed (up to), i.e., honey has not yet been taken from
their beehives' which could be exactly translated with a
Russian passive also, viz., (g) *Ix pčëly ešče ne lažený*.
Eckert, 8, notes that such passive expressions [(h)
nelažený pčely] are known already in the Old Russian
Law Code. According to Eckert, 52, 75 (fn. 1), the
combination of the word denoting 'to climb' plus an
accusative of the word for 'bee' is a linguistic fossil
reflecting earlier syntactic possibilities, i.e., the
use of an intransitive verb of motion with an accusative
of direction. Eckert points out further how the Old
Lithuanian expression has been adapted to a more contemporary syntax in such phrases as (i) *Šiañdien bùs
gerà dienà bìtèms* (dat. pl.) *kõpti* 'today will be a
good day to get honey' (Acad. Dict., Vol. 7, 992; note
the dative of goal, see 32.31); and (k) *Eĩna bìčių*
(gen. pl.) *kopinė́ti* (iterat.) 'goes to take away the
honey' (see 30.42).

34.82 The accusative object is used with *eĩti* 'to go'
in certain fixed expressions which may reflect an
earlier accusative of direction, cf., *eĩti mókslus*
(acc. pl.) 'to study' (*mókslas* 'science, study') *eĩti
páreigas* (acc. pl.) 'to fulfill one's obligations,'
eĩti dárbą (acc. sg.) 'to do one's work, to work,' *eĩti
baũdžiavą* (acc. sg.) 'to work as a serf, to fulfill one's
obligations working as a serf,' *eĩti tarnýbą* 'to do
service.'

The Independent Accusative

35. The accusative to denote a point in time is attested in Mažvydas' Catechism (a) (21, 15) *trete diena* (acc. sg.) 'on the third day'; (b) (54, 17) *kiek wiena cziesa* (acc. sg.) 'every single time.' The accusative may also denote extent of time, cf. Mažvydas' Catechism:

(c) (9, 5) Diena   ir   nakti
          Day   and   night
          (acc.)   (acc.)

          preg   sawęs   mani
          before   yourself   me

          laikikiet (corrected from laitikiet).
          hold.

'Hold me before yourself day and night.' The accusative may denote a time during the course of which something takes place, e.g., from Vilentas' Catechism, (d) (35, 6) *Ritameta* (acc.) *ir Wakara* (acc.) *žegnotisi* 'to bless themselves morning and evening' (Ford, 1969, 122). Klein, 1653, 162, writes that nouns of time are to be used in the accusative case as an answer to the question 'how long?' and gives examples such as (e) *tris metus* (acc. pl.) 'three years,' (f) *tris mėnessis* (acc. pl.) 'three months,' (g) *tris dienas* (acc. pl.) 'three days.' He writes further that the accusative case is to be used as an answer to the question 'when?' and gives the example: (h) *kada swečias tawessp atėjo?* 'when did the guest come to you?' with the answers (i) *szę diena* (acc.) 'this day, today,' (j) *szį mėta* 'this year.' According to the Acad. Gram., Vol. 3, 43, the accusative case may denote the duration of an action or the duration of the result of the action, cf. (k) *ėjo* (imperfective) *vãlandą* (acc.) 'he was going for an hour' with (1) *išėjo* (perfective) *vãlandą* 'he went out for an hour.' The accusative in this function is being replaced by the dative (Ružė, 1969, 100-101).

(m) Výrai   išeĩna   į̃
    The men   are going out   into

    píevas   saváitei.
    the meadows   for a week.
                    (dat. sg.)

(See para. 33.3.) With certain pronouns such as *kàs*, *kiekvíenas* 'each,' *keliñtas* 'which' the accusative can denote repetition, e.g., (n) *kàs diẽną* 'every day,' (o) *kiekvíeną sekmãdienį* 'every Sunday.'

35.1 The accusative to denote extent of space is encountered in Chyliński's Bible:

(a) (13, 12-13) Jeygu   teypag   kas
                 If   thus   someone

      werstu   tawe   eyt   mylia
      would force   you   to go   a mile
                                             (acc. sg.)

      eyk   su   jo   dwi   (mili [acc. dual]).
      go   with   him   two   miles.

242

The Instrumental

36. The instrumental of means develops from the sociative instrumental. Note the examples from Mažvydas' Catechism:

(a) (55, 1) Apgink tu mus tawa
           Protect you us with your

   rąka.
   hand.
   (inst.)
'Protect us with your hand.'

(b) (8, 8-9) Regiety   to   nareia
             to see   it   (they) wanted

   sawa   akimis   Taipyr   ischgirsti
   with their   eyes   and also   to hear
                (inst.)

   sawa   ausimis.
   with their   ears.
                (inst.)
'They wanted to see it with their eyes and also to hear it with their ears.'

(c) (55, 16) Sawa   smerti
             with your   death
                         (inst.)

   ischwadawai...
   you liberated...

(d) (66, 20)   Dwase   schwenta   tu
               With Spirit   Holy   you
               (inst.)

   papildik.
   fill.
'Fill it with the Holy Spirit.'

(e) (77, 12)   Ir   tu   penukslu
               And   with that   with nourishment

   dusche   papeneiei.
   soul   have nourished.
'And you have nourished your soul with nourishment.'

   Differently from standard Russian the instrumental of means may or may not be accompanied by the preposition *su* 'with' in Lithuanian, e.g., (f) *válgo (sù) šáukštu* (inst.) 'eats with a spoon' (= Russ. (g) *est ložkoj*), (h) *siùva (sù) ãdata* (inst.) 'sews with a needle' (= Russ. (i) *š'ět igolkoj*; Musteikis, 1972, 55).[13]

36.1 Certain verbs require an object in the instrumental case in modern Lithuanian (Acad. Gram., Vol. 3, 50-55).

(a) Tėvaĩ   didžiúojas   sãvo
    The parents   boast about   their

   sūnumĩ.
   son.
   (inst. sg.)

(b) Visà   prigimtìs   linksmìnosi,   tarýtum ...
    All   nature   rejoiced,   as if

   džiaũgėsi   pavãsario   grožýbėmis.
   it was rejoicing   at spring's   beauties.
                                        (inst. pl.)

   Some of these verbs can be used with almost the same meaning with a preposition plus case construction instead of the simple case construction: (c) *abejója vìskuo* (inst.) 'doubts everything' or (d) *abejója dė̃l vìsko* (gen.) 'doubts about everything'; (e) *gúodžiasi sãvo neláimėmis* (inst. pl.) 'complains about his misfortunes' or (f) *gúodžiasi dė̃l sãvo neláimių* (gen. pl.) 'id' (see 34.21e and g).

When certain verbs are prefixed the syntactic relationships are changed:

(g) kráuna   valgiùs   ant   stãlo.
      piles   food   on   the table.
                 (acc. pl.)   (gen.)

But

(h) ap-króvė   stãlą   vaĩgiais
      piled   the table   with food.
                  (acc.)   (inst. pl.)

(i) stãto   butè   baldùs
      puts   in the apartment   furniture.
                                     (acc. pl.)
'Puts furniture in the apartment.'   But

(j) ap-stãtė   bùtą   baldais
      outfitted   the apartment   with furniture.
                                        (inst. pl.)

(k) stãto   gubàs   dirvoje.
      sets up   shocks (of grain)   in the field.
                  (acc. pl.)

(l) nu-stãtė   dirvą   gubomìs
      filled up   the field   with shocks (of grain).
                              (inst. pl.)

(m) verčia   šiẽną   į   klojimą.
       throws   hay   into   the barn.
                (acc.)

(n) ùž-vertė   klojimą   šienù.
      filled up   the barn   with hay.
                              (inst.)

The prefixes *ap-*, *nu-* and *už-* denote the completeness of an action in the examples given above.

Klein, 1653, 159, writes that certain reflexive verbs are used with the ablative (i.e., instrumental), e.g., (o) *Diewu* (inst.) *nusitikiu* 'I confide in God,' (p) *ramčiu* (inst.) *pasiremti* 'to support oneself with a stick,' although the preposition *ant* with the genitive could also be used, thus (q) *ant Diewo nusitikieti* 'to confide in God,' (r) *ant ramčio pasiremti* 'to support oneself on a stick.' [14]

The instrumental is used to denote the means with which the action is performed and the object of the action. The instrumental frequently has this meaning when used with iterative, transitive verbs denoting actions susceptible to sight or hearing.

(s) Jı̀s   trỹpė   kójomis,   mojãvo
    He   stamped   (his) feet,   waved
                        (inst.)

rañkomis.
(his) hands.
(inst.)

Some verbs of this group may be used either with an instrumental or an accusative complement. (t) *suskaṁbino rãktais* (inst.) or *raktùs* (acc.) 'jingled the keys,' (u) *trinktelėjo dùrimis* (inst.) or *durìs* (acc.) 'banged the doors,' (v) *sùmušė kulnimìs* (inst.) or *kulnìs* 'beat (his) heels,' (w) *vizgina úodega* (inst.) or *úodegą* 'wags (his) tail.'

The same phenomenon is observed with verbs denoting 'to wear.' E.g., (x) *avėti bãtais* (inst.) or *batùs* (acc.) 'to wear shoes,' (y) *aũtis bãtais* or *batùs* 'to put on (to take off) shoes.'

36.2 The following examples of the instrumental of manner come from Mažvydas' Catechism:

(a) (34, 12) Schytogi   budu   materis
             In this   manner   wives
                           (inst.)

padotas   bukiet   wijramus.
subject   be   to husbands.
'In this manner you wives be subject to (your) husbands.' (b) (8, 7) *ne wenu budu* (inst.) 'in any way.'

(c) (11, 15) Plebanus   kunigus   wenu
             Pastors   priests   with one

>   balsu   praschiikiet.
>   voice   ask.
>   (inst.)

'Ask pastors and priests with one voice.'

A common use of the instrumental of manner in modern Lithuanian is with a substantive in the instrumental cognate with the verb, e.g., (d) *miẽga kíetu miegù* (inst.) 'sleeps a deep sleep,' (e) *risnója smùlkia ristelè* 'trots at a jog-trot' (Acad. Gram., Vol. 3, 57). Klein, 1653, 159, gives the example: (f) *džaugiesi didžiu džaugsmu* (inst.) '(they) rejoiced with great joy.' Sometimes the cognate instrumental is used without a modifying adjective: (g) *Tėvaĩ džiaugsmù* (inst.) *džiaũgèsi* 'the parents rejoiced joyously' (Acad. Gram., Col. 3, 57).

The preposition *su* 'with' may be used or omitted with no difference of meaning in some constructions of the instrumental of manner, e.g., (h) *dìrbo (su) nematýtu užsidegimù* 'worked with unusual enthusiasm.' (i) *kovójo (su) vienódu inirtimù* 'fought with equal fury' (Acad. Gram., Vol. 3, 57). From Mažvydas' Catechism cf. (j) (35, 7) *niekakiu baisumu* (inst.) 'with no fear' but (k) (8, 14) *su džiauksmu* 'with joy.'

36.3 The instrumental of manner can easily be reinterpreted as an instrumental of cause.

>   (a)   Skausmù   iř   ãpmaudu   jõs
>   With pain   and   annoyance   her
>   (inst.)   (inst.)
>
>   kaktà   nuraũdo.
>   forehead   became red.
>
>   (b)   Kuonè   badù   jaũ
>   Almost   with hunger   already
>   (inst.)
>
>   mirštam...
>   we are dying.

'We are almost dying with hunger...' According to the Acad. Gram., Vol. 3, 67, sequences with the instrumental of cause are unproductive and rarely used. In the literary language the cause of the action is more commonly expressed by a preposition such as *iš*, *nuõ* 'from,' *dėl* 'because of.' Thus more commonly (c) *iš skaũsmo* (gen.) 'from pain,' (d) *nuõ bãdo* (gen.) 'from hunger,' and (e) *pradžiùgo dėl mirtiẽs* (gen.) 'rejoiced because of the death' rather than (f) *pradžiùgo mirtimì* (inst.). Klein, 1654, 108, gives the example: (g) *jis baĩdos manimì* (inst.) 'he is afraid of me' and from older sources the Acad. Dict., Vol. 1, 557, quotes similar examples, although also with more modern syntax:

(h) Alkanà várna žmogaũs nesibaĩdo.
    hungry crow man doesn't fear.
                      (gen.)
'A hungry crow is not afraid of a man.'

36.4 Note the following example of an instrumental denoting a spatial relationship from Mažvydas' Catechism:

(a) (50, 12) Vesk mus kieliu
                 Lead us by the road
                          (inst.)
    teisoiu.
    right.
    (inst.)

'Lead us by the right road.' For the most part in modern Lithuanian the instrumental of spatial relationships denotes movement, although occasionally it denotes a place. Thus (b) *eĩna laukù* 'goes through the field' (although such a notion may be expressed by *peř* 'through' plus the accusative, viz. (c) *eĩna peř laũką* [acc.]; Acad. Gram., Vol. 3, 60). Sequences such as (d) *vaĩksto miškù* (inst.) 'walks about in the forest' can also be expressed by *po* plus the accusative, (e) *vaĩksto po mišką* or by the locative (f) *vaĩksto miškè* (Acad. Gram., Vol. 3, 60). Frequently direction is expressed by the instrumental:

(g) Išsiunčiau láišką tuõ pačiù
    I sent letter to that same

    ãdresu.
    address.
    (inst.)

'I sent a letter to the same address.' With a few nouns the instrumental case can denote motion through something: (h) *vanduõ nùteka grioviaĩs* (inst.) 'water flows through the ditches' (Acad. Gram., Vol. 3, 59-60).

36.5 The instrumental case may be used to denote a point in time, e.g., (a) *vidùvasariu* (inst.) *susir̃go* 'in midsummer (he) fell ill.' In this sentence one could have used the locative *vidùvasary* or the accusative *vidùvasari̧* or even the locution *per̃ vidùvasari̧* (acc.) with no difference in meaning (Acad. Gram., Vol. 3, 64).

Sometimes either the instrumental singular or plural can be used to denote a period of time with no difference in meaning, e.g., (b) *pàryčiu* (sg.) or *paryčiais* (pl.) 'early in the morning' (Acad. Gram., Vol. 3, 64).

The instrumental plural may be used with a verb denoting a repeated action.

(c) Ėdžias   véltui   Baltramiejus
    troughs   in vain   Baltramiejus

    rytais   išvalýdavo.
    in the mornings   cleaned out.
    (inst. pl.)

'In the mornings Baltramiejus cleaned out the troughs in vain' (Acad. Gram., Vol. 3, 66).

36.6 According to Fraenkel, 1926, 85, the predicate instrumental played an important role already in the older literature. In his opinion its use resembles more that of Russian than of Polish. From the earliest times the instrumental is common with such transitive verbs as *wadìnti*, *al̃góti* 'to call, to name,' *darýti* 'to make,' *laikýti* 'to consider, to hold,' *turėti* 'to have,' *pastatýti*, *padėti* 'to put, to place,' *ródyti* 'to appear,' *palìkti* 'to leave,' e.g., from Vilentas' Catechism:

(a) (42, 12)   ponu   ghy   wadindama.
               lord   him   calling.
               (inst.)

'Calling him the lord'; Vilentas' Gospel:

(b) (118, 5)   padesiu   neprietelus
               I shall make   enemies

    tawa   sũleliu   koiũ   tawa.
    your   stool   of feet   your.
               (inst.)

'I shall make your enemies your foot-stool.'

Nevertheless, the double accusative occurs, particularly in older texts, but not so commonly, e.g., Vilentas' Gospel:

(c) (123, 16) wissus   daiktus   sau
              all   things   to himself
                        (acc. pl.)

    padůtus   dara.
    subject   makes.
    (acc. pl.)

'(He) makes all things subject to himself.' The double accusative is common when the predicate adjective denotes the state in which someone considers someone else, so it is common with verbs of saying, thinking and perception.

More in competition with the predicate instrumental with verbs of naming is the nominative case, e.g., from Vilentas' Gospel (Fraenkel, 1926, 86):

(d) (54, 8) jaunikaicza   kuri   wadina
             a disciple   whom   they call
                            (acc.)

    Saulus.
    Saul.
    (nom.)

Fraenkel, 1926, 87, writes that the nominative in such instances is to be explained by the fact that the expression of the name is, so to speak, in quotation marks and replaces an entire sentence. The construction is common in other Indo-European languages also, cf. Gothic (Mark 3, 16):

(e) jah   gasatida   Seimona   namo
    and   he gave   to Simon   the name

    Paítrus.
    Peter.
    (nom.)

Even when such transitive verbs as given above are made passive-like with the reflexive particle -*si* the instrumental case remains, thus from Sirvydas' Punktay Sakimu, I, 108, 24-26:

(f) welinas   wadinasi   kunigaykściu
    the devil   is called   the prince
                                         (inst.)

    to   swieto.
    of this   world.

(Punktay sakimu, I, 39, 27-28)

(g) umżinu   esti   karalum   karunawotas.
    eternal   is   as king   crowned.
                               (inst.)

'He is crowned as eternal king.'

    The verbs *tàpti*, *stõtis*, *pastõti* 'to become' and (*pa-*)*wĩrsti* 'to be changed into' are commonly used with the instrumental. From Ledesma's Catechism:

(h) (7, 7)   esch   pastóiu   kriksczónim.
             I   become   a Christian.
                                    (inst.)

(i) (81, 18) dŭna   pawirsta
             The bread   changes into

    kunu   e   winas   krauiú.
    the body   and   the wine   into the blood.
                                         (inst.)

From Sirvydas' Punktay Sakimu:

(j) (I, 182, 4-7)   runka...,   kuri...
                     hand,   which

    raupuotu   tapo.
    leprous   became.
    (inst.)

'The hand which became leprous.'

(k) (I, 304, 28-29) auga   didžiu   ir
                       grows   large   and
                               (inst.)

    tumpa   kayp   medžiu   ssakuotu.
    becomes   like   tree   branchy.
                             (inst.)

'(It) grows large and becomes like a branchy tree' (Fraenkel, 1926, 91).

In general the adjective is rarely in the instrumental case in Lithuanian. Cf. Vilentas' Gospel (1) *esch buwau alkanas* (nom. sg. masc.) 'I was hungry' vs. (m) *esch buwau sweczu* (inst. sg. masc.) 'I was a guest' (Fraenkel, 1926, 93).

Note the examples from Mažvydas' Catechism:

(n) (47, 16) Buk   musu   tu   prawadniku.
             be   our   you   leader.
                                  (inst.)

'You be our leader.'

(o) (48, 5) Swecziu   buk   duschiasu   musu.
            guest   be   in souls   our.
            (inst.)

'Be a guest in our souls.'

Klein, 1653, 160, wrote that the substantive verb *esmi* 'I am' which usually has the nominative before and after it frequently admits the ablative (i.e., instrumental) in a certain elegant construction (*eleganti quadam constructione*) especially when the latter noun is a substantive denoting some kind of office (*officii aliquam rationem*), e.g., (p) *jis yra Karalumi/ Sudźia/ uriedniku* (inst.) 'he is a king (judge, official).' Note from Klein, 1653, 160, also:

(q) Kristus   didžáusu   budams   musu
    Christ   greatest   being   us
               (inst.)

    delei   mažu   tapo.
    for   small   became.
             (inst.)

'Christ (being) the greatest of all became small for us.'

According to Palionis, 1967, 163-164, some authors used the instrumental case to denote even the constant, unchanging state of the predicate. In some cases this may be due to Polish influence, but certainly not always. In the first place in the 16th century the Polish predicate instrumental had not yet been completely generalized and in the second place sometimes the Lithuanian predicate instrumental is used even when the Polish original has a predicate nominative. From Pietkiewicz' Catechism:

(r) (Lith.) kad esme sunumis (inst.)
    (Pol.) żesmy są synowie (nom.)
           that we are sons

    ir   dukterimis (inst.)   Diewa,   ir
    y   corki (nom.)   Boże,   a
    and   daughters   of God,   and

    tewaynimis (inst.)   karalistes...
    dziedzicy (nom.)   krolewstwa...
    heirs   of the kingdom...

(s) (Lith.) buk   pone   mano
    (Pol.) bądź (ty)   panie   ma
            be   (you)   oh Lord   my

    gineiu (inst.)
    obrona (nom.)
    defense.

(Palionis, 1967, 164; Fraenkel, 1947, 64.) In Lithuanian the predicate instrumental is encountered even in a nominal sentence, again from Pietkiewicz' Catechism:

(t) (Lith.)   wirausiu (chief)
    (Pol.)   przednie   mocny
             most   powerful

    gruntu (inst.)   Diewas
    grunt (nom.)   (iest Pan)   Bóg
    foundation   (is   Lord)   God

    musų   ir   ginklu   stipru
    nasz   y   zbroia   mocna
    our   and   armor   strong

    ginančiu (inst.)   mus.
    broniąca (nom.)   nas.
    defending   us.

'Our (Lord) is the chief foundation and strong armor defending us' (Fraenkel, 1947, 64).

Note the following contemporary examples (Acad. Gram., Vol. 3, 68-69) with instrumental complements, e.g.:

(u) Jùras pavir̃to žuvimì...
    Juras turned into a fish...
                    (inst.)

(v) ... agronomù mókosi.
    ... agronomist is studying.
        (inst.)
'He is studying to be an agronomist.'

(w) žmónės išsiriñko ... manè
    The people chose (for themselves) me
                                    (acc.)

    pirmininku.
    as chairman.
    (inst.)

(x) Ir̃ àš apsimèsdavau
    And I used to pretend to be

    vabzdžiù.
    an insect.
    (inst.)

The instrumental is particularly common with the verb *būti* 'to be' when it denotes a change of state or temporary condition.

(y) Teñ ẽsą jõ
    There, they say, he
                    (gen.)

    bū́ta generolù.
    was a general.
    (neut.sg. past (inst.)
     psv. prt.)

(z) Čià jaũ vaikù bū́damas
    Here still child being
                (inst.)

    tampì výru.
    you become a man.
                (inst.)
'Here while you are still a child you become a man.' 15

36.7 According to the Acad. Gram., Vol. 1, 205, the nominalization of a verb can be used with the instrumental case just like the verb itself, e.g., (a) *valýti ką̃ nõrs benzinù* (inst.) 'to clean something with gasoline' and *vãlymas benzinù* 'cleansing with gasoline,' (b) *váikščioti laukaĩs* 'to walk around in the fields' and *váikščiojimas laukaĩs* 'walking around in the fields.'

36.71 According to the Acad. Gram., Vol. 1, 205, in the Samogitian (Low Lithuanian) dialect and in belles-lettres the instrumental of association is used with certain adjectives derived from verbs. This instrumental denotes a person or a thing which is being carried, led, transported or dragged, e.g.:

(a) Pàts   balnù   nẽšinas   parẽjo
    himself   saddle   carrying   went
              (inst.)

    namõ.
    home.
'He himself went home carrying the saddle.'

(b) Baltarãgis,   palšiukù   vẽdinas   ẽjo
    Baltaragis,   light-grey   leading   went
                  (inst.)

    su Cinoku   gretà.
    with Cinokas   side by side.
'Baltaragis, leading the light-grey one went side by side with Cinokas.'

(c) Piemuõ   eĩna   žąsimìs   gẽninas.
    shepherd   goes   geese   driving.
                           (inst.)
'The shepherd goes, driving the geese.'

(d) Žąsiùkas   ẽjo   sparnù   velkinas.
    Gosling   went   wing   dragging.
                           (inst.)
'The gosling went, dragging its wing.'

36.8 According to Palionis, 1967, 165, from the point of view of contemporary Lithuanian the use of the instrumental with such verbs as *mėgti(s)* and *pa(si)mėgti* 'to like, to take pleasure in' seems archaic, e.g.:

(a) taip   kuns   musu   ghrekais   megsta.
    thus   body   our   sins   likes.
'Thus our body likes sins.' From Klein, 1654, 108,
note the example:

(b) Wiespats   mėkstasi   tais
    Lord   is pleased   with those
                              (inst.)

    kurie   jo   bija.
    who   him   fear.
'The Lord is pleased with those who fear him.'
    Palionis, 1967, 166, writes that the instrumental
was used sometimes in 16th and 17th century writings
with certain verbs with which it would occur today only
rarely or not at all, e.g., *áugti* 'to grow' (cf. 35.5
[k]), *atsivėsinti* 'to refresh oneself,' *nuilsti* 'to
weaken,' *patulžti* 'to become soggy,' *pažvilti* 'to bend
over,' *peikti* 'to censure,' *pripildyti* 'to fill,'
pripilti 'to pour into,' *stiprintis* 'to become strong,'
valdyti (*valdžióti*) 'to rule over,' *veldėti* 'to inherit,'
vartóti 'to use.' Examples:

(c) tur   kūpką   rankoie   pripiltą   stipru
    has   glass   in hand   filled   with strong

    winu.
    wine.
    (inst.)
'Has a glass in the hand filled with strong wine, i.e.,
into which had been poured...'

(d) alkanus   pripilde   gerays   dayktays.
    hungry   filled   with good   things.
                                        (inst.)
'Filled the hungry with good things.'

(e) kuris   waldźios   zmonemis   mano
    who   will rule   people   my
                          (inst.)

    Israelo.
    Israel.
'Who will rule my people Israel.'

(f) kántrume   iũsų   weldẽssitę   dũsziomis
    in patience   your   will gain   souls

    sawomis.
    your.
    (inst.)
'In patience you will gain your souls.'

(g) kuriẽ   geraí   wartôie   dowanomis   io.
    who   well   use   gifts   his.
'Who use his gifts well.' Palionis, 1967, 167, writes that in some cases (e.g., with *áugti*, *stìprintis* and perhaps with *pripìlti* and *pripìldyti*) the instrumental developed under Polish influence. Elsewhere, however, (e.g., with *nuĩlsti*, *patulžti*, *pažvìlti*, *valdýti*, *valdžióti*, *veldéti*, *vartóti*) the use of the instrumental may be native Lithuanian, since the originals do not show a slavish copying.

Palionis, 1967, 167, writes that occasionally in writings of the 16th and 17th centuries one encounters the instrumental with the adjectives *nèščià* 'pregnant,' *pìlnas* 'full,' *skalsùs* 'abundant,' *sunkì*, *sunkìnga* 'pregnant,' e.g., (h) *neszcia sunumi* (inst.) 'pregnant with a son':

(i) dangus   szeme   tawimi   pilni.
    heaven and   earth   with you   full.
                                (inst.)
'Heaven and earth are filled with you.' Palionis suggests that the use of various words denoting 'pregnant' with the instrumental may be under Polish influence, cf. Pol. (m) *brzemienna pierwszym synem* (inst.) 'pregnant with the first son.'

37

Simple locative

37. Typically the locative case denotes position in space or time. Palionis, 1967, 168, writes that in the 16th and 17th centuries the locative had in general the same syntactic functions as it does in modern Lithuanian. Note the examples from Mažvydas' Catechism:

(a) (23, 9) Buki   tawa   walia   kaip
                be   your   will   as

        dągui   taip   szemeie.
        in heaven   so   on earth.
        (loc. sg.)   (loc. sg.)

'Thy will be done on earth as it is in heaven.' Similarly Vilentas; Catechism (22, 4-5) has: (b) *Buk walia tawa, kaip Dangui, taip ir Szeme* (loc. sg. shortened from *szemeje*). In the year 1962 in the University of Vilnius library an even earlier manuscript text of a Lord's Prayer was found which apparently dates from the beginning of the 16th century. In this earliest text one reads: (orthography modernized here) (c) *Būki tavo valia, kaip danguj, teip žemėj* (loc. sg.). If a literal translation from Polish had been made one would expect only *ant žėmės* for 'on earth' (Salys, 1979, 147-148).

Although in Mažvydas' Catechism one finds the locative sg. forms of *dangùs* 'heaven' and *žėmė* 'earth' in the Lord's Prayer, elsewhere one encounters such expressions as (12, 12; 53, 12) *ant sweta* 'in the world,' (19, 6) *ant sžemes* 'in the world'; (21, 18) *ant dąngaus* 'in heaven' although two pages later in the first clause of the Lord's Prayer we encounter:

(d) (23, 5-6) Tewe   musu   kuris
                   Father   our   who

258

		essi	dangusu.		
		art	in heaven.		
			(loc. pl.)		

'Our Father who art in heaven...' Still the expression of the locative with *dangùs* 'heaven' seems more current than the locative with *žẽmė* 'earth.' Thus one encounters outside of the Lord's Prayer:

(e)	(73, 7-8)	Rossa	essti	Jesus	Christus,
		Rose	is	Jesus	Christ,

	lelia	esti	Maria,	abu	ssiedu	dangui
	lily	is	Mary,	both	blossoms	in heaven
						(loc. sg.)

'Jesus Christ is a rose. Mary is a lily, both are blossoms in heaven.' Note also:

(f)	(54, 5)	O	Diewe	kurss	dangui
		O	God	who	in heaven
					(loc. sg.)

		essi...
		art...

'Oh God who art in heaven...' Cf. also the use of the loc. sg. of *dangùs* 'heaven' plus the nom. sg. of the personal pronoun to form a semantic definite adjective, thus:

(g)	(48, 19)	Thiewe	musu	Danguię-s-is...
		Father	our	in heaven he...

'Our heavenly Father...' Such a construction must surely be old and it is hard to imagine how it could be transformed into a preposition plus case (genitive) construction.

The first attestation of the expression *añt žẽmės* in the Lord's Prayer comes in S. Chyliński's manuscript translation of the New Testament from 1658-59. K. Sirvydas in his *Punktay sakimu* (1629) uses the expression with the locative singular (h) *danguj ir žemėje* 'in heaven and (on) earth' side by side with the expression (i) *ant dangaus ir ant žemės* (not, however, in the Lord's Prayer). The 18th century Lord's Prayers with all their Polonisms remained right up until the the First World War. The conservative ecclesiastical administration, burdened by Polish tradition did not undertake any reforms. But in 1916 Bishop Pr. Karevičius, who was very pro-Lithuanian, chiefly on the advice of J. Jablonskis gave his approval to the new texts of the Lord's Prayer which contained the expression with the locative žẽmėje rather than the preposition plus case expression añt žẽmės. In 1918 Lithuanian churches were instructed to adopt the locative construction but seven years later (1924) the bishops' conference returned the old preposition plus case construction. In the ritual book (1966) and the liturgical prayer book (1968) published in Vilnius (both of which were approved by the Vatican) we find the phrase: (j) *Teesie Tavo valia, kaip danguje* (loc.) *taip ir žemėje* (loc.). On the other hand the emigré groups tend to hold on to the Polonized *ant žẽmės* (= Pol. *na ziemi*; Salys, 1979, 148-149). Apparently there is an attempt to maintain the difference between the locative notions of on (earth) and in (heaven). One can compare Gk. (Matthew 6, 10) (k) *en ouranȭ kaì epì tễs gễs* 'in heaven and on earth' and German (Luther) (1) *auf Erden wie im Himmel* 'on earth as *in* heaven.' The Gothic version makes the same distinction: (m) *swe in himina jah ana airþai* (Streitberg, 1919, 7).

Although the Old Church Slavic New Testament was obviously translated from Greek the distinction between *in* (*en*) and *on* (*epí*) is apparently not made: in both codices Zographensis and Marianus (Matthew 6, 10) we encounter (n) *na nebesi i na zem(l)i* 'in (on) heaven and on earth.' The Armenian version was apparently translated from Greek (Metzger, 1977, 165), but in the Lord's Prayer the preposition *i* (*y-* in prevocalic position) plus a locative case translates both *in* and *on*: (o) *orpēs y-erkins* (loc. pl.) *ev y-erkri* (loc. sg.) 'both in heaven and on (in) earth' (Jensen, 1964, 12).

According to the Acad. Gram., Vol. 3, 81, in certain expressions denoting spatial position the preposition *añt* plus genitive construction can be replaced by the locative case, (p) *áuga añt kálno* or *kalnè* 'grows on the hill,' (see 41.1 [n]) (q) *gyvẽna añt krañto* or *krantè* 'lives on the bank,' (r) *stóvi añt kẽlio* or *kelyjè* 'stands in the road,' (s) *žiba añt dangaũs* or *dangujè* 'twinkles in the sky,' (t) *supùvo añt laukų̃* or *laukuosè* 'rotted in the fields,' (u) *sėdi añt vežimo* or *vežimè* 'sits in the wagon,' (v) *miẽga añt šiaudų̃* or *šiauduosè* 'sleeps in the straw,' (w) *rãšo añt lentõs* or *lentojè* 'writes on the board.'

The feeling for the differences between the preposition plus the genitive and locative constructions is, apparently quite individual, however. Professor Antanas Klimas of the University of Rochester writes (personal letter) that for him not all of the cases given by the Academy Grammar are, indeed, synonymous. Thus for him *añt kálno* would mean the area beyond the ridge of the hill, whereas *kalnè* means on the very slope or inclination of the hill. The expression *sėdi vežimè* means 'sits (down) in the wagon' whereas *sėdi añt vežimo* means 'sits on top of the wagon.' The expression *miẽga añt šiaudų̃* means 'sleeps on (top of) the straw,' whereas the expression *miẽga šiauduosè* means 'sleeps in the straw.' For him the other expressions mentioned in the preceding paragraph are synonymous, however. In the choice of the syntactic means of expression (either *añt* plus genitive, or locative) we are in one of those gray areas, where native speakers may have slightly different feelings for their language.

Fraenkel, 1928, 209, writes that the expression denoting 'in heaven' is frequently expressed by just the locative case (standardized orthography) *dangujè*, whereas the expression on the earth is prepositional (standardized) *añt žẽmės*.

The earliest and most natural usage for the Lithuanian language is to use the locative constructions *dangujè* 'in heaven' and *žẽmėje* 'on earth.' As a result of the Polish influence, however, the *añt* 'on' plus genitive case construction was introduced.

There emerged an incipient tendency to consider heaven as three-dimensional and to use the locative expression *dangujè* 'in heaven' as opposed to the preposition plus case construction *añt žẽmės* 'on earth' which is considered two-dimensional. This incipient distinction, however, never gained sufficient impetus to be felt by most native speakers of Lithuanian.

37.1 Palionis, 1967, 168, remarks that the chief difference between the modern and the older use of the locative is that in certain functions (e.g., the locative of time) it was more widely used than it is today. Note the examples from Mažvydas' Catechism:

(a) (26, 3) schitage   nakteie,   kuria
            on that   night   on which
                         (loc.)   (loc.)

```
          tureia      buti        ischdotas...
          he was      to be       betrayed.
```

(b) (72, 2) *dienasu* (loc. pl.) *Christaus vszgimima* 'on the days of Christ's birth,' (c) (79, 22) *Metusu* (loc. pl.) *ijr dienagi* (loc. sg.) 'in the year and on the day.' Palionis remarks further that at that time it was particularly common to use the locative with nouns which denote a definite period of time (day, year, night, hour) and that the locative did not only denote a specific moment when something took place, but rather a longer period of time during the course of which something happens repeatedly. (The preceding examples from Mažvydas do not illustrate the notion of repetition of the action.) In contemporary Lithuanian it is more common to denote the point of time with the accusative and the repeated action with the instrumental or with the preposition *per̃* plus the accusative. Klein, 1653, 162, writes that nouns for time are put in the locative case when they denote 'the category of time rather than the duration' (*cum speciem magis significant, quam durationem*) and gives the examples:

```
    (d)  źiemoj'       suszal       wandů.
         in winter     freezes      water.
         (loc.)
'Water freezes in winter.'

    (e)  szwentoj      dienoje      reik
         on the holy   day          it is necessary
                       (loc.)

         bažnyčiona    eiti.
         to church     to go.
         (ill.)
```
'It is necessary to go to church on the holy day.'

37.2 Palionis, 1967, 169, writes that it is difficult to say to what degree other languages have influenced the use of the locative in Lithuanian in the writings of the 16th and 17th centuries. There are frequent translation constructions, cf. from Bretkūnas' Bible (I Kings 6, 12):

(a) ... tu   mana   prisakimosu
          you   in my   commandments
                            (loc. pl.)

    waikschczosi...
    will walk...
'You will walk in my commandments.' Cf. Luther's Bible *in meinen Geboten* 'in my commandments.' From Punktay sakimu II, 132, 11-12:

(b) (Lith.)   kokiey   mokslay   ažusirakina
    (Pol.)   iakie   nauki   zamykaią się
              which   doctrines   are included

          tuose   żodżiose.
    w   tych   słowiech.
    in   these   words.
                    (loc. pl.)

37.3 According to Fraenkel, 1928, 216-217, the shift of the use of the locative as a case denoting position to that of object of motion is conditioned by its use with verbs denoting 'to sit, to place, to lay, to hang, to enter, etc.' Thus, from Mažvydas' Hymns (Gerullis, 1923, 444):

(a) Pona   dangaus   pagulde: Nauyeme
    Lord   of heaven   they lay   in a new

    akmens   grabe.
    stone   grave.
              (loc.)

'They lay the lord of heaven in a new stone grave.'

(b) (Chyliński's Bible, 98, 58)   padejo   ghi
                                   put   him

    prakarte.
    in a manger.
    (loc.)

Fraenkel, 1928, 217, writes that contemporary usage would be *pagulde jį̃ į̃ prãkartą* (acc.), but the Bible Society translation has the loc. *prakartè* (Luke 2, 7,).

37.31 According to Fraenkel, 1928, 218, the use of the locative with verbs denoting 'to heap together, to include, to come together, to hide' furnishes the transition between the locative denoting place and that denoting the direction. He gives the example from Pietkiewicz' Catechism:

(a) (Psalm 143, 3) duszią   mano   ... támsioy
                    soul   my   in a dark

   lindiney   užudáręs   troszkin...
   cave   having enclosed   chokes...
'(my enemy) chokes my soul having enclosed (it) in a dark cave.'

37.32 Fraenkel, 1928, 219, suggests that the locative case can be used as the indirect object of *dúoti* 'to give' and gives the following example from Mažvydas' Catechism:

(a) (47, 7) Dok   malane   szmanesu.
             Give   grace   to men.

Ford, 1971, 63, translates *szmanesu* as 'among men,' and probably Ford's translation is to be preferred. Fraenkel gives the following example from the Margarita Theologica:

(b) Tewuie   pridůdamas   jra
    To the father   attributed   is
    (loc.)

    sutwerimas.
    creation.
'The creation is attributed to the Father.'

Illative

38. According to the Acad. Gram., Vol. 1, 207, the illative as a living case is known today in a part of the Eastern High Lithuanian puntininkai dialect area, in the eastern and western Dzukish area, in certain neighboring central dialects and in the Belorussian Gervėčiai, Lazūnai and Zietela dialects. Certain fossilized forms are still used in the Eastern High Lithuanian pantininkai dialect, and around Pasvalỹs (in a transitional pontininkai-puntininkai dialect the illative singular is commonly used, but the plural is usually replaced by some other means of expression.) In those dialects in which the illative has disappeared as an independent case (Samogitian, Western High Lithuanian and almost all of Central High Lithuanian) the functions of the illative are replaced by the preposition $į$ 'to, into' plus the accusative. This latter means is commonly used in the standard language, although the illative is encountered in the works of many Lithuanian writers, some of whom do not use it consistently but alternate it with the $į$ plus accusative construction.

38.1 Note the following examples from Mažvydas' Catechism:

(a) (11, 13) baszniczian   waiksczati
             to church   to go
             (ill.)

   prisakikiet.
   order.
'Order (them) to go to church.'

(b) (12, 9) Delto   rąkasn   schitą
             Therefore into hands   this
                        (ill. pl.)

   maksla   trumpa   imkiet.
   doctrine   short   take.

'Therefore take this short doctrine into your hands.'
But Mažvydas' Catechism shows the preposition *į* plus
accusative in the same meaning, see 41.10. Examples of
the illative from Vilentas' Catechism: (c) (18, 4)
Nuženge peklosna (ill. pl.) 'descended into hell.'

(d) (50, 8) Tada   asch   yus
             So   I   them

   Wenczawonisten   sudŭmi.
   in matrimony   I join.
   (ill.)

'So I join them in matrimony' (Ford, 1969, 125).

38.2 Klein, 1653, 161, writes that the notion 'to a
place' can be expressed either by 'separable' or
'inseparable' prepositions. By the 'inseparable' preposition he means the illative (and allative) cases and
gives the illative examples (a) *miestana* or *miestan'*
'to the city,' (b) *bažnyciona* or *bazýncion* (for
bažnycion) 'to the church.' By the 'separable'
preposition he means *ing* 'in, to' plus the
accusative, e.g., (c) *eimi ing Karalauczu* 'I am going
to Karaliaučius (Königsberg, Regiomons).' He writes,
however, that it is more elegant (*Elegantius*) when the
'inseparable' prepositions (i.e., illative case forms)
are used (see 41.10).

38.3 According to the Acad. Gram., Vol. 1, 208, the
illative may denote the approximate or approaching time
of an event, e.g., (a) *Vãkaran* (ill.) *kùria pirti*
'Towards evening they heat up the bathhouse.' In the
western Dzukish dialect where the illative is more commonly used it denotes the time during which an event
takes place (i.e., it replaces the simple locative of
the standard language), e.g.:

   (b) Keturiólika   tẽliu   pardavė
        fourteen   calves   sold

šeštādienin.
on Saturday.
(ill.)
'He sold fourteen calves on Saturday.'

38.4 The illative is occasionally used to denote the manner in which an action takes place. From Mažvydas' Catechism:

(a) (24, 11) Vardana   Tiewa
             In the name of the Father
             (ill.)

ir   Suunaus   ir   Dwases   schwentases.
and   Son   and   Ghost   Holy.

'In the name of the Father, Son and Holy Ghost.' The Acad. Gram., Vol. 1, 208, gives the example:

(b) Varlės   vienañ   balsañ
    The frogs   with one   voice
                             (ill.)

    kurkia.
    croak.

38.5 Zinkevičius, 1982, 26, writes that in southern High Lithuanian the inessive (simple locative) and the illative have merged completely. In the singular the form of the illative is retained, but in the plural a form of the inessive is used, thus, (a) *ainù girion* (ill.) 'I am going (in)to the forest' and (b) *gyvenù girion* (ill.) 'I live in the forest,' (c) *vaz(i)ůoju Marcinkonýsa* (loc. pl.) 'I am traveling to Marcinkonis' and (d) *gyvenù Marcinkonýsa* (loc. pl.) 'I live in Marcinkonis.'

39

Adessive

39. According to the Acad. Gram., Vol. 1, 209, the adessive is encountered today only in those isolated dialect areas now located within the Belorussian Republic. The adessive denotes that the actor or action is in the presence of, by, or near the object which is in the adessive case. For the most part the adessive is used with forms of the verb *bū́ti* 'to be,' but it can also function with certain other verbs such as *gyvénti* 'to live,' *kláusti* 'to ask.' Dialect examples:

(a) (Lazū́nai) Kójos   kaĩp
              Legs   as

arkliep
in the possession of a horse.
(adess.)
'Legs like those of a horse.'

(b) (Gervė́čiai)   ... iř
                  ... even

šlúotak   kótas
at a broom   handle
(adess.)
yrà.
is.
'...even the broom has a handle.'

(c) (Zíetela) Svetimáip   momáip
               At somebody else's   mother
                                      (adess.)

tiesõs   nėrà.
justice   is not.

'One does not find justice with somebody else's mother.'
Note the similarity in meaning to that of Russian *u*
plus the genitive. Laigonaitė, 1957, 34, writes that
the adessive used with the verb *kláusti* corresponds to
the usage with the genitive or the accusative in the
standard language, thus *kláusia dukteriak* (adess.) =
kláusia duktefs (gen.), *dùkterį* (acc.) 'asks the
daughter.' An adverbialized adessive *namiẽpi* 'at home'
is still used in the western Dzukish territory, but
sometimes in its place an adverbialized allative *namópi*
is used with the same meaning, viz. 'at home.'

Laigonaitė, 1957, 27, says that as an independent
case the adessive had begun to disappear already in the
16th century and that this disappearance was first manifested in the confusion of the adessive plural with the
locative. This confusion is a result of the shortening
of the postposition. Once the final vowel of the postposition *-pi* was lost, the final consonant *-p* could
easily be lost since it followed immediately the consonant *-m-* as in *žmonesemp* 'among men.' Note the dialect
expressions (d) (Zíetela) *manim̃* (adess.) *niẽko nèrà* 'I
have nothing.' Cf. Russ. *u menja ničego net*.

   (e) (Lazúnai) Bóba   pasitìko   sẽnį
                     woman   met   old man

      vaf̃tuosu.
      at the gate.
      (loc. pl.)

'The woman met the old man at the gate.' From Mažvydas'
Catechism the example:

   (f) (38, 13) tatai ... pamekt   panepi
                      that   pleases   Lord
                                             (adess.)

      Diewepi.
      God.
      (adess.)

Zinkevičius, 1982, 30, notes that in Mažvydas'
writings there is only a single example of the adessive
plural:

(g) Diewas   gijmditosis   Diewas
     God   the begetter   God
                (for gijmditojis)

     gymditas,   abijusump   Dwassie
     the begotten,   in both   Spirit

     schwentoghi   Deiwistes   drauginikie.
     holy   of divinity   partner.

'God the begetter, God the begotten, in both the Holy Spirit is the partner of divinity.' Zinkevičius says that this Samogitian form is to be read *abijūsump*, the High Lithuanian correspondent of which would be **abiejuosump*.

Palionis, 1967, 170, writes that in the 16th and 17th century writings the adessive is frequently used instead of the locative and gives the example from Daukša's Postilla, (h) (115, 9) *iėszkome pàszałpos pasáulip* (adess.) 'we seek help in the world.' Sometimes the locative adjective modified the adessive noun, from Daukša's Postilla, (i) (477, 18) *ne wienamę* (loc.) *žmógup* (adess.) 'in no man,' id.:

žmonese   bediewiůsemp   ir   neysztikumůsemp.
in people   godless   and   unbelieving.
(loc.)   (adess.)   (adess.)

'In godless and unbelieving people.'

Klein, 1653, 161, gives the examples:

(j) Diewiep   newienas   dáiktas   ne
     for God   not one   thing   not
     (adess.)

     esti   negálimas.
     is   impossible.

'For God nothing is impossible'; (k) *manimpi / musimpi* (adess.) *yra* 'near me, us is (Lat. *apud me / nos est*).'

Allative

40. According to the Acad. Gram., Vol. 1, 209, the allative has subsisted only in isolated Lithuanian speech areas. For the most part it is used when one wants to denote a thing towards which or in the direction of which the actor is moving. Laigonaitė, 1957, 34, gives the examples: (a) (Bebrėnai) *Momà daktaróp* (all.) *važiãvo* 'mama went to the doctor's;

(b) (Lazūnai) Kiškis   atbėgo   katinóp.
              The hare ran   to the cat.
                                 (all.)

(c) (Gervėčiai) Tadà   atėjo   mūsunk
                Then   came   to us
                                 (all.)

niẽmčiai.
Germans.
'Then the Germans came to us.'

Mažvydas' Catechism furnishes numerous examples:

(d) (76, 6) Kurs   nar   teisei
             Moreover   wishes   truly

     tap   stalap   prieitij.
     to this   table   to approach.
               (all.)

'Whoever truly wishes to approach this table.'

(e) (8, 23) dągaus   karalistasp
             of heaven   near to the kingdom
                           (all.)

     prisiartysyt.
     you will come.

271

'You will come near to the kingdom of heaven.'

(f) (8, 11)　schitai　　wiss　　iusump
　　　　　　　this　　　all　　　to you
　　　　　　　　　　　　　　　　(all.)

　　　ateia.
　　　has come.
'All this has come to you.'

(g) (50, 16)　Priwersk　　werasp　　　　Turkus
　　　　　　　Turn　　　　to the faith　Turks
　　　　　　　　　　　　(all.)

　　　piktus.
　　　evil.
'Turn the evil Turks to the faith.' (h) (45, 7) *Malda sunauspi* (all.) *Diewa* 'Prayer to the son of God,' (i) (24, 6) *prisakimapi* (all.) *Dewa prerakintas* 'joined to the commandment of God,' (j) (39, 17) *Skaititaiap* 'To the reader.' From Vilentas' Catechism:

(k) (29, 22)　Taip　　turi　　　　　biloti
　　　　　　　Thus　　you should　　speak

　　　Plebonop.
　　　to the pastor.
　　　(all.)

Klein, 1653, 161, gives the forms *miestop* (all. sg.) and *miestump* (all. pl.) 'towards the city, cities.' In a different context Klein, 1653, 162, gives the example (1) *kada swečias tawesp* (all.) *atėjo?* 'when did the guest come to you, your place?'

Prepositions

41. According to Palionis, 1967, 170-171, the use of the prepositions in the language of the 16th and 17th century writings differs considerably from contemporary usage. Certain of the prepositions at this time were used much more commonly and with somewhat different meanings than today, and some even governed different cases.

41.01 For example, in contemporary Lithuanian the preposition *añt* (governing the genitive) usually denotes (1) the place or thing on the surface of which something is put, something happens or something is located, (2) the direction in which someone or something is moving and (3) the person concerning whom certain emotions are expressed. But in the 16th and 17th centuries in addition to these meanings *ant* could denote time, goal or purpose, comparison and separation. Cf. Mažvydas' Catechism: (a) (48, 16) *ant amsziu* (gen. pl.) *amszia* (gen. sg.) 'eternally (lit: for the century of centuries),' the preposition *ant* governing the second genitive.

(b) (26, 10-11) tatai   darikiet   ant
                 this   do   in

   atminima   mana.
   remembrance   of me.
'Do this in remembrance of me.' From Chyliński's Bible:

(c) (103, 25)   nuejo   nog   jo   and
                (he) departed   from   him   for

   wałandos.
   a season.
   (gen. sg.)

Following the King James version I translate *and*
važandos (modern orthography *ant valandos*) 'for a season'
(= Gk. *ákhri kairoũ*).

(d) (291, 30) Kuriemus ney and hadynos
                  to whom not for an hour
                                                            (gen.)

        atstojom su pasidawimu.
        did we stand with subjection.

'To whom we gave place by subjection, no, not for an
hour.' Šukys, 1978, 20, considers the following contemporary example incorrect:

(e) Brólis išvažiãvo añt visõs
    Brother went away for a whole

    savái tės.
    week.
    (gen.)

In his opinion the final expression should be replaced
either by *vìsą savái tę* (acc.) 'the whole week' or *vìsai
savái tei* (dat.) 'for a whole week.' Palionis, 1967, 171-
172, writes that the preposition *ant* used with time
expressions in translated literature corresponds to the
usage of *na* or *nad* in the Polish originals. From
Pietkiewicz' Catechism (Fraenkel, 1947, 77):

(f) Lith. ant smerties iž duota.
    Pol. na śmierć wydanego.
            to death sentenced.
'Sentenced to death.'

(g) Lith. ant numazgoima griekų
    Pol. na obmycie grzechów
            for the absolution of sins

    musų.
    naszych.
    our.
'For the absolution of our sins.'

To express comparison note the example from
Daukša's Postilla (9, 21) with the example from Wuyek's
Postilla immediately below:

(h) râszo   philosóphai,   iog   ant
    piszą   philozophowie, iź   nad
    write   philosophers,   that   than

    diamento   ner   akmenies   kietèsnio.
                is not
    diament   nie   masz   kamienia   twardszego.
    diamond   not   have   stone   harder.
'Philosophers write that there is no (Pol. you don't
have) stone harder than diamond.'

A specific use of 'distinction' is illustrated in the following example from the same two catechisms:

(i) (241, 29-30)   ąnsai   karálus   ąnt
                   on   krol   nad
                   he (is)   king   of

    karâlų   wieszpatis   ąnt   wissų
    krolmi,   pan   nad   wszytkimi
    kings,   lord   of   all

    wieszpatų.
    pany.
    lords.

(Palionis, 1967, 172).

In the 16th and 17th centuries the preposition *ant* could denote 'with respect to' when used with the adjectives *biaurùs* 'ugly,' *gĕras* 'good,' *mãžas* 'small,' *smalstùs* 'fond of good food,' *sunkùs* 'difficult,' etc. From the same two sources:

(j) kuriii   ne   tiektái   ąnt   kûno,
    co by   nie   tylko   na   ćiele,
    who   not   only   in   body,

    bęt   ir   ąnt   dusziós,   ir   ąnt
    ale   y   na   duszy,   y   na
    but   also   in   soul,   and   in

    szirdės,   merga   bûtų.
    heart
    vmyśle,   panną   byłа.
    thought,   maiden   might be.

275

'Who (Pol. so that) not only in body, but also in soul and heart (Pol. thought) might be a maiden' (Palionis, 1967, 173).

Apparently such constructions persist in modern substandard Lithuanian since Šukys, 1978, 19, writes that *añt* should not be used with such adjectives as *gabùs* 'gifted (at),' *gẽras* 'good,' *tiñkamas* 'suitable,' *godùs* 'greedy,' etc., e.g.:

(k) Kárvė   gerà   añt   píeno.
    The cow (is) good   for   milk.

Such a sentence is considered incorrect by Šukys who would replace the expression by the adjective *píeninga* 'good at producing milk.'

The use of *añt* with verbs denoting remembering, verbs of saying, seeing, perceiving, complaining, translation from one language to another, division into parts, etc. is probably the result of Polish influence. Palionis, 1967, 174, remarks, however, that such usage is encountered not only in the Lithuanian Grand Duchy where Polish influence might be clearly expected, but also in the East Prussian territories (e.g., in Vilentas, Bretkūnas), all of which seems to show that Polish influence was strong there also. Nevertheless in these writings we also find German influence. Thus from Bretkūnas' Bible:

(1) (Genesis 4, 4) bei   ponas   mielai
                    and   the Lord   favorably

    pawijsdeia   ant   Habel   ir   io
    looked   at   Abel   and   his

    affiera.
    sacrifice.

'And the Lord regarded Abel and his sacrifice with favor.' Cf. Luther's Bible: *Und Herr sahe gnädiglich an Habel und sein Opffer.* For *ant* Klein, 1653, 167, gives the examples (m) *ant garbês* 'in honor,' (n) *ant kalno* 'on the hill' (see 37 [p]). From Vilentas' Catechism note (o) (title page, 8) *ant Lietuwischka pilnai ir wiernai perguldîtas* 'fully and faithfully translated into Lithuanian.' In modern Lithuanian the locution 'to translate into' is rendered by *veřsti į* plus the accusative.

41.02 Šukys, 1978, 15, writes that the Samogitian usage (a) *Lipk añt mẽdi̦* (acc.) 'climb up the tree' is to be replaced by (b) *Lipk į̃ mẽdi̦*. Similarly in Samogitian where the preposition *añt* can govern the dative case with nouns of the *-(j)ā, *-ē, *-i and consonant stem one encounters, e.g., (c) *Žìrklès añt lõvai* (dat.) 'the pair of scissors is on the bed.' which Šukys would replace with the standard (d) *Žìrklès añt lõvos* (gen.). Zinkevičius, 1966, 416, notes the Samogitian example in which *añt* governs the instrumental: (e) *ant vi̇́ena šakà* (inst.) 'on one branch' for standard *vienõs šakõs* (gen.). Zinkevičius writes further that in northeast Samogitian the preposition *ant* is used with the genitive (with illative meaning).

41.03 The preposition *apie* 'about' had approximately the same meanings in the texts of the 16th and 17th centuries as it has today (Palionis, 1967, 175). From Mažvydas' Catechism:

(a) (18, 6) Pękta   dalis   ape   istatima
             The fifth part   about   the ordinance
                                          (acc.)

(b) (28, 14) Ape   tą   Swetasti   jr
             About   this   sacrament   and
                                 (acc.)

     ape   kitas   swetastis.
     about   other   sacraments.
                            (acc.)

41.04 Klein, 1653, 167, writes that *apie* governs only the accusative and gives the example *apie Krikšta* 'about baptism.' On the other hand in a few writings from East Prussia one encounters the use of the genitive rather than the accusative, e.g., (a) *giesmes ape pakutos* (gen. sg.) 'hymns about penance' (Palionis, 1967, 175).

41.05 The preposition *be* 'without' (which governs the genitive) was used with the same meaning in the older literature as it is today, cf. Mažvydas' Catechism, (a) (10, 15) *B* (for *Be*) *schito maksla* (gen. sg.) 'without this doctrine.'

41.06 The preposition or postposition *dẽl, dẽlei* 'for' (to denote reason or goal) was used in the writings of the 16th and 17th centuries much as it is today (Palionis, 1967, 176). From Mažvydas' Catechism:

(a) (25, 19) kurij   del   musu   wisu
              which   for   us   all

greschnuiu   praleia.
sinners   shed.
(gen. pl.)
'Which he shed for all us sinners.'

(b) (32, 14-15)   Reik   idant
                  It is necessary   in order that

butu   padoti   netektai   del
they be   subject   not only   for the sake of

rustibes,   bet   dęl (for del)
wrath,   but   for the sake of

sumnienes.
conscience.
'It is necessary that they be subject not only for the sake of wrath but for the sake of conscience.' Cf. also (c) (54, 15) *Diel didzia susimilima* 'Because of great mercy.' Although in modern Lithuanian and even according to Klein, 1653, 167, *dẽl* can govern only the genitive case, the use of the accusative is recorded according to Palionis, 1967, 176, who gives the example, (d) *delei grieschna szmogų* (acc.) 'for a sinful man.' For its use as a postposition Palionis gives the example:

(e) kittû   žmonû   dêl   meldžiame.
    other   men   for   we pray.
'We pray for other men.'

41.07 Šukys, 1978, 32, advises against using *dẽl* 'for' to denote purpose in modern Lithuanian, especially with a verbal noun. Thus instead of:

(a) Pirkom   bulvių   dẽl   séklos.
    We bought   some potatoes   for   seed.

He advises the dat. *sė́klai* 'for seed.' Šukys, 1968, 33, advises also against using *dėl* to denote the person for whom something is done. Instead of:

(b) Ne   dėl   tavę̃s   vieno   saulùtė
    Not   for   you   alone (does)   the sun
                             (gen.)

šviẽčia.
shine.

He advises dat. *táu vienám* 'for you alone.' Zinkevičius, 1966, 418, writes that in certain cases in western Samogitian the preposition *dėl* governs the dative singular, e.g., (c) *susìbarė dėl šuniẽ* (dat. sg.) 'they scolded each other about the dog.'

41.08 In the 16th and 17th centuries the preposition *iki* 'until, up to, as far as' had approximately the same meanings that it has today. The chief difference is that at that time particularly in eastern and central Lithuanian it governed the dative case rather than the genitive. Note the examples from Chyliński's Bible: (a) (6, 2) *iki Dowiduy* (dat.) 'to David, as far as David.' (b) (7, 39) *iki smertiy* (dat.) *Heroda* 'until the death of Herod.' (c) (25, 30-31) *kursey isikieley iki dangùy* (dat.) 'who art exalted unto heaven.'
    Klein, 1653, 168, writes that *iki* can govern either the genitive or the dative and gives the examples (d) *iki gálo* (gen.) 'until the end' and (e) *iki szei dienai* (dat.) 'until this day' both of which examples (if put in contemporary orthography) would be perfectly acceptable today, although (e) is more or less a fossilized form (Šukys, 1978, 42). Fraenkel, 1929, 240, writes that the expression from Bretkūnas' Bible (f) *iki wienoliktą maetą* 'until the eleventh year' is to be understood as a genitive rather than an accusative as Bezzenberger had suggested. Palionis, 1967, 177, wrote that the example which he had encountered (g) (40, 2) *bet iki septinias deszymtis ir septinis kartus* (acc. pl.) 'until seventy times seven' was the only one with the accusative known to him. It seems probable to me that he wrote this before he had had the opportunity to look at the index of Chyliński's Bible (44), which lists three additional examples with *iki*. The examples are

(h) (90, 62) *iki pati dwara* 'even into the palace'; (i) (132, 12) *iki kita* 'unto the other'; (j) (225, 34) *iki tą žodi* 'unto this word.' In the preceding examples the ending -*a* (and perhaps even -*ą* [misprint?]) could be interpreted as genitive, but the ending -*i* of *pati* 'very,' and *žodi* 'word' could be interpreted only as accusative. I see no solution to the problem.

Palionis, 1967, 177, lists two examples of *ik* with the instrumental (both with the particle *be* between the preposition and the governed word). From Mažvydas' Hymns: (k) *ik beczesu* (inst.) 'until the time'; from Daukša's Postilla: (1) *ik bẽ mẽtú* 'until the time.' In Chyliński's Bible (199, 53) we encounter the example (m) *iki dienomis* (inst.) *dowida.* 'unto the days of David.' The form *dienomis* may, however, be a dative plural, since dat. pl. forms in -*mis* are known in other Lithuanian texts, see Ambrazas, 1959, 50.

41.09 According to Zinkevičius, 1966, 419, in dialects (Kaniavà) one occasionally finds the instrumental plural with *ik*, e.g.:

(a) vìsa   iškùlsim   ik
    everything we shall thresh by

    Naujaĩs Mẽtais.
    New   Year.
             (inst. pl.)

'We shall thresh everything by the New Year.' Šukys, 1978, 42, warns against the use of the instrumental with *iki*, thus (b) *iki kẽlių* (gen. pl.) 'up to the knees' is preferable to (c) *iki kẽliais* (inst. pl.).

41.10 According to Palionis, 1967, 177, in the 16th and 17th centuries the form *ing(i)* 'in' was commonly used instead of the contemporary *į*. Just as today the preposition governed only the accusative and denoted chiefly goal of motion, direction, manner, time, etc. Since the illative was available to express direction the use of the preposition to denote direction was less common. From Mažvydas' Catechism:

(a) (11, 25) dokiet ig   rąkas
             put   into the hands
                           (acc. pl.)

kiewaika.
of every child.

(b) (20, 12) *ig trete ir ketwirta eyle* (acc.) *gimines*
'unto the third and fourth succession of generation.'

(c) (23, 15) Newed   mus   ingi
            Don't lead us   into

pagundima.
temptation.
(acc.)

(d) (51, 18) Kada   mus   rika   ig
            When   us   chose   into

sunus.
sons.
(acc. pl.)
'When he chose us as sons.'

(e) (65, 1) ijpoliau   asch   ig
            fell   I   into

biauribes.
abominable state.
(acc. pl.)
'I fell into an abominable state.' From Vilentas' Catechism:

(f) (53, 1-2) ing   žeme   pawirsi.
              into   earth   you will change.
                     (acc.)

'You will change to earth.' (g) (68, 19) *ing atleidima* (acc.) *ghrieku* 'for the remission of sins.' Klein, 1653, 167, writes that the preposition *ing/in/y* 'in' governs only the accusative case and gives the examples: (h) *tikiu ing Diewa* (acc.) 'I believe in God' and (i) *y ugni* (acc.) *ymete* 'threw into the fire' (see 34.21, 38.1, and 38.2).

41.11 According to Zinkevičius, 1966, 418, the preposition *i̧, iñ, iñg(i), iñt, iñs, iñč* 'in, into' governs the accusative except in the dialects of eastern High Lithuanian and the Samogitian of the Klaipėda region,

281

where this preposition has been confused with *añt* and, replacing it, can govern the genitive. Šukys, 1978, 34, gives the examples (a) *Sėdi in súolo* (gen.) 'sits on the bench' and (b) *Mèsk in žẽmės* (gen.) 'throw on the ground' which he would correct to (c) *Sėdi ant súolo* and (d) *Mèsk ant žẽmės* respectively. Zinkevičius, 1966, 418, gives the dialect example with the dative: (e) *inlipo in ùgniai* (dat.) 'climbed into the fire.' Šukys, 1978, 35-36, considers the use of *į* plus the accusative construction encountered in the Klaipėda and in places along the Nemunas incorrect. Thus (f) *Į Tilžę* (acc.) *gyvenaũ* 'I lived in Tilžė' should be replaced by *Tilžėje* (loc.).

According to Šukys, 1978, 36, *į* plus the accusative may be used to express approximate time but not exact time, thus (g) *į vãkarą* (acc.) 'toward evening' is correct, but (h) *į trẽčią diẽną* (acc.) 'on the third day' is not acceptable, but should be replaced by the simple accusative expression *trẽčią diẽną* (see 35[a]). Šukys, 1978, 37, considers the use of *į* plus the accusative to denote an approximate number to be incorrect also:

(i) Susiriñko   į   tūkstantį   žmonių.
    gathered   about   a thousand   persons.
                             (acc.)

'About a thousand persons gathered.' More correct would be either *apie tūkstantį* (acc.) or *arti tūkstančio* (gen.). The use of *į* plus the accusative with verbs of speaking, saying is also considered incorrect:

(j) Ilgaĩ   tėvas   kalbėjo   į
    A long time   father   spoke   to

    sū́nų.
    son.
    (acc.)

'The father spoke to (his) son for a long time.' More correct would be *sūnui* (dat.).

41.12 Palionis, 1967, 178, writes that the use of the preposition *iš* 'out of, from' (which governs the genitive) in the 16th and 17th century literary language was used more commonly than now to denote cause. From Mažvydas' Catechism:

(a) (54, 13) Isch   malanes   mums
              from   grace   on us
                       (gen.)

    susimilk.
    have mercy.
'Have mercy on us from grace.'

(b) (57, 14) Muss   isch   teisibes
              us   from   righteousness
                                (gen.)

    suditi.
    to judge.
'To judge us with righteousness.' (c) (67, 14) *isz stiprias weras* (gen.) 'with strong faith.' Other examples parallel modern usage:

(d) (58, 3)   Gielbek   isch   temczias
              Deliver   from   prison
                                 (gen.; for temniczias)

    teisus.
    righteous.
'Deliver the righteous from prison.' (e) (71, 11) *Isch nomirusiuiu* (gen. pl.) *kiele* 'arose from the dead,' (f) (26, 15) *Gierkiet isch ta* (gen. sg.) 'Drink from this.'

(g) (21, 9-10) Kursai   prasideiase   isch
                Who   was conceived   of

    dwases   schwintases,   gimes   isch
    spirit   holy   born   of
    (gen.)

    Marias   mergas   czistas.
    Mary   virgin   pure.
    (gen.)

'Who was conceived of the Holy Spirit, born of the Virgin Mary.' Klein, 1653, 167, writes that *isz* takes only the genitive case and gives the example: (h) *isz Mariôs cžistôs Pannôs* '*ex Mariâ purâ virgine.*'

41.13 Although ordinarily *iš* governs the genitive case in some cases in western Samogitian it governs the dative, e.g.:

(a) iš   ząsiės   úodegai   plùnksną
    from   goose's   tail   feather
                           (dat.)

   ìspešiau.
   I plucked.
'I plucked a feather from the goose's tail';

(b) iš   sẽserie   pinigų   negáusi.
    from   sister   money   you won't get.
              (dat.)

'You won't get any money from sister.' Such usage is branded by Šukys, 1978, 44, as specifically incorrect. Also incorrect in his opinion is the locution, (c) ãnas (jìs) iš po Utenõs (gen.) 'he is from Utena,' although he would permit as conversational:

(d) Iš   po   stãlo   išliñdo
    out from under   table   came out
                          (gen.)

    katẽ.
    cat.

'The cat came out from under the table.' From Šakýna Zinkevičius, 1966, 419, reports:

(e)   Sáulė   išliñdo   iš   ùž
        The sun   appeared   from   behind

        dẽbesio.
        the cloud.
        (gen.)

Šukys, 1978, 49, writes that the locution žíedas iš áukso (gen.) 'ring from gold' is less desirable than áukso (gen.) or áuksinis žíedas 'a gold, golden ring.'

41.14 According to Palionis, 1967, 179, the preposition nuog(i) 'from; by' occurs commonly in 16th and 17th century writings to denote the genitive of agent (see 30.5f-k). Klein, 1653, 167, writes that nůg 'from' takes only the genitive case and gives the example nůg manes (gen.) 'from me.' Meanings similar to those of modern Lithuanian are encountered in Mažvydas' Catechism:

(a) (23, 16) gielbek   mus   nogi   wysa
              deliver   us   from   all

pikta.
evil.
(gen.)

(b) (29, 15) *talims nog lakamstwas* (gen.) 'far from greed.' (c) (34, 17) *nog lauka* (gen.) 'from outside.'

(d) (44, 3-4) Kada   skirsis   nog
              When   will be separated   from

kuna   Duscha.
body   soul.
(gen.)
'When the soul will be separated from the body.'

(e) (53, 20) Vis   mes   nog   tawes
             everything   we   from   you
                                        (gen.)

apturim.
obtain.
'We obtain everything from you.'

(f) (56, 17-18) Nogi   nepreteliaus   Turka,
                from   enemy   Turk,
                       (gen.)   (gen.)

Diewe   saugak.
oh God   protect.
'Oh God, protect us from (our) enemy the Turk.'

41.15 According to Zinkevičius, 1966, 421, in western Samogitian the preposition *nu* is sometimes used with the meaning 'according to' or 'about, approximately,' e.g., (a) *nu tėvo* (gen.) 'according to father':

(b) nu   dvijų   trijų   žmogaũs
    about   two   (or)   three   of a man

áugumų.
heights.

'About two or three times taller than a man.' In western Samogitian the preposition is sometimes used with the dative case, e.g.:

(c) nu marčiaĩ gãvo dovený̨.
 from bride received gifts.
 (dat.)
'(He) received some gifts from the bride.'

(d) nu pat kūdykȳstie esù dárbe
 from very infancy I am at work
 (dat.)

 ir dárbe.
 and at work.
'I have been working since my infancy.'

41.16 Palionis, 1967, 180, writes that the chief difference between the use of *pagal(ei)* 'according to' in the 16th and 17th century writings and those of today is that in earlier times it governed the genitive case more than the accusative case as it does today. From Mažvydas' Catechism: (a) (9, 2) *pagal wales* (gen.) *dewa* 'according to the will of God,' (b) (9, 14) *pagal to schwenta maksla* (gen.) 'according to this holy doctrine,' (c) (54, 12) *Pagal darbu* (gen. pl.) 'according to (our) works.' Similar in meaning and case government to *pagal* is *palig* encountered in some writings of early times. Thus Sirvydas' Punktay sakimu II, 124, 19: (d) *palig žodžiu* (gen.) *anyelo* 'according to the words of the angel.' Klein, 1653, 168, writes that *pagal* and *palig* can govern either the genitive or the accusative case, thus, (e) *pagal/palig tiesôs* (gen.) 'according to the truth,' and (f) *pagal gerybe* (acc.) *Diewo* 'according to the goodness of God.' According to Zinkevičius, 1966, 421, in High Lithuanian *pagal* is used for the most part with the accusative and in Samogitian with the genitive and the instrumental (the latter usage being under the influence of *sulig* 'according to'), although in places such usage is encountered even in High Lithuanian.

41.17 The meaning and use of *pas* 'near, in the vicinity of' in the 16th and 17th century writings is practically no different from the contemporary meaning and use according to Palionis, 1967, 181. Klein, 1653, 167, writes

that the preposition governs only the accusative and gives
the example: (a) *pas dešine* (acc.) 'to, at the right.'
Just as today the preposition for the most part governed
the accusative case and denoted nearness or direction.
From Chyliński's Bible (b) (28, 55) *dalis pože pas kiala*
(acc.) 'a portion fell by the way,' (c) (115, 54) *kurie
pas ghi* (acc.) *stowejo* 'who stood with him,' (d) (116,
32) *pastate ghi pas sawe* (acc.) '(Jesus) put him by
himself.' According to Palionis, 1967, 181, the use of
the genitive with *pas* is also encountered in some writings of this time, e.g., *pas upes* (gen.) 'near the
river.'

41.18 According to Zinkevičius, 1966, 423, in Samogitian
the preposition occurs with the genitive, e.g., (a)
užeĩk kadà pas mūsų (gen.) 'drop in on us sometime.'
An example with dative government comes from Oziai:
(b) *parėjęs pas karãl'ui* (dat.) 'having come to the
king' (Fraenkel, 1929, 83). An example with instrumental
government comes from Šãtės:

   (c) žvakelė   pas manim   atsirado.
        candle   with me   appeared.
                   (inst.)

'A candle was found at my place.' Russian influence is
greatly to be felt in modern Lithuanian syntax. Šukys,
1978, 63-66, expressly advises against many expressions
in which *pas* is an obvious translation of Russian *u*
'near, in the possession of.' Thus:

   (d) Pas   manè   yrà
        In the possession of   me   is

        kláusimas,
        question,

an obvious calque of Russian (e) *u menja est' vopros*, is
to be replaced by (f) *Aš turiù kláusimą* 'I have a question.'

41.19 One of the most characteristic uses of *per* with
the accusative in 16th and 17th century Lithuanian is to
denote the agent (Palionis, 1967, 181). From Mažvydas'
Catechism:

(a) (20, 17-19) DWILIKA   STRAIPSCZIU
                 twelve   articles

   WERAS   KRIKSCZIANIU,   PER
   of the creed   of Christians,   by

   APASCHTALUS   SCHWENTOSIUS   SUGULDITU.
   apostles   holy   put together.
   (acc.)

'The twelve articles of the creed of the Christians put together by the holy apostles.' From Vilentas' Catechism: (b) (title page, 6) *paraschits per Daktara Martina Luthera* (acc.) 'written by Dr. Martin Luther.' The use of *per* frequently corresponds to Polish originals with *przez* and German originals with *durch*, although there are cases where Lithuanian *per* to express agentive usage corresponds to Polish *od* plus the genitive. The agentive use of *per* probably had its origin under the influence of other languages (Polish, German and perhaps even Latin), but then became more widely used by various authors. In addition Palionis, 1967, 182, disputes Fraenkel's, 1929, 128, notion that that agentive use of *per* is found in more modern writings. In Palionis' view all of Fraenkel's examples illustrate the purposive or mediative meaning of the preposition, e.g.:

(c) per̃   tavè   aš   niẽko   nemataũ.
     through   you   I   nothing   see.
                (acc.)

'Because of you I don't see anything, i.e., you are in the way.' Still Šukys, 1978, 73, notes specifically that the agentive usage is wrong in modern Lithuanian. Thus:

(d) Klieñtai   aptarnáujami   tik   per̃
     The customers   are served   only   by

     padavéjas,
     waitresses,
     (acc. pl.)

is incorrect and should be replaced by (e) *Klieñtai aptarnáujami tik padavėjų* (gen. pl.) with an agentive genitive. The instrumental (rather than agentive) use is common in the older writings, from Mažvydas' Catechism:

(f) (33, 14) apczistita   mazgagimu
              cleansed   with the washing
                             (inst.)

    wandens   per   szadi.
    of water   by   the word.
                       (acc.)

(g) (55, 17-18) Ir   per   schwenta
                And   by   holy

    prikielima,   Saugak   per   dangun
    resurrection,   protect   by   to heaven
    (acc.)

    szegima.
    ascension.
    (acc.)

'And protect (them) by (your) holy resurrection and by (your) ascension to heaven.' Klein, 1653, 167, writes that the preposition *per* governs only the accusative case and gives the examples: (h) *per mane* 'through me' and (i) *per áukštus kálnus* 'through the high hills.'

41.20 In the 16th and 17th century writings just as today the preposition *po* (also *pa*) could govern any one of the four following cases: genitive, dative, accusative or instrumental. During this period a particularly common use with the dative was to express time, e.g., from Vilentas' Catechism (a) (36, 6) *potam* 'then, after this,' from Chyliński's Bible (b) (51, 45) *po sielwartuy* (dat.) *anu dienu* 'after the tribulation of those days.' Rather more rarely the preposition with the dative could express position or direction. From Chyliński's Bible (c) (81, 58) *po deszyney (rękey)* (dat.) 'on the right hand.' In general the use of *po* with the dative (in all of the meanings discussed) is encountered more frequently in east and central high Lithuanian dialects at that time than in the works of East Prussian authors. In addition those authors who use *po* with the dative also use *iki* with the dative (Palionis, 1967, 182-183).

41.21 *po* (*pa*) can also govern the genitive case denoting position and time. From Mažvydas' Catechism: (a) (21, 18) *padeschines* (gen.) 'on the right,' (b) (22, 15) *pasmertes* (gen.) 'after death.'

41.22 *po (pa)* denoting 'under' governs the instrumental case. From Mažvydas' Catechism: (a) (8, 20) *pa akimis* (inst. pl.); (9, 4) *po akimis* 'under the eyes'; Chyliński's Bible: (b) (11, 37) *po sudu* 'under a bushel.'

41.23 Palionis, 1967, 184, writes that the use of the accusative with *po* in time constructions is obviously a slavish imitation of Polish syntax. From Chyliński's Bible: (a) (37, 13) *po szeszias dienas* (acc. pl.) 'after six days,' (b) (60, 50) *po tris dienas* (acc. pl.) 'after three days.' *po* with the accusative is also encountered in certain constructions denoting position. From Chyliński's Bible: (c) (50, 32) *po sparnus* (acc. pl.) 'under (her) wings,' (d) (51, 8) *po cieła swieta* (acc.) 'in all the world.'

41.24 Klein, 1653, 168-169, wrote that *po* with the genitive, dative and accusative denotes 'after, near, according to' and gives such examples as: (a) *po kairēs rankõs* (gen.) 'on, at the left hand,' (b) *po senãtwes* (gen.) 'in accordance with old age,' (c) *po triũ dienũ* (gen. pl.) = (d) *po trims dienoms* (dat. pl.) 'after three days,' (e) *po szwentos Traices* (gen.) = (f) *po szwentai Traicei* (dat.) 'after Holy Trinity,' (g) *po mažam* (dat.) 'after a little,' (h) *po senam* (dat.) 'in accordance with antiquity,' (i) *po tiesuma* (acc.) 'in accordance with righteousness,' (j) *po wissa swieta* (acc.) = (k) *po wissam swietui* (dat.) 'in the whole world.' Klein also notes the distributive with the accusative: (l) *eme po graszi* (acc.) 'took one penny a piece.' He writes that with the instrumental *po* denotes 'under': (m) *po kojomis* (inst. pl.) 'under the feet.'

41.25 Zinkevičius, 1966, 423, notes that in dialects *po* with the dative is much more widely used than in the standard language, e.g., (a) (Liubãvas) *po dárbui* (dat.) 'after work,' (b) *dúok visiem po vienám óbuoliui* (dat.) 'give everyone one apple a piece' (for standard *po vieną óbuolį* [acc.]). Šukys, 1978, 76, admonishes strictly against such constructions, but he does allow the fossilized (c) *po kairei* 'on the left,' (d) *po dẽšinei* 'on the right,' (e) *po šiái diẽnai* 'up to this day,' (f) *po tiẽsumui* 'directly.' Šukys, 1978, 80, writes that in principle *po* with the genitive should not denote position, but he allows the common expression (g) *po kóju* (gen.) 'under the feet.'

41.26 Palionis, 1967, 184, writes that in eastern and central standard Lithuanian in the writings of the 16th and 17th centuries the preposition *prie(g)* 'at, before, to, by' was frequently used with the dative. From Mažvydas' Catechism: (a) (39, 7-8) *pregtam* 'in addition to that.' From Chyliński's Bible:

(b) (265, 61-62) kurie   ira   wisados   prieg
                 who   are   always   at the

   altoriuy.
   altar.
   (dat.)

The index of Chyliński's Bible lists three examples with the locative case: (c) (69, 47-48) *prie giarame razume* = (113, 20) *prie gierame razume* (loc.) 'in his right mind.' Palionis, 1967, 185, writes that other instances of the use of *prie* with the locative could be simple typographical errors and that Fraenkel's, 1929, 32, examples are either the result of misprints or misunderstandings. Still the examples above showing both the adjective and the noun in the locative case seem to indicate that at least the locative might be used with *prie*. But *prie* with the genitive is attested as early as Mažvydas' Catechism: (d) (18, 12) *preg manęs* (gen.) 'before me,' (e) (44, 2) *prieg ta cziesa* (gen.) 'at that time,' (f) (55, 20) *Preg teisaus szadzia* (gen.) *palaiki* 'Hold to the true word.' Klein, 1653, 168, writes that *prieg* can be used with either the genitive or the accusative case and gives the examples *prieg manes* (gen.), *mane* (acc.) 'before me,' *prieg tawes* (gen.), *tawe* (acc.) 'before you.'

41.27 Zinkevičius, 1966, 424-423, notes the Lithuanian dialect tendency to confuse the prepositions *priẽ* and *apiẽ* 'about.' In Adùtiškis the preposition *priẽ* with the dative means 'near, towards,' thus: (a) *amète prie ẽžerui* (dat.) 'let's go near the lake' but (b) *visà ùtarka tik prie mergàs* (acc.) 'the entire conversation is only about girls.' In eastern Lithuania the preposition *priẽ* is rather commonly used with the dative singular and somewhat more rarely used with instrumental plural: (c) *priẽ bãlai* (dat. sg.) *prirìštos kárvès* 'the cows are tethered near the swamp,'

(d) jã   prãšė   pabút   prie
    her   asked   to remain   with

   vaĩkaĩs.
   children.
   (inst. pl.)

'(They) asked her to remain with the children a bit.'
Šukys, 1978, 82, brands such expressions as dialectal and considers the standard usage of the genitive case as the only correct possibility, viz., *prie bãlos* (gen.) 'near the swamp' and *prie vaikų̃* (gen.) 'with the children.' In addition the Samogitian use of *prie* with the genitive to denote *pas* 'with, at the place of' is also considered incorrect, thus (e) *prie mū́sų* 'at our place' is to be replaced by *pas mùs*. The eastern High Lithuanian use of *prie* (*pie*) to denote *apie* 'about' is not acceptable either. Thus (f) *prie kãrą* 'about the war' is to be replaced by *apie kãrą*.

41.28 According to Palionis, 1967, 185, in the Lithuanian literary language of the 16th and 17th centuries the preposition *priẽš* for the most part governed the accusative case and denoted place, time, comparison and opposition. From Mažvydas' Catechism: (a) (36, 1-2) *Vredas wijsakiu weschpatu...priesch tarnus* (acc. pl.) 'The duty of all masters towards (their) servants' (a construction which would not conform to the contemporary standard), (b) (56, 8) *prisch tawa szadij* (acc.) 'against thy word.' There are scattered cases of genitive and dative government. From Pietkiewicz' Catechism (c) (61, 7) *priesz io* (gen.) 'against him.' Palionis writes that there are only three examples of *priẽš* governing the dative, a construction which seems to have arisen under Polish influence. Klein, 1653, 167, writes that the preposition governs only the accusative and gives the example: (d) *priesz gimditojus* 'towards the parents.'

41.29 Šukys, 1978, 87, writes that in defining place and manner the short variant *priẽš* can be replaced by the longer variant *priẽšais*. With other meanings (time, object) the longer variant is unsuitable for the standard language. Likewise the dialectal usage of the preposition with the genitive and the dative case are considered incorrect. Thus (a) *priẽšais aikštẽs* (gen.) 'opposite the square' is to be replaced by *priẽšais áikštę* (acc.) and (b) *priẽš trõbai* (dat.) 'opposite the cottage' is to be replaced by *priẽš trõbą* (acc.).

41.30 The use of the preposition *pro* 'through, by' in the 16th and 17th century writings differs little from the modern standard, except that sometimes it is used with the meaning of 'for, out of (figuratively)' (Palionis, 1967, 186). From Chyliński's Bible (a) (33, 7) *rekie pro baÿme* (acc.) '(they) cried out for fear,' (b) (57, 56) *pro wartus* (acc. pl.) 'through the gateway,' (c) (59, 48) *kurie pro szali* (acc.) *ejo* 'who passed by.'

(d) (112, 9-11) nusmelkia pro rupescius,
      are choked with cares,
                        (acc.)

    ir   bagotistes,   ir   raskaszys
    and   riches,   and   pleasures
          (acc.)   (acc.)

    szio   zywata.
    of this   life.

Klein, 1653, 167, writes that the preposition *pra, pro* takes only the accusative and gives the examples: (e) *pro mielą Diewą* (acc.) 'by, through dear God,' (f) *pro szali* (acc.) *eiti* 'to pass by the side,' (g) *pro jį* (acc.) *eit* 'passes by him.'

41.31 Zinkevičius, 1966, 426, notes the dialect use of the instrumental with *prõ*: (a) *invažiãvo pro vaŕtais* (inst. pl.) 'drove in through the gate,' a use which is rejected by Šukys, 1978, 92, who would use rather *prõ vartùs* (acc. pl.). Other uses condemned by Šukys, 1978, 93-94, include: (b) *prõ mìšką* 'through the forest' to be replaced by *peŕ mìšką*; (c) *prõ rãdiją* 'over the radio' for *peŕ rãdiją*; (d) *prõ tamsą* 'when it is dark' for *su tamsà* 'with darkness'; (e) *Mū́sų kárvė prõ juõdi* (acc.) 'our cow is somewhat black' for į juodùmą or the adjective (nom. sg.) juodóka; (f) Vìsą vãkarą prašnekėjom prõ vilkùs (acc. pl.) 'we talked about wolves all evening' for apiẽ vilkùs.

41.32 The use of the preposition *su* 'with' with the instrumental is similar to that encountered in the modern standard language. Examples from Mažvydas' Catechism: (a) (11, 4) *su burtinikie* (inst.) 'with a soothsayer,' (b) 24, 7) *su žadziu* (inst.) *suglaustas* 'connected with (his) word,' (c) (30, 6) *su czista samniene* (inst.) 'with a pure conscience,' (d) (48, 15) *Su dziauksmu* (inst.) *giedakiem Amen* 'let us sing Amen with joy.' Klein, 1653, 168, writes that *su* takes only the ablative (= instrumental) and gives the examples: (e) *su Diewu* 'with God,' (f) *su maldomis* 'with prayers,' (g) *su džaugsmu* 'with joy.'

41.33 The use of the preposition *sulìg* 'according to, up to' with the instrumental is similar to the use in the modern standard language. Note the example from Bretkūnas' Postilla (a) (2, 117) *suligei Diewu Tiewu* 'along with God the Father' (Fraenkel, 1928, 244). From the Acad. Gram., Vol. 3, 225: (b) *sulìg kẽliais* 'up to the knees.'

41.34 The preposition *tar̃p* (*terp*) 'between, among' with the genitive was used in the 16th and 17th century writings much as it is today. From Mažvydas' Catechism (a) (56, 20) *Tarp karaliu kunigaiszcziu* (gen. pl.) 'among kings (and) princes.' From Chyliński's Bible: (b) (7, 2-3) *terp Kunigaykszcziu* (gen. pl.) *Judos* 'among the princes of Juda,' (c) (50, 25) *terp Baznìczios* (gen.) *ir altoriaus* (gen.) 'between the temple and the altar.' Klein, 1653, 167, writes that *tarp* governs only the genitive case and gives the example: (d) *tarp dangaus* (gen.) *bei žémes* (gen.) 'between heaven and earth.'

41.35 The preposition *tiẽs* 'by, at' against, opposite' appears in the writings of the 16th and 17th centuries with meanings similar to those encountered today. From Vilentas' Catechism:

(a) (37, 8-9) Waikai   ir   Scheimina
               children   and   household

    tur   sudeghię   rankas,   patogei
    should   having folded   hands,   reverently

    ties   stalu   staweti...
    at   table   stand...
              (inst.)

'The children and household, having folded (their) hands should stand reverently at the table...' Genitive government is encountered in the example from Bretkūnas' Postilla (b) (2, 457) *ties akiu* (gen. pl.) *Kristaus* 'before the eyes of Christ.' From Chyliński's Bible: (c) (10, 7) *ties mariu* (gen. pl.) 'near the sea,' but for the most part this preposition requires the accusative in this work, (d) (10, 21-22) *ties marius* (acc. pl.) *Galileos* 'by the sea of Galilee,' (e) (62, 49) *ties Marias* (acc. pl.) *Galileos* 'by the sea of Galilee,' (f) (168, 51) *Eykime wel ties Judea* (acc.) 'Let us go into Judaea again.'
Accusative government is not attested in either the contemporary standard language or any of the dialects (Palionis, 1967, 187). Klein, 1653, 168, writes that *ties* governs only the ablative (= instrumental) and gives the examples (g) *ties buttu* 'near the house,' (h) *ties manimi* 'before me.'

41.36 According to Zinkevičius, 1966, 428, in eastern Lithuania sometimes (apparently under the influence of the preposition *prič* 'near') *tiẽs* governs the dative case:

(a) nustójo   keleivìnė   viškui   ties
     stopped   bus   just   opposite

     gryčiai.
     hut.
     (dat.)

'The bus stopped just opposite the hut.'

41.37 The differences between the modern and the older use of the preposition *už* (and numerous variants, e.g., *užu*, *ažu*, etc.) result for the most part from slavish translations of foreign constructions in the 16th and

17th century writings (Palionis, 1967, 187). Ordinarily the preposition denotes 'beyond, behind, in [time expressions]' with the genitive case and '(in return) for; than' with the accusative case. From Mažvydas' Catechism:

(a) (51, 22) ieib   vsz   grekus
              so that for   sins
                             (acc. pl.)

    gailetu.
    may grieve.
'So that (they) may grieve for (their) sins';

(b) (69, 1) Mus   sau   vsz   sunus
             us   for himself   as   sons

    ischrinka.
    chose.
'He chose us as his sons.' From Chyliński's Bible:

(c) (15, 27) Negu   daugiaus   prakilnesni
             not   much   better

    este   uz   jos.
    you are   than   they.
                         (acc. pl.)
'Aren't you much better than they?';

(d) (38, 38) dok   ghi   jems   uz
             give   it   to them   for

    mane   ir   (uz)   sawe
    me   and   for   yourself;
    (acc.)   (acc.)

(e) (40, 22) pagawo   ghi   uz   gurkli
             took   him   by   the throat;
                                   (acc.)

(f) (79, 29-30) Kas   nes   n'est
                whoever   for   is not

    priesz   mus,   tas   ira   uz   mus.
    against   us,   he   is   for   us.
                                            (acc.)

296

'For whoever is not against us is for us'; (g) (83, 42) *iszejo uz Miesta* 'went out of the city';

(h) (140, 52-53) Tey   ira   kunas mano
                  This   is   body   my

kursey dostis   uz   jus.
which   is given   for   you.

'This is my body which is given for you.' Time expressions with the accusative case are also encountered: (i) (65, 22-23) *uz Abiatara Aukszcziausia kuniga* (acc.) 'during the time of Abiathar the high priest'; (j) (54, 59) *uz dwi dieni* (acc. dual) 'in (after) two days.' But note similar expressions with the genitive; (k) (50, 7-8) *uz metu* (gen. pl.) *tewu musu* 'in the days of our fathers'; (1) (88, 31-32) *uz dwieju dienu* (gen. pl.) 'in (after) two days.' With the accusative one encounters: (m) (140, 60) *uz stala* (acc.) 'at the table' but note the genitive: (n) (82, 55-56) *pryryszta uz duru* (gen. pl.) 'tied at the door'; (o) (346, 42) *už antros uždągos* 'after the second vail.' Klein, 1653, 168, writes that *už* with the genitive denotes 'beyond, on the other side of' and gives the examples: (p) *už māriu* (gen. pl.) 'across the sea' and (q) *už pillies* 'beyond the castle.' Klein writes further that *už* with the accusative denotes 'for' and gives the examples: (r) *už manę* (acc.) *užmokėjo* 'paid for me' and *už piktybę* (acc.) *sawo kencze* 'suffers for his own malice.' Palionis, 1967, 187, writes that the use of this preposition with verbs such as *laikýti*, *turėti*, *paskaitýti* in the meaning 'to consider (as, to be)' is under Polish influence, such as the example from Mažvydas' Catechism:

(s) (77, 4)   ia   maksla   sweikiegi
              his   art   the healthy

tur   vsz   ioka.
consider   as   joke.
                  (acc.)

'The healthy consider his art as a joke.' Similarly example (b) above may reflect Polish influence.

41.38 Zinkevičius, 1966, 429, writes that in northern Samogitian *už* governs the instrumental to denote place of rest and the accusative to denote object of motion, thus: (a) *už mìškù* (inst.) 'beyond the forest' instead of the standard *už mìško* (gen.), (b) *užsilindau už medžiùs* (acc. pl.) 'I crawled behind the trees' instead of the standard *užlindaũ už mẽdžių* (gen. pl.). Zinkevičius writes further that in certain instances in the west it is used with the dative singular:

(c) dár   galiùką   už   píevai
    still   little piece   beyond   meadow
                                           (dat.)

     paejési.
     you will go.
'You will go a little piece beyond the meadow.' (d) *ateĩsiu už valandìkei* (dat.) 'I will come in a moment.' The use of the accusative with *už* to denote time is noted in dialects: (e) *už penkiàs minutàs* (acc. pl.) *pareĩs* 'will come in five minutes,' but is specifically condemned by Šukys, 1978, 117.

The Adjective

42. Qualitative adjectives may have a 'definite' form, a form which has its historical origin in the addition of the personal pronoun to the end of the simple or 'indefinite adjective.' Only adjectives expressing a quality, not those expressing a relationship can have the definite form, thus _báltas_ 'white' has the definite form _baltàsis_, but _geležìnis_ 'iron' cannot have a definite form. According to the Acad. Gram., Vol. 1, 505, there are two fundamental meanings of the definite adjective, viz. the determinative and the emphatic.

42.1 One of the determinative meanings consists of distinguishing known items by their lexical meaning, i.e., by spatial, temporal and other physical characteristics, e.g.:

(a) kolūkio   valdýbos
    of the collective farm   of the administration

    didỹsis   kambarỹs.
    the big   room.
    (def.)

'The big room of the collective farm administration.'
The definite adjective _didỹsis_ sets this room off from the other rooms of the collective farm, which, presumably are smaller. It is particularly common when two things are compared, one of which possesses the quality as opposed to another which does not possess the quality, e.g.:

(b) ne   tik   upẽlis,   bet   didžióji
    not   only   the brook,   but   the big
                                          (def.)

        ùpė   bùvo   apsitráukusi   ledù.
        river   was   covered   with ice.
The definite adjective *didžióji* sets off the big river from the brook.

  (c)   jis   tar̃p   krùtančiujų   skarĕlių
       he   among   moving   kerchiefs

       pamãtė   mélynąją.
       caught sight of   the blue.
                                 (def.)

'Among the moving kerchiefs he caught sight of the blue one.' In this case the color of the kerchief is specific, distinguishing it from all of the other kerchiefs.

    Frequently the definite adjective is used in proper names, e.g., (d) *Baltàsis nãmas* 'the White House,' (e) *Juodóji jū́ra* 'the Black Sea,' (f) *Aukščiáusioji Tarýba* 'the Supreme Soviet,' (g) *Didỹsis Tėvỹnės kãras* 'the great Fatherland war,' etc. (Acad. Gram., Vol. 1, 506-507).

42.2 The definite adjective also denotes species or types of things, e.g., (a) *baltàsis lokỹs* 'the white bear,' (b) *plėšrióji žuvėdra* 'the predatory tern,' (c) *kuodúotasis vieversỹs* 'the crested lark,' (d) *mažàsis apúokas* 'the long-eared (lit. small) owl.' This derives from the fact that the definite adjective can denote an inherent as opposed to an ascribed characteristic. The *baltàsis lokỹs* is an inherently white bear, whereas a *báltas lokỹs* is a bear of any species which just happens to be white. Similarly the *mažàsis apúokas* is a certain species of owl whereas the sequence *mãžas apúokas* would denote any owl which happened to be small.

42.3 In the course of a narrative if an object is once identified when it is mentioned again it may be referred to with the definite adjective. This usage is similar to that of the definite article in English.

  (a)   Ìlgainiui   trijų̃
       In the course of time   of the three

Samgori	ežerų	vanduõ...	pasidarė
of Samgori	lakes	water	became

sūrùs...
salty...

'In the course of time the water of the three lakes of Samgori became salty...' Later in the narrative when the lakes are mentioned again they are referred to with the definite adjective sūríeji (def.) ežeraĩ 'the salty lakes' (Acad. Gram., Vol. 1, 508).

In the contemporary Lithuanian there is a tendency for the notion of the definiteness to be expressed by the deictic pronoun instead of (or in addition to) the definite adjective. In the following example a hare has been mentioned in the preceding narrative.

(b)	Antanukas	labaĩ	norė́tų	tą
	Tony	very much	would like	that

gẽrą	kiškutį	pamatýti.
good	hare	to see.

'Tony would like very much to see that good hare.' Note that instead of the collocation tą gẽrą 'that good' it would have been possible to use the definite adjective gẽraji 'the good' or a combination of the deictic pronoun and the definite adjective, viz. tą gẽraji. In such sentences the use of the deictic pronoun plus the indefinite adjective is the norm and the use of the definite adjective is becoming unnecessary.

In dialects the indefinite adjective is commonly encountered in the superlative degree, because functionally the meaning of the superlative is close to that of the definite adjective. Thus when one intends to distinguish the oldest son from the other sons one may use the indefinite form (c) vyriáusias sūnùs 'eldest son' rather than (d) vyriáusiasis sūnùs. In the northeastern corner of eastern High Lithuanian even where the definite form is still used one encounters the indefinite form to distinguish one item from a group, e.g., (e) kanapė́ta višta 'speckled hen' instead of (f) kanapė́toji višta (Acad. Gram., Vol. 1, 511-512).

42.4 The definite adjective may also emphasize a known quality of an object. Such usage is common in artistic epithets and is therefore most common in belles-lettres and in folk songs. These definite adjectives can modify either a common or a proper noun. From a Lithuanian folk song:

(a) Áuga   tàvo   merguželė   pas
    grows up your   little girl   in the home of

    senúosius   tėvužėlius.   Pas senúosius
    old, old   parents.   In the home of

    tėvužėlius,   tarp
    of the old, old parents,   among

    jaunũjų   broluželių.
    young, young   brothers.

'Your little girl is growing up in the home of old, old parents. In the home of the old, old parents and among young, young brothers.' The definite adjective here emphasizes the old age of the parents and the youth of the brothers (Acad. Gram., Vol. 1, 509).

42.5 Klein, 1653, 25, writes that certain adjectives are simple, such as *gḗras* 'good' and certain are emphatic such as *gerassis* (or *gerasis*). As examples Klein gives (a) *asz esmi piemũ gerasis* 'I am the good shepherd' and (b) *Dwãse gerṓji* 'the good Spirit.' Klein, 1654, 12, notes that from the emphatic adjectives (i.e., definite adjectives) certain more emphatic forms are sometimes created, in which the personal pronoun is added to the emphatic adjective, i.e., from *gḗrasis*, *mielasis* and *brángusis* one derives respectively *gerasysis*, *mielasysis*, *brangusysis*, which are in common use.

42.6 Originally the second element (= personal pronoun) did not have to be placed immediately after the simple adjective and one encounters in Old Lithuanian (a) (gen. sg.) *žaysła pa-io-prasta* 'of the ordinary toy' (= modern *pãprasto-jo*), (b) (nom. pl.) *wisi su-gie-spausti* 'all the oppressed' (= modern *suspáustie-ji*), (c) (nom. sg.) *pra-iis-púłęs* 'having perished' (= modern *prapúolęs-is*). Note the doubled pronoun, both preceding and following the simple adjective: (d) (gen. sg.) *ne io-kałto-ia* 'of the innocent' (= modern *nekałto-jo*), see Zinkevičius, 1957, 7-8.

42.7 In Old Lithuanian one encounters the addition of the pronoun to a declined form of the noun, thus (a) (nom. sg.) *danguię-iis ukinikas* 'the heavenly farmer, i.e., the farmer who is in heaven' (< *[loc.] *dangujė̃* + [nom.] *jis* 'in heaven + he'), (b) (dat. sg.) *tewuy danguie-iam* 'to father in heaven' (< *[loc.] *dangujė̃* + [dat.] *jam* 'in heaven + to him'), (c) (inst. pl.) *siłomis szirdiię-iomis* 'with the strength in the heart' (< *[loc.] *širdyję* + [inst. pl.] *jomis* 'in the heart + by means of them'), (d) (nom. sg) *tewas dangu-gis* 'heavenly father' (< *[gen. pl.] *dangų* + [nom. sg.] *jis* 'of the heavens + he'), (e) (nom. sg.) *duona dangu-gi* 'heavenly bread' (< *[gen. pl.] *dangų* [nom. sg. fem.] *ji* 'of the heavens + it'). (See also 37). A similar phenomenon is encountered in contemporary dialects, e.g., from Lazũnai:

(f) dzievõ-   ji   bìtė.
    of god   it   bee.
    (gen.)   (nom. sg. fem.)   (nom. sg.)
'The divine bee.'

(g) žmonių̃-   jai   vaikaĩ.
    of men   they   children.
               (nom. pl. masc.)

(*-jai* here replacing *-jie*) 'the children of men.' In the examples given in this paragraph the locative singular and the genitive singular and plural have functioned as indefinite adjectives to which the personal pronoun has been added to make them definite (see Zinkevičius, 1981, 33).

42.8 There are several theories concerning the origin of the definite adjective. According to one theory the definite pronoun was originally a relative pronoun.
    Evidence for this view comes from Old Church Slavic (which has a similar system of indefinite and definite adjectives) in which the predicate adjective is in the indefinite form since in predicate position it was not originally a subordinate clause, as we presume the definite adjective to have been. In Lithuanian the third declension adjectives were, e.g., possessive compounds like *begė̃dis* 'one who has no shame,' determinative compounds like *sąsenis* 'very old' or complex adjectives such as the patronymic *-aitis*.

Such adjectives were originally nouns and originally stood in apposition with the nouns they came to modify and thus they have no definite form (Lehmann, 1970, 288-289).

The development of the Avestan relative pronoun into a definite pronoun is usually given as a parallel to the Balto-Slavic situation. According to Reichelt, 1909, 370-371, relative clauses which consisted of a relative pronoun plus a predicate noun underwent a special development. Originally the relative pronoun and the noun were both in the nominative case and the relative pronoun agreed with its referent in number and gender (as is typical in Indo-European languages). Later the relative pronoun lost its own meaning and along with the predicate noun came to be felt as being in apposition with its referent. Thus:

(a) daēvō   yō   apaošō.
    demon   which   Apaoša:
    (nom.)   (nom.)   (nom.)

originally meant 'the demon which (is) Apaoša' but came to mean merely 'the demon Apaoša,' i.e., it came to be interpreted as a kind of definite article. The same thing happened in sentences without a surface referent, and (b) (nom.) *yə̄ drəgvā̊* 'whoever is a possessor of falsehood' came to mean 'the possessor of falsehood.' Once the new meaning became established the entire expression assumed the case of the original referent word so that the accusative singular of (a) and (b) are respectively (c) *daēūm yim apaošəm* and (d) *yə̄m drəgvantəm*. The end result is that both the relative pronoun and the predicate are assigned the same case as the referent. Thus an expression:

(e) upa   tąm   čarətąm   yąm
    on   that   race-course   which

    darəγąm.
    long:

in which the preposition *upa* governs the accusative case of all the following words comes to mean 'on *the* long race-course.' Likewise:

(f) hačā   zəmat̰   yat̰   paθanayā̊.
    out of earth   which   wide:

in which the preposition *hača* governs the ablative case
of all the following words comes to mean 'out of *the
wide earth.*' As Zinkevičius, 1957, 10-11, points out,
in Avestan the pronoun occurs before the adjective,
whereas in Baltic it occurs after the adjective. On
the other hand the examples given in 42.6 above in which
the pronoun occurs between the prefix and before the
adjective itself give one a hint that the postadjectival
position may not be the original position.

Held, 1957, 13, found that in Hittite the deter-
minate relative clauses stand after their referent,
whereas indeterminate relative clauses stand before
their referent, e.g.:

(g) | *tăk-ku* | LÚ-*ša* | DUMU.SAL | *na-û-i* |
    | if | man | girl | not yet |

| *da-a-i* | *na-* | *an-* | *za* | *mi-im-ma-i* |
| takes | and | her | particle | refuses |

| *ku-û-ša-ta-ma* | *ku-it* | *píd-da-a-it* | *na-* |
| bride-price but | which | brought | and |

| *aš-* | *kán* | *ša-me-en-zi* |
| he | particle | forfeits. |

'If a man has not yet taken a girl, and he refuses her,
he forfeits the bride-price which he has brought.'
Notice that the subordinate clause *ku-it píd-da-it*
stands after the referent *ku-û-ša-ta* and picks up
the definite referent. Compare, however:

(h) | *nu* | *ku-iš* | DUMU-*aš* | *al-pa-an-za* ... |
    | and | whichever | child | bewitched |

| *na-* | *an* | *tu-i-ik-ku-uš* | *iš-ga-aḫ-ḫi.* |
| and | him | members | I shall anount. |

'Any child who is bewitched...I shall anoint the parts
of its body.' In this event the relative clause which
is indefinite (since it isn't even certain that there
will be a bewitched child) precedes its referent.
Rosenkranz, 1958, 99, calls one's attention to the fact
that from the point of view of example (42.6) *žaysƚa
paioprasta* 'of the ordinary toy' we are dealing with
the same word order as in the determined Hittite relative clause, although the reason for the insertion of

the pronoun following the prefix and before the root is
still unsolved. Benveniste, 1971, 189, considers the
Indo-European pronoun *yo- to have been originally a
marker of definiteness and suggests that even the final
position of the pronoun is encountered in Vedic:

(i) sā́   rā́trī   páritakmyā   yā́.
    this   night   waning   the (which?).

In this example Benveniste suggests the translation of
yā́ as a definite article rather than as a relative, to
give the translation 'this (the) waning night.'
   According to Hirt, 1934, 167, the definite adjective
derives from a postposed deictic pronoun. Similarly
Rosinas, 1975, 167, writes that the pronoun *jis* originally had deictic meaning and it is from this meaning
that the definite meaning developed. Parallels for a
similar development can be found in the history of the
Romance, Germanic, and other language families.
Rosinas, 168, points to the fact that in Old Lithuanian
one may use the preposed article which has developed
from a deictic pronoun, e.g.:

(j) atsiunte   ta   didi   skarba
    sent   the   great   treasure (to)

    sawa   sunu.
    his   son.

(k) Klausik   ka   tas   pirmas
    Listen to   what   the   first (one)

    sā́ko.
    says.

   Rosinas also notes that the pronouns *jis*, *tas*
and *anas* could all be used as third person anaphoric
pronouns in Old Lithuanian. He concludes, 169, that
for both *jis* and *tas* the original function was deictic
and that the secondary functions were anaphoric and as
a definite article.

42.9 Valeckienė, 1984, 124-131, finds that the definite
adjective has its origin in a following pronoun used in
apposition. Thus, e.g., in the Lithuanian folk songs

(*dainos*) we frequently encounter after the person or thing addressed, a definite adjective, commonly with some other repeated words and especially with possessive or 2nd person pronouns, with exclamatory words, repeated predicates. The adjectival group is separated from the noun by a clear pause, e.g.,

(1) Oi dukrãles, ói jáunos'os, tùrit sãnū motùlī.
    Oh daughters, oh young ones, you have an old mother.

(2) Bernẽli màno, jaunàsai màno, išimk áukso žiedẽlī.
    Lad   my,   young one my   take out golden ring.
'My lad, my young one, take out the golden ring.'

Similar definite adjective constructions are attested elsewhere in folk songs in cases where they do not refer directly to the person or thing addressed, generally with repeated possessive or deictic pronouns, prepositions, or repeated predicates, e.g.,

(3) Lakštiñgalė, paukštėlė taĩ tàvo   mergẽlė,
    Nightingale little bird it   your   girl,

    jõs sparnẽliai, jõs eiklíeji, taĩ báltos rankẽlės.
    her wings,   her swift,   it white hands.
'It is your girl, a little nightingale, her swift wings, the white hands.' Note that in the above construction the definite adjective *eiklíeji* 'swift' is isolated from the noun phrase, *jõs sparnẽliai* 'her wings.' The definite adjective along with the repeated possessive pronoun *jõs* 'her' is an emphatic statement defining the item again. The definite adjective in such cases is not used attributively, but in apposition to the noun. Constructions with definite forms or their substitutes can be paraphrased thus: (4) *Jõs sparnẽliai, jõs eiklíeji - *jõs sparnẽliai, jõs eĩklūs kuriẽ* 'her wings, (which) her swift ones.' As we have seen in 42.7 the pronoun was also attached to case forms of nouns. Thus the definite adjective, in Valeckienė's view, does not have its origin in morphological derivation, but rather in syntactic col-

location. Additional evidence that the definite pronoun has a syntactic origin is furnished by Old Lithuanian forms where the adjective and following pronoun have not completely merged, e.g. (allative) *tikrosp-iosp* 'to the true...' Valeckienė, 1984, 127, writes that proof of the fact that the definite adjective derives from a syntactic collocation is also to be found in the preposed forms, such as (DP 170) *praiispūtęs* (*žmógau*) 'lost man' a form which Ivanov, 1965, 238-239, would connect with the enclitic position of the pronoun required by Wackernagel's law. If Ivanov is correct such forms as this, *pa-io-prasta* 'of the ordinary' (with the gen. sg. pronoun *-io-* following the prefix and preceding the root), and *ne-io-kaĩto-ia* 'of the innocent' (with the gen. sg. pronoun *-io-* following the negative and preceding the root [with repetition of the pronominal *-ia* in final position also]) have the position fixed automatically by Wackernagel's law. Ivanov, 1965, 238, compares further Vedic (5) *kakṣívantam yá auśijáḥ* 'Kakshivanta descendant of Ushij' Avestan (6) *azəm yo Ahurō mazdå* 'I who am Ahuramazda,' and Gk. (7) *Teŭkros, hòs áristos Akhaiōn* 'Teukros (which) the best of the Achaeans.' If Ivanov's view is correct, then the preposing of the pronoun is merely a result of Wackernagel's law and does not reflect a parallel with the Hittite definite preposed relative clause. I believe the question needs further research.

Valeckienė, 1984, 131, writes that sometimes definite adjectives, usually of the comparative and superlative degrees, can alternate with the relative adverb *kuř* 'where' with the indefinite adjective, e.g.,

(8) Suriñk kuř didesnės (= didesniąsias) [bùlves]
    Gather which bigger   (bigger)   [potatoes]
                          (def. adj.)

    o mažesnės palìk.
    and smaller leave.
'Gather the bigger potatoes and leave the smaller ones behind.'

(9) Retaĩ   kàs   turėdavo tekiùs bagotėsniai
    Rarely someone had   boars richer

    kuř   (= bagotėsniaji)
    which (richer)
           (def. adj.)
'Rarely did anyone have boars, only the richer people!

Thus Valeckienė concludes that the pronoun *$\underset{\sim}{i}$o- originally had the nuance of anaphoric meaning, but was not a true anaphoric demonstrative pronoun. The relative pronoun *$\underset{\sim}{i}$o- could get the nuance of anaphoric meaning when it occurred with an adjective in appositional position with a noun and again emphasizing the same object which the noun denoted. The syntactic position determined the nuance of the anaphoric meaning of the pronoun. Otherwise the pronoun *$\underset{\sim}{i}$o- does not have an anaphoric meaning. Thus the pronoun *$\underset{\sim}{i}$o-, which over a long period formed the Baltic and Slavic definite adjective, is neither a pure relative nor a real anaphoric. In origin it is a relative with a nuance of anaphoric meaning determined by its syntactic position. This notion explains the inconsistency of the usage for the attribution of definiteness in the Baltic and Slavic languages.

43

Anatolian and Lithuanian Word Order

43. On the basis of the Anatolian languages, Ivanov, 1965, 216, writes that the most ancient word order which one can reconstruct is represented by:

$N + E_1 (+ E_2 \ldots + E_n) + \ldots + V_f$ where N is a noun, or a pronoun or perhaps a conjunction having its origin in a pronoun. (The initial noun could later have become adverbialized and then passed to a preverb.) E stands for an enclitic whereas V_f stands for the verb in sentence final position. Thus it is possible to suppose that the typical Hittite sequence *nu-ši...* 'and (to) him ...' can be compared with Lith. *nu-si-mazgok* 'wash yourself off' (Ambrazas, 1967, 120). The etymological initial nominal element is represented by the conjunction *nu-* in Hittite and the preverb *nu-* in Lithuanian. The Hittite dative-accusative 3rd sg. pronoun *-ši(-)* corresponds to the Lithuanian dative-accusative reflexive particle (Ivanov, 1965, 233). According to Ivanov, 1965, 232, the pronominal elements **s-*, **t-*, **n-* reconstructed on the basis of Celtic and Hittite correspondences are reflected in the initial elements of the corresponding Baltic constructions. The element *sa* is encountered in Latv. *sa-sa-tikties* 'to meet' and the element *t-* is encountered in the Lithuanian permissive particle *te-*. Ivanov, 1965, 230, compares the position of Lith. *-si-*, Hitt. *-ši-* on the one hand with the Lithuanian strengthening particle *-gi-* and Hitt. *-kan-* on the other hand, i.e., just as Hitt. *-kan-* follows *-ši-* so does Lith. *-gi-* follow *-si-* cf. Lith. *pa-si-gi-žiūrėjau* 'I looked (for myself),' *pa-si-gi-dėjau* 'I put for myself.' **Ambrazas**, 1967, 122, notes, however, that although more rarely, another word order is encountered, e.g. *at-gi-si-(i)lsėk* 'rest!', *ne-gi-si-tikėjau* 'I did not hope.'

The expected order with enclitic following the initial element of the sentence may be reflected by cases where the pronoun follows elements other than the preverb, e.g., (Daukša's Postilla) *kuriõs-mi daveĩ* 'which you gave to me' and *kaĩp-mi regis* 'as it seems to me' (Ivanov, 1974, 110).

Functional Sentence Perspective

According to Ambrazas, 1986, 93, in sentences which can be divided into theme and rheme, the rheme can be expressed by (1) the verb [V] and the object [O], (2) the subject [S] and the V, (3) the O, (4) the S. In those sentences in which the theme is expressed by S and the rheme by V and O, at the present time the neutral word order is SVO, e.g.,

(1) Svẽčias   nusivil̃ko   káilinius
    The guest   took off   the fur.

Similar sentences without an expressed subject can be formed according to the model VO, e.g.,

(2) Miškè   pamačiaũ   trobẽlę
    In the forest I saw   the hut.

Such a model is predominant for the style of the official language. An object preceding the verb is somewhat more emphasized, e.g.,

(3) Mykoliùkas   laimẽs   nemãtė
    Mike   luck   didn't see.
'Mike didn't have any luck.'

On the other hand the (S)OV model is stylistically marked only in places. In many cases it can alternate with the (S)VO model with somewhat unclear semantic nuances. When O is a pronoun, its position before the V is not only neutral, but predominant, e.g.,

(4) Vìsas   miẽstas   manè   ger̃bė
    The whole   city   me   respected.
'The whole city respected me.' The (S)OV model is customary in statements having a generalized meaning (sometimes fossilized) denoting continuous actions or a state e.g.,

(5) Dárbas   dárbą   vẽja
    Work   work   chases.   'Work chases away work'

This word order is most commonly found in the folk language and folklore where the (S)OV word order is sometimes more frequent than the (S)VO. Since the greatest semantic burden is usually carried by the verbal object, the (S)OV model is common in conversational language where there is a tendency to put the center of the rheme in penultimate position. But the position of the object can depend upon the meaning of the verb. For example the SVO order clearly predominates with verbs denoting speaking, feeling, comprehension, e.g.,

(6) Sesuõ   pasãkė   naujíeną
    Sister   told   the news.

(7) Mẽs nežinójom   kẽlio
    We didn't know the way.

(8) Pamačiaũ kìškį
    I saw the hare.

Note the following sentences formed according to the SVO and SOV patterns:

(9) Tà   žinià   labaĩ   sujáudino   mótiną
    That news   very much   excited   mother.

(10) Tà   žinià   mótiną   labaĩ   sujáudino
     That news   mother   very much   excited.
'That news excited mother very much.'

But in addition to the preceding patterns others are possible, patterns which can be made more obvious by a following context, cf. the VSO and VOS models:

(11) Labaĩ   sujáudino   tà   žinià   mótiną,   vìs   dár
     Very much   excited   that   news   mother,   still

     láukiančią   sūnaũs   sugrį̃žtant
     waiting   son   returning.   'That piece of news very much excited mother who was still waiting for her son's return.'

(12) Labaĩ   sujáudino   mótiną   tà   žinià,   kurią̃
     Very much   excited   mother   that   news   which

     ilgaĩ   slėpiaũ
     a long time   I hid.   'The news which I had hidden for a long time excited mother.'

For example, in answer to the question:

(18) *Ką dėdė nušóvė* 'What did uncle shoot?' possible answers with neutral word order are (SOV):

(19) Dėdė   lãpę   nušóvė
      Uncle   fox   shot

or (SVO):

(20) Dėdė   nušóvė   lãpę
      Uncle   shot   the fox.

In sentence (19) the object which is the rheme is in penultimate position which is more characteristic of the spoken language, and in sentence (20) in final position which is more characteristic of the literary language.

In the sentences in which the rheme is the subject the most customary neutral word order models are OVS or OSV, cf. the question:

(21) Kàs nušóvė lãpę? 'Who shot the fox?' Possible answers are (OVS):

(22) Lãpę   nušóvė   dėdė
      The fox   shot   uncle.   'Uncle shot the fox'

or (OSV):

(23) Lãpę   dėdė   nušóvė
      The fox   uncle   shot.   'Uncle shot the fox.'

Here the rheme (which is the subject) is in penultimate or sentence-final position and the uncommon position of the subject after the object helps to indicate the functional sentence perspective. In sentences with a different word order, viz. (SVO)

(24) Dėdė nušóvė lãpę

or (SOV):

(25) Dėdė lãpę nušóvė

a similar functional perspective would have to be indicated by the intonation of the sentence.

According to Ambrazas, 1986, 93, in sentences in which the theme is not clearly distinguished from the rheme the neutral sentence model is VS, e.g.,

(26) Išaũšo   rýtas
      Dawned   morning.   'Morning dawned.'

(27) Viršum̃ pilkų̃, tuščių̃ laukų̃ skrìdo sẽnas var̃nas
     Above the gray empty fields flew an old raven.

If there is an object in such sentences the usual word order is VSO or OVS, e.g.:

(28) Pàkvietė žvìrblis visùs paukštelìùs.
     Invited sparrow all birds.
'The sparrow invited all the birds.'

(29) Atvãrė vėjas dėbesį ir̃ ėmė pìlti líetų
     Brought wind cloud and began to pour rain.
'The wind brought a cloud and it began to pour raining.'

(30) Píevas ir ežerėlį sùpo aukštì kalnaĩ
     Meadows and lake surrounded high hills.
'High hills surrounded the meadows and the lake.'

(31) Príešus skýrė šviesì ùpė
     Enemies separated clear river.
'A clear river separated the enemies.'

If there is no expressed subject the usual order is VO, e.g.,

(32) Kažkur̃ kãlė daĩgį
     Somewhere were forging scythe.
'Somewhere (someone [they]) was/were forging a scythe.'

In sentences which have a second object in addition to the direct object this latter usually precedes the second object, e.g.:

(33) Kaimýnas paródė vaĩkui kẽlią
     The neighbor showed the child the way.

If, however, the indirect object contains more information (if it is somewhat rhematized), then the indirect object can follow the direct object, e.g.:

(34) Senẽlė kai kadà váišino Antanùką
     Grandmother sometimes treated Tony

    medumì (inst.)
    to some honey.

Word forms with adverbial meaning which are rather closely bound to verbs, for the most part precede the direct object, e.g.,

(35) Vaikaĩ riñko miškè úogas
     Children gathered in the forest berries.
'The children were gathering berries in the forest.'

If it is more rhematized, then the adverbial phrase may occur either before the verb or the object, e.g.:

(36) Vaikaĩ   riñko   úogas   miškè
     Children gathered berries in the forest.

or

(37) *Miškè vaikaĩ riñko úogas* 'id.'

Position of the Adjective

45. According to Ambrazas, 1986, 96, the neutral position for the adjective is to precede the noun, e.g.,

(1) *sẽnas var̃nas* 'old raven,' (2) *gražùs ruduõ* 'beautiful autumn,' etc. The reverse word order with the adjective following the noun, gives the phrase expressive or emphatic value, e.g.

(3) galė́jau   atsimiñti apiẽ   mū́sų   mókytoją brángų.
    I could   remember   about   our   teacher dear.

(4) mótina... malónės   didelė̃s   neturė́davo
    mother   pleasure great   did not have.
'Mother did not have great pleasure.'

Adjectives following nouns are sometimes used for stylistic effect in poetic language or they may be used as permanent epithets, e.g. (5) *rūtà žalióji* 'the green rue,' (6) *ą́žuolas pláčiašakis* 'the broad-rooted oak.'

Preposed adjectives which do not immediately precede the modified noun also have expressive effect:

(7) Iš   mažõs   kibirkštiẽs didìs   kỹla   gaĩsras
    From small   spark   great   arises fire.
'A great fire arises from a small spark.'

Postposition is characteristic for adjectives which are expanded by further modifiers or for two adjectives which are separated by meaning and intonation:

(8) Rãdo   óbelę,   pìlną labaĩ gražių̃   obuolių̃
    found   apple-tree   full of very beautiful apples.
'(He) found an apple tree full of very beautiful apples.'

(9) Atė̃jo   ruduõ,   liū̃dnas, nelaimìngas
    Arrived   autumn, sad,   unhappy.
'Autumn, sad and unhappy, arrived.'

Adjectival position after an indefinite pronoun is common and neutral, e.g.,

(10) *kas nõrs įdomaũs* (gen.) 'something interesting,'
(11) *šis tàs gẽro* (gen. sg.)/ *gẽra* (neut.) 'this and that good (thing),' (12) *kažkàs nežinomo* (gen. sg.)/ *nežinoma* (neut.) 'something unknown.'

The usual position for adjectival participles, pronouns and numerals is before the noun, e.g. (13) *gẽriamas vanduõ* 'potable water,' (14) *kažkóks žmogùs* 'some man (or other),' (15) *kìtas krãštas* 'another country,' (16) *dù kareĩviai* 'two soldiers,' (17) *pìrmas mokinỹs* 'the first pupil.'

The usual position for the adnominal genitive is before the determined noun, e.g.,

(18) áukso žíedas
 of gold ring. 'ring of gold, golden ring.'

(19) paũkščio   sparnaĩ.
 of the   bird wings. 'wings of the bird, bird's wings.'

The reverse word order is encountered if one wishes to emphasize the genitive, particularly in poetic language, e.g., (20) *kalnaĩ Nemunẽlio* 'hills of the Nemunas,' (21) *dũmas tėvỹnės* 'native smoke.' Such word order is also encountered if there is a modifying subordinate clause or participle construction:

(22) Sunkùs   gyvẽnimas   žmogaũs, kurìs   negãli
   Difficult   life   of man, who   cannot

 paeĩti/ negãlinčio paeĩti.
 walk   unable   to walk. 'Difficult is the
life of a man who cannot walk/is unable to walk.'

If an adjective and a genitive noun both determine a noun, the usual word order is (a) adjective, (b) genitive noun, (c) noun, e.g.:

(23) báltas   óbels   žíedas.
   white   of apple tree   bloom.
   (nom.)   (gen.)   (nom.) 'the white bloom
of the apple tree.'

(24) sunkùs   vãrio   varpas.
   heavy   of copper   bell.
   (nom.)   (gen.)   (nom.) 'heavy copper bell.'

318

(25) mãžos   mū́sų   núodėmes.
     small   our   sins   'our small sins.'

Nevertheless in such cases from the point of view of the adjective the position of the genitive depends upon the semantic division of the word sequence. The adjectival attribute goes directly before the modified word if it makes a closer or terminological unit with the modified word, e.g.,

(26) mótinos   vestùvinė   suknẽlė.
     mother's   wedding   dress.

(27) árklio   príekinės   kójos.
     horse's   front   legs.

Nominal modifiers in the instrumental usually follow the modified noun, e.g.,

(28) peiliùkas   káulinėm   kriaunõm
     knife   with a bone (inst.)   handle (inst.)

(29) vyrìškis   júodu   švarkù
     man   with a black (inst.)   coat (inst.)

Occasionally the instrumental modifier precedes the modified noun, e.g.,

(30) Taĩ   bùvo   dìdelė,   žemaĩ   paliñkusiomis
     It   was   big,   low   bending (inst. pl.)

     šakomìs   ẽglė
     branches   spruce.
'It was a big spruce with branches bent low.'

In general the locative and pronoun constructions follow the modified noun, e.g.,

(31) gaĩsras   dvarè
     fire   in the manor

(32) eĩgeta   bè   pastóges
     beggar   without a   home

(33) lángas   į̃   sõdą
     window opening onto the garden.

According to Ambrazas, 1986, 97, in comparative constructions the preposition ùž 'than' plus the accusative which denotes the standard can go either before the comparative adjective or after it. The model with the standard plus the comparative is more common to popular

319

speech, folklore and, in part to belles lettres, e.g., (34) *ùž árklį didèsnis* 'larger than a horse,' (35) *ùž mẽdų saldèsnis* 'sweeter than honey.' On the other hand the model with the order comparative plus the standard is typical of the official and scientific style, e.g., (36) *sunkèsnis ùž gẽležį* 'heavier than iron,' (37) *greitèsnis ùž gařsą* 'faster than sound.' In constructions with the preposition *peř* 'than' the prepositional phrase precedes, e.g., (38) *peř visùs vertèsnis* 'more valuable than all.' Similarly in expressions with the gen. pl. pronoun *visũ* 'of all' or the adverbs *užvìs, pervìs* 'than all' the pronouns or the adverb respectively precedes, e.g., (39) *visũ kalnũ aukščiáusias* 'the highest of all the hills,' (40) *užvìs didžiáusias/didèsnis* 'greatest of all/greater than all.' On the other hand in more recent constructions with the comparative particles *negù, neĩ, kaĩp, nekaĩp* 'than' the standard follows the comparative e.g., (41) *kietèsnis negù/neĩ geležìs* 'harder than iron, (42) *baltèsnis kaĩp/nekaĩp sniẽgas* 'whiter than snow.'

Position of the Adverb

46. In general, according to Ambrazas, 1986, 95, the neutral and usual place for the adverb of manner and similar prepositional and case constructions is directly before the verb, e.g.:

(1) geraĩ   dìrba.
    well   works.   'works well'

(2) ramiaĩ   kaĩba.
    calmly   talks.   'talks calmly'

(3) añt   rañkų   nešiójo.
    on   hands   carried.   'carried on (his/her) hands'

Adverbs of place, time and cause are similarly placed, e.g.:

(4) visì   teñ   sugrĩšime.
    all   there   we shall return.
'We shall all return there.'

(5) dabař   visuř   palĩjo.
    now   everywhere   began to rain.
'Now it began to rain everywhere.'

Such adverbs follow the verb only if there is some semantic functional load involved, e.g.:

(6) mẽs   gyvẽname   geraĩ.
    we   live   well.
This would be in answer to a question such as 'How do you live?'

(7) kalbė́k   ramiaĩ.
    speak   calmly.
This sentence tells you how you should speak, not that you should say something.

The usual position for other adverbs, case constructions and prepositional phrases is before the verb although with verbs of motion and change of state the position is after the verb, e.g.:

(8) žeñgė atgál.
 stepped back.

(9) išvažiãvo namõ.
 went home.

(10) pasidãrė nebegeraĩ.
 became no longer well. 'No longer began (to feel) well.'

Forms and constructions denoting purpose usually follow the verb also, e.g.:

(11) pàkvietė pietų̃.
 invited for dinner.

(12) susė́dom pùsryčiauti.
 We sat down to eat breakfast.

If the forms or constructions have a heavier semantic burden, they may be shifted to the position following the verb, e.g.:

(13) sustójom tiẽs vartẽliais.
 We stopped opposite the gate.

Such forms or constructions may be shifted to sentence initial position, but in this case their meaning is connected with the entire sentence, their function is less of a logical argument than that of a secondary predicate, e.g.:

(14) Apliñk ẽžerą áugo tánkus mìškas.
 Around the lake grew a thick forest.

In a sequence of adverb plus adjective the adverb usually precedes according to Ambrazas, 1986, 97, e.g.:

(15) nepaprastaĩ tvankùs óras.
 unusually close air.

(16) labaĩ gẽras žmogùs.
 very good man.

Similarly a prepositional phrase modifying an adjective usually precedes, e.g.:

(17) bè gãlo gẽras.
 without end good 'infinitely good.'

(18) iš   esmės   klaidìngas.
    from   essence   erroneous.   'essentially
                                    erroneous.'

The instrumental noun usually precedes adjectives in *-inas*, e.g.:

(19) ėjo   kibìrais   nẽšinas.
     went   pails (inst. pl.)   carrying.
'(someone) went carrying the pails.'

(20) grìžo   árkliu   vẽdinas.
     returned horse (inst. pl.)   leading.
'(He) returned leading the horse.'

The place of other case and prepositional constructions from the point of view of the adjective can vary, i.e., it can occur either before or after the word modified, e.g.:

(21) vandeñs   pìlnas   ąsõtis
     of water (gen.) full (nom.)   jug. (nom.)

or

(22) pìlnas   vandeñs   ąsõtis.
     full (nom.) of water (gen.)   jug. (nom.)
'jug full of water.'

(23) tėvui   reikalìngas   kir̃vis.
     for father   necessary   axe.

or

(24) reikalìngas   tėvui   kir̃vis.
     necessary   for father   axe.
'axe necessary for father.'

(25) iš   pažiūrõs   gražì   kepùrė.
     from   view   beautiful   hat.

or

(26) gražì   iš   pažiūrõs kepùrė.
     beautiful   from   view   hat.
'a hat that is pretty to look at.'

Adverbial modifiers precede the adverb which they modify, e.g.:

(27) visái   blogaĩ   dìrba.
     quite   badly   works.   'works quite badly.'

(28) labaĩ   greĩtai   skreñda.
    very   fast   flies.   'flies very fast.'

(29) mãto   daũg   geriaũ.
    sees   much   better.

Adverbs of quantity usually precede the noun quantified, e.g.: (30) *daũg vandeñs* 'much water,' (31) *mažaĩ grỹbų* 'few mushrooms.' (Ambrazas, 1986, 98).

The order of the standard and the comparative in adverbial sentences is similar to that encountered with the adjective. Thus one can say either:

(31) ùž vė́ją greičiaũ   or (32) greičiaũ ùž vė́ją.
    than wind faster   faster than the wind.

Only the order standard plus comparison is possible in the following sentences: (33) *užvìs geriaũ* 'better than all,' (34) *pervìs toliaũ* 'farther than all.' Only the order comparison plus standard is possible in the following sentences: (35) *ankščiaũ negù/neĩ vãkar* 'earlier than yesterday,' (36) *gražiaũ nekaĩp/neĩ kitì* 'more beautifully than the others.'

Conclusions About Word Order

Ambrazas, 1986, 98, concludes that for the most part the word order shows that the modifier precedes the element modified, thus, e.g., adverb plus verb, particle plus verb, adjective plus noun, pronoun plus noun, numeral plus noun, genitive plus noun, adverb plus adjective and modifying adverb plus adverb. The only exceptions are when a noun is modified by an instrumental, see 45.27-32 and when the order is preposition plus noun, (see appropriate paragraphs on prepositions). The order of the verb, subject and object is governed by the functional sentence perspective, but even here the most usual order is SVO. The tendency for the dependent and the fundamental member of a group to follow the same order is observed in many languages and is variously called natural serialization, natural word order, or cross category harmony.

It is frequently thought that the position of the subject and object in relation to the verb is the decisive factor in determining the relationship of the other elements mentioned above. The data of the Lithuanian (and Latvian) language(s) do not confirm this rule, since the SVO word order has become dominant during the epoch of the Lithuanian literary language, i.e., much later than the time when the preposition plus noun and certain comparative constructions with the word order comparative plus standard came into existence. Typological studies of various languages have shown that the SVO model is harmonious with various word order combinations and does not imply any of these directly. A clearer correlation has been established between prepositional constructions and SOV order on the one hand and postpositions and an SVO order on the other hand.

The preposition plus noun order implies strongly the order of the noun plus genitive, and the noun plus genitive in turn implies noun plus adjective order. Nevertheless the Lithuanian data contradict this implication. Along with the preposition plus noun constructions the neutral or unmarked word order is adjective plus noun, pronoun plus noun and genitive plus noun (except for certain expressions of quantity, see fn. 11). Such a relationship would seem to be maximally disharmonic but Ambrazas, 1986, 99, would explain this diachronically by the way in which the prepositional constructions arose. In Lithuanian, as in other related languages, prepositions and prefixes had their origin in earlier adverbs or preverbs. In fact the change of adverbs into prepositions is in Lithuanian a live process: such words as *apliñk* 'around,' *artì* 'near,' *gretà* 'side by side,' *išilgaĩ* 'along,' *pãskui* 'after,' *pirmà* 'before,' *príešais* 'opposite,' *skersaĩ* 'across,' *šalià* 'beside,' *viršum̃* 'above,' *viršùj* 'above,' are sometimes used like adverbs and other times like prepositions. As adverbs they modify the semantic relationships expressed by the sequence of words, i.e., they are modifiers, e.g.,

(1) apẽjom   laukùs apliñk.
    we went   fields around. 'We went around the fields'

(2) gyvẽnom   gretà   pamiškėjè
    we lived side by side   on the forest's edge.

(3) viršùj lentàs užkalė.
    above   boards nailed up
'(They) nailed up boards up above.'

In other contexts they have taken on a prepositional function because of their semantic proximity to prepositions of similar meaning, cf., e.g.,

(4) bė́go apliñk (cf. apiẽ) namùs.
    ran   around (around)   house (acc.).
'(He) ran around the house.'

(5) stóvi   gretà (cf. priẽ) manę̃s.
    stands beside (near)   me (gen.)
'(He) is standing near me.'

(6) viršùj (cf. añt) stógo   tupė́jo.
    on   (on)   roof (gen.) perched
'(It) perched on the roof.'

An etymological analysis would lead us to believe that those adverbs from which the older prepositions developed (*añt* 'on,' *bè* 'without,' *per̃* 'through,' *nuõ* 'from') were also formerly used as modifiers of the relationships expressed by the noun cases, i.e., they were dependent members. They could go either before or after the modified noun in a certain case. The word order model according to which the adverbs went before the noun or verb according to the position of the dependent member was then not 'disharmonic' and could be harmonized with the word order of genitive before noun, adjective before noun, etc.

When preposed adverbs (preverbs) became prepositions and postposed adverbs (preverbs) became postpositions, their relationship to the noun changed. From being syntactically dependent they became fundamental, i.e., they determined the case of the noun. In the course of time the prepositional constructions began to oust the postpositional constructions. The process took place in the different Indo-European language groups at various times and its results are nowhere exactly the same, but the victory of the prepositional constructions is observed in nearly all the related languages and in the Germanic languages along with the genitive plus noun order.

My own comment on all this is to suggest that the facts which Ambrazas has revealed are a counter-example to the various theories of word order. In my view it has to be explained why exactly a disharmonic word order, viz., preposition plus noun became predominant in view of the fact that the word order of genitive and adjective plus noun was the standard. Since postpositions were (and still are to a limited extent) possible, exactly why did the prepositional constructions gain the upper hand over the postpositional constructions? The theory of word order development predicts exactly the opposite of what actually did happen. Since clever patching and repairing can save most theories, possibly there can be found an answer that would satisfy at least the proponents of theories of word order harmony. But until such clever repairs and/or patches have been made, the facts adduced by Ambrazas must be considered evidence that the entire theory of word order universals is deficient. On this matter one should see also Reklaitis, 1982, for a shift from SVO to SOV order within Indo-European.

FOOTNOTES

1. A sentence such as (a) *àš daviaũ vaĩkui óbuolį* could be passivized with either the direct or the indirect object as the subject, vz. (b) *obuolỹs (yrà) dúotas vaĩkui* 'the apple was given to the child' or (c) *vaĩkas (yrà) dúotas óbuolį* 'The child was given the apple.' The acc. *óbuolį* remains from the underlying sentence (a) from which (c) was derived. There are several impersonal paraphrases of sentence (a), viz. (d) *obuolỹs* (nom.) *(yrà) dúota* (neut.) *vaĩkui* 'the apple was given to the child' and (e) *óbuolį* (acc.) *(yrà) dúota* (neut.) *vaĩkui* 'id.' In sentence (e) the acc. *óbuolį* is to be explained in the same way as the acc. *láišką* in such a sentence as *rãšoma láišką* 'a letter is written' (see chapter 6, sentences (q), (r), (s) ff.) (Ambrazas, personal communication, September 19, 1986.)
2. Kazlauskas, 1968, 301, suggests that the Baltic languages never had a third plural form, but even if this is the case, it seems likely that the present active participle is of Indo-European age.
3. If I understand Trost, 1986, correctly he would connect the appearance of the nominative object of the infinitive with the impersonal nature of the sentence. He gives the following sentences:
  (1) Reĩkia   dárbas   dìrbti
      is necessary work   to work. 'It is necessary to
             (nom.)
      do the work; the work must be done.'
  (2) Kitíem   laiškaĩ   rašýti   sunkù
      For others letters   to write difficult.
      (dat.pl.) (nom. pl.)
      'It is difficult for others to write letters.
      Letters are difficult for others to write.'
  (3) Girdéti   bùvo   šùnys   lójant
      to hear   was   dogs   barking.
                      (nom. pl.)
      'One could hear dogs barking.'
  (4) Mą   lìko   púdymas   árti
      To me remained fallow   to plow. 'It remained
      (dat.)
      for me to plow the fallow land.'

Sentences (1) through (3) are transformations of a normal sentence into a subjectless sentence, such that the unoccupied slot (*Leerstelle*) of the nominative subject is filled by the object (sentences (1) and (2)) or the subject (sentence (3)). In sentences (1) and (2) the object case is raised to the nominative subject. In sentence (3) where there is no object case the subject case remains as such in the condensed sentence. In sentence (4) the object of the infinitive sentence is raised to the subject of the impersonal predicate.

4. Ambrazas, 1987, gives a complete analysis of the nominative plus infinitive construction and supports the notion of its Indo-European origin.

5. According to the *Grammatika litovskogo jazyka*, p. 431, the last of the following impressive sequences of infinitives can still require a genitive case as a result of the negation of a governing main verb:

nenorėjo	(1) léisti	(2) pradėti	(3) lankýti
did not want	to allow	to begin	to attend

mokỹklos
school

(gen. sg.) '(They) did not want to allow (him/her/them/) to begin to attend school.'

6. According to Ambrazas (personal communication, Sept. 15, 1986) the verb *eĩti* 'to go' in such sentences as *àš einù árklio pir̃kt*ų (*pir̃kti*) 'I am going (some placé) to buy a horse' could have been semantically influenced by such verbs as *norėti* 'to wish,' *ieškóti* 'to search for' and *siekti* 'to try to reach, to achieve' which govern the genitive case. Thus when *eĩti* is used with the meaning 'to go for something' (with ellipse of the infinitive or supine) it is construed with a genitive object.

7. The use of the accusative as the direct object of the supine in place of the genitive in sentences such as (c) *puolė visi bučiuot*ų *rankas seneliui* and (d) *Stankūnas nubėgo sudėt*ų *pinigus advokatui* must be an innovation as we can see from the Old Lithuanian example (30.4/a/) *ateis suditu giwu ir numirusiu* where there can be no notion of 'getting something for oneself.'

8. On the model *Jõnas* (nom.) *bùvo mókytoju* (inst.) 'John was a teacher,' it is also possible to have *Jõno* (gen.) *búta* (neut. past passive participle) *mókytoju* (inst.) 'id.' (Gramatika litovskogo jazyka, p. 641).

9. Jablonskis felt that the use of the instrumental with such verbs as *pripíldyti* 'to fill,' *prikim̃šti* 'to stuff

with,' *pritviñkti* 'to swell up with,' *primir̃kti* 'to be soaked with' was incorrect. Thus he corrected (1) *ródos, vìskas džiaũgsmù* (inst.) *prisipìldytų* 'it seems, everything would become full of joy' with the gen. *džiaũgsmo* 'by, with joy.' In the sentence (2) *Jõ véidas pritviñksta kraujù* (inst.) 'His face swells with blood' he replaced the inst. *kraujù* 'with blood' by the gen. *kraũjo*. In the sentence (3) *Žùs alkoholiù* (inst.) *pérmirkusiame kūne* '(It) will perish in a body soaked with alcohol' he replaced the inst. *alkoholiù* 'with alcohol' by the gen. *alkohòlio*. Cf. sentence (4):

Sukìlėliai paléido dinamitù prikráuta
Rebels set in motion with dynamite loaded
                                   (inst.)

gárvežį
locomotive. 'The rebels set the locomotive loaded with dynamite in motion.'

In this sentence Jablonskis replaced the instrumental with the genitive. In these examples it seems to me that the genitive is used with a clear instrumental meaning rather than an agentive meaning which we might expect. The verbal government requires the genitive with the instrumental meaning (Piročkinas, 1986, 194).

10. It is interesting to note that Jonas Jablonskis felt that the use of the instrumental as agent with the passive participle was a result of the influence of Slavic languages. Thus:

(1) Kalbétojai palinkéjo, kàd sutvirtétų ryšiaĩ
    Speakers wished that would become firm bonds

ir̃ tar̃p atstováujamų jaĩs tautų̃
even between being represented by them nations

'The speakers wished that the bonds between the nations represented by them would become firm.' Jablonskis would correct the instrumental *jaĩs* 'by them' with the genitive *jų̃* 'by them.' In certain cases either the instrumental or the genitive is possible, but with a different meaning. Thus the phrase

(2) àpsuptas žmonių̃ minià
    surrounded of people with a crowd
                            (inst.)

Jablonskis translated into German as *mit einer Menschenmenge umringt, umgeben* 'surrounded with a crowd of people!'

The phrase
(3) didelės   žmonių   miniõs   àpsuptas
    by a big   of people   crowd   surrounded
    (gen. sg.) (gen. pl.)   (gen. sg.)

Jablonskis translated into German as *von einer groszen Menschenmenge umringt* 'surrounded by a big crowd of people' (Piročkinas, 1986, 194).

11. According to Ambrazas, 1986, 97, when the noun denotes quantity and the genitive the object being measured, then the noun in this meaning is close to that of the adverb of quantity which also precedes the genitive. In such cases word order can be used to differentiate meaning, e.g. *vežimas šiẽno* and *šiẽno vežimas* can both mean 'a wagon (load) of hay,' but only the latter could alternatively have the meaning 'a hay wagon, a wagon for transporting hay.' Likewise both *stiklìnė arbãtos* and *arbãtos stiklìnė* can mean 'a glass of tea,' but only the latter can mean 'a glass for tea.' Similarly *maĩšas bùlvių* and *bùlvių maĩšas* can both mean 'a sack of potatoes,' but only the latter can mean 'a sack for potatoes.'

12. In sentence (a) the acc. *úodegą* is explained as the result of the influence of an underlying sentence such as *kãtinui úodegą láužo* '(someone) is twisting the cat's tail.' In sentence (b) the acc. *šìrdį* might be explained from such an underlying impersonal sentence as *man* (dat.) *šìrdį sópa* 'my heart aches.' (Ambrazas, personal communication, Sept. 19, 1986.)

13. Jablonskis considered the sociative instrumental a dialectism and would correct it by adding the preposition *su* 'with.' Thus instead of:
  Atvỹko   pasiuntiniaĩ   láuro   šakẽlėmis   rañkose
  Arrived   ambassadors   of laurel with branches in hands
  'The ambassadors arrived with branches of laurel in their hands' Jablonskis would have *sù láuro šakẽlėmis* 'with branches of laurel' (Piročkinas, 1986, 198).

14. Jablonskis demanded that a semantic distinction be made between the use of the instrumental and the use of the accusative as complements of the verb *tikėti* 'to believe' (Piročkinas, 1986, 196). Thus he condemned the following sentence:
  (1) Tù   vìs   dár   tikì   senaĩs   dievaĩs
      You still   believe in the old gods
                                  (inst.)   (inst.)

and would replace the instrumental with the accusative *senùs dievùs* 'old gods.' On the other hand such a phrase as

(2) *tikėk manim̃* (inst.) 'believe me' he found perfectly correct. Later in life, however, he decided that the distinction could no longer be maintained and wrote that

(3) *tikėti kã* (acc.) and *kuõ* (inst.) 'to believe someone have exactly the same meaning and are to be used the same way in the standard language.

15. The use of the instrumental with such verbs as *būti* 'to be,' *tàpti* 'to become,' *ródytis* 'to appear,' *apsimèsti* 'to pretend,' *jaũstis* 'to feel,' *likti* 'to remain,' *gim̃ti* 'to be born' was condemned by Jablonskis (Piročkinas, 1986, 190-191). Thus instead of:

(1) *bañgos...tãpo tam̃siai mėlynomis* (inst. pl.) 'the waves...became dark blue' Jablonskis recommended *mėlynos* (nom. pl.) 'blue.' Instead of:

(2) *Jìs apsimetė sergančiu* 'he pretended to be sick' Jablonskis recommended *sergą̃s* (nom. sg.) 'sick.' As a result of Russian and Polish influence the second member of the double accusative construction was sometimes replaced by the instrumental, a practice which Jablonskis also condemned (Piročkinas, 1986, 192-193). Thus instead of:

(3) Paprašýkite jį̃ gerù būti
    Ask him good to be.
    (acc.) (inst.)

'Ask him to be good' Jablonskis would substitute *gẽrą* (acc.) 'good.' With a negated object the accusative of course should be replaced by the genitive. Thus instead of:

(4) Àš ne šveñtas ir̃ tavè šventù nenóriu
    I not saint and you saint I don't want

darýti   (inst.)
to make.

'I am not a saint and I don't want to make you a saint.'

Jablonski would have '...*tavę̃s* (gen.) *šveñto* (gen.) *nenóriu darýti*. Instead of the instrumental the double dative is advised with impersonal constructions. Thus instead of:

(5) Bèt studeñtams reĩkia būti ir̃
    But for students it is necessary to be also

sveikaĩs
healthy (inst. pl.)

Jablonskis recommends *sveikíems* (dat. pl.) 'healthy' (Piročkinas, 1986, 193).

REFERENCES

Academy Dictionary = Lietuvių kalbos žodynas, Kruopas, J. et al., eds. Vilnius, Mintis, Mokslas.
Academy Grammar = Lietuvių kalbos gramatika. K. Ulvydas et al., eds. Vilnius, Mintis.
Ambrazas, V. 1959. Dėl vadinamojo 'absoliutinio įnagininko' XVI-XVII a. lietuvių kalbos paminkluose. Lietuvių kalbotyros klausimai 2.47-54.
―――――. 1962. Absoliutinis naudininkas XVI-XVII a. lietuvių kalbos paminkluose. Lietuvių kalbotyros klausimai 5.3-146.
―――――. 1967. Review of Ivanov, Vjač. Vs. Obščeindoevropejskaja, praslavjanskaja i anatolijskaja jazykovye sistemy. Baltistica 3.117-123.
―――――. 1979. Lietuvių kalbos dalyvių istorinė sintaksė. Vilnius, Mokslas.
―――――. 1981. Zur Geschichte einer indoeuropäischen Konstruktion: Dativus cum Infinitivo im Baltischen. Kalbotyra 32, No. 3, 12-24.
―――――. 1986. Dabartinės lietuvų kalbos žodžiu tvarkos modeliai. Lietuvos TSR Mokslų Akademijos darbai. A serija 3(96) : 92.102.
―――――. 1987. Indogermanische Grundlage des Dativus und Nominativus cum infinitivo im Baltischen. Indogermanische Forschungen 92.
Andersen, Henning. 1970. The dative of subordination in Baltic and Slavic. 1-9. Baltic Linguistics, eds. Thomas F. Magner and William R. Schmalstieg. University Park and London, The Pennsylvania State University Press.
Aronson, Howard I. 1982. Georgian: A reading grammar. Columbus, Ohio, Slavica Press.
Balkevičius, J. 1963. Dabartinės lietuvių kalbos sintaksė. Vilnius.
Bammesberger, A. 1971. Litauisch *byla/bila* bei Mažvydas. Baltistica 7.185-187.
Bech, G. 1971. Beiträge zur genetischen indogermanischen Verbalmorphologie. Copenhagen.
Bednarczuk, L. 1966. On certain participial constructions in Balto-Slavic, Germanic and Celtic. Acta Baltico-Slavica 3.29-32.

Benveniste, E. 1962. Les substantifs en *-ant-* du hittite. Bulletin de la société de linguistique de Paris. 57.44-51.
——————. 1971. Problems in general linguistics. (English translation by Mary Elizabeth Meeks). Coral Gables, University of Miami Press.
Bielenstein, A. 1863. Handbuch der lettischen Sprache I. Lettische Grammatik. Mitau, Fr. Lucas' Buchhandlung. Repr. 1972 by the Zentralantiquariat der Deutschen Demokratischen Republik, Leipzig.
Boeder, Winfried. 1979. Ergative syntax and morphology in language change: The South Caucasian languages. Pp. 435-480 in Ergativity, ed. by Frans Plank. London, New York, Academic Press.
Bogoliubov, M.N. 1982. Typological parallels of the Old Armenian perfect with a transitive verb. Pp. 20-21. Abstracts. International Symposium on Armenian Linguistics. Erevan, Academy of Sciences of the Armenian SSR.
Brugmann, Karl and Berthold Delbrück. 1906. Grundriss der vergleichenden Grammatik der indogermanischen Sprachen. Vol. 2, Pt. 1. Strassburg, Karl J. Trübner.
——————. 1916. Grundriss der vergleichenden Grammatik der indogermanischen Sprachen. Vol. 2, Pt. 3 (2nd half). Strassburg, Karl J. Trübner.
Buch, Tamara. 1962. Użycie participiów w utworach Ch. Donełajtisa. Biuletyn polskiego towarzystwa językoznawczego. 21.147-159.
Buch(ienė), Tamara and J. Palionis. 1957. Introductory comments on D. Klein and his grammar in Kabelka, 1957.
Būga, K. 1958. Rinktiniai raštai I. Vilnius, Valstybinė politinės ir mokslinės literatūros leidykla.
——————. 1959. Rinktiniai raštai II. Vilnius, Valstybinė politinės ir mokslinės literatūros leidykla.
——————. 1961. Rinktiniai raštai III. Vilnius, Valstybinė politinės ir mokslinės literatūros leidykla.
Bulygina, T. V. 1959a. O sočetanijax s roditel'nym padežom v sovremennom litovskom literaturnom jazyke. Lietuvių kalbotyros klausimai 2.90-108.
——————. 1959b. Neglagol'nye sočetanija s roditel'nym padežom v sovremennom litovskom literaturnom jazyke. Slavjanskoe jazykoznanie. Moscow, pp. 217-18.
Burrow, T. 1965. The Sanskrit language. 2nd ed. Glasgow, The University Press.

Cardona, George. 1970. The Indo-Iranian construction *mana (mama) kr̥tam*. Language 46.1-12.
Chvany, Catherine V. and Richard D. Brecht, eds. 1980. Morphosyntax in Slavic. Columbus, Ohio, Slavica Publishers.
Chyliński's Bible = Biblią litewska Chylińskiego. Vol. 2, Text, 1958, Vol. 3, Index, 1964. Poznań, Ossolineum in Wrocław. Ed. by Czesław Kudzinowski and Jan Otrębski. (Numbers denote page and line from this edition.)
Čikobava, Arn. 1948. Istoričeskoe vzaimootnošenie nominativnoj i ergativnoj konstrukcii po dannym drevnegruzinskogo jazyka. Izvestija AN SSSR. Otdelenie literatury i jazyka 8, No. 3.221-234.
Classen, J. 1879. Beobachtungen über den homerischen Sprachgebrauch. Frankfurt a. M., Carl Winter
Collitz, H. 1888. II.-Die Herkunft des schwachen Präteritums der germanischen Sprachen. The American Journal of Philology 9.42-57.
—————. 1891. Die herkunft des schwachen präteritums der germanischen sprachen. Beiträge zur kunde der indogermanischen sprachen 17.227-244. Reprt. from Collitz 1888.
Comrie, Bernard. 1979. Definite and animate direct objects: A natural class. Linguistica Silesiana 3.13-21.
—————. 1981. Language universals and linguistic typology. Chicago, University of Chicago Press.
Cowgill, Warren. 1970. The nominative plural and the preterit singular of the active participles in Baltic. Pp. 23-37. In Magner and Schmalstieg, Baltic Linguistics. University Park and London, Pennsylvania State University Press.
—————. 1975. The origins of the insular Celtic conjunct and absolute verbal endings. Pp. 40-70. In Helmut Rix, ed., Flexion und Wortbildung. Wiesbaden, Dr. Ludwig Reichert Verlag.
Delbrück, B. 1888. Altindische Syntax. Halle A. S., Verlag des Waisenhauses.
—————. 1897. Vergleichende Syntax der indogermanischen Sprachen. Strassburg.
Disterheft, Dorothy. 1980. The syntactic development of the infinitive in Indo-European. Columbus, Ohio, Slavica Publishers.

D'jakonov, I. M. 1967. Ėrgativnaja konstrukcija i
sub"ektno-ob"ektnye otnošenija. Pp. 95-115. In Ėrgativnaja konstrukcija predloženija v jazykax različnyx tipov, ed., V.M. Žirmunskij, et al. Leningrad, Nauka.

Eckert, Rainer. 1981. Untersuchungen zur historischen Phraseologie und Lexikologie des Slawischen und Baltischen: Systemfragmente aus der Terminologie der Waldimkerei. = Reihe A, Arbeitsberichte 81. Akademie der Wissenschaften der DDR, Zentral Sprachwissenschaft, Berlin.

Elizarenkova, T. Ja. 1967. Ėrgativnaja konstrukcija v novoindijskix jazykax. Pp. 116-125. In Ėrgativnaja konstrukcija predloženija v jazykax različnyx tipov, ed., V. M. Žirmunskij, et al. Leningrad, Nauka.

Elzbutas, J. 1967. Antrasis naudininkas lietuvių ir rusų kalbose. Kalbotyra 16.143-157.

Endzelīns, J. 1951. Latviešu valodas gramatika. Riga, Latvijos valsts izdevniecība. (= Latvian translation of his Lettische Grammatik, Riga, 1922.)

Ėrgativnaja konstrukcija predloženija v jazykax različnyx tipov. 1967. Žirmunskij, V. M., S. D. Kacnel'son et al., eds. Leningrad, Nauka.

Erhart, Adolf. 1980. Struktura indoíranských jazyků. Brno, Univerzita J. E. Purkyně.

Fennell, T. G. and Gelsen, H. 1980. A grammar of modern Latvian. The Hague, Mouton.

Fillmore, Charles J. 1968. The case for case. Pp. 1-88 in Universals in linguistic theory, ed., by Emmon Bach and Robert T. Harms. New York, Holt, Rinehart, and Winston.

Ford, Gordon B., Jr. 1969. The Old Lithuanian Catechism of Baltramiejus Vilentas (1579): A phonological morphological and syntactical investigation. The Hague, Paris, Mouton.

—————. 1971. The Old Lithuanian Catechism of Martynas Mažvydas (1547), edited and translated by Gordon B. Ford. Assen, Van Gorcum and Comp. N.V.

Fraenkel, Ernst. 1925. Zur baltoslavischen Grammatik II. KZ 53.36-65.

—————. 1926. Der prädikative Instrumental im Slavischen und Baltischen und seine syntaktischen Grundlagen. Archiv für slavische Philologie 40.77-117.

—————. 1928. Syntax der litauischen Kasus. Kaunas.

—————. 1929. Syntax der litauischen Postpositionen und Präpositionen. Heidelberg, Carl Winter.

Fraenkel, Ernst. 1947. Sprachliche, besonders syntaktische Untersuchung des kalvinistischen litauischen Katechismus des Malcher Pietkiewicz von 1598. Göttingen, Vandenhoeck and Ruprecht.
—————. 1950. Die baltischen Sprachen. Heidelberg, Carl Winter.
Friedrich, Johannes. 1960. Hethitisches Elementarbuch. Vol. 1, 2nd ed. Heidelberg, Carl Winter.
Gerullis, Georg, ed. 1923. Mosvid: Die ältesten litauischen Sprachdenkmäler bis zum Jahre 1570. Heidelberg, Carl Winter.
Girdenienė, D. 1981. Derinamojo pažyminio vieta tarminėje ir bendrinėje lietuvių kalboje. Baltistica 17.156-169.
Givón, Talmy. 1976. Topic, pronoun, and grammatical agreement. Pp. 151-188. In Subject and topic, ed. by Charles N. Li. New York, San Francisco and London, Academic Press, Inc.
Godel, Robert. 1975. An introduction to the study of classical Armenian. Wiesbaden, Dr. Ludwig Reichert Verlag.
Gołąb, Zbigniew. 1975. Endocentricity and endocentrization of verbal predicates: illustrated with Latin and Slavic material. General Linguistics 15.1-35.
Gonda, Jan. 1966. A concise elementary grammar of the Sanskrit language. Tr. by Gordon B. Ford, Jr. University, Alabama.
Goodwin, William Watson and Charles Burton Gulick. 1958. Greek grammar. Waltham, Mass., Blaisdell.
Grabauskas, V. 1971. Dabartinės lietuvių kalbos naudininko reikšmės ir funkcijos. Kalbotyra 22, No. 1, 49-59.
Grammatika litovskogo jazyka. 1985. Ambrazas, V., ed. in chief. Vilnius, Mokslas.
Grenda, Č. 1965. Veiksmažodžių junginiai su objekto bendratimi. Kalbotyra 13.29-55.
—————. 1967. Pastabos dėl vadinamųjų infinityvinių sakinių. Kalbotyra 17.81-87.
—————. 1979. Apibrėžtumo/neapibrėžtumo požymių opozicija veiksmazodžių konstrukcijose su daiktavardžiu. Kalbotyra 30, No. 1, 32-38.
Güterbock, Hans G. and Harry A. Hoffner. 1980. The Hittite Dictionary. Vol. 3, Fasc. 1. Chicago, Oriental Institute of the University of Chicago.

Haarmann, Harald, ed. 1977. Daniel Klein: Grammatica Lituanica, Compendium Lituanico-Germanicum, Oder Kurtze und gantz deutliche Anführung zur Littauschen Sprache. Hamburg, Helmut Buske Verlag.

Hakulinen, L. 1957. Handbuch der finnischen Sprache. Vol. 1. Wiesbaden, Otto Harrassowitz.

Hamp, Eric P. 1973. On Baltic, Luwian and Albanian participles in *-m-. Baltistica 9.45-50.

Havránek, B. 1928. Genera verbi v slovanských jazycích. Vol. 1. Prague.

——————. 1937. Genera verbi v slovanských jazycích. Vol. 2. Prague, Náklad kr. české spol. nauk.

Hawkins, J. D., Anna Morpurgo-Davies, and Günter Neumann. 1973. Hittite hieroglyphs and Luwian: New evidence for the connection. Pp. 144-197. Nachrichten der Akad. der Wiss. in Göttingen I. Phil-Hist. Klasse.

Held, Warren. 1957. The Hittite relative sentence. Language 33 = Supplement. Language Dissertation No. 55.

Hermann, Eduard. 1926. Litauische Studien (= Abhandlungen der Gesellschaft der Wissenschaften zu Göttingen. Philologisch-historische Klasse, Neue Folge. Bd XIX, 1). Berlin, Weidmannsche Buchhandlung.

——————. 1926. Die subjektlosen Sätze bei Homer und der Ausdruck der Tätigkeit, des Vorgangs und des Zustands. Nachrichten der Gesellschaft der Wissenschaften zu Göttingen aus dem Jahre 1926. Philologisch-Historische Klasse. Berlin, Weidmannsche Buchhandlung (1927).

Hirt, Hermann. 1928. Indogermanische Grammatik. Part 4. Heidelberg, Carl Winter.

——————. 1934. Indogermanische Grammatik. Syntax I, Part 6. Heidelberg, Carl Winter.

Hofmann, Erich. 1970. Das Halbpartizip in Daukšas Postille. Pp. 198-205 in Donum Balticum, ed. by Velta Rūķe-Draviņa. Stockholm, Almqvist and Wiksell.

Hopper, P. J. and S. A. Thompson. 1980. Transitivity in grammar and discourse. Language 56.251-299.

Humbert, Jean. 1954. Syntaxe grecque. Paris, Librairie C. Klincksieck.

Ivanov, V. V. 1963. Xettskij jazyk. Moscow, Izdatel'stvo vostočnoj literatury.

——————. 1965. Obščeindoevropejskaja, praslavjanskaja i anatolijskaja jazykovye sistemy: Sravnitel'no-tipologičeskie očerki. Moscow, Nauka.

Ivanov, Vjač. Vs. 1974. Rekonstrukcija obščebaltijskix sintaksičeskix struktur. Pp. 106-115 in Balto-slavjanskie issledovanija, ed. by T. Sudnik. Moscow, Nauka.

Jablonskis, J. 1957. Rinktiniai raštai. Vol. 1, J. Palionis, ed. Vilnius, Valstybinė politinės ir mokslinės literatūros leidykla.

Jensen, Hans. 1964. Altarmenische Chrestomathie. Heidelberg, Carl Winter.

Jokojama, Ol'ga. 1983. V. zaščitu zapretnyx deepričastij. Pp. 373-381 in Flier, Michael S., ed. American contributions to the ninth international congress of slavists, Vol. 1. Linguistics. Columbus, Ohio, Slavica Publishers.

Kabelka, J., ed. 1957. Pirmoji lietuvių kalbos gramatika, 1653 metai. Vilnius, Valstybinė politinės ir mokslinės literatūros leidykla. (Daniel Klein's Grammatica Lituanica et Compendium Lit anico-Germanicum with Lithuanian translation.)

Károly, Sándor. 1972. The grammatical system of Hungarian. Pp. 85-170, in Benkő, Loránd and Samu Imre, eds., The Hungarian language. The Hague and Paris, Mouton and Co.

Kazlauskas, J. 1961. Iš optatyvo istorijos. Lietuvių kalbotyros klausimai 4.73-91.

————. 1968. Lietuvių kalbos istorinė gramatika. Vilnius, Mintis.

Kent, Roland G. 1953. Old Persian: Grammar, texts, lexicon. 2nd ed. New Haven (= American Oriental Series, Vol. 33).

Kerns, J. A., and Benjamin Schwartz. 1972. A sketch of the Indo-European finite verb. Leiden, E. J. Brill.

Kiparsky, Valentin. 1969. Das Nominativobjekt des Infinitivs im Slavischen, Baltischen und Ostseefinnischen. Baltistica 5.141-148.

Klein, Daniel. 1653. Grammatica Lituanica. Regiomonti (Königsberg), Typis et sumptibus Johannis Reusneri. (See Buch and Palionis, 1957; Haarmann, 1977.)

————. 1654. Compendium Lituanico-Germanicum, Oder Kurtze und gantz deutliche Anführung zur Littauschen Sprache. Gedruckt und verlegt durch Johann Reussnern. (See Buch and Palionis, 1957; Haarmann, 1977.)

Klenin, Emily. 1983. Animacy in Russian: A new interpretation. Columbus, Ohio, Slavica Publishers.

Klimov, G. 1962. Sklonenie v kartvel'skix jazykax v sravnitel'noistoričeskom aspekte. Moscow, Izdatel'stvo AN SSSR.

——————. 1973. Očerk obščej teorii èrgativnosti. Moscow, Nauka.

Krause, Wolfgang and Werner Thomas. 1960. Tocharisches Elementarbuch, Vol. 1. Heidelberg, Carl Winter

Kronasser, Heinz. 1956. Vergleichende Laut- und Formenlehre des Hethitischen. Heidelberg, Carl Winter.

Kruopas, J., ed. 1972. Dabartinės lietuvių kalbos žodynas. Vilnius, Mintis.

Kühner, Raphael and Carl Stegmann. 1962. Ausführliche Grammatik der lateinischen Sprache. 4th ed. Vol. 1, Pt. 2. Munich, Max Hueber Verlag.

Kuryłowicz, Jerzy. 1964. The inflectional categories of Indo-European. Heidelberg, Carl Winter.

Labutis, V. 1980. Kilmininkas ir savybiniai įvardžiai. Baltistica 16.53-57.

——————. 1981. Vadinamųjų kiekio kilmininkų valdymas ir semantika. Baltistica 17.194-199.

Laigonaitė, Ad. 1957. Pašalio vietininkai dabartinėje lietuvių kalboje. Pp. 21-39 in Kai kurie lietuvių kalbos gramatikos klausimai. Vilnius, Valstybinė politinės ir mokslinės leidykla.

Laroche, E. 1959. Dictionnaire de la langue louvite. Paris, Librairie Adrien-Maisonneuve.

——————. 1962. Un 'ergatif' en indo-européen d'Asie Mineure. Bulletin de la société de linguistique de Paris 57.23-43.

Lehmann, Winfred P. 1970. Definite adjective declensions and syntactic types. Pp. 286-290 in Donum Balticum, ed. by Velta Rūķe-Draviņa. Stockholm, Almqvist and Wiksell.

Macdonell, Arthur A. 1916. A Vedic grammar for students. Bombay, Calcutta, Madras, Oxford University Press. (1962 reprt.)

Marr, N. and M. Brière. 1931. La langue géorgienne. Paris, Firmin-Didot et Cie.

Marvan, Jiří. 1962. O nekotoryx predikativnyx funkcijax litovskogo pričastija. Kalbotyra 4.33-42.

——————. 1969. K voprosu o lingvo-geografičeskom položenii balto-slavjanskix jazykov. Baltistica 5.17-19.

——————. 1973. Baltic and Indo-European ergative: Based on Professor Pavel Trost's pioneering work. Lituanus 19.31-38.

Matthews, W. K. 1955. Lithuanian constructions with neuter passive participles. Slavonic and East European Review 33.350-371.
Mažiulis, V. 1970. Baltų ir kitų indoeuropiečių kalbų santykiai. Vilnius, Mintis.
Mažvydas' Catechism - see Ford, 1971.
Mažvydas' Hymns - see Gerullis, Georg., ed. 1923.
Meillet, Antoine. 1964. Introduction à l'étude comparative des langues indo-européennes. Alabama Linguistic and Philological Series No. 3, Reprint of 1937 ed.
Meriggi, Piero. 1962. Hieroglyphisch-Hethitisches Glossar. Wiesbaden, Otto Harrassowitz.
Metzger, Bruce. 1977. The early versions of the New Testament: Their origin, transmission, and limitations. Oxford, Clarendon Press.
Moulton, Janice and George M. Robinson. 1981. The organization of language. Cambridge, Cambridge University Press.
Mühlenbachs, K. and J. Endzelīns. 1923-1925. Latviešu valodas vārdnīca. Vol. 1. Riga; 1925-27, Vol. 2; 1927-29, Vol. 3; 1929, Vol. 4; 1934-38, Supplement.
Murray, A. T. 1975. Homer, The Iliad with an English translation. Cambridge, Harvard University Press; London, William Heinemann Ltd.
Musteikienė, I. 1967a. Glagol'nye celevye slovosočetanija s roditel'nym bespredložnym v sovremennom litovskom jazyke i ix ėkvivalenty v russkom. Kalbotyra 16.23-48. (Lith. resume.)
————. 1967b. Veiksmažodiniai žodžių junginiai su tikslo naudininku dabartinėje lietuvių literatūrinėje kalboje. Kalbotyra 16.5-22.
Musteikis, K. 1972. Sopostavitel'naja morfologija russkogo i litovskogo jazykov. Vilnius, Mintis.
Neu, Erich. 1979. Einige Überlegungen zu den hethitischen Kasusendungen. Pp. 177-196. Hethitisch und Indogermanisch, ed. by Erich Neu and Wolfgang Meid. Innsbruck (= Innsbrucker Beiträge zur Sprachwissenschaft, Vol. 25).
Nichols, Johanna. 1981. Predicate nominals: A partial surface syntax of Russian. Berkeley and Los Angeles, University of California Press.
Otrębski, J. 1956. Gramatyka języka litewskiego. Vol. 3, Warsaw, Państwowe Wydawnictwo Naukowe.

Palionis, J. 1967. Lietuvių literatūrinė kalba XVI-XVII a. Vilnius, Mintis.

——————. 1972. Über einen Typ des Infinitivsatzes im Litauischen. Baltistica. Supplement 1.125-129.

Palmaitis, L. 1977. Dėl baltų kalbų nenominatyvinės praeities. Baltistica. Supplement 2.114-123

Paternost, J. and W. R. Schmalstieg. 1977. Slovanski edninski rodilnik kot izvor dejanja pri deležnikih na -no- in -to-. Jezik in slovstvo 5.146-149.

Paul, Hermann. 1920. Prinzipien der Sprachgeschichte. 5th ed. Halle a. S., Max Niemeyer.

Paulauskienė, A. 1979. Gramatinės lietuvių kalbos veiksmažodžio kategorijos. Vilnius, Mokslas.

——————. 1980. Review of V. Ambrazas' Lietuvių kalbos dalyvių istorinė sintaksė. Baltistica 16.170-175.

Piročkinas, A. 1972. Dėl kilmininko ir galininko su bendratimi vartojimo tikslo aplinkybei reikšti. Baltistica. Supplement 1.131-134.

——————. Jono Jablonskio kalbos taisymai. Kaunas, Šviesa.

Potebnja, A. A. 1958. Iz zapisok po russkoj grammatike. Moscow

Reichelt, Hans. 1909. Awestisches Elementarbuch. Heidelberg, Carl Winter.

Reklaitis, Janine. 1982. The PIE word order controversy and word order in Lithuanian. Pp. 369-385. Papers from the 3rd international conference on historical linguistics, ed. by J. Peter Maher, Allan R. Bomhard and E. F. Konrad Koerner. Amsterdam, John Benjamins B.V.

Renou, Louis. 1952. Grammaire de la langue védique. Lyon, Paris, Édition IAC.

Rosenkranz, Bernhard. 1958. Zur Entstehungsgeschichte des bestimmten Adjektivs des Baltischen und Slavischen. Die Welt der Slaven 3.97-100.

Rosinas, A. 1972. Žymimasis artikelis lietuvių kalbos tarmėse ir senuosiuose raštuose. Kalbotyra 24.83-90.

——————. 1975. Ar baltų $*i$-, $*i̯o$- resp. $*i$, $*i̯a$-kamienai buvo reliatyviniai? Baltistica 11.165-170.

——————. 1981. Kelios pastabos parodomųjų ir nežymimųjų įvardžių evoliucijos klausimu. Baltistica 17.16-26.

Ruipérez, Martín S. 1968. Some remarks on the Mycenean verbal ending -toi. Minos 9.156-160.

Ružė, A. 1969. Dabartinės lietuvių literatūrinės kalbos laiko konstrukcijos su galininku. Lietuvių kalbotyros klausimai 11.85-105.
Salys, Antanas. 1979. Raštai I. Bendrinė kalba. Rome, Lietuvių Katalikų Mokslo Akademija.
Savvina kniga = Ščepkin, V. 1903. Savvina kniga. Pamjatniki staroslavjanskago jazyka. Vol. 1, fasc. 2. Izdanie otdelenija russkago jazyka i slovesnosti imperatorskoj akademii nauk. Photomechanic reprint by the Akademische Druck- u. Verlagsanstalt, Graz, 1959.
Schanidze, Akaki. 1982. Altgeorgisches Elementarbuch. Tbilisi, Universitetis gamocemloba.
Schleicher, August. 1856. Litauische Grammatik. Prague.
—————————. 1857. Litauisches Lesebuch und Glossar. Prague.
Schmalstieg, William R. 1971. Die Entwicklung der a-Deklination im Slavischen. Zeitschrift für slavische Philologie 36.130-146.
—————————. 1973. New thoughts on Indo-European phonology. KZ 87.99-157.
—————————. 1974. An Old Prussian grammar: The phonology and morphology of the three catechisms. University Park and London, The Pennsylvania State University Press.
—————————. 1974. Some morphological implications of the Indo-European passage of *-oN to *-$\bar{o}$. KZ 88.187-198.
—————————. 1976. Studies in Old Prussian. University Park and London, The Pennsylvania State University Press.
—————————. 1980. Indo-European linguistics: A new synthesis. University Park and London, The Pennsylvania State University Press.
Schmid, Wolfgang P. 1963. Studien zum baltischen und indogermanischen Verbum. Wiesbaden, Otto Harrassowitz.
Schmidt, Karl Horst. 1972. Probleme der Typologie (Indogermanisch/Kaukasisch). Pp. 449-454. Homenaja a Antonio Tovar. Madrid, Gredos.
Schwyzer, Eduard. 1942. Zum persönlichen Agens beim Passiv, besonders im Griechischen. Berl. Ak. Abh. Nr. 10.
—————————. 1966. Griechische Grammatik. Vol. 2. Munich, C. H. Beck.

Shaumyan, Sebastian. 1985. Ergativity and universal grammar. Pp. 311-338 in Relational typology, ed. by Frans Plank. Berlin, New York, Mouton.
Sirtautas, V. 1967. Infinityvas lietuvių kalbos dvinariame sakinyje (*Aš bėgti*). Kalbotyra 17.51-60.
――――――. 1971. Konstrukcijų *buvo matyti, girdėti*... struktūra. Kalbotyra 22. No. 1, 71-79.
Skardžius, Pranas. 1935. Daukšos akcentologija. (Humanitarinių Mokslų Fakulteto raštai XVIIt.) Kaunas, V.D.U. Humanitarinių Mokslų Fakultetas.
Sommer, F. 1916. Zur Syntax des slavischen Genitiv-Akkusativ bei belebten Wesen. Indogermanische Forschungen 36.302-319.
Specht, Franz. 1947. Der Ursprung der indogermanischen Deklination. Göttingen, Vandenhoeck and Ruprecht.
Stang, Chr. S. 1942. Das slavische und baltische Verbum = Skrifter utgitt av Det Norske Videnskaps-Akademi i Oslo II. Hist.-Filos. Klasse. Oslo, I kommisjon hos Jacob Dybwad.
――――――. 1957. Slavonic accentuation. Oslo, I kommisjon hos H. Aschehoug and Co.
――――――. 1958. Die litauische Konjunktion *jeib* und der lit.-lett. Optativ. Norsk Tidskrift for Sprogvidenskap 18.348-56.
――――――. 1970. Opuscula linguistica. Oslo, Bergen, Tromsö, Universitetsforlaget. (Article cited originally published in 1958, see Stang, 1958.)
Stepanov, Ju. S. 1978. Slavjanskij glagol'nyj vid i baltijskaja diateza. Slavjanskoe jazykoznanie. VIII meždunarodnyj s"ezd slavistov. Doklady Sovetskoj delegacii. Moscow, Nauka.
Streitberg, Wilhelm. 1919. Die Gotische Bibel. 2nd ed. Heidelberg, Carl Winter.
Sturtevant, Edgar. 1951. A comparative grammar of the Hittite language. New Haven and London, Yale University Press, (Reprt. 1964).
Šukys, Jonas. 1978. Prielinksnių vartojimas. Kaunas, Šviesa.
Tangl, E. 1928. Der Accusativus und Nominativus cum Participio im Altlitauischen. Weimar.
Tchekhoff, Claude. 1978. Aux fondements de la syntaxe: l'ergatif. Paris, Presses universitaires de France.
Thurneysen, Rudolf. 1946. A Grammar of Old Irish. Revised and enlarged edition translated from the German by D. A. Binchy and Osborn Bergin. Dublin, Institute for Advanced Studies.

Trautmann, Reinhold. 1910. Die altpreussischen Sprachdenkmäler. Göttingen, Vandenhoeck and Ruprecht.
Trost, Pavel. 1986. Nochmals zum Nominativobjekt des Infinitivs im Baltischen. Baltistica 22.35-36.
Tschenkéli, Kita. 1958. Einführung in die georgische Sprache. Vols. 1 & 2, Zürich, Amirani Verlag.
Ulvydas, K. 1957. Vienaskaitos naudininko prieveiksmėjimas ir prieveiksmiai su formantais -(i)ui, -i lietuvių kalboje. Pp. 115-169 in Kai kurie lietuvių kalbos gramatikos klausimai. Vilnius, Politinės ir mokslinės literatūros leidykla.
———. 1959. Dėl vienaskaitos galininko prieveiksmėjimo dabartinėje lietuvių kalboje. Lietuvių kalbotyros klausimai 2.75-89.
———. 1969. Vienaskaitos vardininko kilmės prieveiksmiai. Lietuvių kalbotyros klausimai 11.7-16.
Vaillant, André. 1964. Manuel du vieux slave. 2nd ed. Paris, Institut d'études slaves.
Valeckienė, A. 1957. Dabartinės lietuvių kalbos įvardžiuotinių būdvardžių vartojimas. Literatūra ir kalba 2.162-304.
———. 1984. Lietuvių kalbos gramatinė sistema: Giminės kategorija. Vilnius, Mokslas.
Van Windekens, A. J. 1979. Le tokharien confronté avec les autres langues indo-européennes, Vol. 2. Louvain, Centre international de dialectologie générale de l'Université catholique néerlandaise de Louvain.
Vilentas' Catechism - see Ford, 1969.
Villar, Francisco. 1983. Ergatividad accusatividad y género: en la familia lingüística indoeuropea. Salamanca, Ediciones Universidad de Salamanca.
Villar (-Liebana), Francisco. 1974. Origen de la flexion nominal indoeuropea. Madrid, Instituto 'Antonio de Nebrija.' Consejo superior de investigaciones cientificas: Manuales y anejos de 'Emerita' XXX.
Watkins, Calvert. 1962. The Indo-European Origins of the Celtic verb. Dublin, The Dublin Institute for Advanced Studies.
———. 1969. Indogermanische Grammatik, Vol. 3. Formenlehre. Heidelberg, Carl Winter.
Whitney, William Dwight. 1885. The roots, verb-forms and primary derivatives of the Sanskrit language. Leipzig, Breitkopf and Härtel (= American Oriental Series, Vol. 30, New Haven, 1945).

Woodcock, E. 1959. A new Latin syntax. Cambridge, Mass., Harvard University Press.
Zinkevičius, Z. 1957. Lietuvių kalbos įvardžiuotinių būdvardžių istorijos bruožai. Vilnius, Valstybinė politinės ir mokslinės literatūros leidykla.
——————. 1966. Lietuvių dialektologija. Vilnius, Mintis.
——————. 1977. M. Mažvydo raštų kalba. Baltistica 13.358-371.
——————. 1981. Lietuvių kalbos istorinė gramatika. Vol. 2. Vilnius, Mokslas.
——————. 1982. Lietuvių kalbos postpoziciniai vietininkai. Baltistica 18.21-38.
Zubatý, Josef. 1889. Review of B. Delbrück's Altindische Syntax. Listy filologické 16.62-65.
Žulys, V. 1969. Vadinamųjų nekaitomųjų įvardžių vieta lietuvių kalbos gramatinėje sistemoje. Baltistica 5.167-177.

USE OF THE WORD INDEX

Since the normalized forms of the Lithuanian words do not always occur in the text the decision was made to list each Lithuanian word in the form in which it occurs in the text. In a few cases in which a word occurs once or more with a stress mark and once or more without the stress mark the stress mark is included even though it may be lacking in some citations in the text. The usual principles of Lithuanian alphabetization are used except that the letter w follows v and the letters $\check{z}$, $\dot{z}$ and $\acute{z}$ occur in that order.

The alphabetization principles used are those customary for the language in question except for Sanskrit, (Old Indic), Old Persian, Avestan and Tocharian for which the Latin alphabetization is used (although even here the long vowels follow the short vowels). In addition the modern American transliteration of Devanagari replaces the German transliteration occurring in the direct quotations from German authors (particularly Hirt). Sumerian and Akkadian words are included in the Hittite index since these words occur only in the Hittite texts quoted. These are also alphabetized according to the customary manner of alphabetizing Hittite texts, i.e., the voiced stops are alphabetized along with the voiceless stops and doubled consonants are disregarded, e.g., Sumerian DUMU is alphabetized as though it had an initial t-. Hittite transcribed $\underset{\smile}{i}$ is alphabetized like y.

In the index a slash is inserted before the letter l in order to avoid confusion with the number 1. Similarly a slash is inserted before the letter o in order to avoid confusion with the number 0 (zero).

WORD INDEX

abawem - 33f
abeioiamas - 5
abejója - 36.1c,36.1d
abejójamas - 2.4
abejóti - 5,16
abejotinas - 5
Abiatara - 41.37i
*abiejuosump - 39g
abijoienti - 2.4
abijusump - 39g
abu - 13/1,37e
ãdata - 5,36h
ãdresu - 36.4g
advokãtui - 30.42d
affiera - 5,6
affiera - 41.01/1
afieros - 5
afieru - 5
agronomù - 36.6v
agur̃kai - 6
aikštę - 41.29a
aikštẽs - 41.29a
aĩna - 13b
ainù - 38.5a
akẽčių - 30.43c
akim - 4.3
akimis - 36b,41,22a
akìs - 6,14i,21d
ãkys - 3.3,30.51u,31.1/o
akýtas - 6
akýti - 6
akiu - 41.35b
akmenéti - 29.8
akmenies - 41.01h
akmeniuy - 32.1/1
akmeñs - 31.1n,37.3a

alaũs - 5
alba - 4.3,31.1d
aleių - 5
algas - 29.3a
ałgoiasi - 29.3b
algõs - 30.42f, 31.3b
ałgóti - 36.6
algótis - 29.3
alkohòlio, alkoholiù -
  Fn 9(3)
alkanà - 36.3h
alkanas - 36.6/1
alkanus - 36.8d
altoriaus - 31.1b,41.34c
altoriuy - 41.26b
altorui - 2.5
Amen - 41.32d
amète - 41.27a
amatiniñkai - 30.2/1
amatininkų - 30.2/1
amszia - 31.6c,40.01a
amszinamui - 32.2b
amsziu - 31.6c,40.01a
ámžius - 29.6a,32.42b
ana - 13e
anam̃ - 25h
ãnas - 41.13c
and - 41.01c,41.01d,
anga - 21g
angelas - 11p
Ánglijos - 31.1a
aniełas - 12b
anyelo - 41.16d
anis - 11/o,13j,22h,28f
anksčiaũ - 29.81a,46(35)
annus - 19i

annus - 19i
anoy - 28e
anóks - 23s
ans - 22a,23g,26h
ąnsai - 41.01i
ansjen - 11k
añt - 6q,11a,36.1q,36.1r,
　37p,27q,37r,37s,37t,
　37u,37v,37w,40.01a,
　40.01b,40.01e,40.01f,
　40.01g,40.01h,40.01k,
　40.01/1,40.01m,40.01n,
　40.01/o,41.01k,41.01m,
　41.01n,41.01/o,41.02a,
　41.02c,41.02d,41.02e,
　41.11c,41.11d,46(3),
　47(6)
ąnt - 41.01i,41.01j
antaĩ - 30.7b
Antãnas - 31.1z$_2$
Antanùką - 44(34)
Antanukas - 42.3b
Antiochia - 21d
antra - 12a
antros - 41.37/o
anu - 14j, 41.20b
Anùpras - 31.1z$_3$
apaschtalus - 30.5i,41.19a
apáugę - 23k,23/1
apczistita - 41.19f
ape - 4.3,34.6c,41.03a,
　41.03b,41.04a
apeĩti - 34.8a
apẽjom - 47(1)
àpėmė - 44(17)
apgink - 36a
apiẽ - 34.8a,41.03,41.04,
　41.11i,41.27f,41.31f,
　45(3),47(4)
apieškóti - 34.2b
apkróvė - 36.1h
apłaydżia - 10
aplei - 8a
apliñk - 23k,46(14),47((1),
　(4))

ãpmaudu - 36.3a
apreisskie - 32.14b
apsake - 11p
apsiaũt - 11h
apsiãvus - 32.41f
apsiãvusiems - 32.41f
apsiblaũsę - 3.3
apsidruñstę - 23j
apsigyvẽno - 30.2/1
apsiimti - 16
apsimèsdavau - 36.6x
apsimesta - 30.5w
apsimèsti - 16,Fn 15
apsìmetė - Fn 15(2)
apsir̃go - 23t
apsitráukusi - 42.1b
apsnúdusiai - 3.8
apstãtė - 36.1j
apstìrę - 23k
apstodami - 10
àpsuptas - Fn 10(2),(3)
aptarnáujami - 41.19d,
　41.19e
apteisintas - 12e
áptureius - 21n
apturim - 41.14e
apúokas - 42.2d
ãpvalkalo, ãpvalkalu -
　30.5/1
apver̃sti - 30.43c
apweyzdet - 22h
apwogs - 2.2
árams - 5
arbãtos - Fn 11
ariamì - 5
arimui - 32.31/1
árklį - 30.42g, 32.31k,
　32.31/1,45(34)
arkliaĩ - 6,31.7e
arklíep - 39a
árklio - 30.42e,32.3c,
　Fn 6,45(27)
arklỹs - 3.1,6,18b
árkliu - 46(20)
arklių̃ - 31.7c

árklius - 32.42f
ármijoj - 23i
ártas - 6
arti (about) - 41.11i,47
árti - 13d,32.3c,32.31k,
　Fn 3(4)
artimims - 32f
arúodai - 30.51j
arúodus - 30.51i
asch - 38.1d,41.10e
asiłaycio - 8
asliczios - 8
ąsõtis - 46(21),(22)
aš̆ - 44(14), Fn 15(4)
asz - 42.5a
āš - 16a,23i,23/o,26h,27h,
　29.71a,30.3c,30.42h,
　33.3a,33.3b,34.7e,36.6x,
　41.18f,41.19c,Fn 1(a)
ataiusiam - 21d
atbė́go - 40b
ateia - 32.11j,40f
ateiens - 11p
atêįęs - 30.12b
ateija - 10,22k
ateijusi - 4.3
ateĩna - 19d
ateĩnantį - 19c
ateis - Fn 7
ateĩs - 27b,30.4a
ateisenti - 4.3
ateĩsiant - 27a
ateisiantį - 27a
ateĩsiąs - 27c,27d,27h
ateĩsiu - 41.38d
ateyt - 8
ateĩti - 4.4
ateitỹ - 29.6a
ateiwiu - 30.14a
atė́jaũ - 30.4h,30.4i,30.4j
atė̃jęs - 18g,27j,27k,27/1,
　27m
atė́jo - 35h
atė̃jo - 40c,40/1,45a
atė̃jusį - 27i
àtėmė - 32.31a

atgál - 46(8)
atgalos - 28e
at-gi-si-(i)lsėk - 43
àtgrę̃žia - 29.8
atjója - 14f
atłaydimą - 21n
atleidem - 32f
atleidima - 21.1t,34.21a,
　41.10g
atlikens - 11m
atlikus - 23i
atmenu - 30.11f
atminima - 40.01b
atmiñk - 30.11b,30.11j
atminkite - 30.11a
atpilditu - 3.5
atrasti - 31.5
atródyti - 16
atsakimams - 32.11b
atsakit - 12b
atsigrę̃žęs - 22p
atsìgulė - 8,13a
atsiiñti - 30.4i
atsikándo - 30.16b
at(si)miñti - 16,45(3)
atsinešiaũ - 32.31f
atsirado - 41.18c
atsisė́dęs - 14a
atsisė́do - 23c
atsiskýręs - 26j
atsitikìmo - 30.31a
atsiunte - 42.8j
atsìveria - 29.6c
atsivė́sinti - 36.8
âtskałùnis - 2.3
atstojom - 41.01d
atstováuja - 32.13a
atstováujamas - 32.13b
atstováujamų - Fn 10(1)
atsĩpo - 32.31b
attadokiet - 34.4a
atvãrė - 44(29)
atvažiãvo - 29.6b,30.2e
atvažiãvome - 33.3b
atvažiãvusiems - 30.15c
àtvežė - 32.31j

atvežiaũ - 32.31c
atvỹkęs - 30.41b
atvỹko - 30.41a,Fn 13
áudinį - 17r
audinỹs - 17s
áuga - 10,36.6k,37p,42.4a
áugęs - 3.1
augĩndamas - 10
augiwes - 12f
áugo - 46(14)
augszczéus - 31.7a
áugti - 32.42a,34.2,36.8
áugum - 41.15b
auksa - 2.5
áuksas - 6
áuksinis - 41.13
áukso - 28m,41.13,42.9(2) 45(18)
auksúotas - 6
auksúoti - 6
aukszcziausia - 41.37i
aukščiáusioji - 42.1f
aukštà - 30.15e
aukštĩ - 44(30)
aukštùmo - 31.21
áukśtus - 41.19i
ausimĩs - 34.21g,36b
ausĩs - 2.3,11i
aušrelei - 21m
aušrytėlė - 22m
aũštant - 21k
avĕlė - 6x
avĕlių - 5
avéti - 36.1x
ãvį - 29b
avĩs - 4.2
avižų̃ - 30.2n
awinaelio - 22i
awis - 5,10,22k
awiu - 10
ažu - 41.37
ąžuolas - 45(6)
ažu - 10
ažumirszk - 30.11e
ažusirakina - 37.2b

badù - 36.3b
bãdo - 30.12c,36.3d
bagotas - 9
bagotèsniai - 42.9(9)
bagotesnieji - 42.9(9)
bagotistes - 41.30d
baidos - 36.3g
baĩgti - 18
baÿme - 41.30a
báimė - 44(17)
báimės - 14c,29.81b
baisĩ - 44(17)
baĩsiai - 32.4g
baisumu - 36.2j
balà - 23p
bãlai - 41.27c
baĩdais - 36.1j
baldùs - 36.1i
balnù - 36.71a
bãlos - 41.27
balsañ - 38.4b
baĩso - 30.1/1
balsu - 36.2c
balsus - 34.1b
Baltarãgio - 30.7a
Baltarãgis - 36.71b
báltas - 6,42,42.2,45(23)
baltàsis - 42,42.1d,42.2a
baltèsnis - 45(41)
bálti - 6
báltos - 42.9(3)
Baltramiejaus - 30.51i
Baltramiejus - 36.5c
bañgos - Fn 15(1)
Barabôszių - 31.7a
basám - 32.41b
basznicczian - 38.1a
batùs - 34.2d,36.1x,36.1y
bãtais - 36.1x,36.1y
baũdžiavą - 34.82
bazniczios - 41.34c
bažnićia - 13d
bažnycion, bažnyciona - 38.2d
bažnyćiona - 37.1e

be -- 41.05a
be- - 2.2,22g,2.3
bè - 45(31),46(17),47
bẽ - 41.08/1
beaustančiai - 21m
beaustanti - 22m
bebėginėdamas - 30.1q
bebūnančiam - 32.41e
beczesu - 41.08k
beda - 2.5
bėdà - 29.72a
bediewiůsemp - 39i
bedirbąs - 15j
bėdõs - 32.12d
beeĩdamam - 10
bėgamas - 6
beganans - 22k
beganczius
bėgantis - 2.1
begėdis - 42.8
bėgo - 47(4)
bėgtas - 6
bėgti - 30.4
bei - 11/o, 41.01/1
beliko - 30.2n
belỹnąs - 26/1
bemiẽgąs - 17e,17f
bendrúomenės - 30.5m
benè - 26j
benzinù - 36.7a
bepiauia - 22j
bẽrė - 17p
bérnas - 13f,18a
berneleis - 23n
berneli - 20g
Bernẽli - 42.9(2)
besą̃ - 26n
besiruošiąs - 22q
besiskùndžiąs - 18a
beskaudanti - 22n
besóčiui - 32.41g
bestypsinąs - 4.2
besusieĩčiau - 23/o
beszelùienti - 2.2
beszindans - 22i

bèt - 14,21d,27t,41.06b, 41.08g,42.1b, Fn 15(5)
bęt - 41.01j
betekančiai - 21m
betekanti - 22n
BethSęmitai - 22j
beveřkiąs - 18a
bewelidams - 18s
bezaydziantiam - 28e
bi - 27n,27/o
biauri - 2.3
biauribes - 41.10e
biaurybes - 34.7e
biaurùs - 41.01
bìčių - 34.81k
bigusiu - 3.2
bija - 36.8b
bijadomos - 8c
bìjo - 30.6k
bijojos - 27e
bijóti(s) - 5,16,30.1a, 30.61
byla - 31.1m
bilaia - 21f
biloia - 11a,12f
biloti - 40k
biotiesi - 30.1g
biro - 17q
Birùtės - 31.1v
bìškį - 22b
bìtė - 42.7f
bìtėms - 34.81i
bitès - 34.81b
bìtės - 34.81f
biti - 23f
bliũdo - 26n
blõga - 16a
blogaĩ - 46(27)
blùsų - 28n
bóba - 3.1,4.2,13/1,39e
bralei - 34.7f
brángų - 45(3)
brángusis - 42.5
brangusysis - 42.5
bredamà - 5

bréndę - 3.1
bristi - 34.2
broléliai - 14f,14g
broli̇̀ - 14i
bróli̇̀ - 19e,19f,19h,23d
bróliai - 15c
brólio - 1a,30.5v
brólis - 18g,19g,23i,30.5u, 41.01e
brolyti - 11e
brolýti̇̀ - 19a
bróliui - 28c
broluželių - 42.4a
búčiau - 22
bučiúotų - 30.42c,Fn 7(c)
buday - 5h
búdamas - 36.6z
budams - 36.6q
budanti - 2.2
budu - 36.2a,36.2b
buk - 27r,27s,27t,36.6n, 36.6/o,36.6s,37b
būk - 27e
bukám - 32.4d
buki - 32.2b,37a
būki - 37c
bukiet - 36.2a
bukit - 33e
bùksvoms - 6
bùlbių - 30.31b
bùlves - 42.9(8)
bùlvės - 30.2n
bùlvių - 32.31j, 41.07a, Fn 11
bũnam - 25h
bũrams - 30.51i,30.51j
bùrnos - 32.31g
burõkai - 5,5e
burtinikie - 41.32a
bùs - 12d,22c,26d,30.2/o, 34.81i
bųsenti - 4.3
būsi - 7
būsią - 26g
būsiantis - 4.2
bųsiąs - 4.1
bųsimas - 4.2,7
būsintis - 4.2
bųsit - 24d
būsiu - 22
but - 24c
būt - 32.41g
bùtą - 36.1j
butè - 36.1i
būta - 30.5r,30.5t,36.6y Fn 8
bútas - 5,6
buti - 32.41a,34.22a,37.1a
būti - 2.6,4.4,6,7,15,16c, 23,24,27,29.3,32.4c, 32.4d,32.41h,39,Fn 15(3), (5)
butischkai - 27s
buttu - 41.35g
butu - 22f,22h,41.06b
butų - 21b
bųtų́ - 41.01j
būtų - 15m,32.42g
buvaũ - 22
bùvę - 23t,26/o
bùvęs - 23g,23h,23w,26f
bùvo - 3.3,15,22b,23a,24, 25g,26d,29.5j,29.51j, 29.81a,30.5/1,30.5s,31.7c, 31.7e,42.1b,45(30),Fn 3 (3),Fn 8
buwa - 13j,21d,22g,22j,22k, 23d,23e,23n,24g
buwau - 36.6/1,36.6m
buwens - 23f

catechismusa - 29.73a,31.1h
Christaus - 31.7a,37.1b
Christus - 10,27p,30.14b, 37e
Christusa - 30.5e
cieła - 41.23d
Cinoko - 30.7a
Cinoku - 36.71b
cziesa - 35b

cziésas – 5
cziesti – 32.14e
cziestis – 32.2b
czista – 41.32c
czistas – 41.12g
czístôs – 41.12h
čià – 6r,6s,10,29.2c,30.5j,
  30.5r,32.42b,36.6z
čyrúoja – 14a
čiulbė́jimas – 31.1z
čiuõžtas – 6

dabař – 25h,29.6c,30.18c
  46(5)
dabokites – 32.1a,32.1c
dągaus – 31.1i,31.1j,40e
dągui – 37a
dáigui – 32.42a
daykta – 21n
daiktai – 5,29.5f
dayktay – 5
dayktays – 36.8d
daiktáms – 32.31a,32.31e
dáiktas – 5,39j
daiktĭnis – 30.5/1
daykto – 2.3
daiktu – 30.1f
daiktus – 36.6c
dayktus – 13i
dainà – 31.1v
daktara – 41.19b
dăktaro – 30.12e
daktaróp – 40a
daĩgi – 32.3a,44(32)
daliié – 29.8
dalỹkas – 2.4
dalis – 41.03a,41.17b
dangaũs – 11p,28e,31.1k,
  31.1/1,37i,37s,37.3a,
  41.34d
dągaus – 37
dangu – 22g
dangy – 42.7d,e
dangugi – 42.7e
dangugis – 42.7d
dangui – 37b

dągui – 34.1a,37e,37f
danguy – 41.07c
danguieiam – 42.7b
danguięiis – 42.7a
dąnguię-s-is – 37g
danguj – 36.7c,37h
dangujè – 37j,37s
*danguję́ – 42.7a,b
dągun – 41.19g
dangùs – 36.8i,37
dangusu – 37d
dañtį – 32.14k
dantis – 32.14k
dañtys – 28h
dár – 26g,29.6a,30.7a,
  30.7b,34.7e,34.81f,
  41.38c,44(11),Fn 14(1)
dara – 36.6c
darą̃ – 15n
dãrąs – 15a
dárbą – 34.82,44(5)
darbai – 32.11/o
dárbas – 31.1x,Fn 3(1),
  44(5)
dárbe – 41.15d
darbè – 30.2i
darbinikas – 29.3a,31.3b
darbininko – 22/1
dárbo – 30.2j
darbu – 32g,41.16c
dárbui – 41.25a
darbus – 3.5
darens – 13j,23e,23m
darỹk – 15e
darikiet – 41.01b
darisens – 23n
darit – 29.5h
dariti – 29.5f
darýti – 32.42c,32.42d,
  36.6
dăro – 17v
dăromas – 5
dărosi – 17w
daũg – 16b,21c,21/o,23d,
  29.51j,46(29),46(30)
daugė́ti – 29.8

355

daugiaũ - 18i,23/o,31.7b,
 31.7d
daugiaus - 41.37c
daveĩ - 43
daviaũ - 15f,Fn 1(a)
dawė - 29.32a
dczauxmas - 2.4
dẽbesi̧ - 44(29)
dẽbesio - 41.13e
dẽdanti - 2.1
dẽdasi - 17e
dẽdė - 44(18),(19),(20),
 (22),(23),(24),(25)
dedù - 9
dẽga - 42.8
degamos - 5
deganciu - 5
dẽgant - 29.5j
degantesnis - 2.6
degina - 12c
Deiwistes - 39g
deiwiu - 31.5
dekawotumbim - 32.11n
del - 41.06a,41.06b
dẽl - 36.1d,36.3e,41.06,
 41.07a,41.07b,41.07c
dę̃l - 41.06b
delei - 36.6q,41.06d
delto - 38.1b
dėltõ - 30.15d
dėmẽ - 6
dėmétas - 6
dėmė́ti - 6
derėti - 21
deschimtis - 31.5
dėsianti - 4.2
deszymtis - 41.08g
deszyney - 41.20c
dẽšimt - 31.5
dẽšimti̧ - 31.7d
dešimties - 31.7b
dešimti̇̀s - 31.5
dẽšinei - 41.25d
dešine - 41.17a
dešiney - 10

deti - 2.5
dė́ti - 4.2,9
dė́tis - 16,27f
devýnetas - 31.51
devyngaĩvis - 14h
devyni - 29.6
devýniasdešimt - 31.5
devyniólika - 31.5
devýnios - 23r
devýnis - 30.5k
Dewa - 30.5g,40h,41.16a
Dewui - 32.14e,32.2b
diamento - 41.01h
di̧dei - 8c
di̧delė - 45(30)
di̧delẽs - 45(4),Fn 10(3)
di̧delio - 30.5t
di̧delis - 29.8d
didesnès - 42.9(8)
didesnią́sias - 42.9(8)
didèsnis - 45(34),(40)
didi̧ - 29.8b,42.8j
didis - 29.3c
didi̇̀s - 45(7)
didỹsis - 42.1a,g
didùmo - 31.21a
di̧dvyrio - 30.5w
didzia - 41.06c
didžiáusias - 45(40)
didžióji - 42.1b
didžiúojas - 36.1a
di̧dziu - 36.6k
didźáusu - 36.6q
didźei - 30.14b
didźiu - 36.2f
didźiùia̧s - 2.5
diegiamà - 5
diel - 41.06c
dienà - 2.1,5,6,29.74b,
 35a,c,i
diẽną - 2.1,5,29.74e,
 32.11e,34.5,35n,41.11h
dienagi - 37.1c
diẽnai - 41.08e,41.25e
dienas - 11n,32.11j,35g,
 41.23a,b

dienasu - 37.1b
dieni - 41.37j
dienoje - 37.1e
dienomis - 41.08m
dienoms - 41.24d
dienu - 13d,32.14a,41.20b, 41.37/1
dienų - 33.3b,41.24c
diẽvą - 34.21b,34.21c
dievaĩs - Fn 14(1)
diẽvo - 30.5
diẽvui - 33.1a
dievùs - Fn 14(1)
Diewa - 31.1y,31.5,33f, 36.6r,40h,41.10h
Diewą - 41.30e
Diewas - 22g,29.3b,36.6t, 39g
Diewe - 31.3a,37f,41.14f
Diewepi - 39f
Diewiep - 39j
Diewo - 10,30.1i,30.1j, 30.5c,36.1q,41.16f
diéwo - 20.14h
Diews - 27q
diewu - 2.6,18s,30.3a, 36.1/o,41.32e,41.33a
diewui - 32b,32.2a,33c
dinamitù - Fn 9(4)
dìrba - 31.1x,46(1),46(27)
dirbamą - 5
dìrbdavęs - 16b
dìrbęs - 11,16a
dìrbo - 16b,36.2h
dìrbsime - 4
dirbsį̃s - 4
dìrbti - 11n,15/1 Fn 3(1)
dirbtì - 6
dir̃vą - 36.1/1
dir̃voje - 36.1k
diwijos - 32.1d
dodi - 32.14a
dok - 37.32a,41.37d
dokiet - 41.10a
dona - 32.14a
dostis - 41.37h

dovenų̃ - 41.15c
dowanomis - 36.8g
dowida - 41.08m
Dowidas - 21e
Dowiduy - 41.08a
draũgas - 29.71a,31.6b
drauginikie - 39g
draũgo - 30.1b
draugų̃ - 21/o,31.6b
drẽba - 14f
drum̃stas - 6
dù - 45(16)
duchawniems - 32.11m
dukrãles - 42.9(1)
duktẽ - 7b,23t
dùkterį - 29.7b,39
dùkteriai - 32.14/1
dukteriak - 39
dukterimis - 36.6r
duktẽrs - 39
dū̃mas - 45(21)
dūmodami - 27e
dūmók - 11e
dūmóti - 27
dunojų - 21m
duobẽ - 30.51x
duodamà - 5k,5/1
dúodamas - 5j,9
dùdami - 24a
dúodu - 5i,9
dúok - 30.17a,41.25a
dúona - 5,5k,6,42.7e
dùna - 27s,36.6i
dúoną - 5i
dúonos - 3.7,29.8e,30.16b
dùnos - 6
dúosiąs - 4.1
dúota - 6, Fn 1(d),(e)
dúotas - 1,30.5,Fn 1(b),(c)
dúoti - 9
dùrimis - 36.1u
durìs - 36.1u
dùrys - 5c
duru - 41.37n
duscha - 33b,41.14d
dusche - 36e

duschiasu - 36.6/o
duszią - 37.31a
dûsziomis - 36.8f
dusziós - 41.01j
duśios - 13i
dvarè - 45(30)
dvējetas - 31.51
dvijũ - 41.15b
dvýlikai - 33.3b
dviračio - 30.4h,30.4i,
   30.4j
dwara - 41.08h
dwase - 27e,34.21d,36d,
   42.5b
dwases - 38.4a,41.12g
dwassie - 39g
dwi - 35.1a,41.37j
dwieju - 41.37/1
dwilika - 31.5,41.19a
dzaugenczies - 8c
dziauksmu - 36.2k,41.32d
dzievõji - 42.7f
džiaũgėsi - 36.1b,36.2g
džiaũgsmo - Fn 9(1)
džiaugsmù - 36.2g,Fn 9(1)
džiaũgtis - 16,32.1i
džiovytą - 6
džiūnantesnė - 2.6
džiúvusi - 3.1
dźaugies - 32.1g
dźaugiesi - 36.2f
dźaugiùs - 32.1h,32.1i
dźaugsmu - 36.2f,41.32g

ę - 36.6i
ėda - 14h
ędzu - 20g
ėdžias - 36.5c
ẽglė - 29.2c,45(30)
Ẽglei - 15c
eiantiemus - 21f
eĩdamas - 9,18b
eiens - 11a
ęija - 2.5
eĩk - 11h,14d
eyk - 35.1a

eĩkim - 25i
eykime - 41.35f
eiklíeji - 42.9(3)
éiklūs - 42.9(4)
eyle - 41.10b
eimì - 9,34.11b,38.2c
eĩna - 30.42f,30.42h,34.81k,
   36.4b,36.4c,36.71c
einą̃ - 22,25i
eĩnamas - 6
einą̃s - 22
einù - 5,9,26m,30.42a,
   30.42b,30.42i,Fn 6
eis - 13k
eĩt (3rd present) - 41.30g
eit - 15n,29.1c
eyt - 35.1a
eĩta - 6n
eĩtas - 6
eĩti - 9,30.4b,30.4d,30.4f,
   30.4g,30.4i,30.4k,30.42,
   30.43,32.41b,32.41f,
   34.11c,34.82,37.1e,41.30f,
   Fn 6
ẽjęs - 11h
ejo - 41.30c
ẽjo - 35k,36.71b,36.71d,
   46(19)
eĩgeta - 45(31)
Eliosiaus - 30.12a
eme - 3.6,41.24/1
ẽmė - 44(29)
ẽmęs - 14
ẽmus - 14e
enèrgijos - 31.3c
ẽsą - 27f,32.43,36.6y
ẽsama - 30.5w
ẽsamas - 5
esans - 22g
esanti - 10
ẽsąs - 2,15i
esą̃s - 26f,26j
esch - 21d,36.6h,36.6/1,
   36.6m
esme - 36.6r
esmẽs - 46(18)

esmi - 31.2g,42.5a
ēssanczei - 2.6
essansis - 2.5
essant - 27t
essąs - 27r
essi - 32.2c,33a,34.4b,37d, 37f
essti - 37e
essus - 18s,22h
est - 30.5h,33c,41.37f
este - 41.37c
ēsti - 29.3a,30.5k,32.4b, 33f,36.6g,37e,39j
esù - 22,23h,41.15d
euangelijstu - 30.5f
ēžį - 26m
ēžerą - 46(14)
ežerai - 42.3a
ežerelį - 34.81a
ežerēlį - 44(30)
ežerų - 42.3a
ēžerui - 41.27a

fabrikaĩ - 31.1p,31.1q
fãktai - 32.13c
fãktų - 32.13d
fanãtikui - 32.4d
fìgų - 32.4g

gabùs - 41.01
gádíná - 29.8
gaĩla - 29.8c
gailétis - 16
gailetu - 41.37a
gailetus - 18s
gáinioti - 32.42f,32.42g
gaĩsras - 45(7),(31)
gal - 2.2,21c,29.6a,32a
gãlą - 14c
galè - 25h
galéjau - 45(3)
galéti - 7,32.12
galì - 7,15h
galýbės - 29.81c
Galileos - 41.35d,e
gãlimas - 7

gãlime - 4,7
galinczias - 2.3
galincziausias - 2.6
galingas - 2.3
gãlintis - 2.6
galis - 22h
galĩs - 4
galiùką - 41.38c
gálo - 41.08d
gãlo - 46(17)
gálvą - 32.14i
gálvas - 23v
galvelė - 22/o
galvódamas - 15g
gaminti - 30.4k
gamuri - 12c
ganà - 27,29.8d,29.8e
ganéja - 29.8f
ganéti - 29.8
ganna - 27t
garbe - 32.14e,32.2a,32.2b, 33c
garbē̃ - 29.8b
garbês - 41.01m
garbintumbime - 2.6
gar̃są - 45(37)
garstićios - 12c
gárvėžį - Fn 9(4)
gaũbė - 44(16)
gáudyti - 32.31h
gauti - 11m
gãvęs - 13b,14d
gãvo - 41.15c
géda - 29.8b
gédytis - 16
Gegrėnų - 4.2
geidáujama - 5
gélbėk - 32.12d,32.12e
gélbeti - 32.12
gélbėti - 32.12f
gélbmi - 32.12
gelbt - 32.12c
gēležį - 45(36)
geležiẽs - 31.1p
geležìnis - 42

geležis - 45(41)
gélmês - 5
genczių - 30.12b
generolù - 36.6y
gēninas - 36.71c
gēra - 21/o,34.11a,34.11b
gerà - 34.81i,41.01k
gēra - 45(11)
gērą - 42.3b,Fn 15(3)
geraî - 19i,26h,29.8b,
 36.8g,46(1),46(6)
geraus - 36.8d
gērąji - 42.3b
gerama - 5
géras - 42.5
gēras - 41.01,46(16),46(17)
gerasis - 42.5a
gerasysis - 42.5
gerassis - 42.5
gerbė - 44(4)
géręs - 11e
geresnia - 21b
gerî - 30.2c
gēriamas - 45(13)
geriaũ - 46(29),(33)
gerybe - 41.16f
gérk - 11e
gēro - 16c,
 45(11)
gerόji - 42.5b
gēros - 32.31g
gérôs - 31.2g
gerù - 31.21a,34.11c,Fn 15(3)
gerų̃ - 30.2a
ghadnas - 29.3a
ghi - 12f,37.3b,41.17c,
 41.17d,41.37d,e
ghi - 2.5,11c
ghie - 27r
ghiems - 20g,27t
ghis - 11c,15b
ghrekais - 36.8a
ghrieku - 30.14d,41.10g
-gi- - 43
giarame - 41.26c
Gibeona - 13j

gýdantis - 5
gýdo - 5
gýdomas - 5
giadakiem - 41.32d
gíedamosios - 5
gieisk - 32.14g
gielbek - 41.12d,41.14a
giełeżies - 5
giemus - 32.11h
gierays - 3.5
gierame - 41.26c
gierens - 11b
gierkiet - 41.12f
giesmes - 29.73a,41.04a
gįją - 13h
gilų - 30.15e
gymditas - 39g
gimditojus - 41.28d
gijmditosis - 39g
gimens - 3.5
gimes - 41.12g
gimęs - 3,3.1
gimines - 41.10b
gimmusiam - 21b
giñtas - 6
gimti - 6,Fn 15
gimtóji - 6
gimus - 32.11p
gimusį - 3
gimusius - 3.6
gieray - 3.5
ginančiu - 36.6t
gineiu - 36.6s
ginkłu - 36.6t
gintis - 16
girdeiens - 13g
girdėjau - 22q,26h
girdes - 30.14c
girdḗt - 16c
girdḗti - Fn 3(3)
girdḗti(s) - 29.5,30.21e
girdinčiai - 2.6
gìrdytą - 6
girdžiù - 19b
gìrgždinamos - 5c

giria - 3.8
girią - 29.1a
girieciui - 32.41e
girioie - 21g
girion - 38.5a,38.5b
gyrtas - 11b
girti - 5
girtis - 16
girtuokliãvimo - 30.21e
gývas - 29.31d,30.5u
gyvẽna - 26b,37q
gyvẽnamas - 5,6
gyvẽname - 46(6)
gyvenąs - 26a
gyvẽnęs - 3.3
gyvẽnimas - 2.4,4.2,45(22)
gyvẽno - 6,10
gyvẽnom - 47(2)
gyvénsi - 30.5j
gyvéntas - 5,6
gyvénti - 32.42b,39
gyvenù - 38.5b,38.5d
gývo - 30.5v
gyvs - 34.7e
giwám' - 21q
giwen - 3.5
giwená - 29.8
giwenamą - 5
giwenáncziámuy - 21n
giwenanczìu - 2.4
giwenimas - 2.4
giwu - 30.4a, Fn 7
godùs - 31.3,41.01
grabe - 37.3a
grabo - 8c
grasìnti - 16
graszi - 41.24/1
graszu - 20g
graudžiai - 8b
grazì - 46(25),(26)
gražiaũ - 46(36)
gražiũ - 45(8)
gražūmas - 30.15c
gražùs - 45(2)
greičiaũ - 46(31),(32)
greĩtai - 46(28)

greitėsnis - 45(37)
greku - 31.1s,31.1t,34.21a
grekus - 41.37a
greschnuiu - 41.06a
gressnasis - 29.1c
gretà - 36.71b,47(2),47(5)
griáunamas - 5
grỹbų - 46(31)
grỹčiai - 41.36a
grieku - 21n,27r
griekų - 41.01g
grieschna - 41.06d
grieztas - 6
griežti - 6
grinas - 2.5
grioviaĩs - 36.4h
gristas - 6
grišias - 16e

grĩžęs - 3.1,8,19g,19h,27u
grĩžo - 8,19g,19h,46(20)
grĩžta - 18q
grĩžtanti - 18n,18/o,19a
grĩžtąs - 18/1,18r,18w
grĩžti - 16e,30.4,34.7c
grĩžusi - 28d
gryžo - 28e
grožýbėmis - 36.1b
grūdą - 17p
grudas - 12c
grūdas - 17q
grūdintas - 6
gruntu - 36.6t
grūstà - 6
gubàs - 36.1k
gubomìs - 36.1/1
gudrèsniam - 32.4c
gulėta - 30.5w
guléti - 5,29.31d,34.2
gùli - 17j
guliamà - 5
gulima - 5
gulinti - 20g
guliù - 11f
gundina - 3.8
gúodžiasi - 36.1e,36.1f
gurkli - 41.37e

Habel - 41.01/1
hadynos - 41.01d
heretikay - 29.32c
Heroda - 41.08b
Herodui - 23n
hukinikas - 34.6a

į̃ - 14b,14d,37.3,38,38.1,
    41.01/o,41.02b,41.11f,
    41.11g,41.11h,41.11i,
    41.11j,41.31e,45(33)
y (into) - 41.10i
ia - 21d,41.37s
iam - 21g,21q,23e,29.32a,
    29.74e
iamije - 30.21d
yamui - 32.11n,33d
Ianas - 4.3
iapi - 21f
iau - 2.2,13d,22g
iauczessi - 10
iaunikaicziu - 31.1e
idant - 3.5,18s,28g,32d,
    32.11/o,41.06b
idanti - 34.7h
įdomaũs - 45(10)
ieib - 41.37a
iem - 32,12, yem - 33d
yemimp - 30.21c
iems - 32.11f
iemus - 21f
ieszkome - 39h
íeško - 32.3c
ieškójau - 34.2a
ieškóti - 5,13e,30.4e,34.2,
    Fn 6
ieškótų - 30.4b
iey - 30.1e
ig - 41.10a, 41.10b,41.10d,
    41.10e
igùdusiai - 3.8
ijngistatitas - 30.5g
ijpoliau - 41.10e
ijra - 30.5g
ik - 41.08k,41.08/1,41.09a

ikì - 15,41.08a,41.08b,
    41.08c,41.08d,41.08e,
    41.08f,41.08g,41.08h,
    41.08i,41.08j,41.08m,
    41.09b,41.09c
įkyrėjo - 32.41e
ikki - 29.3c
ilgaĩ - 30.5w,41.11j,44(12)
ìlgainiui 42.3a
ìlgas - 29.6a
ilgùmo - 31.21b
ymete - 41.10i
iñk - 5,9,10
imkiet - 38.1b
impuołys - 18s
iñti - 14
iñ - 41.10,41.11a,41.11b,
    41.11e
iñč - 41.11
ing - 38.2c,41.10f,41.10g,
    41.10h,41.11
iñgi - 41.10c,41.11
įnirtimù - 36.2i
inkirschusi - 3.4
inlipo - 41.11e
institùtas - 32.13b
institùtui - 32.13a
iñš - 41.11
iñt - 41.11
invažiãvo - 41.31a
io - 19i,23e,30.14f,32.11b,
    34.7a,36.8g,41.01/1,
    41.28c
iog - 27r,27s,30.14h,41.01h
ioka - 41.37s
iospi - 11a
įpýliau - 32.31m
iř̃ - 14
ira - 2.5,2c,3.5,22d,22i,
    24a,24b,24f,31.3b,41.26b,
    41.37f,h
yrà - 1d,1e,21/o,22,23/1
    23m,24,25b,25d,26d,30.2a,
    30.2c,30.2g,32.31h,32.41a,
    36.6p,39k,41.18d

įrankis - 32.3b
isch - 3.5,11p,14j,32.1i,
 41.12a,41.12b,41.12c,
 41.12d,41.12e,41.12f,
 41.12g,41.12h
ischdotas - 37.1a
ischeijo - 8c
ischgirdę - 13j
ischgirskiet - 34.1b
ischgirsti - 36b
ischgrabo - 8c
ischkaitimas - 27r
ischkenteiens - 11m
ischlegimu - 31.1r
ischmanans - 2.3
ischmintiei - 32e
ischpaszinti - 30.14d
ischpilditi - 29.5g
ischrinka - 41.37b
ischtirtumbei - 28g
ischwadawai - 36c
ischwida - 14i
isikieley - 41.08c
įsimi-ejo - 30.14b
įspūdį - 30.15e
įspūdžio - 30.15c
Israelo - 36.8e
issipilde - 24g
istatima - 41.03a
istrowos - 5
iszejemoji - 5
iszejo - 41.03a
iszganima - 32.1/1
iszmanidamas - 32.11
iszmanimuy - 32.11b
iszriszá - 29.8
iš - 14c,32.1i,32.1k,32.12d,
 36.3c,41.12,41.13a,41.13b,
 41.13c,41.13d,41.13e,
 45(7),46(18),(25),(26)
išárta - 29.5b
išárti - 29.5d,29.5e
išáušo - 44(26)
išbėgo - 13e
išbrìsti - 34.2d
išdalýsi - 9

išdýkęs - 3.3
išdýkusiai - 3.8
išdriko - 30.5w
išeĩna - 35m
išeinù - 26/1
išeit - 8b
išėjaũ - 33.3a
išėjo - 35/1
išgélbėję - 14g
išgerąs - 26h
išgiřdę - 11,14f
išgiřdęs - 14f
išgiřdo - 28i
išilgaĩ - 47
išiñk - 42.9(2)
išklausiaũ - 30.1k
išklěrę - 3.3
iškùlsim - 41.09a
išlãksto - 28h
išlikìmas - 30.5v
išlìko - 30.5u
išlìkti - 32.41j
išliñdo - 41.13d,41.13e
išmanýti - 32.11
išmintingas - 2.3
išpeikt - 34.7g
išpešiau - 41.13a
išrinkti - 30.5d
išrugělėm - 6y
issìbaigė - 23r
išsidúoti - 16
išsiriñko - 36.6w
issiunčiau - 36.4g
issprendìmas - 31.1u
ištisas - 29.31d
ištìžus - 3.3
ištvìrkęs - 3.3,24
išvalýdavo - 36.5c
išvažiavaũ - 30.42k
išvažiãvo - 41.01e
 46(9)
iums - 2.5
yums - 33.2a
iùksis - 30.14c
ius - 5.d,30.14a,34.7h
yus - 38.1d

iuss - 34.1a
yussu - 33e
iusu - 24d,32.11d,34.1b
iusu - 2.5
iûsų - 36.8f
iusump - 40f
i̇wárstomà - 5
iwedei - 2.5
iżduota - 41.01f
iżgánima - 21n
iżgirdi - 11/1
iżmanomas - 5
iżbĩłoma - 5

ją̃ - 41.27d
jái - 29.6a
jaĩs - Fn 10(1)
Jakubas - 14i
jám - 10,11i,21a,26i,28e,
  30.15e,32.4f,32.41c,
  34.43,34.22b,42.7b
Jana - 34.6c
jaũ - 5e,29.2b,30.7a,30.7b,
  30.7c,36.6z
jauczui - 32.14h
jaunàsai - 42.9(2)
jaunikaicza - 36.6d
jáunos'os - 42.9(1)
jaunų̃jų - 42.4a
jaũsti(s) - 16, Fn 15
jáutis - 5
javáms - 32.3b
jei - 34.7f
jéib - 27p,27q
jeygu - 35.1a
jems - 41.37d
Jesus - 29.32b,37e
jèszkomas - 5
Jėzus - 29.32a
jį̃ - Fn 15(3)
jĩ - 44(13)
jíems - 32.42b
jĩs - Fn 15(2)
jõ - 6r,6s,14e,23p,23q,23r,
  30.1g,30.11k,30.5r,30.5t,
  30.5w,32.1d,32.1e,32.1f,
  34.21h,36.6y,36.8b,41.01c,
  Fn 9(2)
jódamas - 9
jóg - 19,27
jója - 14g
Jõnas - 32.13a,33.3c,
  Fn 8
Jõno - 32.13b,
  Fn 8
Joníenė - 18c
Jõnui - 33.4d
jõs - 36.2a,42.9(3),(4)
Josua - 13j
jóti - 9
jra - 22e,33.2a,37.32b
jstatimui - 32.11/1
jų̃ - Fn 10(1)
Judeą - 41.35f
Judos - 41.34b
juodà - 29.2a
juõdį̇ - 41.31e
juodóji - 42.1e
juodóka - 41.31e
júodu - 45(29)
juodùmą - 41.31e
juõkiasi - 28c
juomi - 7b
Jùras - 36.6u
jus - 41.37h

ka - 23e,23n,42.8k
ką̃ - 13j,15a,15c,15e,15f,
  15g,32.42c,32.42d,34.21,
  34.22b,34.4a,34.4b,44(18)
  Fn 14(3)
ką̃ nors - 36.7a
kabìnta - 6q
kačiùkams - 32.31m
kà(d) - 15k
kàd - 11g,11h,15m,16b,19,
  23/o,26h,26i,27k,27/1,
  30.51u,32.4d,32.42b,36.6r
kàd iř - 11f

kadà - 15,22f,22g,35h,40/1,
 41.10d,41.14d,41.18a
kaĩ - 29.1a
kai kadà - 44(34)
kai kuriẽ - 30.15f
káilinius - 44(1)
káime - 26a,26b
kaimýnai - 30.7c
kaimýnas - 3.3,44(33)
kaimýnų - 30.7b
káimo - 25h
kaĩp - 13f,15,22d,22f,27,
 31.7d,31.7e,34.3a,37a,
 37b,37c,37j,39a,43,45(42)
kayp - 3.5,12d,22h,36.6k
kaipo - 34.6a
káypo - 21n
kaĩrei - 41.25c
kaires - 41.24a
kãklas - 6
kaktà - 36.3a
kalavìjo - 30.43a
kaĩba - 46(2)
kaĩbą - 30.1k
kalbant - 13c
kalbeia - 21e
kalbéjo - 18t,41.11j
kalbék - 46(7)
kalbéti - 29.8b
kalbétojai - Fn 10(1)
kalbomìs - 29.8b
kalbù - 29.71a
kãlé - 44(32)
kalnaĩ - 44(30),45(20)
kalnè - 37p
kálno - 37p,41.01n
kálnus - 41.19i
kaltas - 34.4b
kaltinti - 34.7h
kaltus - 34.6b
kám - 15/1,15m,32.12c,32.31h,
 32.42e,32.42f
kamara - 5
kamãrą - 32.31a,32.31e
kambario - 32.4a

kambarỹs - 6,42.1a
kambariũ - 30.43b
kan - 15b
kanapéta - 42.3e
kanapétoji - 42.3f
kąntrume - 36.8f
kapóti - 32.31b,32.31f
kapų̃ - 26k
kãrą - 41.27f
Karalauczu - 38.2c
karãliaus - 6n,31.1a
karalista - 31.1/1
karalistas - 31.1j
karalistasp - 40e
karaliste - 31.1i
karalỹstė - 31.1k
karalistes - 36.6r
karaliu - 41.34a
karãlium - 15n
karalius - 3.5
karãlų - 41.01i
karãl'ui - 41.18b
karalum - 36.6g
karalumi - 36.6p
karálus - 8,41.01i
kãras - 42.1g
kárčių - 32.31c
kareĩviai - 45(16)
kareĩvis - 3.1
karsztas - 12c
kartą - 32.4c
kartùs - 34.11f,41.08g
karunawotas - 36.6g
kárvė - 4.2,41.01k,41.31e
kárves - 7a
kárvės - 41.27c
kàs - 15i,15j,15k,15n,24f,
 24g,29.4,29.5h,29.5i,
 29.6c,29.71b,32.11d,
 32.31h,34.21f,35n,35.1a,
 41.37f,42.9(9),44(21)
kasani - 4.3
kas nóris - 45(10)
kąstà - 6x
kàsti - 30.31b

kaszna - 33b
kasznam - 32a
katẽ - 41.13d
katinaĩ - 26n
kãtinas - 34.3a
katinóp - 40b
kãtinui - Fn 12(a)
káulinėm - 45(28)
kaušeliũ - 31.21a
kavõs - 31.4d,31.4e
Kazakáuskų - 31.1z$_3$
kažkàs - 45(12)
kažkóks - 45(14)
kažkuř - 44(32)
kẽdę - 30.15g
keĩstas - 6
keĩsti - 6
kela - 34.11b
kelame - 31.7a
kelauiá - 29.8
keleivinė - 41.36a
kęles - 27p
kélės - 10
kelĩ - 29.6
kẽlią - 34.11e,38.8b,44(33)
kẽliais - 41.09c,41.33b
kẽlias - 6
keliàs - 31.21b
keliáuti - 34.11e
kelyjè - 37r
keliñtas - 35
kelio - 11a,37r
kẽlio - 44(7)
kẽlių - 41.09b
keliũs - 29.2c
kélsi - 29.31e
kelu - 34.11c
kencze - 41.37r
keñčiančiam - 21/o
keñčiant - 21/o
kẽpa - 29a,29b,30.15b
kepams - 12a
keptà - 6
kepùrė - 2.1,46(25),(26)
kepùrės - 34.2a

kepusias - 3.2
keřpamos - 5
ketinti - 16
ketu - 20g
keturì - 6s,29.5f
keturiólika - 38.3b
kẽturis - 6r
ketwirta - 41.10b
kiala - 41.17b
kiaũliaberio - 30.51q
kiaũliaberis - 30.51r
kiáurą - 28n
kiaušìnių - 29.81d
kibìrais - 46(19)
kibirkštiẽs - 45(7)
kìbti - 5
kíek - 15
kiek wiena - 35b
kiekvíeną - 35/o
kiekvíenas - 35,44(15)
kiele - 41.12e
kiełęs - 11k,14j
kieley - 5
kiely - 29.1b
kieliu - 21f,30.14e,36.4a
kielius - 32.14b
kiẽmą - 30.51/o,30.51s
kiẽmas - 30.51m
kietẽsnio - 41.01h
kietõm - 6y
kietèsnis - 45(41)
kíetu - 36.2d
kieturiu - 30.5f
kiewaika - 41.10a
kỹla - 45(7)
kilogrãmas - 31.4a,31.4b,
   31.4c
kilomètrai - 29.6
kilomètro - 30.32b
kilpẽlės - 28m
kìlpinio - 30.43a
kìltas - 6
kìlti - 6
kimbamà - 5
kimšdavos - 9

kiřtęs - 23v
kiřto - 34.11f
kiřvis - 32.31b,46(23),(24)
kìškį - 44(8)
kìškis - 40b
kìškių - 30.2g
kiškutį - 42.3b
kita - 41.08i
kìtą - 10,22p
kitas - 11n,13i,45(15)
kitas (acc.pl.) - 41.03b
kitì - 26i,29.6a,30.14g,
 46(36)
kitíem - 29.51j, Fn 3(2)
kitiemus - 32.12a
kìto - 18s,32.1k,32.42e
kits - 32.42e
kittû - 41.06e
kitu - 10,30.3a
kitų̃ - 30.2g
kiũtinti - 30.4
klaidìngas - 46(18)
klaidų̃ - 30.15a,30.2i
klaiojme - 27s
klajójime laikytis - 27
klãną - 29.31e
klãsėje - 30.2a
klausa - 32.11d
klausau - 30.1
klause - 13g,32.11b
kláusia - 5,14f,39
kláusiamas - 5,12b
kláusiantis - 5
klausiaũ - 30.1/1
klausik - 32.11a,42.8k
klausyk - 30.1h
klausima - 2.4
kláusimą - 41.18f
kláusimas - 41.18d
klausyti - 30.1i,30.1j,32.11
klausitoius - 5d
kláusti - 39
kleodama - 10
klieñtai - 41.19d,41.19e
Klìmo - 31.1z$_2$

kliùvę - 26i
klojìmą - 36.1m,36.1n
klùpo - 29.1a
knygà - 5
knigieles - 31.1m
knỹgos - 5,6,30.1d,30.3c
kõ - 15d,15h,30.63c
kodẽl - 32.41c
koiũ - 36.6b
koja - 5
kójas - 33.4c,33.4d
kójomis - 36.1s,41.24m
kójos - 24c,31.1n,39a,
 45(27)
kójų - 41.25g
kokę - 27e
kokiey - 37.2b
kol - 34.7e
kolei - 22i
kolúkio - 42.1a
kopinéti - 34.81k
koplyčią - 13c
kópti - 34.81b,34.81i
kosznam - 29.5f
kosznas - 11m
kõšė - 6
kótas - 23q,39b
kovójo - 36.2i
krañtas - 29.2c
krantè, krañto - 37q
krãštas - 6,45(15)
kraughi - 2.5
krauia - 31.1r
krauiú - 36.6i
Kraujelį - 18t
kraũjo, kraujũ - Fn 9(2)
kráuna - 36.1g
krẽpšį - 30.16d
kriaunõm - 45(28)
krikschczonis - 2.3
krikschtitoghi - 34.6c
krikscziniu - 34.21e,
 41.19a
krikscziniu - 31.2c
kriksczónim - 36.6h

krikščionis - 29.7
krikščioniškas - 31.2d
Krikšta - 41.04
krimtamas - 12c
krimtimas - 2.3
Kristaus - 41.35b
Kristu - 4.3
Kristus - 36.6q
kropštinėja - 8a
krõsytų - 6
krùtančiųjų - 42.1c
kùbilas - 5
kudì - 11g
kudikis - 5
kũdikis - 3.1
kūdykỹstie - 41.15d
kuiną - 34.7d
kulameys - 5
kulantem - 32.14h
kulnimìs - 36.1v
kulnìs - 36.1v
kumẽlės - 23v
kuna - 41.14d
kunas - 41.37h
kũne - 2.3
kũne - Fn 9(3)
kuniga - 41.37i
kunigaykśc̀iu - 36.6f
kunigaiszscziu - 41.34a
kunigų - 2.5
kunigus - 36.2c
kũno - 41.01j
kuns - 34.6b,36.8a
kunu - 36.6i
kuõ - 11h, Fn 14(3)
kuodúotasis - 42.2c
kuonè - 36.3b
kuonorint - 18s
kùpinas - 31.3c
kûpką - 36.8c
kuř - 10,15,23s,23t,23x,24b,
    29.7a,30.5k,42.9(8),(9)
kure - 32e
kūrénti - 32.31i
kuri - 34.6c,36.6d,36.6j

kùria (verb) - 38.3a
kuria - 37.1a
kurią̃ - 44(12)
kuriẽ - 2.5,3.7,32.11b,
    33.2a,36.8b,36.8g,41.17c,
    41.26b,41.30c,42.9(4)
kuriemus - 41.01d
kuriii - 41.01j
kurij - 41.06a
kūrìmas - 30.5m
kūrinỹs - 31.2e
kuriõs - 43
kurìs - 12d,27,36.8e,37d,
    42.8,45(22)
kuriū - 30.14d
kuřkia - 38.4b
kurpiu - 34.7b
kurs - 29.74e,30.5h,32.11/1,
    40d
kursaĩ - 27,30.14c,41.12g
kursey - 41.08c,41.37h
kurss - 37f
kvalifikãcija - 30.15e
kviẽsti - 30.4
kwapas - 5
kwepiamas - 5

labà - 29.74b
lãbą - 34.5
labaĩ - 42.3b,44(9-14),
    45(8),46(16),(28)
labãnaktis - 29.74c
lãbas - 29.74a,29.74d
labiaũ - 29.81a
laĩkantis - 2
laiką̃s - 2
laikikiet - 35c
laikýti - 36.6,41.37
laĩko - 2
laikomóji - 5b
laikosi - 27s
laĩks - 5
laimẽjo - 31.7b,31.7d
láimės - 30.4b,44(3)
láiptai - 3.3

laisvų̃ - 30.2/o
láišką - 1b,6,26c,26d,36.4g, Fn 1
láiškai - 29.51j, Fn 3(2)
láiškas - 1b,6
laĩvas - 30.51w
łaizdącze - 2.5
lakamstwas - 41.14b
lakštiñgalė - 42.9(3)
langą - 14b
langaĩ - 29.5a,29.5c
lángas - 45(33)
lango - 14b
lankýti - Fn 5
lañkomas - 16c,16d
łápinimu - 3.2
lãpę - 44(19),(20),(21),(22),(23),(24),(25)
lãpių - 30.2g
lásziniû - 5
lãšant - 28/1
lauka - 41.14c
laũką - 26/1
laukaĩ - 5
laukaĩs - 36.7b
laukáms - 32.31k,32.31/1
láukiama - 1a,5
láukiamas - 5
láukiančią - 44(11)
láukiant - 28k
laũko - 30.11c,30.7b,32.1a
láukti - 5,30.1b
laukù - 36.4b
laukų̃ - 37t,44(27)
laukuosè - 37t
laukùs - 47(1)
laũmė - 13h
Laurins - 12a
láuro - Fn 13
láužo - Fn 12(a)
láužomas - 34.3a
Lazdíenės - 26g
lẽdas - 6
ledù - 42.1b
léisti - Fn 5

léistis - 30.4
lelia - 37e
lengviaũ - 29.51j,32.43
leñktas - 6
lenktu - 30.13b
lentàs - 47(3)
lentojè, lentõs - 36w
Letuuinikump - 31.1m
Leuitai - 2.5
Leuitas - 2.5
Lęwas - 22k
liáuti(s) - 18
liekariaus - 32.4b
liepe - 34.22a
liẽpia - 34.22b
liepk - 32i
liepsna - 2.5
liẽpti - 34.22
lieta - 6
lietaũs - 30.51k
líetų - 44(29)
lietùs - 30.18a,30.51/1
lietuvininkus - 34.7g
lietuwischka - 41.01/o
liežùvio - 26g
ligà - 2.4,5
ligą - 2.4
ligaus - 28g
ligga - 2.3
ligi̇̀ - 15
ligóni̇ - 44(15)
ligónis - 5,16c,16d,30.12e
ligus - 33c
lýgūs - 33.1a
lỹja - 2.1,30.18a
lĩko - 17f, Fn 3(4)
likos - 3.7
lìkti - 32.41i, Fn 15
liliamus - 32.1a
limpamà - 5
liṁpanti - 2.3,5
linaĩ - 30.2n
lynantesnė - 2.6
lỹnanti - 2.1
lỹnantie - 21

lindiney - 37.31a
liñkęs - 3.1
liñksmas - 25g
linksminkim - 32.1/1
lìnksminosi - 36.1b
linksmos - 34.22a
lìno - 31.2f
Linu - 5
linùs - 30.7b,30.7c
linxmibaeie - 22e
lìpk - 41.02a,41.02b
lìpti - 5
lytaũs - 22c
lytẽlis - 26/1
lìtų - 31.7b,31.7d
lytùs - 30.51i
liũdnas - 45(9)
lójant - Fn 3(3)
lójęs - 23u
lóki̇ - 30.1q
lokỹs - 42.2a
lopytoms - 6
lóvai - 41.02c
lóvos - 41.02d
luktelėjęs - 13k
Luthera - 41.19b
lúžęs - 3.1

Mą - Fn 3(4)
macze - 33c
maczems - 33b
maczes - 30.5g
mačiaũ - 19a
maedumi - 2.5
maedus - 2.5
maetą - 41.08f
maĩšas - Fn 11
maksla - 38.1b,41.05a,41.16b, 41.37s
makslas - 29.73a
malane - 32.14c,32.14d,37.32a
malanes - 41.12a
malanus - 32.2c,33a
maldà - 32.4d,40h
maldiniñkas - 23s

maldomis - 41.32f
málkoms - 32.31b,32.31f
málkų - 32.31i
malones - 31.3a
malonù - 21
malónės - 45(4)
mama - 22/1
Mamre - 21g
mán - 23w,28g,29.6a,29.8c,
    30.1h,30.17a,32.12b,
    32.4a,32.4g,32.41d,
    32.42c,32.42d,33.4a,
    Fn 12(b)
mana - 5d,29.3c,32.11/o,
    37.2a,41.01b
mane - 21m,32.11d,31.19h,
    41.26,41.37d,r
manè - 32.12d,32.12e,36.6w,
    41.18d,44(4),(17)
mãnė - 18i
manens - 30.14c
manes - 30.14e,30.3a
manę̃s - 28j,41.26d,47(5)
manęs - 30.11b
mani - 35c
maniñ - 39d,41.18c, Fn 14
    (2)
manimi - 36.3g,41.35h
manimpi - 39k
manýti - 16
màno - 30.11j,36.6s,36.8e,
    37.31a,41.37h,42.9(2)
Marcinkonýsa - 38.5c,38.5d
marčiai - 32.14k
marčiaĩ - 41.15c
marginių - 6
Maria - 37e
Marias (Mary) - 41.12g
marias - 14j,41.35e
marìnamas - 5
Mariôs - 41.12h
mariu - 41.35c
máriu - 41.37p
marius - 41.35d
martẽlę - 34.7c

Martina - 41.19b
Màskvą - 30.41a
maszas - 23e
màt - 23j,26g
mataũ - 8,19c,19d,19e,19f,
  19h,42.8
mãtė - 15d
mãtę - 18t
materis - 36.2a
matýsiantis - 4.2
matýti(s) - 16,26/o,29.5,
  30.21e
mãto - 46(29)
maũdžia - 32.14k
maxlas - 29.1b
mazgagimu - 41.19f
mazgotos - 24c
mažaĩ - 46(31)
mãžas - 41.01,42.2
mažàsis - 42.2d
mažėja - 30.18d
mažesnės - 42.9(8)
mažiaũ - 31.7c,31.7e
mãžmožis - 44(13)
mãžos - 45(25)
mažõs - 45(7)
mažam - 41.24g
mažu - 36.6q
mẽdį - 41.02a,41.02b
mẽdų - 45(35)
medùkais - 23/1
medumì - 44(34)
medžiójamieji - 2.4
mẽdžių - 5,41.38b
medžiùs - 41.38b
medžias - 3.5
medžiu - 36.6k
medžioiančius - 2.4
mėgsta - 36.8a
mėgtis - 36.8
megztìniui - 32.14/1
meldė - 13/1
meldziu - 5d
meldžiame - 41.06e
mėlynąja - 42.1c

mėnesius - 30.5k
mėnessis - 35f
mẽno - 31.2e
mérda - 9
mérdėti - 9
mergà - 3.3,41.01j
mergáičių - 30.15c
mergàs - 41.12g,41.27b
mergĕle - 5b
mergĕlė - 42.9(3)
mergytė - 8b
mergužĕle - 28j
mergužĕlė - 42.4a
mẽs - 25h,32d,41.14e,44(7),
  46(6)
mėsà - 3.1,6
mėsk - 41.11d
Messioschu - 4.3,30.5c
mèsti - 18,26
meškõs - 30.1r
mėšlo - 30.42j,30.42k
méta - 35j
mẽtą - 28n
mẽtai - 29.6a
mẽtais - 41.09a
mẽtamas - 26
meteliùs - 5b
mètrai - 29.6
metu - 41.37k
mêtu - 41.08/1
metùs - 30.5k,35e
metusu - 37.1c
mėžemoji - 5
mi - 34.4b,43
miadžias - 12d
miẽga - 34.11a,36.2d,37v
mieganti - 2.2
miegmi - 34.11a
miẽgo - 30.1c,30.62d
miegóti - 1,5c
miegù - 36.2d
miẽlą - 41.30e
mielai - 41.01/1
mielasis - 42.5
mielasysis - 42.5

371

mieschczionis - 13j
miesta - 41.37g
miẽstą - 4.2
miestan, miestana - 38.2a
miẽstas - 30.15d, 31.1z$_1$, 44(4)
miestop - 40
miestump - 40
mieżienes - 3.7
Mykoliùkas - 44(3)
Mykoliuko - 30.3b
myléta - 6k, 30.5j
mileti - 30.14a
myléti - 6/1
mili - 35.1a
mylia - 35.1a
milijárdas - 31.5
milijõnas - 31.5
mýlimas - 5
milimus - 5d
milins - 22d
minià - Fn 10(2)
mìnios - 31.6a
miniõs - Fn 10(3)
minių̃ - 31.6a
minutàs - 41.38e
minùtei - 33.3a
minùtės - 29.6b
mìrę - 23m
mîrsiancziam' - 4.4
myrstanczion - 2.4
mirsztątime - 2.3
mìrštam - 36.3b
mìrštamà - 2.4, 5
mir̃tas - 6
mir̃ti - 4.4, 5, 6
mirtiẽs - 36.3e
mirtimì - 36.3f
mirtóji - 6
mìrusį - 19b
mìską - 32.41b, 32.41f, 36.4e, 41.31b
miškaĩ - 6k, 6/1
mìškas - 46(14)
miškè - 30.2g, 36.4f, 44(2), (35-37)

mìško - 29.5j, 41.38a
miškù - 36.4d, 41.38a
miškų̃ - 30.18d
miškuosè - 6
močiùtės - 33.4a
mojàvo - 36.1s
mokantiemus - 2.5
mókė - 30.43a
mókestį - 30.42h
mokét - 21p
mokéti - 30.42h
mokieti - 29.5i
mokik - 30.14e
mokỹklos - Fn 5
mokiniaĩ - 30.2c
mokinỹs - 30.15a, 45(17)
mokinių̃ - 30.2a
mokinti - 34.6a
mókytas - 6
mokýti - 30.43a
mokitiniey - 11/1
mókytoją - 45(3)
mokitojems - 33e
mókytoju - Fn 8
mókytos - 6
mókosi - 36.6v
moksłay - 37.2b
moksłuy - 32.1d, 32.1e
mókslus - 34.82
momà - 40a
momáip - 39c
mótė - 29a, 29b
moterischkes - 3.5
móteriška - 5
mótina - 45(4)
mótiną - 44(9), (10), (11), (12), (13), (14)
motynėlė - 21m
mótinos - 45(26)
motinu - 10
mótriška - 5
motùlĩ - 42.9(1)
muitenikas - 12e
muka - 5f

mums - 27q,29.5g,32g,32.11j,
  32.11m,32.14a,32.2c,32.4e,
  32.42e,33a,41.12a
mumus - 21c,32.14a
mus - 23f,34.6b,36a,36.4a,
  36.6t,41.10c,41.10d,
  41.14a,41.27e,41.37b,f
muschti - 24d
musimpi - 39k
muss - 41.12b
musu - 31.1s,32.14a,36.6n,
  36.6/o,36.6q,36.6t,36.8a,
  37d,37g,41.06a,41.37k
musų - 41.01g
mūsų - 5e, 30.7b,32.41e,
  41.18a,41.27e,41.31e,
  45(3),(25)
mūsunk - 40c
mùšamas - 13f
muštỹnių - 30.21e
muzikañtas - 14a
mùzikos - 30.3b

nagà - 31.21a
nãkčiai - 32.31n
nakteie - 37.1a
nakti - 35c
nãktį - 34.5
naktìs - 2.1,2.3j,29.2a,
  44(16)
nãmą - 34.8a,42.8
nãmas - 6,42.1d
namie - 3.6,12e
namiẽpi - 39
nammû - 30.11d
nãmo - 29.7a,46(9)
namõ - 6n,11e,13a,13b,14d,
  14g,22,25i,30.12d,36.71a
namõpi - 39
namosna - 11k
namu - 30.11e
namû - 30.11g
namų̃ - 30.43d
namùs - 47(4)
namusn - 30.12b

namùs - 8a,10,30.11g,34.2b
nar - 40d
nareia - 36b
naschliu - 31.1f
nasru - 32.14h
nauiei - 3.5
nauyeme - 37.3a
naujíenų - 44(6)
naujaĩs - 41.09a
neãpkenčia - 29.8
neapleisk - 11n
neatwersk - 32g
nebagams - 21c
nebebùvę - 23/o
nebegeraĩ - 46(10)
nebeĩs - 6x
nebereikent - 27t
nebẽsant - 28m
nèbjaũris - 29.8
neburbė́jęs - 11j
nebū́ti - 32.41c
nebùvęs - 23w
nebùvo - 15j
nedãręs - 15e
nedeket - 34.7a
nedėlios - 32.11e
nederunčio - 2.3
nedìdelė - 29.8b
neẽsant - 28n
negal - 32.12a
negaleczia - 31.5
negaletu - 34.7h
negãli - 45(22)
negalì - 29.74e,32.13f
negálimas - 39j
negaliñčio - 45(22)
negaliù - 30.31a,32.1b
negáusi - 41.13b
negáusiąs - 16c
negelbąs - 27n
negelbt - 32.12b
neger - 32.41a
negerai - 10
negérus - 21p
negérusiam - 21p

negi - 18s
negirdė́t - 30.21e
negiriamą - 5
ne-gi-si-tikėjau - 43
negývas - 13f
negývo - 30.5w
negu - 31.7d,41.37c,45(41), 46(35)
negudrùs - 30.5s
negudraũs - 30.5t
néi - 27,34.7b,45(41), 46(35),(36)
ney - 27f,41.01d
neimsiu - 34.7b
neiokałtoia - 42.6d,42.9
neischkalbama - 5f
neischkepto - 6
neysztikumùsemp - 39i
neišsilaĩžę - 26n
neĩšvirė - 30.7a
neįveĩkia - 30.31b
neįvertino - 30.3b
neįžveĩgiama, neįžveĩgiamos - 30.5m
nejuntĩ - 28j
nekaip - 31.7d,45(42),46(36)
nekaĩtojo - 42.6d
nekenčia - 6
nekenteia - 2.4
nekeptą - 6
nekir̃tęs - 23v
neklaũso - 23u
nekópt os - 34.81f
nekultĩ - 6
nekuštėk - 2.6
neláimėmis - 36.1e
neláimės - 32.1k
nelaimìngą - 17t,17v
nelaimìngas - 17u,w,45(9)
neláimių - 36.1f
neléido - 5c
neliáunas - 18b
nelĩko - 30.21a
nemãtę - 23p,23q,23r
nemelúok - 2.6

nemãtanti - 2.1
nemataũ - 41.19c
nemãtė - 44(3)
nemãtęs - 15d
nematýt - 30.21e
nematýti - 29.6c
nematýtu - 36.2h
nemelúok - 2.6
nemokė́ti - 29.8b
Nemunė̃lio - 45(20)
nemušk - 34.7d
nenorė́jo - Fn 5
nenóriu - Fn 15(4)
nenuė̃jo - 30.32b
nenùjėgančiamui - 32.12e
nenusekami - 5
nepadaritu - 34.6b
nepadest - 29.74e
nepagelbas - 27q
nepagendansis - 2.3
nepakeĩčiamas - 24
nepaláubąsis - 2.3
nepapeiksit - 34.7f
nepastebimaĩ - 32.41i
nepàtelpams - 10
nepatõgu - 32.41b
nepazistamas - 5g
nepertamsĩ - 23j
neprasĩtarė - 15c
nepaprastaĩ - 46(15)
nepasíekė - 44(13)
nepreteliaus - 41.14f
nepridulkė́tų - 30.51u
neprietelių - 24d
neprietelus - 36.6b
ner - 41.01h
nẽr - 11h,15n,23g,33.4a
nera - 21n,30.21c,30.21d
nėrà - 15/1,30.21b,39c,39d
nerãgina - 34.7c
neraudók - 5b
neregė́jęs - 34.7e
neregimi - 5
neregiunćiey - 2.6
nereik - 32.41g

374

nes - 4.3,21d,41.37f
nesa - 28f,30.14c,30.21d
nesą - 22c
nesãkęs - 11i
nesanczio - 28g
nesche - 6
nesibaĩdo - 7b,36.3h
nesidžiaūk - 32.1j,32.1k
nesigėdi - 34.7g
nesijaučiù - 16a
nesilióvė - 18a
nesìmeldęs - 23s
nesisaugaienti - 2.2
neskaičiaũ - 30.3c
neszcia - 36.8h
nẽša - 2
nẽšamas - 1Ba
nẽšantis - 1Aa,2
nẽšąs - 1Aa,2
nėščią - 36.8
nẽšdavęs - 1Ac
nẽšęs - 1Ab
nẽšiąs - 1Ad
nẽšimas - 1Bc
nẽšinas - 36.71a,46(19)
nesiójo - 46(3)
nešókęs - 11g
nẽštas - 1Bb
nẽšti - 2
net - 14f
netektai - 41.06b
neteptì - 6
netikḗk - 34.21h
nètikiu - 34.21g
neturḗdavo - 45(4)
neturḗjau - 44(14)
neturiù - 33.4b
neužgul - 32.11m
neužmingù - 11f
nevalgydama - 13e
nevažiúoja - 30.32a
newalgikjte - 6
newed - 41.10c
newenge - 14j
newienas - 39j

newirk - 22i
nežinaĩ - 15g
nežĩnanti - 26g
nežinaũ - 27h
nežinójęs - 23x
nežinójo - 15a
nežinójom - 44(7)
nežĩnoma - 45(12)
nežĩnomo - 45(12)
nežinomas - 5g
niaũzgia - 34.3a
nieka - 32.12b
niekakiu - 36.2j
niekas - 23f,30.3b
niẽko - 16a,16c,21p,39d,
    41.19c
niekursai - 21f
niẽmčiai - 40c
niéžanczes - 2.3
nýkščio - 31.21a
nog - 30.5h,41.01c,41.14b,
    41.14c,41.14d,41.14e
nogi - 30.5f,30.5g,41.14a,
    41.14f
nomirusiuiu - 41.12e
nopkeñčia - 29.8
noraetu - 27t
nóras - 32.41i,32.41j
norḗdami - 30.14g
norḗdams - 15h
norḗjo - 16c,16d
norḗjosi - 32.4g
noręs - 30.1e
norḗti - 5,30.1c, Fn 6
norḗtų - 42.3b
nóri - 30.62d
norimi - 5
nósis - 6
nosytikiedamas - 32b
nu - 4.3,41.15a,41.15b,
    41.15c,41.15d
nubḗgo - 30.4e,30.42d, Fn 7
nudžiùgino - 30.5v
nueiens - 11d
nueinąs - 15k

nueĩti - 15m
nuejo - 11k,41.01c
nuė̃jo - 11
nugalė́ti - 34.2e
nuiĩsti - 36.8
nùkasė - 30.7b
nuklójo - 30.51s,30.51t
nuklóta - 30.5k
nulė́idusios - 23v
nulė́idžia - 11i
nulieta - 6
numanaũ - 16c
numanýti - 16
numazgoima - 41.01g
numien - 22/1
numirė - 29.74e
numìręs - 3.7
numirre - 9
nunokens - 3.4
nuõ - 14e,26j,29.1a,30.1r, 30.5j,32.42e,36.3d,47
núodėmė - 2.4
núodėmės - 45(25)
nùdemen - 2.4
nuog - 30.5e,41.14
nůg - 10,30.1e,41.14
nuolačiaĩ - 32.41e
nùmirusiu - 30.4a, Fn 7
nùženge - 38.1c
nupiřko - 32.14/1
nupúolė - 29.1a
nuráminti - 21n
nuraũdo - 36.3a
nurìmti - 18
nurõvė - 30.7b,30.7c
nusideimu - 30.14i
nusideis - 3.5
nusidė́jęs - 3.7
nusilė́idžiąs - 2.1
nu-si-mazgok - 43
nusistebė́jau - 32.1f
nusitikieti - 36.1q
nusitikiu - 36.1/o
nusivìjęs - 14h
nusivilko - 44(1)

nusmełkia - 41.30d
nusprę́sti - 16
nustãtė - 36.1/1
nustìpo - 14c
nustójo - 41.36a
nustóti - 18
nuščiúti - 18
nušóvė - 44(18),(19),(20), (21),(22),(23),(24),(25)
nùteka - 36.4h
nutekiedama - 10
nutìlo - 18c
nutìlti - 18
nuvažiãvęs - 23h

õ - 14,21f,23n,29.6a, 30.12b,30.14g,30.7a
óbelę - 45(8)
óbels - 45(23)
óbuolį - 1,41.25b, Fn 1(a), (c),(e)
obuoliaĩ - 1d,1e
obuolỹs - 1, Fn 1(b),(d)
óbuoliui - 41.25b
obuolių̃ - 45(8)
óbuolius - 1c
oficialiám - 30.41b
oficialaũs - 30.41a
oi - 42.9(1)
oleumi - 6
Onýtė, Onýtę - 29.7b
órą - 32.31d
óras - 46(15)
ožėlį - 6y

pa - 41.20,41.21,41.22a
pabė́gėjęs - 14c
pabė́go - 14e
pabucziawa - 11c
pabugusi - 10
pabūt - 41.27d
paczias - 31.1m
pačià - 32.4d
pačiù - 36.4g

padare - 2.5,6
padãrė - 30.15a,30.15c,30.15e
padãrę - 15c
padãręs - 16a
padarisiu - 33d
(pa-)darýti - 34.6
padaugėjo - 30.18c
padaugẽs - 30.18a
pàdavė - 30.15g
padavėjas - 41.19d
padavėjų - 41.19a
padawę - 15b
padėjėjas - 31.1w
padėjo - 37.3b
padėjo - 33.4c,33.4d
padeschines - 41.21a
padesiu - 36.6b
padėt - 29.74e
padėti - 31.1w,36.6
padety - 32a
padota - 33b
padotas - 36.2a
padoti - 41.06b
padūkiausias - 3.8
padùtus - 36.6c
pædo - 30.11c
paeĩti - 45(22)
pagal - 32g,41.16a,41.16b, 41.16c,41.16e,41.16f
pagalba - 33d
pagalei - 41.16
pagalį - 6
pagą̃sdinti - 32.31d
pagawo - 41.37e
pageidáuti - 5
pagelbami - 5
pagélbejo - 32.12a
pagelbetumbim - 32.12
pagélbmi - 32.12
pagieszansis - 2.5
pagulde - 37.3a
paguĩdė - 37
pagundima - 41.10c
paĩkti - 29.8
pailsėti - 13a
paiĩsti - 18

paioprasta - 42.6a,42.8, 42.9
pajési - 41.38c
pajutaũ - 28/1
pakaiuie - 22e
pakàkti - 21
pakañkamas - 2.4
pakañkantis - 2.6
pakañkąs - 2.4
pakankąsis - 2.4
pakasti - 24e
pakieles - 14i
paklidusiái - 3.8
paklusni - 33e
pakretami - 24b
pakutos - 41.04a
pàkvietė - 44(28),46(11)
palaiki - 41.26f
paléido - Fn 9(4)
palig - 41.16d,41.16e
palìjo - 46(5)
palìk - 42.9(8)
palikaũ - 34.3b
palìksim - 30.43d
palìkti - 30.43,36.6
palinkėjo - Fn 10(1)
paliñkusiomis - 45(30)
palitêio - 30.14f
palójantis - 2.1
palšiukù - 36.71b
pamačiaũ - 44(2),(8)
pamãtė - 42.1c
pamatýti - 42.3b
pamegdamij - 32.11p
pamekt - 39f
pamektas - 30.5h
pamiškėjè - 47(2)
pamokita - 12f
pamókytam - 32.4c
pamoksla - 13g
pana - 34.1a
panams - 32i
panepi - 39f
paniekins - 13i
Pannôs - 41.12h

panu - 31.1d
panui - 32c
papeneiei - 36e
papenėjęs - 7a
papildik - 36d
pàprastojo - 42.6a
paprãšė - 30.43c
paprašýkite - Fn 15(3)
par - 4.2,14b
paradik - 32.14c
paraschitas - 30.5f
paraschits - 41.19b
pařdavė - 38.3b
pardúok - 7a
pardúosimas - 7a
pardúoti - 30.42g
pareia - 12e
pãreigas - 34.82
pareis - 41.38e
pareitis - 29.5g
pareitissi - 29.5f
parėjąs - 42.18b
parėjęs - 13a
parėjo - 36.71a
paryčiaĩs - 36.5b
pãryčiu - 36.5b
parjójančio - 28j
paródė - 44(33)
(pa-)rodýti - 16
parsivežė - 32.31i
parvažiãvo - 30.4c
pas - 21e,21g,22f,41.17a,
    41.17b,41.17c,41.17d,
    41.18a,41.18b,41.18c,
    41.18d,41.27e,42.4a
pasãkė - 44(6)
pasáulip - 39h
pasáulo - 30.14b
paschak - 32.11k
pasėnusiam - 28h
pasidãrė - 42.3a,46(10)
pasidáugino - 30.18b
pasidawimu - 41.01d
pasidéti - 32.31a,32.31e
pasièmė - 32.31n

pa-si-gi-dėjau - 43
pa-si-gi-žiurėjau - 43
pasigùlęs - 11f
pasiim̃ti - 30.42f
pasiim̃tų - 30.4c
pasilabinusi - 13/1
pa(si)mėgti - 36.8
pasiremti - 36.1p,36.1r
pasiródyta - 30.5w
pasiskólinti - 30.4j
pasitáikė - 10
pasitáiko - 30.2i
pasitìko - 39e
pa(si)tìrti - 16
pasituris - 2.5
pasiučiausias - 3.8
pasiuntiniaĩ - Fn 13
pasiutesnis - 3.8
pasiùtusiai - 3.8
paskaitýti - 41.37
paskõlink - 30.17b,30.17c
pãskui - 11m,47
paslaptiẽs, paslaptim̃ -
    30.5m
pãslikas - 17j
pasmertes - 41.21b
pasnìgę - 25e
passidabotu - 32.11/o
passirode - 21g
passistengiau - 21d
pastačiaũ - 32.31e
pastate - 41.17d
pastatydino - 13c
pastatitas - 30.5e
pastatýti - 36.6
pastìprinti - 27
pastógės - 45(31)
pastóiu - 36.6h
pastóti - 29.3,36.6
paszadetu - 30.5c
pászałpos - 39h
paszinsti - 19i
paszławina - 32.11e
paszławink - 32.11g
pašãlus - 21

pašálusie - 21
pàšauké - 30.43b
pasélesnis - 3.8
(pa-)šlóvinti - 32.11
pat - 41.15d
patam - 30.5g
paténkintas - 24
pati - 41.08h
patogei - 41.35a
patogiey - 29.32c
pàts - 11k,15a,30.13a,
　36.71a
patuĩžti - 36.8
paũkščio - 31.1z,45(19)
paukštēlé - 42.9(3)
paukšteliùs - 44(28)
paválgęs - 23a,23b,23c
paválgymui - 32.31j
paválgyti - 32.31j
pãvardę - 30.11k
pavar̃gęs - 3.7,25c,25d,
　26e,26f
pavar̃gęsis - 3.7
pavãsario - 36.1b
(pà)ver̃té - 17t
(pa)vir̃to - 17u,36.6u
pawadino - 30.12c
pawijsdeia - 41.01/1
pawirsi - 41.10f
pawirsta - 36.6i
(pa-)wir̃sti - 36.6
pawisti - 2.2
pazinimas - 31.1s
pažadaĩs - 32.1j
pažinęs - 13c
pažįstamas - 5
pažiūrėt - 13k
pažiūrõs - 46(25),(26)
pažvìlti - 36.8
pažieydis - 18s
pēčius - 30.51q
peĩkti - 36.8
peĩļio - 30.17a
peĩlis - 5,6
peiliùkas - 45(28)

peklosna - 38.1c
pękta - 41.03a
pelaĩ - 30.51/o,30.51s
pellinai - 24b
pelų̃ - 30.51m
penekslu - 36e
penétą - 6y
penkì - 29.6,31.7e
penkiàs - 41.38e
peñkios - 29.6b
penkių̃ - 31.7c
Pentepolėj - 10
per̃ - 30.5i,30.5k,31.21b,
　32.41b,34.8b,36.4c,36.5a,
　41.19a-d,41.19f-i,41.31b-c,
　45(38),47
péraugti - 34.2c
perdaũg - 32.41d
péreiti - 34.8b
pergulditas - 41.01/o
perkalbeti - 27t
pérkalbéti - 27
pérmirkusiame - Fn 9(3)
pérsigérusiam - 21a
persimainanti - 27s
personu - 30.21c
pertjre - 11/o
pérveda - 29.8
pervìs - 46(34)
Petras - 13g
Petrui - 21d
piauiemosos - 5
pharaonas - 22f
philosóphai - 41.01h
piáutas - 6
piáutuvas - 6
piemuõ - 36.71c,42.5a
pienas - 2.5
píeno - 32.31m,41.01k
pienu - 2.5
pieštùko - 30.17b
pietų̃ - 30.4f,30.4g,30.4k,
　30.4i,46(11)
píevai - 41.38c
píevas - 35m,44(30)

piggai - 2.2
pikta - 23n,41.14a
piktái - 2.4,30.14h
pìktas - 17i,32.11j
pikti - 5h
piktybę - 41.37r
pikto - 18s
piktus - 3.5,40g
pìldo - 30.51i
pìldomi - 30.51j
pilìs - 31.21b
pilkų̃ - 44(27)
pillies - 41.37q
pìlną - 45(8)
pilnai - 41.01/o
pìlnas - 30.51q,31.3,36.8,
    46(21-22)
pilnasis - 31.3a
pilni - 36.8i
pìlti - 44(29)
pinigaĩs - 32.12f
pìnigų - 32.4f
pìnigus - 29.72a,30.42d,
    Fn 7
piningų̃ - 41.13b
pinkieto - 3.7
pyrãgų - 30.16a
pirkaũ - 32.3a,32.31k,32.31/1
pirkéjai - 30.2m
pirklio - 6w
pirkom - 41.07a
pirkti - 30.42e, Fn 6
pirktų - Fn 6
pirm - 2.5
pìrma - 47
pìrmas - 42.8k,45(17)
pirmiausei - 11p
pìrmininku - 32.41h,36.6w
pirštas - 5
pirti - 38.3a
pjáuna - 5
pjáunamas - 5
pjáunantis - 5
pjáuta - 6a
pjáuti - 32.3a,32.3b

plačiašãkis - 45(6)
platink - 32.14e
plaukaĩ - 31.2f
plaukiama - 5
plebanus - 36.2c
plebonop - 40k
pléšė - 17r
plėšrióji - 42.2b
pliẽnas - 6
plýšo - 17s

plùnksną - 41.13a
plusta - 2.5
plustancze - 2.5
plùtom - 6y
po - 4.3,5,10,13h,41.13c,
    41.13d,41.20b-c,41.21,
    41.22b,41.23a-d,41.24a-m,
    41.25a-g
połe - 41.17b
pona - 30.5e,37.3a
põną - 19b
ponačiai - 6
põnas - 13k,21g,22d,29.71b,
    29.72a,30.13a,32.11e,
    41.01/1
pone - 31.3a,36.6s
põno - 23t
ponop - 21n
pons - 27q
ponu - 36.6a
popieżischkei - 27s
potam - 41.20a
pra - 41.30
pràdeda - 21a
pradėti - Fn 5
pradžiùgo - 36.3e,36.3f
praiispùłęs - 42.6c,42.9
praìlgsta - 28k
prákaitû - 5
prãkartą - 37.3
prakartè - 37.3b
prakiłnesni - 41.37c
praleia - 41.06a
pràleñkia - 29.8

prałobint - 30.14g
pramane - 13j
praminsi - 29.32b
pramiñti - 29.3
pranesche - 4.3
prapúolęsis - 42.6c
prarakai - 4.3
praschiikiet - 36.2c
praschom - 30.1f
prasideiase - 41.12g
prastèsnio - 29.8f
prasty - 29.73a,31.1h
praszakusius - 3.5
prãšė - 41.27d
prašýt - 15h
prašýti - 5,30.1d
prašnekėjom - 41.31f
prãšo - 14g
prawadniku - 36.6n
preg - 35c,41.26d,f
pregtam - 41.26a
prerakintas - 40i
pribėgo - 30.51x
pribėrė - 30.51/o
pribertas - 30.51q
pribiro - 30.51m
pridengtas - 30.5m
pridera - 29.5h
prideránczios - 2.3
priderančiai - 2.6
priderąs - 2.3
priderencziu - 2.5
pridrebe - 30.51p
pridribo - 30.51n
pridūdamas - 37.32b
priẽ - 14b,41.26c,41.36, 47(5)
prieg - 30.3a,41.26b,e
prieglaudělę - 29.7a
prieiens - 11c
prieitij - 40d
priėjo - 30.51v,30.51w
príekinės - 45(27)
priesch - 31.1d,41.28a
prieschtarau - 32.11/1

priesz - 41.27c,d,41.37f
priẽš - 29.6b,41.28,41. 29b
priešais - 41.29a,47
priešus - 44(31)
prieštaráuja - 31.13c
prieštaráujamas - 32.13d
prietam - 21n
príežasti̧ - 20e,20f
priežasties - 2.3
prigawa - 2.2
prigimtìs - 36.1b
priimamas - 5
prikielima - 41.19g
prikimšti - Fn 9
prikráutą - Fn 9(4)
primerkė - 30.51/1
primirko - 30.51k
primirkti - Fn 9
pripilde - 36.8d
pripildyti - 36.8,Fn 9
pripiltą - 36.8c
pripilti - 36.8
pririñko - 30.16c,30.16d
pririštos - 41.27c
prisakikiet - 38.1a
prisakimapi - 40i
prisakimas - 31.1y
prisakimosu - 37.2a
prisakimu - 31.5
prisch - 31.1c,41.28b
prischtariaudamij - 32.11p
prisiartinęs - 14b
prisiartinti - 21n
prisiartysyt - 40e
prisikepė - 30.16a
prisimiñti - 16
prisiweyzdet - 32.1b
pritviñksta - Fn 9(2)
pritviñkti - Fn 9
priwalimu - 32.14g
priwalingas - 27r
priwalu - 27
priwersk - 40g
prižiūrėt - 30.43d

prõ - 11i,41.30a-g,41.31
   a-f
prõtas - 34.22b
protìngas - 31.2b
prõto - 31.2
pryryszta - 41.37n
pūdymas - Fn 3(4)
puikì - 31.21b
puikyste - 32.12c
pułkey - 32.1e
pùlti - 5
puodělis - 31.4d,31.4e
puolamóji - 2.4
puołancię - 2.4
puołe - 11/1
púolė - 30.42c,Fn 7(c)
púolęs - 29.31e
puolimóji - 5
pùpose - 26/o
puschczoie - 10
pùsę - 22p
pùsryčiauti - 46(12)
pūti - 9
pùtrai - 32.31g

rādęs - 26m
rādiją - 41.31c
rādo - 45(8)
rādusi - 13h
ragaĩ - 6
ráišioti - 33.4c,33.4d
raiteliùko - 28m
rąka - 36a
rąkas - 41.10a
rąkasn - 38.1b
rāktais - 36.1t
raktùs - 36.1t
ramćio - 36.1r
ramćiu - 36.1p
ramiaĩ - 46(2),(7)
rañdasi - 30.2h
rañką - 34.2e
ranka - 34.7a
rankàs - 2.3,30.42c,41.35a,
   Fn 7(c)

rankoie - 36.8c
rañkomis - 31.1x,36.1s
rañkon - 6x
rankôs - 41.24a
rañkų - 31.1x,46(3)
rankělės - 42.9(3)
rañkose - Fn 13
ràs - 29.7a
raschta - 2.5
ràsis - 30.2j
raskaszys - 41.30d
râszo - 41.01h
raszoma-tobliczią - 5
rāšęs - 26c,26d
rašýti - 27,29.51j,Fn 3(2)
rāšo - 36w
rāšoma - 1b,6,Fn 1
rašta - 29.73a
rātai - 6,30,42j
rātais - 30.42k
raugìnti - 6
raugintos - 6
raupuoti - 29.32c
raupuotu - 36.6j
razume - 41.26c
rediti - 32i
rėdýti - 6
regedams - 14j
regeiens - 11m
regéti(s) - 16,21,29.5
regì - 27e
regiedama - 13d
regiedamas - 13i
regiety - 36b
regimì - 5,5h
reginčiaĩ - 2.6
regiuncey - 2.6
reik - 22/1,30.14d,37.1e,
   41.06b
reika - 32.4b
reĩkalą - 29.71a
reikalãvimu - 32.1f
reikalìngas - 31.3,46(23-
   24)
reykalingiasnia - 21n

382

reĩkalo - 30.21b,34.42f,
　34.7d
reikĕdavo - 32.42g
reikėję - 32.42g
reikėjo - 32.4c,32.42g
reikent - 27
reikės - 32.42g
reikėti - 32.4a,32.42f
reĩkia - 15n,29.5e,30.63c,
　32.4a,32.4d,32.41f,
　32.42d,32.42e,Fn 3(1)
reykia - 30.14i
reikią - 27
reĩkiamas - 5
reikiamieghi - 5
reykiamu - 5
réikšmę - 30.15f
reikšmės - 30.15d
reĩkta - 29.5c,29.5d
reĩkti - 5
rękey - 41.20c
rekie - 41.30a
retaĩ - 42.9(9)
riẽstas - 6
riešutẽliai - 3.1
rika - 41.10d
rinkens - 23d
riñko - 44(35),(36),(37)
risnója - 36.2e
ristelè - 36.2e
ryšiaĩ - Fn 10(1)
rýtą - 34.5
rytaĩs - 36.5c
ritameta - 35d
rýtas - 29.4,29.74d,44(26)
rýtui - 21k
roda - 29.1b
ródyti - 36.6
ródytis - 16,21,Fn 15
ródos - 26k,Fn 9(1)
roputès - 30.7b
rossa - 37e
rubo - 30.14f
ruduõ - 29.2b,45(2),(9)
rugiaĩ - 6a,25f,30.51n

rùgio - 32.42a
rugiùs - 30.51p,30.51t
rúgtas - 6
rúgti - 6
rūkýta - 6
runka - 36.6j
rupescius - 41.30d
rūpintis - 16
rupliùkai - 26/o
rustibe - 3.4
rustibes - 30.1g,41.06b
rūta - 45(5)

sacramentas - 31.1b
saka - 4.3,12a,27r
*sakā - 2.7
sake - 20g
sãkė - 18n,18p,18q,18r,27a,
　27b,27c,27d
sãkęs - 23u
sãkės - 16b
sãkėsi - 18/1,27u
sakýk - 11i
sakita - 24g
sakýti(s) - 16,27
sãko - 16b,19j,20e,20f,
　26i,27i,27k,27/1,28d,
　28n,42.8k
sãkos - 18g
sãkosi - 16a,19k,27j
saldèsnis - 45(35)
Samgori - 42.3a
samniene - 41.32c
sanczius - 19i
sánti - 4.3,21p
sãnū - 42.9(1)
sapnawa - 22f
sarmačiaũ - 29.81
sarmatà - 29.81
sąs - 2
sąsenis - 42.8
sąsiuviniai - 6s
sąsiuvinius - 6r
saũ - 6,23v,29.7a,36.6c,
　41.37b

saua - 29.3a
saugak - 41.14f,41.19g
saugotusi - 30.13b
saulelei - 21m
sáulės - 32.4e
saulytėlė - 22n
Saulus - 36.6d
saulùtė - 41.07b
saũsą - 17p
saũsas - 17q,29.31e
saváitę - 41.01e
saváitei - 35m,41.01e
saváitės - 41.01e
savè - 19j,27i
sàvo - 26n,30.1/1,30.15d,
   34.21g,34.3b,36.1a,36.1e,
   36.1f
savõsios - 29.8b
sawa - 12f,14i,14j,19i,
   21g,22k,31.3b,32e,32f,
   32.1/1,32.14b,34.6a,36b,
   36c,42.8j
sawe - 21e,41.17c,41.37d
sawę - 32.12a
sawęs - 35c
sawo - 11/1,13i,41.37r
sawomis - 36.8f
sawų - 30.14g
sążinę - 21n
schale - 12a
schaudai - 24a
scheimina - 34.6a,41.35a
schętro - 21g
schimta - 31.5
schimty - 31.5
schirdies - 34.22a
schitą - 38.1b
schitage - 37.1a
schitai - 40f
schito - 41.05a
schytogi - 36.2a
schitokius - 11m
schwenta - 36d,41.16b
schwęnta - 41.19g
schwentąge - 34.21d

schwentas - 11p,13g
schwentases - 38.4a
schwentibei - 32e
schwentoghi - 39g
schwentoj - 37.1e
schwentosius - 30.5i,41.19a
schwentu - 34.21e
schwiesibe - 30.21d
schwintases - 41.12g
sededamas - 10
sėdėjo - 23b
sėdi - 17i, 37u,41.11a
sedinczam - 21g
sedins - 8
sėjama - 25f
sėjamas - 5
sėjams - 5
sẽkantis - 2.3
sėklai - 41.07a
sėklos - 41.07a
sekmadienį - 35/o
sémti - 30.42a
sémtų - 30.42i
senaĩs - Fn 14(1)
senam - 41.24h
sẽnas - 44(27),45(1)
senei - 2.2
senẽlė - 44(34)
senẽliai - 30.16a
senẽlis - 6y
senẽliui - 30.42c,Fn 7(c)
sẽnį - 39e
sẽnis - 3.3
sennu - 31.1e
senų̃ - 6k,6l
senúosius - 42.4a
senùs - Fn 14(1)
septinias - 41.08g
septinis - 41.08g
seredós - 5
sergancziams - 32.11k
serñganciam - 28c
serñganciu - Fn 15(2)
serganti - 22/1
serñgantį - 20h,20i

sergantis - 2.1
sergą̃s - 8a,22a,22b,
  Fn 15(2)
serkti - 30.13a
sermė̃gą - 13h
sesė̃lę - 14g
sẽserie - 41.13b
seseris - 34.7f
sesuõ - 44(6)
sė́ti - 30.4d
siaũrą - 30.15f
siekti - Fn 6
sielwartuy - 41.20b
sijõnas - 2.6
silams - 32e
sĩłomis - 42.7c
sylpnams - 32.11j
simbolis - 30.5/1
siūbúoja - 28m
siula - 34.7b
siū́las - 6
siū́lytis - 16
siū́lų - 32.14/1
siuntė - 21m
siųsti - 30.4,30.42
siùtusi - 3.1
siutusiay - 3.8
siùva - 36h
skayčiaus - 30.14i
skaititaiap - 40j
skayto - 13d
skaldo - 6
skalsùs - 36.8
skarba - 42.8j
skarė̃lių - 42.1c
skaũda - 9,32,14i,32.14j
skaudama - 5
skaũdamas - 5,9,10
skaũdantis - 5
skaudė́ti - 9,21,29.8
skaũsmo - 36.3c
skausmù - 36.3a
skaũsta - 29.8
skélbtis - 16
skélda - 9

skéldéti - 9
skeléti - 34.4
skersą - 17r
skersaĩ - 47
skersas - 17s
skielat - 34.4a
skylélė - 5
skìna - 1c
skìnama - 1e
skinamì - 1d
skýrė - 44(31)
skirsis - 41.14d
skìrtas - 32.31h
skìrtos - 32.31g
skýstas - 6
skýsti - 6
skreñda - 46(28)
skrìdo - 44(27)
skunsta - 21d
skų́stis - 16
slėpiaũ - 44(12)
sluszba - 11n
sluszidamy - 32c
smãkas - 14f,14h
smalà - 6
smalstùs - 41.01
smalúotas - 6
smalúoti - 6
smarãgdai - 6w
smercziop - 2.5
smerti - 11m,14j,36c
smerties - 41.01f
smertiy - 41.08b
smilčių̃ - 30.51u
smirdunćiey - 2.6
smùlkia - 36.2e
snaudzanti - 2.2
sniẽgas - 30.51p,30.51t,
  45(42)
sniẽgo - 30.5k,30.51n
sniegù - 30.5k
sniñgantie - 21p
sõdą - 45(33)
sodýbą - 44(16)
sodintas - 12d

sópa - Fn 12(b)
sópamas - 34.3b
sparnaĩ - 45(19)
sparnêliai - 42.9(3),(4)
sparnù - 36.71d
sparnus - 41.23c
spausdamies - 9
spawiedniie - 27r
speciãlią - 30.15f
spend - 32.14f
sprándą - 13f,14d
srẽbti - 32.31g
ssadzius - 34.7f
ssakuotu - 36.6k
ssiedu - 37e
ssmaniu - 34.1b
stãčias - 29.31a
staghisi - 21f
stala - 41.37m
stãlą - 36.1h
stãlo - 36.1g,41.13d
stáltiesę - 13b
stalu - 41.35a
Stankūnas - Fn 7(d)
stãto - 36.1i,36.1k
staweti - 41.35a
stebẹiosi - 32.1e
stebétis - 16
stebuklamus - 32.1b
stebuklingas - 29.3b
stebuklùs - 20e,20f
stìgti - 21
stiklìnė - Fn 11
stìlo - 31.1/o
stiñga - 32.4f
stiprias - 41.12c
stìprintis - 36.8
stipru - 36.6t,36.8c
stiprus - 19i
stýroti - 5
stógo - 47(6)
stóti(s) - 29.3,36.6
stõtį - 29.6b
stotku - 2.5
stóvi - 23v,37r,47(5)

stovį̃s - 22p
stoviũ - 29.31a
stow - 12d
stowejo - 41.17c
stowins - 22f
stowintiems - 21e
straipsczĭu - 31.5,41.19a
strela - 28e
stubą - 14b
studeñtams - Fn 15(5)
sù - 15n,29.6a,32.12f,35.1a,
    36f,36h,36.2h,36.2i,
    36.71b,41.01d,41.32a-g
suáugęs - 3.1
suaugesnis - 3.8
subréndę - 3.1
sudeghię - 41.35a
sudereghimas - 2.3
sudétų - 30.42d,Fn 7
sudyta - 6
suditi - 41.12b
suditu - 30.4a,Fn 7
sudraude - 14j
sudu - 41.22b
sudûmi - 38.1d
sudźia - 36.6p
sugiespausti - 42.6b
suglaustas - 41.32b
sugrisza - 11/o
sugrį̃s - 33.3c
sugrį̃šime - 46(4)
sugrį̃žtant - 44(11)
sugrį̃žusį - 8
sugulditu - 30.5i,41.19a
sujáudino - 44(9),(10),
    (11),(12),(13),(14)
sukìlėliai - Fn 9(4)
suknẽlė - 45(26)
suknẽlės - 30.4c
sùktas - 6
sukúrę - 30.15b
sulìg - 31.2]a,41.16,
    44.33b
suligei - 41.33a
sumaischita - 6

sumnienes - 41.06b
sùmušė - 36.1v
sūnaũs - 44(11)
sunauspi - 40h
sūnytėlis - 10
sunkèsnis - 45(36)
sunki - 36.8
sunkibes - 30.14i
sunkinga - 36.8
sunkų̃ - 21,32.41d,Fn 3(2)
sunkùmų - 30.1a
sunkùs - 41.01,45(22),(24)
sunt - 13d
sųnu - 22h,42.8j
sū́nų - 41.11j
sùnui - 41.11j
sūnum̃ - 36.1a
sunumi - 36.8h
sunumis - 36.6r
sunus - 23e,29.3c,31.1c,
   41.10d,41.37b
sū́nùs - 42.3c,d
sùleliu - 36.6b
súolo - 41.11a,41.11c
supáustieji - 42.6b
suplḗšė - 13h
sùpo - 44(30)
suprañtamas - 5
supràsti - 16
supùvo - 37t
surastì - 6w
surašýta - 6r
surašýti - 6s
sūriéji - 42.3a
suriñk - 42.9(8)
surinkaĩ - 29.72a
surynkimu - 34.21e
sūrùs - 42.3a
susḗdo - 30.7a
susḗdom - 46(12)
susìbarė - 41.07c
susiédų - 30.12b
susimilima - 41.06c
susimilk - 41.12a
susimilstąs - 2.4

susir̃go - 36.5a
susiriñko - 30.2k,41.11i
susitiko - 2.5
suskam̃bino - 36.1t
sussimilstas - 2.4
sustójom - 46(13)
sustóti - 18
suszal - 37.1d
sušãlo - 5e
sutẽmus - 21
sutvirtétų - Fn 10(1)
sutwere - 22g
sutwerima - 37.32b
suunaus - 38.4a
suvėjęs - 26k
suwadina - 30.12b
sużieduotine - 10
svẽčias - 5,44(1)
svẽčių - 1a,30.2e
sveikaĩs, Fn 15(5)
sveikám - 29.8f
sveĩkas - 25a,25b
sveikíems - Fn 15(5)
sver̃da - 9
svetimáip - 39c
svetimomìs - 29.8b
svíestas - 23w
svíesto - 30.4b,31.4c
svíetas - 26k
swecziu - 36.6/o
sweczu - 36.6m
swéćias - 35h,40/1
sweikiegi - 41.37s
sweikims - 32.4b
sweta - 37
swetasti - 41.03b
swetastis - 41.03b
swieta - 21n,41.23d,41.24j
swieto - 32.12c,36.6f
swietui - 41.24k
swietuy - 32.11i
szabągha - 32.14f
szadei - 29.73a,31.1h
szadeiei - 32.14d
szadi - 41.19f

szadij - 41.28b
szadzia - 41.26f
szakė - 5
szali - 41.30c,f
szaudomieij - 5
szaukia - 30.12a
szę - 35i
szegima - 41.19g
szei - 41.08e
szemaicziump - 31.1m
szeme - 2.5,22g,36.8i
szemę - 11/o
szemeie - 36.7a,37b
szemena - 2.5
szeszias - 41.23a
szį - 35j
szinnodams - 14j
szio - 41.30d
szirdės - 41.01j
szirdiês - 31.2g
szirdiięiomis - 42.7c
szławina - 32.11f
szławint - 32.11h
szmaguį - 32a
szmagus - 29.1c
szmanemus - 32c
szmanesu - 37.32a
szmaniu - 31.1g,31.5
szmogu - 2.2
szmogų - 41.06d
szmogui - 5f,21b
szmogus - 3.5
szmones - 10,19i,22d
szmoniu - 2.4
szmoniû - 30.11d
szodis - 22g
szodzio - 30.11a
szolie - 2.2
sztey - 8
szuwies - 3.2
szwentai - 41.24f
szwentos - 41.24e
szwinnas - 5
szemes - 37

šakà - 41.02e
šakė̃lėmis - Fn 13
šakė̃lių - 6q
šakomĩs - 45(30)
šakõs - 41.02e
šalià - 28m,47
šáltas - 6
šálti - 6
šašlỹkų - 30.15b
šaũk - 30.12d
šaũkėsi - 30.12e
šáukštu - 36f
šaũkusi - 18c
šeimininkais - 32.41j
šeimininkams - 32.41j
šeĩpti - 32.12
šeštãdienin - 38.3b
šẽšuras - 34.7c
šiái - 41.25e
šiañdien - 34.81i
šiaudaĩ - 6
šiaudų̃, šiauduosè - 36v
šiẽną - 36.1m
šienáuti - 22q
šiẽno - 31.3d,Fn 11
šienù - 36.1n
šiẽnui - 32.3a
šiĩtas - 26/1
šiltà - 44(16)
šiñtas - 31.5
šĩrdį - 34.3b,Fn 12(b)
širdyj - 5b
širdyję - 42.7c
širdĩs - 2.6,34.22b
širdžiai - 32.43
šĩs tàs - 45(11)
šlóvinti - 32.11d
šlúotak - 39b
šoka - 3.8
šõkį - 34.11d
šõks - 11g
šókti - 34.11d
šóvė - 32.31d
šulnỹ - 30.18b
šùnie - 26m

šuniẽ - 41.07c
šùnys - Fn 3(3)
šuniũ - 23u
šuõ - 2.1,2.7
švarkù - 45(29)
šveñtas - Fn 15(4)
šveñto - Fn 15(4)
šveñtù - Fn 15(4)
šviẽčia - 41.07b
šviesì - 44(31)

tà - (nom.sg.) - 44(9-14)
ta - (gen.sg.) - 41.12f, 41.26e
tą - 41.03b,41.08j,42.3b
tacziau - 14j
tačiaũ - 14,44(13-14)
tadà - 14j,30.14d,32.11m, 38.1d,40c,44(17)
tadda - 21e
tadrin - 34.4a
tádu - 13d
taĩ - 42.9(3),45(30)
taĩp - 30.15f,34.21f, 36.8a,37a,37b,37j,40k
tais - 36.8b
tãkas - 6
talims - 41.14b
tam - 21b,32.11a
tampa - 24e
tampì - 36.6z
tampýti - 30.43a
tamsà - 41.31d
tam̃są - 41.31d
tam̃siai - Fn 15(1)
támsioy - 37.31a
tamuy - 32.1g,32.11
tánkiai - 10
tánkus - 46(14)
tap - 40d
tapa - 11b
tapo - 36.6j,36.6q, Fn 15(1)
taps - 29.3c
tàpti - 24,29.3,36.6, Fn 15
tarýba - 42.1f

tarýti - 27
tarýtum - 36.1b
tarnamus - 24a
tar̃nas - 6,22k,33f
tarnautumbim - 32d
tarnýbą - 34.82
tarnus - 3.6,31.1d,41.28a
tar̃p - 41.34a,d,42.1c,42.4a, Fn 10(1)
tars - 28f
tassai - 23n,29.1b,32a,32.11d
tatai - 39f,41.01b
táu - 30.63c,32d,32.41h,33f, 41.07b
tautų - Fn 10(1)
tavè - 30.5v,41.19c,Fn 15(4)
tavę̃s - 41.07b,Fn 15(4)
tavo - 37c,37j,42.4a,42.9(3)
taw - 32.11/o
tawa - 2.5,22k,24a,30.14e, 36.6b,37a,37b,41.28b
tawe - 35.1a,41.26
tawes - 41.14e,41.26
tawęs - 30.13a,30.5h
tawesp - 29.1c,40/1
tawessp - 35h
tawimi - 36.8i
tawo - 8, 30.11d,30.11e,30.5d
teesie - 37j
teiginỹs - 32.13d
téiginiui - 32.13c
teip - 13/1,30.14b,36.7c
teyp - 12b
teypag - 35.1a
teipaieig - 27r
teipo - 29.5g
teisaus - 41.26f
teisei - 32i,40d
teisibe - 29.5g
teisybę - 13c
teisibes - 41.12b
teisinĩkas - 2.5
téisintis - 16
teisoiu - 36.4a
teisu - 34.11c

teisus (acc.pl.) - 41.12d
teisūs - 27f
tek - 34.81a
tekėsima - 7b
tekėti - 29.8
tekinis - 3.1
tẽkintojų - 30.15e
tekiùs - 42.9(9)
tẽko - 21p
tèks - 29.6a,32.41g
tekstìlės - 31.1q
telia - 6
tẽlių - 38.3b
temczias - 41.12d
tẽmė - 29.1a
tempiù - 5
témstant - 21
teñ - 3.2,36.6y,46(4)
tenaĩ - 16b
tenuplesch - 2.5
tepamaghi - 5
tereikią - 27
tereikiant - 27
terp - 41.34b,c
teschla - 6
testa - 32.2a
testamentas - 30.5f
testawi - 33b
tėvą - 8,19c,27a,34.2c
tėvaĩ - 36.1a,36.2g
tėvas - 1c,8,13a,16a,16b,16e,
   17p,17r,17t,19d,25a,25b,
   25c,25d,25g,27b,27c,27d,
   27/1,27m,30.6k,32.31i,
   41.11j
tėvẽlio - 33.4a,33.4b
tėvynę - 34.3b
tėvỹnės - 42.1g,45(21)
tėvo - 1d,1e,30.1/1,31.1w,
   41.15a,44(13-14)
tėvų̃ - 29.7a
tėvužėlio - 10
tėvui - 46(23),(24)
tėvužėliùs - 42.4a
tewaynimis - 36.6r
tewas - 42.7d

tewe - 37d
tewo - 30.1d,30.11e
tewu - 10,41.37k
tewui - 32.2a
tewuy - 42.7b
tewuie - 37.32b
thiewe - 37g
tíek - 23u
tiėktai - 41.01j
tiemus - 32.1b
ties - 41.35a-h,41.36a,
   46(13)
tiesà - 29.71b
tiesõs - 39c,41.16e
tiesuma - 41.24i
tiẽsumui - 41.25f
tiewa - 19i,38.4a
tiewe - 31.3a
tiewo - 22k
tiews - 32.2c,33a
tiewu - 31.1c,41.33a
tik - 32e,34.21f,41.19d,
   41.19e,41.27b,42.1b
tikėk - Fn 14(2)
tikėti - 16,34.21b,34.21c,
   Fn]4(3)
tikėtum - 32.4d
tikì - Fn 14(1)
tikincze - 2.4
tikintiemus - 2.3
tikintis - 24
tikiu - 34.21a,34.21d,
   34.21e,41.10h
tikra - 29.1b
tikroms - 32.11h
tikrosp-iosp - 42.9
tylėjo - 13f
tylėk - 11j
tylėti - 2
tỹli - 2
tỹlintis - 2
tylĩs - 2
Tilžę - 41.11f
Tilžėje - 41.11f
tinginio - 30.5t
tiñka - 32.31g

tiñkamas - 41.01
tinklaĩ - 2.4
tiñklas - 32.31h
tinklus - 2.4
tò - 30.13b,32.1c,32.1h,
　32.1i,36b,36.6f
tobulibes - 13i
todėl - 34.7c
todryn - 29.32c
tókią - 13b
tokiám - 32.41g
tokias - 34.7e
tókiu - 15n,32.1f
tola - 14j
toliau - 46(34)
tólintis - 32.42e
Traicei - 41.24f
Traices - 41.24e
tráukiniui - 29.6b
tráukti - 30.4
trẽčią - 41.11h
trejùs - 5b
trete - 35a,41.10b
trijų̃ - 41.15b,42.3a
trims - 41.24d
trinktelėjo - 36.1u
trỹpė - 36.1s
tris - 34.11f,35e,35b,35g,
　41.23b
triû - 41.24c
trobà - 5,5/1,30.51v
tróbą - 41.29b
tróbai - 32.31i,41.29b
trobẽlę - 44(2)
troszkin - 37.31a
truba - 2.5
trubijenczių - 2.5
trúkti - 21
trumpa - 38.1b
trumpai - 3.5
tù - 19i,22i,29.32f,30.5j,
　32.2c,33a,36a,36d,36.6m,
　37.2a,Fn 14(1)
túkstančio - 41.11i
túkstančių - 31.5

tū́kstantį - 41.11i
tū́kstantis - 31.5
tulžti - 21a
tumpa - 36.6k
tuõ - 36.4g
tù - 27t
tùiaus - 2.2
tuojaũ - 22c
tuose - 37.2b
tupėjo - 47(6)
tur - 2.5,11m,24c,34.6a,
　36.8c,41.35a,41.37s
turėdama - 15f
tureia - 37.1a
turėdavo - 42.9(9)
turėjo - 6y,27f,29.7b,
　30.15d
turek - 30.3a
turėsianti - 4.2
turėta - 29.5c,29.5d
turėti - 21/o,33.4b,36.6,
　41.37
tur̃guj - 29.81d
tùri - 12b,30.15f,40k
turim - 30.1g
tùrimė - 29.8
turinczias - 31.51
turinsis - 2.5
turit - 30.14a,34.1a,
　42.9(1)
turiù - 41.18f
Turka - 41.14f
Turkus - 40g
turrins - 15b
tur̃tą - 9
turtingas - 31.3
tuščių̃ - 44(27)
tvankùs - 46(15)
tvarkýti - 30.43b
tvérti - 32.31c
tvórai - 32.31c

ugni - 41.10i
ùgnį - 30.15b
ùgniai - 41.11e

úkvedžio - 30.4e
umžinu - 36.6g
úodega - 36.1w
úodegą - 34.3a,36.1w,
 Fn 12 a
úodegai - 41.13a
úogas - 44(35),(36),(37)
úogos - 5
úogų - 30.16c,30.16d,30.2h,
 31.4a
upe - 5
ùpė - 5,42.1b,44(31)
upělis - 42.1b
upes - 41.17
upiteła - 34.81a
uriedniku - 36.6p
uszgimens - 3.5
uszkeikta - 24f
uszmirschai - 30.11c
ùtarka - 41.27b
Utenõs - 41.13c
uz - 41.37c-n
ùž - 29.5j,41.13e,41.37,
 41.38a-e,45(34-37),46(31-32)
užbėgsi - 30.1q,30.1r
uždągos - 41.37/o
uždarýta - 29.5a
uždarýti - 29.5c
ùždavinio - 31.1u
užeĩk - 41.18a
ùžkalė - 47(3)
užlàkti - 32.31m
užlindaũ - 41.38b
užmiršaũ - 30.11k
užmiřšti - 30.31a
užmokiek - 34.4b
užplúdo - 30.2m
užsidegimù - 36.2h
užsidengia - 6
užsìlindau - 41.38b
užsimérk - 30.51u
už(si)miřšti - 16
ùžstelbtas - 30.5/1
užtémdytas - 30.5/1
užteňka - 32.4e

užtìkrinti - 16
užu - 41.37
užudárę̨s - 37.31a
ùžvertė - 36.1n
užvìs - 45(40),46(33)
uź - 41.37p-r
uźmirśk - 30.11g
uźmokėjo - 41.37r

vabzdžiù - 36.6x
vadìnti(s) - 29.3
vagà - 6
vagỹstės - 30.21e
vãgos - 29.5b,29.5e
vagótas - 6
vagóti - 6
vaikaĩ - 26/o,42.7g,
 44(35-37)
vaikaĩs - 41.27d
vaikáms - 32.41f
vaĩkas - 1,3.3,5j,Fn 1(c)
váikščiojimas - 36.7b
váikščioti - 36.7b
váikšto - 36.4d,36.4e,
 36.4f
vaikù - 36.6z
vaikų̃ - 29.81c,41.27
vaĩkui - 5i,44(33),
 Fn 1(a-e)
vaikùs - 30.12d
vainìkai - 6q
váišino - 44(34)
vaitóti - 9
vaizdaĩ - 29.6c
vãkar - 30.41b,46(35)
vãkarą - 41.11g,41.31f
vãkaran - 38.3a
vãkaras - 29.1a,29.74a
vakarìenės - 13e
vãlandą - 35k,35i
valandìkei - 41.38d
valandõs - 30.32a
valdýbos - 42.1a
valdýti - 36.8
valdžióti - 36.8

vaĺgiais - 36.1h
vaĺgio - 29.8f,30.15b
válgyti - 5i,30.4g,30.7a
válgytojų - 30.18c
valgiùs - 36.1g
válgo - 36f
válgomi - 5e
válgomieji - 5
válgomos - 5
valià - 29.8,29.81a,37c,37j
valiaũ - 29.81a
vãlymas - 36.7a
valýti - 36.7a
vandenėlio - 21m
vándenio - 30.18a,30.18b
vándeniu - 5
vandeñs - 30.15g,30.42a,
  30.42b,30.42i,30.51w,
  30.51x,46(21-22),(30)
vanduõ - 2.1,5,6,36.4h,42.3a,
  45(13)
vardana - 38.4a
vardũ - 29.7b
vargšėlis - 29.7a
vãrio - 45(24)
varýti - 30.4,30.42
vařlės - 38.4b
várna - 36.3h
vařnas - 44(27), 45(1)
vařpas - 45(24)
Varšuvą - 30.41b
vařtais - 41.31a
vartėliais - 46(13)
vartóti - 30.43a,36.8
vartuosu - 39e
vartùs - 41.31a
vãsara - 2.6
vãsarai - 33.3c
vasarójaus - 30.4d
vasarójus - 30.7b
vãsaros - 44(16)
važiãvo - 40a
važiúoja - 30.42e,30.42g
važ(i)úoju - 38.5c
važiúosįs - 4

važiúoti - 30.4,30.42
*vedan - 2.7
vedantes - 2.7
vedą̃s - 3
*veden - 3
vẽdęs - 3,23g
vėdinas - 36.71b,46(20)
véidas - 21a,Fn 9(2)
veiksmìnis - 30.5/1
veizd - 14b
vė́ja - 44(5)
vė́ją - 46(31),(32)
vė́jas - 5,44(29)
vė́jo - 5c
vẽl - 11
veldėti - 36.8
vėlývas - 29.2b
veĺkinas - 36.71d
véĺmias - 22p,29.81d
véltui - 36.5c
veřčia - 36.1m
vérda - 30.15b
vérdamas - 9
verkianti - 8b
veřkti - 16
verpalų̃ - 32.31n
veřpti - 32.31n
veřsti - 41.01/o
veřtas - 31.3
veršis - 5
vertèsnis - 45(38)
veržždavos - 9
vėsinti - 4.2
vesk - 36.4a
vèsti - 4.2
vestùvinė - 45(26)
vežìmas - Fn 11
vežimè, vežìmo - 37u
vežtì - 30.42j
vèžtų - 30.42k
vidų - 34.7c
vidùvasari̇̀ - 36.5a
vidùvasary - 36.5a
vidùvasariu - 36.5a
víena - 41.02e

vienà - 23i
víeną - 13h,32.4c,41.25b
vienám - 32.41d,32.41e,34.21h,
    41.07b,41.25b
vienañ - 38.4b
víenas - 23i
vienì - 30.15h
víeno - 30.31a,41.07b
vienódu - 36.2i
vienók - 14
vienõs - 41.02e
vienúolika - 31.5
viešpatáuti - 32.11
viẽtą - 10
vietų̃ - 30.2/o
vieversỹs - 42.2c
viežlybus - 34.7g
vikriám - 32.41c
viĩkas - 14c
viĩke - 29
viĩko - 6x,30.1q,30.1r,30.6k
vilkų̃ - 30.2g
viĩkui - 28h,33.4c
vilkùs - 41.31f
Vilniaũs - 31.1z$_1$
výrai - 35m
výras - 4.2,29
vyriáusias - 42.3c
vyriáusiasis - 42.3d
vyrìškis - 45(29)
výro - 29,30.5j
viršùj - 47(3),(6)
viršuñ - 44(27),47
virtà - 6
vìrti - 9,30.4/1
výru - 29.6a,36.6z
vis - 41.14e,44(11),Fn 14(1)
vìsa - 23k,41.09a
visà - 36.1b,41.27b
vìsą - 9,30.1k,41.01e,41.31f
visadà - 30.2j
vìsai - 41.01e
visái - 5e,23g,30.11k,32.4d
    46(27)
vìsas - 44(4)

visì - 23m,30.42c,33.1a,
    46(4), Fn 7(c)
visíem - 41.25b
vìsiškai - 32.31a
vìskas - 23/1,29.81a
vìsko - 36.1d
vìskuo - 36.1c
vyskups - 13c
visõs - 41.01e
vissu - 31.1g
visų̃ - 32.31g,45(39)
visuomèt - 28k
visur̃ - 46(5)
visùs - 29.2c,44(28),
    45(38)
vìškui - 41.36a
vištà - 2.1,42.3e,f
vìzgina - 36.1w
vizìto - 30.41a
vizìtui - 30.41b
vredas - 31.1c,31.1d,31.1e,
    31.1f,31.1g,41.28a
vsz - 41.37a-b,s
vszmirschk - 30.11d
vszrischi - 32.14h
vżgawimôsios - 5
vżgul - 29.5i

wádina - 29.8,36.6d
wadinam - 34.6c
wadinasi - 29.32c,36.6f
wadindama - 36.6a
wadìnti - 36.6
wagis - 2.2
waikai - 41.35a
waikschczosi - 37.2a
waikscziati - 38.1a
waikų - 30.14g
waikus - 34.6a
waisius - 3.4
waitodams - 9
wakar - 29.74e
wakara - 35d
wałandos - 41.01c
waldźios - 36.8e

394

wales - 41.16a
walgiusiemus - 3.7
walgjti - 27t
walgomosios - 5
walia - 37a,37b
wandeni - 22f
wandens - 41.19f
wandů - 37.1d
warda - 29.32b
wardą - 29.32a
wárdo - 30.14h
wargus - 11m,14j
wartôie - 30.14h,36.8g
wartosa - 2.5
wartůsu - 2.5
wartus - 41.30b
waźeys - 5
weydu - 11/1
weisdeghima - 30.21c
weisdek - 11d
wejus - 14j
wel - 41.35f
weldêssitę - 36.8f
welinas - 21c,36.6f
wena - 31.5
wenas - 32a,34.7h
wenczawonisten - 38.1d
wenu - 36.2b,36.2c
weras - 41.12c,41.19a
werasp - 40g
werschi - 6
wersk - 12a
werstu - 35.1a
werta - 33d
wertas - 31.3b
weschpatu - 31.1d,41.28a
wienam - 5g,32.41a
wienamę - 39i
wienolikta - 41.08f
wiera - 2.4
wiernai - 41.01/o
wieschpatije - 33.2a
wiespats - 36.8b
wieszpatauia - 32.11i
wieszpatis - 41.01i

wieszpatų́ - 41.01i
wijramus - 36.2a
wijsakiu - 31.1d,41.28a
wilaiie - 2.3
wiliu - 13
winas - 36.6i
wyno - 11b
winu - 36.8c
wirams - 2.3,21e
wirausibei - 32.11/1
wirausiu - 36.6t
wiresnieghi - 33.2a
wiresniams - 33b
wiro - 10
wiru - 31.1e
wirui - 29.5f
wis - 15b,24f
wysa - 41.14a
wisados - 41.26b
wisam - 32.11i
wisi - 5,52.6b
wisims - 32.14d
wiss - 40f
wissa - 29.5g,41.24j
wissam - 41.24k
wissems - 34.4a
wissi - 4.3,32.11/o
wissokios - 31.3a
wissokiu - 2.5
wissu - 27r
wissų́ - 41.01i
wyssu - 32.14a
wissus - 36.6c
wisu - 41.06a
wisus - 3.6,13i

zmoguy - 21n
zmonemis - 36.8e
zuīkis - 11g
žadéjo - 16e
žadéti(s) - 16
žalióji - 45(5)
žaliů́ju - 6q
žaliúoti - 32.42a

žąsiės – 41.13a
žąsimìs – 36.71c
žąsiùkas – 36.71d
žegnotisi – 35d
žemaĩ – 45(30)
žeme – 41.10f
žẽmė – 14f,30.5k,30.51k,37
žẽmę – 30.51/1
žẽmei – 32.3c
žemėj – 36.7c
žẽmėje – 30.15b,37h,37j
žẽmės – 30.21a,37i,41.11b,
  41.11d
žeñgė – 46(8)
ženteliai – 5
žéntu – 29.6a
žìba – 37s
žíedas – 41.13,45(18),(23)
žiedẽlī – 42.9(2)
žiemės – 30.12c
žìlą – 6y
žìnantį – 19j
žìnąs – 18i,19k
žinaũ – 20h,20i,23x
žìndamas – 5
žìndantis – 5
žiñgsniai – 29.6
žiñgsnis – 29.6c
žinià – 29.8,44(9-14)
žìno – 29.2c
žinódami – 32.42b
žinójo – 15i,18/o,18p
žinójosi – 18m
žìnomas – 5
žinóti – 16
žìrgas – 29.1a
žìrklės – 5,41.02c,41.02d
žìrklių – 30.17c
žįsti – 5
žiūrét – 26m
žiūri – 22p
žiūriù – 26m
žywata – 41.30d
žiwatas – 32.11/o
žmagus – 31.2c
žmogaũs – 36.3h,41.15b,
  45(22)

žmõgui – 29.8f,32.41b
žmogùs – 2.1,2.4,3.1,4.2,
  5,6,14i,17i,29.7,31.2a,
  31.2b,31.2d,45(14),
  46(16)
žmonéms – 32.11h,32.31d
žmónės – 18t,30.2k,30.31b,
  33.1a,36.6w
žmonesemp – 39
žmoniŲ – 29.81b,30.2k,
  30.51v,31.5,41.11i,
  Fn 10(2-3)
žmoniŲjai – 42.7g
žmonõs – 26j
žodi – 41.08j
žõdinio, zõdiniu – 30.5/1
žodis – 29.74e
žõdžiai – 30.15f
žõdžiui – 34.21h
žodžiùs – 30.11j
žõlei – 32.3b
žùs – Fn 9 3
žuvédra – 42.2b
žùvęs – 23i
žuvimì – 36.6u
žuvìms – 32.31h
žuvìs – 6
žuvŲ – 30.18d
žvakelė – 41.18c
žvėrių – 30.2g
žvìlgsnis – 5
žvìrblis – 44(28)
żała – 5
żaysła – 42.6a,42.8
żała – 5
żalas – 3.5
żę́klas – 2.3
żiemes – 13i
żindams – 5
żmog' – 3.5
żmógau – 42.9
żmõgui – 32.41a
żmóguy – 4.4
żmogus – 2.5,2.6,13i,18s
żmones – 5
żodis – 5
żodżiu – 5

żadems - 34.21f
żadis - 31.1j
żadziu - 41.32b
żąmbo - 30.14f
żémes - 41.34d
żibancziąie - 2.3
żiemoj - 37.1d
żinomé - 29.8
żinot - 30.14i
żmógup - 39i

źmonese - 39i
źmoniu - 5g, 30.1e
źmonû - 41.06e
źodi - 30.1i
źodźio - 30.1j
źodźiose - 37.2b
źodźiû - 30.11f, 41.16d
źodźius - 30.11f
żwaké - 2.3

ALBANIAN

dhanëm - 5
mish - 5
pjekëm - 5
punuem - 5

AVESTAN

Ahurō - 42.9(6)
apaošəm - 42.8c
apaošō - 42.8a
Azəm - 42.9(6)
čarətąm - 42.8e
dāēum - 42.8c
daēvō - 42.8a
darəθąm - 42.8e
drəgvā̊ - 42.8b
drəgvantəm - 42.8d
gāuš - 29.51c
hača - 42.8f
ǰaidyāi - 29.51c
maraēta - 32.3f
mazdå - 42.9(6)
mąθrəm - 32.3f
mərəta - 6
pa anayā̊ - 42.8f
spənəm - 32.3f

tąm - 42.8e
upa - 42.8e
uxšne - 32.3f
xraθwe - 32.3f
yąm - 42.8e
yat̰ - 42.8f
yo - 42.9(6)
yə̄ - 42.8b
*yə̄m - 42.8d
yim - 42.8c
yō - 42.8a
zəmat̰ - 42.8f

CZECH

hřésti - 32.3d
kúpichu - 32.3d
lakomý - 5
nevidomý - 5
pole - 32.3d
pútníkóm - 32.3d

ENGLISH

began - 21j
down - 21j
going - 21j
to rain - 21j

FARSI

kardam - 6

FINNISH

juoda - 6
juotu - 6
päästän - 6
quivettijn - 6
saada - 6
saatiin - 6
siemen - 6

FRENCH

été - 29c
livres - 29c,29e
ont - 29c
se - 29e
vendent - 29e
vendus - 29c

GEORGIAN

Abraam(-man) - 29
ar - 30.6h,30.63d
araperi - 30.63d
axsovso - 30.6j
gvčirdeba - 30.63d
damvicqebia - 30.6h
dedas - 30.6i
dedasa - 30.6f
erti - 30.6e
esmis - 30.6f
ešinoda - 30.6d
vačarta - 6v
vačarman - 6u
tkveni - 30.6h
kacma - 6
margalitni - 6u,6v
mas - 30.6e,30.62
maxsovs - 30.6g
melas - 30.6j
movida - 6

mokvda - 6
mters - 30.6d
povna - 6u
povnes - 6v
saxeli - 30.6h
unda - 30.6e
uqvars - 30.6i
katami - 30.6j
kartvelebis - 30.6d
qvelaperi - 30.6g
qmay - 30.6f
qomisay - 30.6f
šeertebuli - 30.6d
šva - 29
švili - 30.6i
čemgan - 30.6e
jalisa - 30.6d
jilšidac - 30.6j
cigni - 30.6e
Jsaak - 29

GERMAN

Acker - 30.11c
an - 41.01/1
angeneme - 5
auf - 37/1
*augen - 14
Bleywurf - 5
Brot - 6
Bund - 2.3
deines - 30.11d,30.11h
denn - 30.14c
durch - 41.19
erdachten - 13
Erden - 37/1
eschene - 29k,29m
folgender - 2.3
Fuss - 5
Garbe - 30.11c
gedencke - 30.11b
gedenket - 30.11a
gehe - 11
gessammelt - 23

GERMAN (continued)

gesewrt - 6
gewesen - 23f
gnädiglich - 41.01/1
Hauss - 30.11d
Herr - 41.01/1
Himmel - 37/1
hinter - 29
hören - 30.14c
höreten - 13
hub - 14
im - 37/1
küsset - 11
lachen - 30.14c
List - 13j
mein - 30.14c
meiner - 30.11b
menschenmenge - Fn 10(2),(3)
mit - Fn 10(2)
nach - 29k,29m
Opffer - 41.01/1
Räucherns - 5
Saatzeit - 5
sahe - 14,41.01/1
Säugling - 5
schleifte - 29k,29m
schlimmer - 5
Schweissloch - 5
sein - 41.01/1
sich - 29
sihe - 11
Speer - 29k,29m
Spicknadel - 5
trat - 11
umgeben - Fn 10(3)
umringt - Fn 10(2),(3)
Vaters - 30.11d
vergessen - 30.11c
vergiss - 30.11d,30.11h
vnuerwesenlich - 2.3
Volcks - 30.11d,30.11h
von - Fn 10(3)
ward - 23f
werckeltage - 5

wie - 37/1
wird - 30.14c
Wort - 30.11a
wurde - 29/1

GOTHIC

airþai - 37m
ana - 37m
ataugidedun - 14
athaitands - 14
bairan - 3
baurg - 14
bērusjōs - 3
du - 14,30.62b
duatiddja - 21i
frijōnds - 2.7
galaiþ - 17/1
garaihtana - 20a
gasatida - 36.6e
gaurs - 17/1
haírdeis - 29
harjis - 29
himina - 37m
hundafaþs - 21i
im - 14
imma - 21i
in - 14,37m
ina - 20a
innatgaggandans - 14
innatgaggandin - 21i
izos - 30.62b
jah - 14,36.6e,37m
Kafarnaum - 21i
kunnands - 20a
luston - 30.62b
managaim - 14
namo - 36.6e
nasjada - 29
nasjands - 2.7
nasjaza - 29
Paítrus - 36.6e
qaþ - 14
Seimona - 36.6e
sik - 14

GOTHIC (continued)

siponjans - 14
stoþ - 6
swe - 37m
-uh - 14
wair - 20a
weihon - 14
weitwōþs - 3
witan - 3

GREEK

agathòn - 6
anablépsas - 14
anémois - 14
ap' - 30.5q
hápasan - 30.51e
apéstrepsan - 11/o
ápiston - 6
apostéllein - 14
áristos - 42.9(7)
autón - 11
autō̃i - 29.51t
autō̃n - 30.5q
Akhaiō̃n - 42.9(7)
ákhri - 41.01c
batós - 6
blē̃to - 6
blētós - 6
gàr - 30.51e
gē̃n - 11
gē̃s - 37k
dakrúoisi - 30.51e
dakrúōn - 30.51f
dépas - 30.51d
dḗmou - 30.5p
didóāsi - 2.7
dídōsi - 2.7
Diósdotos - 30.5
dotós - 6
do̰ũpon - 30.1m
dṓdeka - 14
eggísas - 11
egéneto - 6

egertheìs - 14
égkhos - 29j
edóthēs - 29
edómēn - 29
édoto - 6,29
édou - 29
étheto - 6
ei̇́ - 30.5p
eĩde - 14
eidós - 3
FeidFós - 3
eirṓtā̰s - 28b
eisē̃lthon - 14
ek - 29.51r
ekeĩthen - 11
éklue - 30.1m,30.1n
elthónta - 28b
Hellád' - 30.51e
emé - 30.51f
emnēsteuménēi - 29.51t
en - 37k
enephanísthēsan - 14
enípleion - 30.51c
éntes - 2
epaúsato - 18f
epetímēsen - 14
epì - 37k
éplēse - 30.51e
éplēsen - 30.51f
eprákhthē - 30.5q
éssuto - 6
etimãto - 30.5p
hetós - 6
euergétēn - 20c
éphato - 6
ephélketo - 29j
éphthito - 6
ephílēsen - 11
ékhuto - 6
dzugón - 29
hēgoũnto - 20c
ē̃n - 29.51r
ḗrksato - 14
thalássḛ̄ - 14
thetós - 6

400

GREEK (continued)

thumiamátos - 5
Iakṑb - 14
íde - 11
iduĩa - 3
kaì - 11,14,37k
kairoũ - 41.01c
kataskepsámenoi - 11
kúōn - 2.7
lalõn - 18f
lékto - 6
lektós - 6
lelatomēménon - 29.51r
lúke - 29
Mariàm - 29.51t
mḗ - 30.63a
meílinon - 29j
méllon - 4
mḗtēr - 29,30.1n
ksúneto - 6
oínoio - 30.51d
oínou - 30.51c
holokautōmátōn - 5
orthós - 17/o,29.31b
hòs - 42.9(7)
oudén - 30.5q
ouranõ̀ - 37k
ophthalmoĩs - 14
páter - 29
pétras - 29.51r
plēsámenos - 30.51d
plḗto - 6
poimḗn - 30.1m
politeíais - 6
polukoiraníē - 6
poreutheìs - 11
pótnia - 30.1n
proskaleĩtai - 14
púthō - 9
sḗ - 30.63b
soí - 30.63b
statós - 6
stḗ - 17/o,29.31b
sùn - 29.51t

Teũkros - 42.9(7)
tē̃s - 37k
tinos - 30.63a,30.63b
tis - 30.5p
tò - 29j
toũ - 5,30.1n,30.5p
turannís - 6
hupò - 30.5p
phatós - 6
phéreai - 29
phéretai - 29
phéromai - 29
pherómenos - 5
phérōn - 2.7
Philippon - 20c
khrḗ - 30.63a,30.63b

HIEROGLYPHIC HITTITE

á-š^1-za-mi-a-s - 5
ki-i-ša-am-mi-iš - 5

HITTITE

akkanza - 2
al-pa-an-za - 42.8h
an- - 42.8g,h
ANA - 32.3h
an-tu-uḫ-ša-aš - 29
arḫa - 29.51d
arḫaḫat - 29
Arnuandan - 20d
artat - 29
aš - 42.8g
ašanza - 2.7
adanza - 2.7
EGIR-an - 32.3h
EGIR-pa - 32.3h
ḫaštiyaš - 32.3g
irman - 20d
iš-ga-aḫ-ḫi - 42.8h
ištamaššir - 20d
iịahḫaḫat - 29
iịattati - 29
iyauwanzi - 32.3h

GA.KIN.AG - 29.51e
kán - 42.8g,43
kattan - 29.51d
kišat - 29
kišati - 29
ku-iš - 42.8h
ku-it - 42.8g
kunanza - 2.7
ku-ú-ša-ta - 42.8g
leššuwanzi - 32.3g
LÚ-ša - 42.8g
ma - 42.8g
mi-im-ma-i - 42.8g
na-ú-i - 42.8g
nepišaš - 29.51d
nu - 32.3g,42.8h
nu-ši - 43
panza - 2.7
pānzi - 32.3g
paršiwanzi - 29.51e
petummanzi - 29.51d
píd-da-a-it - 42.8g
SAL.MEŠ - 32.3g
ŠEŠ-ya - 20d
da-a-i - 42.8g
daganzipaš - 29.51d
ták-ku - 42.8g
tannattan - 29
tayazil - 29
DINGIR.MEŠ-ŠU - 32.3h
tu-i-ik-ku-uš - 42.8h
DUMU-aš - 42.8h
DUMU.SAL - 42.8g
uizzi - 32.3h
ukturiya - 32.3g
uddār - 29.51d
^{D}UTU-ŠI - 32.3h
-ši- - 43
waštul - 29
waštulaš - 30.7
za - 42.8g

HUNGARIAN

eltette - 6e
ember - 6g
én - 6g
jött - 6g
kosár - 6f
megszámolt - 6e
megtelt - 6f
messziről - 6g
pénzt - 6e
pénztáros - 6e
szeméttel - 6f
választottam - 6g

LATIN

ā - 30.6c
ad - 32.12c
adjuvo - 32.12
aliis - 32.12
alios - 32.12
amant - 2.7
amat - 2.7
ambiguus - 5
amor - 6
apud - 39k
aquae - 30.51b
attonitus - 30.5a,30.6c
bonae - 31.2g
bonis - 30.51g
circumventus - 6
compleo - 30.51h
complētus - 6
comprehensibilis - 5
convivium - 30.51h
cotidie - 30.51h
credas - 20b
cupiunt - 30.62a
datus - 6
deus - 30.51g
divitem - 17b
dixit - 17b
doctus - 17g

LATIN (continued)

est - 39k
ēuidēns - 2.7
explevit - 30.51g
facere - 32.12
facilis ad intelligendum - 5
facit - 32.12c
famam - 30.12c
fecit - 32.12
felix - 17m
flumen - 5
genitus - 6
grātus - 6
hujus - 32.12c
ignorantes - 5
invocavit - 30.12c
iugum - 29
juvare - 32.12
juvo - 32.13
me - 20b,39k
mentis - 31.2g
mihi - 32.12b
mundi - 32.12c
mundum - 30.51g
mutabile - 6
nascitur - 17g
navigabile - 5
nemo - 17g
nequit - 32.12
nihil - 32.12b
nos - 39k
omnibus - 30.51g
opem - 32.12
parentes - 2.7
plēnus - 30.51b
potest - 32.12
praesēns - 2
prodest - 32.12b
quae - 30.62a
quid - 32.12c
regēbar - 29
regēbāris - 29
regēbātur - 29
regeris - 29
regis - 29
regit - 29
regitur - 29
regor - 29
salvos - 32.12
salvum - 32.12
se - 17b
seipsum - 32.12
semper - 6
senex - 6
senilis - 6
sequens - 2.3
serpentē - 30.6c
serpentis - 30.5a,30.6c
status - 6
sum - 31.2g
terram - 30.12c
tristem - 20a
tui - 30.62a
tulit - 32.12
turpe - 6
varium - 6
vehēns - 2.7
vicinorum - 30.51h
vivas - 17m

LATVIAN

akmins - 29.51i
bagāts - 17
balts - 6
bites - 34.81c
bîtîes - 5
braucis - 18d
brūtes - 5m
bûsit - 4
bûšus - 4.1
bûts - 6
darba - 20k
dędzams - 5
diena - 6
dzimtā - 6
dzimts - 6
dzimušu - 3

LATVIAN (continued)

ej - 10
ejamā - 10
grūti - 29.51i
ir - 33.4b
jautā - 8
kâpt - 34.81c
kustinât - 29.51i
labi - 8,17a
laĩks - 5
linu - 5
ļaunprātigi - 8
man - 5,33.4b
māsas - 20k
māsiņa - 10
nams - 33.4b
nemâkuošas - 20k
nieka - 20k
nuostâja - 18d
nuosûnuojis - 29.51i
plūcams - 5
salts - 6
sa-sa-tikties - 43
silts - 6
sirmi - 5m
strādājuoši - 17a
šie - 17a
šķindêt - 9
teicās - 17a
teicat - 20k
upuris - 5
vedamie - 5m
viņš - 8,17
ziņuots - 8
zirgi - 5m

MARATHI

pustak - 6t
tũ - 6t
vācalẽs - 6t

OLD ARMENIAN

ayn - 29.51n

ařeal - 29.51/o,30.6b
ařnem - 29.51
arareal - 29.51n
arcat'n - 29.51u
gerezmani - 29.51q
gorc - 29.51p
gorceal - 29.51p
ed - 29.51q
ekeal - 29.51m
em - 29.51k
es - 29.51k
ev - 37/o
ē - 29.51/1,29.51p
ēr - 29.51m,29.51n,29.51/o,
    29.51q,29.51u,30.6b
žamanak - 29.51/1
i - 29.51q,30.6b
xawseal - 29.51s
cařaysn - 29.51u
cneal - 29.51k
handerj - 29.51s
haseal - 29.51/1
hraman - 29.51/o,30.6b
y-erkins - 37/o
y-erkri - 37/o
Yisus - 29.51m
Maremaw - 29.51s
nma - 29.51s
nmanē - 30.6b
nšan - 29.51n
novaw - 30.6b
nora - 29.51n,29.51/o,29.51p
    30.6b
or - 29.51q,29.51s
oroc' - 29.51u
orpēs - 37/o
varem - 29
varim - 29
vimē - 29.51q
tueal - 29.51u
p'oreal - 29.51q

OLD CHURCH SLAVIC

aky - 27g
bytъ - 6

OLD CHURCH SLAVIC (continued)

byšęšteje - 4
vidęšte - 18j,27g
*viždǫ - 42.8
vlъče - 29
vědъši - 3
glagolanyxъ - 30.5b
glagolę - 18e
goněti - 29.8
goritъ - 42.8
divišę - 30.5b
domъ - 42.8
duxъ - 18j,27g
želěti - 30.64
želěxъ - 30.62c
zapovědei - 30.62c
zem(l)i - 37n
igo - 29
idǫ - 9
iže (jьže) - 42.8
imъ - 21h
iskati - 30.64
kъ - 30.5b
mati - 29
mьněaxǫ - 18j,27g
město - 29
na - 37n
načętъ - 14
nebesi - 37n
nimъ - 30.5b
oba na desęte - 14
otъ - 30.5b
pastuxъ - 30.5b
pitŭ - 6
prizъvavъ - 14
prěsta - 18e
reče - 21h
rodi sę - 17k
slěpъ - 17k
sъbъravъšemъ - 21h
sъlati - 14
tvoixъ - 30.62c
xotěti - 30.64
jadǫ - 9

OLD ENGLISH

háeland - 2.7

OLD HIGH GERMAN

stuot - 6

OLD IRISH

*bretha - 29
breth(a)e - 29
carth(a)ir - 29
midiur - 29
no-m·charthar - 29
suidigidir - 29
suidigther - 29

OLD PERSIAN

arikā - 30.64a
auramazdā - 30.64a
auramazdām - 30.64a
avaiya - 30.64a
ayadaiy - 30.64a
ayadiya - 30.64a
āha - 30.64a
naiy - 30.64a
utāšām - 30.64a
ūvjiyā - 30.64a

OLD PRUSSIAN

ainangimmusin - 3
deiwas - 29
*enimaman - 5
enimumne - 5
giwa - 29.8
giwammai - 29.8
giwāntei - 29.8
giwassi - 29.8
naunagemmons - 6
naunagimton - 6
perweddā - 29.8
poklausīmanas - 5

OLD PRUSSIAN (continued)

popaikā – 29.8
ructandadan – 6
skijstan – 6

OLD RUSSIAN

volxvъ – 17h
Dvdvъ – 14
době – 29.51g
dьjakona – 5a
dětьska – 5a
Eremeja – 14
estь – 29.51g
znajutь – 5a
znajemyja – 5a
ida – 17c
knjazь – 14
loviti – 29.51g
molodъ – 17h
Mьstislavъ – 14
na – 29.51g
ovo – 17h
ostaneši – 17d
otca – 20/1
povědaša – 20/1
popa – 5a
postavętь – 5a
preměnjašetsja – 17h
prizovutь – 5a
prisla – 14
Rigu – 14
ryba – 29.51g
sam – 17h
Simonъ – 17h
Smolenьskij – 14
snъ – 14
starъ – 17h
susědi – 5a
sъdumavъ – 14
tvoritьsja – 17c
tvorja – 17d
umerša – 20/1
xotętь – 5a

jemu – 20/1
jepiskopi – 5a

POLISH

ale – 41.01j
bądź – 36.6s
bez – 2.3
błogosławić – 32.11h
błogosławił – 32.11e, 32.11f
bogaty – 2.5
Boże – 36.6r
broniąca – 36.6t
brzemienna – 36.8m
by – 41.01j
być – 32.41a
była – 41.01j
Chrystusa – 30.5e
co – 41.01j
corki – 36.6r
człowiek – 2.5
człowiekowi – 4.4, 32.41a
ciele – 2.3, 41.01j
dali – 29.32
diament – 41.01h
dobranoc – 29.74c
dobrze – 32.41a
dom – 6/o, 6p
domu – 30.11e, 30.12b
dotknęła – 30.14f
duszy – 41.01j
dźiedźicy – 36.6r
dzień – 32.11e
dzisia – 29.74f
dziwom – 32.1b
głodu – 30.12c
grunt – 36.6t
gryzienie – 2.3
grzechów – 41.01g
grzechu – 2.4
Heliasza – 30.12a
heretycy – 29.32
iakie – 37.2b
iego – 32.11c
iest – 32.41a, 36.6t

POLISH (continued)

im - 32.11f
imię - 29.32
istotnie - 2.6
iy - 32.11h
iż - 41.01h
jasną - 2.3
Jezus - 29.32
kamienia - 41.01h
komora - 5
kraiu - 30.14f
krol - 41.01i
krolewstwa - 36.6r
krolmi - 41.01i
ktorzy - 32.11c
lud - 32.11h
ładunek - 5
łażbić - 34.81d
ma - 36.6s
masz - 41.01h
miałem - 6
mocna - 36.6t
mocny - 36.6t
mogę - 32.1b
mu - 29.32
na - 37,41.01e,41.01b,41.01g
nad - 41.01e,41.01h,41.01i
nam - 32.11g
narodu - 30.11e,30.11i
nas - 36.6t
następający - 2.3
nasz - 36.6t
naszych - 41.01g
nauki - 37.2b
niepewna - 5
niepotrzebnych - 5
nieprzystoyną - 2.3
niewiadomi - 5
niewidomy - 5,5g
obmycie - 41.01g
obrona - 36.6s
od - 30.5e,41.19
odpoczynienia - 32.11e
odpowiedźiom - 32.11c
odszczepieńcy - 2.3

on - 41.01i
oyca - 30.11e
ósmiej - 29i
Pan - 32.11e,36.6t,41.01i
Pana - 30.5e
panie - 36.6s
panną - 41.01j
pany - 41.01i
philozophowie - 41.01h
pierwszym - 36.8m
piszą - 41.01h
pojętny rozumem - 5
postanowiony - 30.5e
pracę - 29i
przednie - 36.6t
przeto - 29.32
przez - 41.19
przyaćioły - 30.12b
przyczyny - 2.3
przypatrzyć - 32.1b
przystoyne - 2.3
przyszedszy - 30.12b
psczoły - 34.81d
rozpoczyna - 29i
rozumieiącz
rozumowi - 32.11c
rzecz - 2.3
samemu - 32.41a
są - 36.6r
sąsiady - 30.12b
się - 29i,30.14f,37.2b
słowo - 29.74f
słowiech - 37.2b
słuchali - 32.11c
słusznej - 2.3
słusznie - 2.6,29.32
służy - 29.74f
smrodliwie - 2.6
spustny - 5
srzodę - 5
strzelby - 5
synem - 36.8m
synowie - 36.6r
sypialnia - 5
szaty - 30.14f
śię - 29.32c

POLISH (continued)

śmierć - 41.01f
śmiertelnego - 2.4
śmiertelnemu - 4.4
śmiertelny - 4.4
śmiertelnym - 2.3
świecą - 2.3
temu - 32.11
trędowaći - 29.32
twardszego - 41.01h
twego - 30.11e,30.11i
twoi - 30.5d
tych - 37.2b
tylko - 41.01j
ubogi - 2.5
umarł - 29.74f
vmyśle - 41.01j
ustawiczne - 2.3
w - 2.3,37.2b
wczora - 29.74f
widome - 5
wierny - 32.11h
woła - 30.12a
wstępa - 5
wszytkimi - 41.01i
wybadáne - 5
wybrani - 30.5d
wydanego - 41.01f
wzywa - 30.12b
zamykaią - 37.2b
zapomni - 30.11e,30.11i
zawołał - 30.12c
zbroia - 36.6t
zbudowano - 6p
zbudowany - 6/o
zdradliwi - 2.3
ziemi - 37
ziemię - 30.12c
známie - 2.3
został - 6o
zowią - 29.32
żadnemu - 5g
żesmy - 36.6r

RUSSIAN

batьka - 6b
byli - 29d
v - 30.2b
vernut'sja - 34.7c
vetrom - 30.5n
vidno - 29h
volkóv - 29g
vopros - 41.18e
glaza - 21
goreli - 21
gosti - 30.2f
grex - 6
domoj - 34.7c
dopustil - 30.15a
est - 36g
est' - 30.2b,41.18e
znaemyja - 5a
znat' - 29.51h
jídeno - 29g
igolkoj - 36i
izdaleka - 29h
ix - 34.81g
knigi - 29d,29f,30.3c
koróvu - 29g
laženy - 34.81g
lazit' - 34.81e
lovit' - 29.51f
ložkoj - 36g
menja - 21,39d
nado - 29.51f
nevestku - 34.7c
nelaženy - 34.81h
net - 39d
ničego - 39d
oficiantom - 30.5/o
ošibki - 30.15a
padko - 6
perju - 29.51h
po - 29.51h
polëtu - 29.51h
poètomu - 34.7c
priexali - 30.2f
pródany - 29d

RUSSIAN (continued)

prodajutsja - 29f
pčel - 34.81e
pčely - 34.81g,h
ryba - 29.51f
svekor - 34.7c
sladko - 6
slušaja - 21
sova - 29.51h
sokol - 29.51h
susědi - 5a
tut - 29g
toropit - 34.7c
u - 29g,39d,41.18e
ubito - 6b
unosilo - 30.5n,30.5/o
učenik - 30.15a
učeniki - 30.2b
xorošie - 30.2b
čelovek - 6
čital - 30.3c
šljapu - 30.5n,30.5/o
š'ět - 36i
sčeki - 21
ètoj - 30.3c
ètu - 29h

SANSKRIT

abhakta - 6
ábhavanta - 2.7
ábhavata - 2.7
adhita - 6
adi - 29
ádita - 6
adithās - 29
agata - 6
agnír - 29.51b
agūrta - 6
áhaye - 32.3e
ákr̥ta - 6
amata - 6
amatta - 6
amr̥ta - 6
ánnasya - 30.64b

apr̥kta - 6
arkáir - 32.3e
asakta - 6
áspaṣṭa - 6
aspr̥ta - 6
asr̥ṣṭa - 6
ásthita - 6
astr̥ta - 6
astr̥tás - 6
asya - 6i,6j
átho - 32.31/o
auśijáḥ - 42.9(5)
avardhayann - 32.3e
ávr̥kta - 6
avr̥ta - 6
ayukta - 6
ārta - 6
bhaktás - 6
bháramāṇas - 5
bhárase - 29
bhárate - 29
bháre - 29
bhavanti - 2.7
bhavati - 2.7
bhayate - 30.61a,30.61b
bhīmás - 5
bhūtáh - 6
brahmā́ṇa - 32.3e
cakr̥vā́n - 3
cyutás - 6
dāsyán - 4.1
devásya - 30.1p
devébhyo - 6j
gataḥ - 6m
gr̥ham - 6m
gūrtás - 6
hantavā́ - 32.3e
havyaír - 29.51b
havyáṁ - 6j
hitás - 6
hutás - 6
id - 30.6a
índram - 32.3e
índrāya - 32.31/o
īrayádhyai - 29.51b
járant- - 2.7

SANSKRIT (continued)

jatháram - 30.51a
jātasya - 28a
kakṣī́vantam - 42.9(5)
krītā́ - 6h
kr̥ṇoti - 8
kr̥tás - 6
kṣitás - 6
kuryāt - 28a
maháyanto - 32.3e
mama - 30.6a
máméd - 30.6a
mā́nuṣa - 29.51b
manyate - 18k
mat - 30.6a
matás - 6
mattas - 6
mayā́ - 30.6a
mātā́ - 29
mr̥tás - 6
mr̥taḥ - 6c
nā́ma - 28a
páritakmyā - 42.8i
pátyuḥ - 6h
pā́tave - 32.31/o
pítar - 29
pitā - 30.61b
pītas - 6
prajā́ḥ - 6i
prastīmas - 5
prayā́taḥ - 6d
prītā́ni - 6j
pr̥ktás - 6
pr̥ṇā́ti - 30.5a
pŕ̥ṣant - 2.7
putrasya - 28a
pūrtás - 6
rā́jā - 6c,m
rā́trī - 42.8i
r̥tás - 6
saktás - 6
sā́ntam - 2
satī́ - 2,6h
Savitā - 29.31c

sā́ - 42.8i
sómam - 18k,32.31/o
sómasya - 30.51a
spaṣṭas - 6
sr̥ṣṭā́ḥ - 6i
stavā́n - 2.7
'sthād - 17n,29.31c
sthitás - 6
sunú - 32.31/o
śr̥ṇóti - 30.1/o,30.1p
śvā́ - 2.7
tasmāt - 28a
tr̥pyati - 30.64b
uchántī - 8
uchántyām - 21/1
ūrdhvas - 17n,29.31c
uṣási - 21/1
uṣā́ - 8
vahanti - 6j
vardhasva - 30.6a
vayúnā - 8
vā́cam - 30.1/o
vidúṣī - 3
viktá - 6
viktás - 6
vis - 29
ves - 29
vr̥ka - 29
vr̥kasya - 30.61b
vr̥kāt - 30.61a
vr̥ktás - 6
vr̥tás - 6
ya - 42.9(5)
Yamaḥ - 6d
yā - 42.8i
yugám - 29
yuktás - 6

SPANISH

a - 29n,34
diferencia - 29n
géneros - 29n
morfológico - 29n
ningún - 29n
rasgo - 29n

TOKHARIAN

cämpamo - 5
kautāmai - 29
kautātai - 29
kautāte - 29
kolokmar - 29
kotat - 29
kote - 29
kotte - 29
lkātsi - 29.51a
pälkamo - 5
pälkäs - 29
pälkät - 29

salamo - 5
sūk - 29.51a
tränkmār - 29
wsāyokyats - 29.51a
ynamo - 5

VENETIC

zoto - 6

ZAN

bičik - 29/o
kulanis - 29/o
qozops - 29/o

ABBREVIATIONS

Acad. Dict. – Academy Dictionary
Acad. Gram. – Academy Grammar
acc. – accusative
act. – active
adess. – adessive
all. – allative
aor. – aorist
BB – Bretkūnas' Bible
ChB – Chyliński's Bible
dat. – dative
DP – Daukša's Postilla Catholicka, Vilnius 1599
erg. – ergative
fem. – feminine
fut. – future
gen. – genitive
Gk. – Greek
Hitt. – Hittite
ill. – illative
inf. – infinitive
inst., instr. – instrumental
intr. – intransitive
Lat. – Latin
Latv. – Latvian
lit. – literally
Lith. – Lithuanian
loc. – locative
masc. – masculine
neut. – neuter
nom. – nominative
OCS – Old Church Slavic
para. – paragraph
part. – participle
pl. – plural
Pol. – Polish
prep. – preposition
pres. – present
pret. – preterite
prt. – participle
pst. – past
psv. – passive
refl. – reflexive
Russ. – Russian
sg. – singular
Skt. – Sanskrit, Old Indic
subj. – subjunctive
sup. – supine
tr. – transitive
voc. – vocative
Zograph. = Codex Zographensis

OTHER SLAVICA BOOKS

Ronelle Alexander: *The Structure of Vasko Popa's Poetry*, 1986
American Contributions to the Ninth International Congress of Slavists (Kiev 1983) Vol. 1: *Linguistics*, ed. by Michael S. Flier, 1983
American Contributions to the Ninth International Congress of Slavists, (Kiev 1983) Vol. 2: *Literature, Poetics, History*, ed. by Paul Debreczeny, 1983
American Contributions to the Eighth International Congress of Slavists (Zagreb and Ljubljana, Sept. 3-9, 1978), Vol 1: *Linguistics and Poetics*, ed. by Henrik Birnbaum, 1978
American Contributions to the Eighth International Congress of Slavists (Zagreb and Ljubljana, Sept. 3-9, 1978) Vol. 2: *Literature*, ed. by Victor Terras, 1978
Patricia M. Arant: *Russian for Reading*, 1981
Howard I. Aronson: *Georgian: A Reading Grammar*, 1982
James E. Augerot and Florin D. Popescu: *Modern Romanian*, 1983
Adele Marie Barker: *The Mother Syndrome in the Russian Folk Imagination*, 1986
John D. Basil: *The Mensheviks in the Revolution of 1917*, 1984
Henrik Birnbaum: *Lord Novgorod the Great Essays in the History and Culture of a Medieval City-State Part One: The Historical Background*, 1981
Henrik Birnbaum & Thomas Eekman, eds.: *Fiction and Drama in Eastern and Southeastern Europe: Evolution and Experiment in the Postwar Period*, 1980
Henrik Birnbaum and Peter T. Merrill: *Recent Advances in the Reconstruction of Common Slavic (1971-1982)*, 1985
Marianna D. Birnbaum: *Humanists in a Shattered World: Croatian and Hungarian Latinity in the Sixteenth Century*, 1986
Feliks J. Bister and Herbert Kuhner, eds.: *Carinthian Slovenian Poetry*, 1984
Karen L. Black, ed.: *A Biobibliographical Handbook of Bulgarian Authors*, 1982
Marianna Bogojavlensky: *Russian Review Grammar*, 1982
Rodica C. Boțoman, Donald E. Corbin, E. Garrison Walters: *Îmi Place Limba Română/A Romanian Reader*, 1982
Richard D. Brecht and James S. Levine, eds: *Case in Slavic*, 1986
Gary L. Browning: *Workbook to Russian Root List*, 1985
R. L. Busch: *Humor in the Major Novels of Dostoevsky*, 1987

OTHER SLAVICA BOOKS

Catherine V. Chvany and Richard D. Brecht, eds.: *Morphosyntax in Slavic*, 1980

Jozef Cíger-Hronský: *Jozef Mak* (a novel), translated from Slovak by Andrew Cincura, Afterword by Peter Petro, 1985

Frederick Columbus: *Introductory Workbook in Historical Phonology*, 1974

Julian W. Connolly & Sonia I. Ketchian, eds.: *Studies in Honor of Vsevolod Setchkarev*, 1987

Gary Cox: *Tyrant and Victim in Dostoevsky*, 1984

Anna Lisa Crone & Catherine V. Chvany, eds.: *New Studies in Russian Language and Literature*, 1987

R. G. A. de Bray: *Guide to the South Slavonic Languages (Guide to the Slavonic Languages, Third Edition, Revised and Expanded, Part 1);*, 1980

Carolina De Maegd Soep: *Chekhov and Women: Women in the Life and Work of Chekhov*, 1987

Bruce L. Derwing and Tom M. S. Priestly: *Reading Rules for Russian: A Systematic Approach to Russian Spelling and Pronunciation, with Notes on Dialectal and Stylistic Variation*, 1980

Dorothy Disterheft: *The Syntactic Development of the Infinitive in Indo-European*, 1980

Thomas Eekman and Dean S. Worth, eds.: *Russian Poetics Proceedings of the International Colloquium at UCLA, September 22-26, 1975*, 1983

James S. Elliott: *Russian for Trade Negotiations with the USSR*, 1981

Ralph Carter Elwood, ed.: *Reconsiderations on the Russian Revolution*, 1976

Michael S. Flier and Richard D. Brecht, eds.: *Issues in Russian Morphosyntax*, 1985

Michael S. Flier and Alan Timberlake, eds: *The Scope of Slavic Aspect*, 1985

John Miles Foley, ed.: *Comparative Research on Oral Traditions: A Memorial for Milman Parry*, 1987

John M. Foley, ed.: *Oral Traditional Literature A Festschrift for Albert Bates Lord*, 1981

Diana Greene: *Insidious Intent: An Interpretation of Fedor Sologub's <u>The Petty Demon</u>*, 1986

Charles E. Gribble, ed.: *Medieval Slavic Texts, Vol. 1, Old and Middle Russian Texts*, 1973

OTHER SLAVICA BOOKS

Charles E. Gribble: *Reading Bulgarian Through Russian*, 1987
Charles E. Gribble: *Russian Root List with a Sketch of Word Formation, Second Edition*, 1982
Charles E. Gribble: *A Short Dictionary of 18th-Century Russian*/Словарик Русского Языка 18-го Века, 1976
Charles E. Gribble, ed.: *Studies Presented to Professor Roman Jakobson by His Students*, 1968
George J. Gutsche and Lauren G. Leighton, eds., 1982
Morris Halle, ed.: *Roman Jakobson: What He Taught Us*, 1983
Charles J. Halperin: *The Tatar Yoke*, 1986
William S. Hamilton: *Introduction to Russian Phonology and Word Structure*, 1980
Pierre R. Hart: *G. R. Derzhavin: A Poet's Progress*, 1978
Michael Heim: *Contemporary Czech*, 1982
Michael Heim, Zlata Meyerstein, and Dean Worth: *Readings in Czech*, 1985
M. Hubenova & others: *A Course in Modern Bulgarian, Parts 1 and 2*, 1983
Martin E. Huld: *Basic Albanian Etymologies*, 1984
Charles Isenberg: *Substantial Proofs of Being: Osip Mandelstam's Literary Prose*, 1987
Roman Jakobson, with the assistance of Kathy Santilli: *Brain and Language Cerebral Hemispheres and Linguistic Structure in Mutual Light*, 1980
Donald K. Jarvis and Elena D. Lifshitz: *Viewpoints: A Listening and Conversation Course in Russian, Third Edition*, 1985; plus *Instructor's Manual*
Leslie A. Johnson: *The Experience of Time in Crime and Punishment*, 1985
Raina Katzarova-Kukudova and Kiril Djenev: *Bulgarian Folk Dances*, 1976
Emily R. Klenin: *Animacy in Russian: A New Interpretation*, 1983
Andrej Kodjak, Krystyna Pomorska, and Kiril Taranovsky, eds.: *Alexander Puškin Symposium II*, 1980
Andrej Kodjak, Krystyna Pomorska, Stephen Rudy, eds.: *Myth in Literature*, 1985
Andrej Kodjak: *Pushkin's I. P. Belkin*, 1979
Andrej Kodjak, Michael J. Connolly, Krystyna Pomorska, eds.: *Structural Analysis of Narrative Texts (Conference Papers)*, 1980
Demetrius J. Koubourlis, ed.: *Topics in Slavic Phonology*, 1974

OTHER SLAVICA BOOKS

Ronald D. LeBlanc: *The Russianization of Gil Blas: A Study in Literary Appropriation*, 1986

Richard L. Leed and Slava Paperno: *5000 Russian Words With All Their Inflected Forms: A Russian-English Dictionary*, 1987

Richard L. Leed, Alexander D. Nakhimovsky, and Alice S. Nakhimovsky: *Beginning Russian, Vol. 1*, 1981; *Vol. 2*, 1982

Edgar H. Lehrman: *A Handbook to Eighty-Six of Chekhov's Stories in Russian*, 1985

Lauren Leighton, ed.: *Studies in Honor of Xenia Gąsiorowska*, 1983

Rado L. Lencek: *The Structure and History of the Slovene Language*, 1982

Jules F. Levin and Peter D. Haikalis, with Anatole A. Forostenko: *Reading Modern Russian*, 1979

Maurice I. Levin: *Russian Declension and Conjugation: A Structural Description with Exercises*, 1978

Alexander Lipson: *A Russian Course. Part 1, Part 2, and Part 3*, 1981; *Teacher's Manual* by Stephen J. Molinsky 1981

Yvonne R. Lockwood: *Text and Context Folksong in a Bosnian Muslim Village*, 1983

Sophia Lubensky & Donald K. Jarvis, eds.: *Teaching, Learning, Acquiring Russian*, 1984

Horace G. Lunt: *Fundamentals of Russian*, 1982

Paul Macura: *Russian-English Botanical Dictionary*, 1982

Thomas G. Magner, ed.: *Slavic Linguistics and Language Teaching*, 1976

Vladimir Markov and Dean S. Worth, eds.: *From Los Angeles to Kiev Papers on the Occasion of the Ninth International Congress of Slavists*, 1983

Mateja Matejić and Dragan Milivojević: *An Anthology of Medieval Serbian Literature in English*, 1978

Peter J. Mayo: *The Morphology of Aspect in Seventeenth-Century Russian (Based on Texts of the Smutnoe Vremja)*, 1985

Vasa D. Mihailovich and Mateja Matejić: *A Comprehensive Bibliography of Yugoslav Literature in English, 1593-1980*, 1984

Edward Możejko, ed.: *Vasiliy Pavlovich Aksënov: A Writer in Quest of Himself*, 1986

Edward Możejko: *Yordan Yovkov*, 1984

Alexander D. Nakhimovsky and Richard L. Leed: *Advanced Russian, Second Edition, Revised*, 1987

OTHER SLAVICA BOOKS

The Comprehensive Russian Grammar of A. A. Barsov/ Обстоятельная грамматика А. А. Барсова, Critical Edition by Lawrence W. Newman, 1980

Felix J. Oinas: *Essays on Russian Folklore and Mythology*, 1985

Hongor Oulanoff: *The Prose Fiction of Veniamin Kaverin*, 1976

Lora Paperno: *Getting Around Town in Russian: Situational Dialogs*, English translation and photographs by Richard D. Sylvester, 1987

Slava Paperno, Alexander D. Nakhimovsky, Alice S. Nakhimovsky, and Richard L. Leed: *Intermediate Russian: The Twelve Chairs*, 1985

Ruth L. Pearce: *Russian For Expository Prose, Vol. 1 Introductory Course*, 1983

Gerald Pirog: *Aleksandr Blok's* Итальянские Стихи *Confrontation and Disillusionment*, 1983

Stanley J. Rabinowitz: *Sologub's Literary Children: Keys to a Symbolist's Prose*, 1980

Gilbert C. Rappaport: *Grammatical Function and Syntactic Structure: The Adverbial Participle of Russian*, 1984

Lester A. Rice: *Hungarian Morphological Irregularities*, 1970

David F. Robinson: *Lithuanian Reverse Dictionary*, 1976

Don K. Rowney & G. Edward Orchard, eds.: *Russian and Slavic History*, 1977

Catherine Rudin: *Aspects of Bulgarian Syntax: Complementizers and WH Constructions*, 1986

Ernest A. Scatton: *Bulgarian Phonology*, 1975

Ernest A. Scatton: *A Reference Grammar of Modern Bulgarian*, 1984

William R. Schmalstieg: *Introduction to Old Church Slavic, second edition, revised and expanded*, 1983

R. D. Schupbach: *Lexical Specialization in Russian*, 1984

Peter Seyffert: *Soviet Literary Structuralism: Background Debate Issues*, 1985

Kot K. Shangriladze and Erica W. Townsend, eds.: Papers for the V. Congress of Southeast European Studies (Belgrade, September 1984), 1984

Michael Shapiro: *Aspects of Russian Morphology, A Semiotic Investigation*, 1969

J. Thomas Shaw: *Pushkin A Concordance to the Poetry*, 1985

Efraim Sicher: *Style and Structure in the Prose of Isaak Babel'*, 1986

OTHER SLAVICA BOOKS

Mark S. Simpson: *The Russian Gothic Novel and its British Antecedents*, 1986

Greta N. Slobin, ed.: *Aleksej Remizov: Approaches to a Protean Writer*, 1987

Theofanis G. Stavrou and Peter R. Weisensel: *Russian Travelers to the Christian East from the Twelfth to the Twentieth Century*, 1985

Gerald Stone and Dean S. Worth, eds.: *The Formation of the Slavonic Literary Languages, Proceedings of a Conference Held in Memory of Robert Auty and Anne Pennington at Oxford 6-11 July 1981*, 1985

Roland Sussex and J. C. Eade, eds.: *Culture and Nationalism in Nineteenth-Century Eastern Europe*, 1985

Oscar E. Swan: *First Year Polish, second edition, revised and expanded*, 1983

Oscar E. Swan: *Intermediate Polish*, 1986

Charles E. Townsend: *Continuing With Russian*, 1981

Charles E. Townsend: *Czech Through Russian*, 1981

Charles E. Townsend: *The Memoirs of Princess Natal'ja Borisovna Dolgorukaja*, 1977

Charles E. Townsend: *Russian Word Formation, corrected reprint*, 1975 (1980)

Charles E. Townsend & Veronica N. Dolenko: *Instructor's Manual to Accompany Continuing With Russian*, 1987

Janet G. Tucker: *Innokentij Annenskij and the Acmeist Doctrine*, 1987

Walter N. Vickery, ed.: *Aleksandr Blok Centennial Conference*, 1984

Daniel C. Waugh, ed.: *Essays in Honor of A. A. Zimin*, 1985

Daniel C. Waugh: *The Great Turkes Defiance On the History of the Apocryphal Correspondence of the Ottoman Sultan in its Muscovite and Russian Variants*, 1978

Susan Wobst: *Russian Readings and Grammatical Terminology*, 1978

James B. Woodward: *The Symbolic Art of Gogol: Essays on His Short Fiction*, 1982

Dean S. Worth: *Origins of Russian Grammar Notes on the state of Russian philology before the advent of printed grammars*, 1983

OTHER SLAVICA BOOKS
JOURNALS
Folia Slavica
International Journal of Slavic Linguistics and Poetics
Oral Tradition